Rise Up and Walk

†

STUDIES IN WORLD CATHOLICISM

Michael L. Budde and William T. Cavanaugh, Series Editors

Karen M. Kraft, Managing Editor

Studies in World Catholicism offers scholarly, pastoral, and general readers alike the best of interdisciplinary research about and from the multifaceted worlds of Catholicism, which has seen its center of gravity shift from the so-called global North to Africa, Asia, and Latin America. In this series, authors from around the globe engage with both large-gauge theoretical questions and the particularities of specific communities and contexts, crossing disciplinary boundaries between theology, social ethics, history, cultural studies, political science, and more.

This series is a project of the Center for World Catholicism and Intercultural Theology (CWCIT) at DePaul University in Chicago, one of the leading scholarly institutes focusing on Christianity as a transnational reality. More information on the center and its work is available at http://cwcit.depaul.edu. Proposals for the series may be sent to series editors William T. Cavanaugh at wcavana1@depaul.edu or Michael L. Budde at mbudde@depaul.edu.

Recent Titles in This Series

Put Away Your Sword: Gospel Nonviolence in a Violent World. Vol. 14, 2024.

Fratelli Tutti: A Global Commentary. Vol. 13, 2023.

Daughters of Wisdom: Women and Leadership in the Global Church. Vol. 12, 2023.

African Ecological Ethics and Spirituality for Cosmic Flourishing: An African Commentary on Laudato Sí. Vol. 11, 2022.

For God and My Country: Catholic Leadership in Modern Uganda. Vol. 10, 2020.

Gathered in My Name: Ecumenism in the World Church. Vol. 9, 2020.

For the complete list and ordering information, please visit www.wipfandstock.com/series and click on "Studies in World Catholicism."

Rise Up and Walk

Catholicism and Health Care Across the Globe

EDITED BY
William T. Cavanaugh

CONTRIBUTORS

Kochurani Abraham
Abraham Castañeda-Chávez, MD, MPH
David Cayley
David Gaus, MD, MPH/TM
Diego Herrera, MD
Frank Hutchins
Stan Chu Ilo
Pyeong Man Kim
Soojung Kim
Carolina Martínez Haro, MD

Alexandre A. Martins
Joan Mumaw, IHM
Susan Nedza, MD
Sam Orochi Orach, MD
Claudio de Oliveira Ribeiro
Elisee Rutagambwa, SJ
David Toole
Bernhard Udelhoven, MAfr
Maria Vasantha, SCC, MD
Barbra Mann Wall, RN, FAAN

 CASCADE Books · Eugene, Oregon

RISE UP AND WALK

Catholicism and Health Care Across the Globe

Studies in World Catholicism 15

Copyright © 2025 Wipf and Stock Publishers. All rights reserved. Except for brief quotations in critical publications or reviews, no part of this book may be reproduced in any manner without prior written permission from the publisher. Write: Permissions, Wipf and Stock Publishers, 199 W. 8th Ave., Suite 3, Eugene, OR 97401.

Cascade Books
An Imprint of Wipf and Stock Publishers
199 W. 8th Ave., Suite 3
Eugene, OR 97401

www.wipfandstock.com

PAPERBACK ISBN: 978-1-6667-7280-7
HARDCOVER ISBN: 978-1-6667-7281-4
EBOOK ISBN: 978-1-6667-7282-1

Cataloguing-in-Publication data:

Names: Cavanaugh, William T., editor.

Title: Rise up and walk : catholicism and health care across the globe / edited by William T. Cavanaugh.

Description: Eugene, OR : Cascade Books, 2025 | Series: Studies in World Catholicism 15 | Includes bibliographical references and index.

Identifiers: ISBN 978-1-6667-7280-7 (paperback) | ISBN 978-1-6667-7281-4 (hardcover) | ISBN 978-1-6667-7282-1 (ebook)

Subjects: LCSH: Catholic Church—Doctrines. | Health—Religious aspects—Catholic Church. | Medical care.

Classification: BX1795.H4 .R64 2025 (paperback) | BX1795.H4 .R64 (ebook)

01/05/26

Scripture texts marked (JB) are taken from The Jerusalem Bible © 1966 by Darton, Longman & Todd, Ltd., and Doubleday and Company, Ltd.

Scripture texts marked (NAB) are taken from the New American Bible, revised edition © 2010, 1991, 1986, 1970 Confraternity of Christian Doctrine, Washington, DC, and are used by permission of the copyright owner. All Rights Reserved. No part of the New American Bible may be reproduced in any form without permission in writing from the copyright owner.

Scripture quotations marked (NIV) are from the Holy Bible, New International Version®, NIV®. Copyright © 1973, 1978, 1984, 2011 by Biblica, Inc.™ Used by permission of Zondervan. All rights reserved worldwide. www.zondervan.com The "NIV" and "New International Version" are trademarks registered in the United States Patent and Trademark Office by Biblica, Inc.®

Scripture quotations marked (RSVCE) are from the Revised Standard Version of the Bible: Catholic Edition, copyright © 1965, 1966 the Division of Christian Education of the National Council of the Churches of Christ in the United States of America. Used by permission. All rights reserved.

Contents

Contributors | ix

Introduction by William T. Cavanaugh | 1

Part One: Biblical and Theological Narratives of Health and Healing

1: The Centrality of the Sick, the Poor, and the Oppressed
in Jesus's Mission | 11
ALEXANDRE A. MARTINS

2: "Rise Up and Walk": A Biblical Theology of Healing and Hope
for the Sick | 28
STAN CHU ILO

Part Two: Catholic Health Care Services and Strategies

3: Catholic Sisters in Health Care: Conflict, Entanglements,
and Crossovers in Medicine, Nursing, and Religion | 49
BARBRA MANN WALL, RN, FAAN

4: Catholic Health Care in the Global South:
Does the Giant Matter? A Perspective from Africa | 67
SAM OROCHI ORACH, MD

5: The History and Mission of Korea's Catholic Medical Center | 89
SOOJUNG KIM AND PYEONG MAN KIM

Part Three: Western and Non-Western Traditions of Medicine

6: *Medical Nemesis* Revisited | 109
DAVID CAYLEY

7: Concepts of Health: Challenges to the Healing Ministry from a Zambian Perspective | 128
BERNHARD UDELHOVEN, MAFR

8: Western Medicine and Ethnomedicine: How Culture and Cost Affect Access to Quality Care in Chiapas, Mexico | 148
ABRAHAM CASTAÑEDA-CHÁVEZ, MD, MPH, AND CAROLINA MARTÍNEZ HARO, MD, WITH KAREN M. KRAFT

9: Connecting Western and Eastern Medicine from a Rural and Christian Perspective in India | 162
MARIA VASANTHA, SCC, MD

Part Four: Catholic Partnerships Between the Global North and Global South

10: Responding to the Call to Go Forth: Embracing Accompaniment in the Catholic Medical Mission Model | 189
SUSAN NEDZA, MD

11: Fields, Forms of Capital, and Power in a Global North-South Health Partnership: Lessons from Ecuador | 206
DAVID GAUS, MD, MPH/TM, DIEGO HERRERA, MD, AND FRANK HUTCHINS

12: Solidarity with South Sudan: Paradigm of Promise in a Challenging Context | 227
JOAN MUMAW, IHM

Part Five: Healing Trauma and Invisible Wounds

13: Trauma Healing and Reconciliation in Post-Genocide Rwanda: A Complementary and Dialectical Approach | 251
ELISEE RUTAGAMBWA, SJ

14: "It Is Like That": The Moral Imagination of Maggy Barankitse | 276
DAVID TOOLE

15: Gendered Wounds That Clamor for Healing | 295
KOCHURANI ABRAHAM

16: The Pandemic in the Context of Necropolitics and Liberation Spiritualities | 311
CLAUDIO DE OLIVEIRA RIBEIRO

Index | 327

Contributors

Kochurani Abraham is a feminist theologian, gender researcher, and trainer from Kerala, India. She has an MA in child development from Kerala University, a licentiate in systematic theology from the Pontifical University of Comillas, Madrid, and a PhD in feminist theology from the University of Madras, India. The former national convener of the Indian Christian Women's Movement (ICWM), she currently serves as a member of the World Forum on Theology and Liberation's executive committee and as a consultant on the Ecclesia Women of Asia's coordinating team.

Abraham Castañeda-Chávez, MD, MPH, is a Mexican doctor and diabetes educator with over thirty years of experience; he specializes in public health and epidemiology with a focus on human rights, community mobilization, and peer education. Since 1999, he has served as a consultant for SerBien (Servicios de Bienestar en Salud) and Project HOPE in Mexico City, Central America, and the Caribbean. From 1985 to 1990, he worked at Hospital San Carlos, which serves the indigenous communities of Altamirano, Chiapas, Mexico; while there, he developed a successful, indigenous community health project focused on the prevention and control of pulmonary tuberculosis.

David Cayley is a writer and retired broadcaster living in Toronto. For more than thirty years, he made radio documentaries for CBC Radio's Ideas series. He is also the author of nine books, the most recent of which is *Ivan Illich: An Intellectual Journey* (Pennsylvania State University Press, 2021). More of his work is available at www.davidcayley.com.

David Gaus, MD, MPH/TM, began as an accounting graduate from the University of Notre Dame but, after a transformative volunteering experience in Ecuador, was inspired to pursue medicine at Tulane University. He is the founder/CEO of Andean Health Development (AHD), established in rural Ecuador in 1996. AHD provides quality, sustainable medical services in two hospitals/clinics while training family physicians to become tomorrow's rural health care leaders. Gaus and his AHD team are also involved in research, the writing of medical manuals, and the publication of the online journal *Práctica Familiar Rural*. Gaus has received numerous awards for his work including the World Economic Forum's Social Entrepreneur for Latin America (2010) and Tulane University's International Award for Exceptional Achievement (2023).

Diego Herrera, MD, sits on the Ecuadorian Foundation Board of Directors for Andean Health Development (AHD). He earned his MD at the Universidad Central de Ecuador and completed a residency in family medicine at the Pontificia Universidad Católica del Ecuador (PUCE) in Quito. Subsequently, he studied medical anthropology and earned an MA in pedagogy and research. He is the vice president of Saludesa, AHD's counterpart in Ecuador, and teaches at PUCE and the Universidad Técnica Luis Vargas Torres in Esmeraldas, two of AHD's partner universities in Ecuador.

Frank Hutchins is associate professor of anthropology at Bellarmine University (Louisville, KY). He earned his MA from the Patterson School of Diplomacy at the University of Kentucky and his PhD in cultural anthropology from the University of Wisconsin-Madison. His research focuses on cultural change among indigenous peoples in the Amazonian and Andean regions of Ecuador. He was a Peace Corps volunteer in Ecuador and continues to do research and work there as director of the University of Wisconsin-Madison Summer Field School in Ecuador for the Study of Language, Culture, and Community Health. He is the coeditor, along with Dr. Patrick Wilson, of *Editing Eden: A Reconsideration of Identity, Politics, and Place in Amazonia* (University of Nebraska Press, 2010).

Stan Chu Ilo is a priest of Awgu Diocese, Nigeria, and a research professor at DePaul University's Center for World Catholicism and Intercultural Theology (Chicago, IL). The coordinating servant of the Pan-African Catholic Theology and Pastoral Network (PACTPAN), he is also the North American coordinator of Doing Theology from the Existential Peripheries, a project of the Vatican's Dicastery for Integral Human Development. He is also an editor and director of *Concilium: International Journal of Theology* and serves on the editorial boards of numerous other journals. In addition, he sits on the senior advisory board of a Templeton Religious Trust grant project on global spiritual formation for religious leaders and represents Africa in a project on the ethics of philanthropy and stewardship supported by the Dicastery for Integral Human Development and a number of Catholic charities. His numerous authored/edited works include the *Handbook of African Catholicism* (Orbis, 2022) and *A Poor and Merciful Church* (Orbis, 2019).

Pyeong Man Kim is a Catholic priest and a professor in the department of medical humanities and social sciences at the Catholic University of Korea's College of Medicine in Seoul, South Korea. He is a contributing author to the edited volume (in Korean) *A Case-Based Guide to Catholic Clinical Medical Ethics* (Catholic Medical Center, 2014).

Soojung Kim is a professor in the department of medical humanities and social sciences at the Catholic University of Korea's College of Medicine in Seoul, South Korea. She holds an MA in philosophy from Ewha Woman's University (Seoul) and received her PhD in the same field from the Catholic University of America in Washington, DC. Author of *Alasdair MacIntyre's Criticism of Modern Moral Philosophy: The Relationship of Moral Agency to Community* (VDM Verlag Dr. Müller, 2009), she is also a contributing author to the edited volume (in Korean) *A Case-Based Guide to Catholic Clinical Medical Ethics* (Catholic Medical Center, 2014). Her research interests include virtue ethics, bioethics, and medical professionalism, and she sits on the editorial boards of the journals *Personalist Bioethics*, the *Korean Journal of Ethics*, and the *Korean Journal of Medical Ethics*.

Carolina Martínez Haro, MD, is a general physician from Ciudad Juárez, Chihuahua, Mexico, where she studied medicine at the Universidad Autónoma de Ciudad Juárez. While in medical school, she spent her *pasante* year of mandatory social service working with Compañeros en Salud in the Sierra Madre mountains of Chiapas, providing primary care to the area's underserved coffee farmer families. While there, she obtained a certificate in social medicine and global health. Following this, she worked for at least six years serving the indigenous at Hospital San Carlos in Altamirano, Chiapas, working with inpatient/outpatient services, caring for tuberculosis patients, and managing the child malnutrition program.

Alexandre A. Martins is the William J. Kelly, SJ, Chair in Theology at Marquette University (Milwaukee, WI), where he holds a joint position in the College of Nursing. He holds a PhD from Marquette and completed postdoctoral work at the University of Coimbra (Coimbra, Portugal). Specializing in health care ethics and social ethics, especially in the areas of public health, global health, Catholic social teaching, and liberation theology, Martins advocates for universal health care coverage through grassroots and social movements as well as through his scholarship and publications. The vice president of the Brazilian Society of Moral Theology and a member of the International Association of Catholic Bioethics' academic committee, Martins has numerous publications that include *Christology and Global Ethics: Encountering the Poor in a Pluralist Reality* (Paulist, 2023) and *The Cry of the Poor: Liberation Ethics and Justice in Health Care* (Lexington, 2020).

Joan Mumaw, IHM, is the founder and president emerita of Friends in Solidarity, a nonprofit based in the Washington, DC area that supports the mission of solidarity with South Sudan, a collaborative commitment of religious men and women from different congregations and countries. It works to train teachers, nurses, midwives, farmers, and pastoral teams, empowering the South Sudanese people to build a just, peaceful society. A member of the Servants of the Immaculate Heart of Mary (Monroe, MI), Sr. Mumaw holds an MA in cultural anthropology (Wayne State University, Detroit, MI). She spent sixteen years in ministry in Africa, teaching at the major seminary in Uganda and also serving as the development director of the Catholic Institute of Education in South Africa.

Susan Nedza, MD, is a physician executive who assists hospitals and specialty societies in examining and responding to changes in health policy. She has served in various roles across the health care industry including as a regional chief medical officer at the Centers for Medicare and Medicaid Services (CMS) and as vice president of quality and patient safety at the American Medical Association (AMA). She is also a past president of the Olancho Aid Foundation, a Catholic 501(c)3 focused on education, health, and clean water projects in Olancho, Honduras. She holds a medical degree from Loyola-Stritch School of Medicine (Chicago, IL), an MBA from Northwestern's Kellogg Graduate School of Management (Evanston, IL), and an MA from the University of Chicago.

Sam Orochi Orach, MD, is the executive secretary of the Uganda Catholic Medical Bureau, which is responsible for the coordination of all health services of the Catholic Church in Uganda, and he also sits on the Health Policy Advisory Committee of the Ugandan Ministry of Health. He holds an MD from Uganda's Makerere University Medical School and an MA in primary health care management from Istituto Superiore di Sanita (Rome) and, in 2000, participated in a Hubert H. Humphrey Fellowship in health policy and management at Emory University (Atlanta, GA). In 2012, Pope Benedict XVI appointed him as a consultant/advisor to the Pontifical Council for the Pastoral Assistance to Health Care Workers, now part of the Dicastery for Integral Human Development.

Claudio de Oliveira Ribeiro is a Methodist pastor in Brazil, professor of religious studies at the Methodist University of São Paulo, and a researcher with the Institute of Human Sciences at the Federal University of Juiz de Fora (Juiz de Fora, Brazil). He obtained his MA and PhD in religious studies and theology at the Pontifical Catholic University of Rio de Janeiro (Brazil) and completed postdoctoral work at both Southern Methodist University (Dallas, TX) and the Pontifical Catholic University of Campinas, São Paulo.

His areas of interest are religious pluralism, theology and culture, theological anthropology, ecumenism, popular pastoral care, and human rights.

Elisee Rutagambwa, SJ, is a Jesuit priest from Rwanda who serves as a senior lecturer at Hekima Institute of Peace Studies and International Relations at Hekima University College (Nairobi). He holds an MA and PhD in social ethics from Weston Jesuit School of Theology (Cambridge, MA) and Boston College (Boston, MA), respectively. Previously, he worked as director of the Jesuit Social Research Center and St. Ignatius School Complex in Kigali, Rwanda, while also serving as formation assistant to the Jesuit regional superior in the Rwanda-Burundi Region. His research interests include social ethics, Catholic social teaching, political theology, human rights, genocide studies, peacebuilding, and postcolonial studies.

David Toole is an associate professor of the practice of theology, ethics, and global health at Duke University (Durham, NC), where he holds a joint appointment in the Global Health Institute, Kenan Institute for Ethics, and Divinity School. He also serves as the Nannerl O. Keohane Director of the Kenan Institute. He holds an MTS and PhD from Duke University as well as an MPH from the University of North Carolina at Chapel Hill. He is the author of *Waiting for Godot in Sarajevo: Theological Reflections on Nihilism, Tragedy and Apocalypse* (Pendle Hill, 2010) and *The Morgue in the Garden of Eden: An Essay on Hope . . . in the Dark* (forthcoming) about a Burundian woman and the hospital she founded during her nation's protracted civil war.

Bernhard Udelhoven, MAfr, is a priest with the Missionaries of Africa and holds an MA in social anthropology from SOAS University of London (UK). He has lived and worked in Zambia for nearly thirty years, both in rural and urban areas. As a result of an eight-year research project he led on Satanism and occultism in Zambia, the "Fingers of Thomas" support group was established to assist those who have had occult experiences, feel afflicted by demons or witchcraft, identify with forms of Satanism as portrayed by Christian preaching, or are accused of Satanism or witchcraft. Its pastoral approach is culturally sensitive, addressing people's fears without foregoing the fight for justice for those who are victims of moral panics, witch hunts, and minority demonization. Udelhoven outlines this approach in *Unseen Worlds: Dealing with Spirits, Witchcraft, and Satanism*, published in 2015 in Lusaka by FENZA, a Catholic resource center on faiths and cultures in Zambia.

Maria Vasantha, SCC, MD, belongs to the Congregation of the Sisters of the Cross of Chavanod, popularly known as the Holy Cross Sisters. She holds numerous positions at Leonard Hospital in the town of Batlagundu in India's Tamil Nadu State, including that of director, consultant, and surgeon within the Department of Obstetrics and Gynecology. Proficient in the practice of contemplative and Zen meditation, she is also certified in Bach flower medicine, reflexology, and yoga. She follows an integrative approach to women's health, using a balance of Western science and alternative and spiritual therapies of Eastern science. Her passion is to bring the healing touch of Christ to everyone she meets, particularly the indigenous poor.

Barbra Mann Wall, RN, FAAN, is an internationally recognized nurse historian whose research demonstrates nurses' strong influences on the development of hospitals and nursing schools. She is a visiting professor at the University of Texas at Austin's School of Nursing (Austin, TX) and professor emerita of nursing at the University of Virginia (Charlottesville, VA). A fellow of the American Academy of Nursing, she holds an MS in nursing from Texas Woman's University (Denton, TX) and a PhD in history from the University of Notre Dame. She has been funded by the NIH and private grants. Her publications include *Into Africa: A Transitional History of Catholic Medical Missions and Social Change* (Rutgers University Press, 2015) and *Unlikely Entrepreneurs: Catholic Sisters and the Hospital Marketplace, 1965–1925* (Ohio State University Press, 2005).

Introduction

WILLIAM T. CAVANAUGH

IT IS OFTEN NOTED that the Catholic Church is the world's largest nongovernmental provider of health care. More than a quarter of all the health care facilities in the world are under Catholic auspices.¹ The church, however, is not a provider of health care in the way that some governments or corporations are. There is no central administration in the Vatican running Catholic health care worldwide. There is rather a wide spectrum of facilities that have sprung up from the initiatives of Catholic religious and laypeople, which range from hospitals in the US boasting the latest in sophisticated—and expensive—technology to small clinics in the Peruvian altiplano staffed by villagers with very few resources at their disposal. Church teaching has emphasized what Pope Francis has called "each person's fundamental right to basic and decent health care"; as Francis has remarked "health care is not a luxury; it is for everyone."² But the gap between health care for those with means to pay and those without continues to widen. This volume gathers scholars and practitioners from around the world to reflect on some of the most pressing challenges to Catholic health care among some of the globe's most underserved people. In addition to local narratives and analysis, the

---

1. "Catholic Hospitals Comprise One Quarter of World's Healthcare, Council Reports," *Catholic News Agency*, February 10, 2010, https://www.catholicnewsagency.com/news/18624/catholic-hospitals-comprise-one-quarter-of-worlds-healthcare-council-reports. The announcement was made by the Pontifical Council for Pastoral Assistance to Health Care Workers. Despite the title of the article, the total includes not only Catholic hospitals but also clinics, orphanages, pharmacies, and leprosy centers.

2. Carol Glatz, "Health Care Is a Universal Right, Not a Luxury, Pope Says," *National Catholic Reporter*, January 17, 2023, https://www.ncronline.org/vatican/vatican-news/health-care-universal-right-not-luxury-pope-says.

volume also reflects dialogues between care providers in different parts of the global South and between practitioners in the global South and the global North. The chapters in this volume question the missionary model of the rich North rescuing the poor South and show how a universal church can promote dialogue between Western and non-Western medicine and traditions of care.

Health care in the West has been technologized over the last century. Tremendous advances in treatment have been accompanied by a certain distancing of ourselves from our bodies; the body has become a machine we inhabit or a field of war on which, if obituaries are to be believed, we fight various—inevitably losing—battles ("So-and-so lost her fight against cancer. . . ."). But the reason the Catholic Church has been so involved in health care since its beginnings—the early Christians stood out in Roman society for tending instead of shunning the sick, and the first hospitals grew out of the Christian imperative to provide hospitality to the suffering—is the inability, from the Christian point of view, of separating the body from the soul. The many instances of bodily healing that Jesus performed were not just a side gig meant to impress people and attract them to his main purpose, the salvation of the soul. The Gospels make abundantly clear that Jesus has come to redeem the whole person, body and soul. In this way, Jesus stands in continuity with the Jewish tradition and the Old Testament, in which God both "forgives all your iniquity" and "heals all your diseases" (Ps 103:3). In this sense, the Bible itself is "non-Western." The unity of body and soul found in the Scriptures and in Christian origins is something that many people in the global South—both Christians and non-Christians—take for granted. This unity explains the popularity in the global South of both the prosperity gospel and liberation theology; though their methods for achieving it are opposed, both seek the unity of the spiritual and the material.

Another factor that separates the West (or global North[3]) from the Two-Thirds World is access to technologically advanced forms of medicine.

---

3. In this volume, the terms "West" and "global North" are both used to refer to Europe and North America. Both are inexact terms with different histories. "West" originally referred to the Western Roman Empire, as opposed to the Eastern, or Byzantine, Roman Empire. Eventually, "the West" and "Western civilization" came to refer to the type of culture and political structures formed in Western Europe and English-speaking former colonies in North America and Australia. People commonly refer to "Western" medicine, rather than "Northern" medicine. The term "global North" has been used more recently to refer to Europe and North America, as opposed to the global South, meaning Africa, Asia, and Latin America. Although these are also inexact terms—Seoul is as far north as New York City—"global South" is preferable to outdated and pejorative terms like "Third World" or "underdeveloped countries."

The gap between rich and poor exists certainly within the United States, where health care remains a commodity and not a right, but the gap is most pronounced when viewing the world as a whole and noting the large disparities in health outcomes between, for example, Western Europe and sub-Saharan Africa. Lack of access to quality health care is a kind of structural violence visited upon the world's poorest people. The fact that some of the places with the worst health outcomes were formerly colonized by some of the places with the best health outcomes has not escaped notice. The relationship of the Catholic Church to colonialism is a mixed legacy. On the one hand, Catholic institution-building in the global South is historically connected to colonialism and paternalism toward the inhabitants of colonized lands. On the other hand, Catholic agencies are crucial providers of health care today, especially in places where "failed states" neglect the needs of the people. The colonial legacy complicates well-meaning attempts by Catholics from the North today to support health care initiatives in the South. How to get resources to those most in need without paternalism, without cultural imperialism, and without fostering dependence on foreign money is a significant concern of the authors in this volume.

The Catholic Church is an institution and has been particularly focused on institution-building since the mid-nineteenth century. In focusing on institutions and the Catholic Church as a provider of health care, however, we are tempted to bypass the question of what, if anything, distinguishes Catholic health care from health care provided under other auspices. Catholic organizations worldwide grapple with these questions, especially where the founding religious community has given up control. If body and soul are a unity, then it is not only the case that Catholics are concerned about health care, but also that Catholics might bring something valuable and distinctive from Catholic tradition to bear on the care of bodies and souls. What is Catholic about Catholic health care is an underlying question addressed in different ways in this volume. There may not be anything distinctive about the way Catholic institutions use antiretroviral drugs to treat HIV/AIDS. But Catholic doctrine discouraging condom use has famously and controversially intervened in the arguments about strategies to combat the spread of the disease. Behind such headline-grabbing controversies, there are a host of other ways in which what Catholics believe can and does affect the way health care is provided. In its prioritizing of the poor, the Gospel has something to say about a system that bases access to treatment on the ability to pay. In its belief in eternal life, the Gospel has something to say about the meaning of death, and the lengths to which medicine is required to go to forestall it. Catholic belief has much to say about the sanctity of life, the status of the spirit world, the building of community and the common good in face of fear and social isolation, the healing of trauma, and the unity of the body and the soul. Technology is an important tool in the treatment of bodily illness, but in the Catholic view of health, it is not reducible to the physical; health is rather one element of what the Catechism calls "what is needed to lead a truly human life."[4] In the Catholic view, a truly human life is one that participates in the love of God.

The first two chapters, which constitute the first section of this volume, lay down a biblical and theological basis for thinking about Catholicism and health care from the Two-Thirds World. Brazilian theologian Alexandre Martins reflects on the need to base health care provision on the preferential option for the poor. Rather than simply cite this principle of Catholic social teaching, however, Martins uncovers its biblical foundations, most notably in the healing ministry of Jesus. He concludes by sketching a liberation approach to health care, one that goes beyond health care philanthropy to overturn top-down and market-based approaches to medicine. The next chapter, by Nigerian theologian Stan Chu Ilo, focuses on three healing miracles from the Gospel of Luke to draw out theological principles for a Catholic approach to health care. Ilo focuses not only on Jesus but also on those healed of sickness and the crowds that accompany them to ask foundational questions about what it means to be sick and what it means to be healed. Ilo ends with practical recommendations for servant leaders in Catholic health care, advocating a holistic approach that both addresses the social causes of illness and accompanies and listens to those who are sick.

The second section of the volume focuses on Catholic institution-building. Barbra Mann Wall begins this section with a historical account of Catholic sisters who built hospitals in the United States and then did the same in sub-Saharan Africa. Wall discusses the ambiguities of the enterprise, in which sisters first collaborated with colonial authorities but—especially after Vatican II—eventually showed greater respect for local African cultures, even collaborating with indigenous healers and incorporating some of their practices alongside more Western-oriented therapies. Wall shows how Catholic sisters' work in health care has been characterized by "conflict, cooperation, entanglements, and crossovers." The next chapter, by Sam Orochi Orach, addresses the reality of Catholic health care systems in

---

4. *Catechism of the Catholic Church*, §1908 (https://www.vatican.va/content/catechism/en/part_three/section_one/chapter_two/article_2/ii_the_common_good.html): "Development is the epitome of all social duties. Certainly, it is the proper function of authority to arbitrate, in the name of the common good, between various particular interests, but it should make accessible to each what is needed to lead a truly human life: food, clothing, health, work, education and culture, suitable information, the right to establish a family, and so on."

Africa today. Orach—a physician and head of the Uganda Catholic Medical Bureau—describes the tension between financial exigencies and trying to remain faithful to the Catholic mission of the organization. Catholic hospitals are expected to provide inexpensive or free health care to impoverished people at the same time that already poor funding for health care has been decreasing in many African countries. Orach tries to measure the impact of Catholic health care systems in various African countries, despite a lack of good data. He argues that the church must do a better job of measuring and touting its impact on health care in Africa if it is to surmount the many challenges it faces. In the final chapter of this section, physicians Soojung Kim and Pyeong Man Kim tell the story of the Catholic Medical Center (CMC) in South Korea. Founded in 1936 as St. Mary's Hospital, it is now one of the largest medical centers in South Korea and includes a medical college and nursing college. The chapter describes both the achievements of the CMC and its challenges, which include the tension between commodification and technologization on the one hand, and the Catholic mission to reach out to the poor and to treat patients holistically on the other hand. The chapter describes how the CMC has responded to these challenges with an educational program for the staff to focus on the core values of the CMC and an extensive program of care for the underprivileged and marginalized.

The third section of the volume considers encounters between Western and non-Western traditions of medicine in Catholic contexts. We begin with David Cayley's exposition of Ivan Illich's critique of Western medicine and Cayley's attempt to bring Illich to bear on the present moment. Illich was a famed Catholic intellectual who lived and worked for decades in Latin America; Cayley is Illich's friend and most astute intellectual biographer. Cayley revisits Illich's famous 1974 book *Medical Nemesis*, in which Illich lays bare the detrimental effects of the Western medical establishment on individuals, society, and culture. The Western medical establishment, argues Illich, has become the high priesthood of a new religious ideology, arrogating social power to itself, creating dependence and sapping people's ability to experience their own bodily reality. Cayley then applies this analysis to the Western medical and political establishment's response to the COVID-19 epidemic. In the following chapter, Bernhard Udelhoven discusses his priestly ministry in rural Zambia, where the Western biomedical paradigm operates in parallel to a large variety of traditional healers. People have ideas about sickness, health, and the body that often diverge from those of the biomedical establishment and include contact between the body and the spirit world. Udelhoven outlines an approach to Catholic healing ministry that neither simply dismisses local cultural understandings as primitive and superstitious, nor simply accepts them and tries to do battle with the many malign spirits that people believe cause sickness. Instead of a demon-centered approach, Udelhoven outlines a person-centered approach, informed by Catholic theology, that works with people's own understandings of what is happening to them in order to achieve healing. Physicians Abraham Castañeda-Chávez and Carolina Martínez Haro likewise discuss their work in Chiapas, Mexico, in terms of the encounter between Western biomedical and traditional or ethno-medical approaches. The indigenous population of the state of Chiapas has been marginalized and excluded since the Spanish conquest in the sixteenth century. This chapter offers the Hospital San Carlos in Chiapas as an experiment in healing that marginalization through what the authors call "intercultural health care." The authors describe how the physical environment of the hospital is open to nature, how local people who speak indigenous languages are hired and trained, and how traditional practices and spirituality are incorporated alongside biomedical approaches for more holistic treatment. The final chapter in this section takes us to rural India, where Maria Vasantha, who is both a Catholic sister and a medical doctor, describes the integration of Eastern and Western approaches to health care in Catholic contexts. Vasantha argues that traditional Eastern practices are not only culturally important but often more effective, inexpensive, and accessible than Western medicine, which is frequently beyond the reach of the rural poor. Using the model of Jesus as holistic healer, Catholic organizations like the Catholic Health Association of India and the Sister Doctors Forum of India have taken a leading role in promoting Indian traditional medicine. Vasantha discusses her own experience of complementing Western biomedical approaches with traditional flower remedies in rural India.

In the fourth section of the volume, our authors address the promise and challenges of cooperation between Catholic organizations in the global North and those in the global South. Given its nature as the world's only truly global grassroots organization, the Catholic Church is ideally situated to promote transnational solidarity, but given its history with colonialism, caution is warranted. Susan Nedza, a lay Catholic physician from the United States, describes her experiences with short-term medical missions in Central America. Nedza marshals evidence from research and her own experience to mount a critique of such missions, which often perpetuate colonial and paternalistic relationships, despite good intentions. She then describes a better model of engagement, based both on Pope Francis's teaching and on the experience of Dr. Paul Farmer's Partners in Health. Finally, Nedza describes the decision by her own organization, the Olancho Aid Foundation, to move from short-term medical missions to long-term accompaniment of their partners in Honduras. In the next chapter, a US medical doctor, an

Ecuadorian MD, and a US sociologist—David Gaus, Diego Herrera, and Frank Hutchins, respectively—describe the power dynamics involved in the experience of an NGO uniting US and Ecuadorian health professionals to build a decentralized health care network in an impoverished area of Ecuador. Drawing on Pierre Bourdieu's concept of "fields" of power, the authors describe the way power worked among federal and local government officials, church officials, and informal leaders to erect obstacles to the project. Besides trespassing on others' turf, there was resistance to the dominance of the biomedical model over medical alternatives. The authors draw on Ivan Illich's concept of iatrogenesis to critique the dominant model and discuss the eventual adaptation and success of the NGO in Ecuador. In the final chapter in this section, Joan Mumaw, an IHM sister from the US, analyzes Solidarity with South Sudan (SWSS), a new model of ministry born of the collaboration of many religious orders, both women and men, from as many as twenty different countries. After summarizing the history of South Sudan and the dire state of health indicators there, Mumaw describes the structure, financing, and work of SWSS, then discusses what the organization has learned and how it has adapted, moving, for example, from a diocesan to a national model in order to try to overcome the ethnic divisions that plague the country. Mumaw gives a detailed analysis of the challenges of North-South collaboration, including questions of control, sustainable financing, and the tension between addressing immediate needs and building long-term capacity among the South Sudanese.

The fifth and final section of the volume consists of four chapters outlining Catholic approaches to violence, trauma, and wounds both visible and invisible. Jesuit Elisee Rutagambwa begins with a consideration of post-genocide efforts in Rwanda. He outlines disputes between advocates of two different approaches—trauma healing and reconciliation—and argues that a complementary and dialectical approach is better than a reliance on one or the other. Drawing lessons from the experiences of two different programs—Healing Life Wounds and Christian Gacaca initiatives—Rutagambwa also provides a theological basis for a complementary approach to healing and reconciliation rooted in the event of Christ and the work of the Spirit. In the next chapter, theologian David Toole tells the story of Maggy Barankitse, who started a home for Hutu and Tutsi orphans together after being forced to witness the massacre of seventy-two Hutus in Burundi in 1993. While telling the remarkable story of Barankitse's Maison Shalom, Toole highlights her theological and moral imagination rooted in the sacraments and the imperative of forgiveness. Toole shows the importance Barankitse places on the morgue and the chapel in her hospital. Rather than hide the morgue by the loading dock in the back, as Western hospitals do, Barankitse's hospital gives it a prominent place, to highlight the sanctity of death, and thereby highlight the sanctity of life. In the following chapter, theologian Kochurani Abraham describes the layers of woundedness inflicted by sexual and gendered violence in India. The pressures on women to remain silent and keep their wounds invisible can be intensified by a culture of patriarchy and secrecy within the church. Abraham argues that healing abuse victims requires therapeutic accompaniment of victims but also rethinking and reform of the church's own functioning. The crisis is ecclesiological and requires the undoing of clericalism. Brazilian theologian Claudio de Oliveira Ribeiro concludes the volume with a reflection on the COVID-19 pandemic. He discusses what the pandemic has revealed about the fragility and injustices of our economic, social, and political systems; the poor are left to bear the brunt of disease and isolation, but all of us are vulnerable. Ribeiro then looks at various religious responses to the pandemic. The first set of responses involves misinformation, including denial, attributing the pandemic to God's wrath, scapegoating communism, and bypassing science to offer ritual cures. The second set focuses on interior spiritual practices as ways of coping with the pandemic. The third set of religious responses is more liberationist in its approach, focusing on responsibility, solidarity, and communion to overcome the injustices of our current systems. Ribeiro concludes with an extended meditation on the type of spirituality needed to embrace others and commit to the creation and recreation of life in the face of death.

This volume is the product of an international conference held under the auspices of DePaul University's Center for World Catholicism and Intercultural Theology in April 2021 at the height of the global pandemic. Rather than meeting in Chicago, we were forced to conduct the conference online. While the online format curtailed the side conversations and budding friendships that are often among the richest fruits of our annual conferences, the pandemic did have a way of focusing our attention on the importance of health care to the mission of the universal church. I hope that this volume will serve to foster continued conversations among the many Catholic actors across the globe who are trying, in ways large and small, to bring Jesus's words—"rise up and walk"—to a hurting world.

PART ONE

Biblical and Theological Narratives of Health and Healing

I

The Centrality of the Sick, the Poor, and the Oppressed in Jesus's Mission

ALEXANDRE A. MARTINS

Introduction

I OFTEN BEGIN PRESENTATIONS about global health and the mission of the Catholic Church to care for the sick by directly addressing where this care should be delivered. I then talk about how to promote this care, as well as who must be partnered with in providing it. With consideration for the global health context, we are placed in the reality of the poor, where those most vulnerable to illness are ill, and suffer due to a lack of proper health care. This leads us to focus on the need for a preferential option for the poor[1] in health care, a Catholic social principle that I present as a guide for

---

1. The preferential option for the poor is a principle of Catholic social teaching that appeared for the first time in a church document in 1987, Pope John Paul II's encyclical letter *Sollicitudo Rei Socialis* (39). He incorporated this principle into the official magisterium after its development in Latin American theology. Pope Francis continued developing the meaning of the preferential option for the poor as a choice from christological faith (Francis, *Evangelii Gaudium*, 198) and as an ethical imperative (Francis, *Laudato Si'*, 158). Although the preferential option for the poor has been broadly accepted in theological circles around the world, this understanding has a more conceptual-theoretical aspect than it does practical implications as a way of life and perspective for building justice. These practical implications were discussed in the first writings about this option, which expressed theologically an experience embodied by Latin American communities in the 1950s, sixties, and seventies. To understand this

efforts in promoting health and well-being for the most disadvantaged of our societies.

It is a fact that the main cause of health issues, diseases, and premature death is poverty.[2] This single cause creates a vicious cycle[3] that begins with injustice and ends with death. Poverty is not a natural phenomenon, but a socioeconomic creation that makes people vulnerable to falling ill. Once sick, a poor person does not have access to medical care needed to recover. This leads to more suffering, making people even poorer and sicker. As a result, the poor person dies in a process of the denial of his/her dignity. Even rich countries suffer with this reality, with poverty and a lack of access to proper health care, which impacts marginalized, impoverished communities. The way the COVID-19 pandemic has disproportionately impacted African American and Latino communities in the US reveals this connection between poverty, socioeconomic injustice, and health care.

Considering this fact, the preferential option for the poor guides us to a perspective that places the poor at the center of global health efforts in order to break this vicious cycle. This Catholic social principle inverts the most common logic of global health governance from a top-down to a bottom-up approach. In this light, we look at global health challenges from the point of view of the social *locus* where these victims of structural violence are in a perspective *from below*. This approach recognizes value in the experience of the poor and includes their voices at the center of our discussion and actions relating to global and public health.

That being said, I have to offer a self-criticism, which also applies to many works of scholarship in theological ethics and Catholic bioethics. This criticism concerns the presentation of Catholic social principles, such as the preferential option for the poor, as important resources for global and public health, especially in a reality marked by poverty. These presentations often show the pragmatic aspect of these principles but sometimes forget to present their foundations, most notably their biblical foundations. The goal of this paper is to reflect on the biblical foundations of the option for the poor and the Christian mission of caring for the sick and poor. I conclude

---

Latin American experience, see Martins, *Cry of the Poor*, chapter 4, "The Preferential Option for the Poor as an Existential Commitment."

2. There are many comprehensive reports showing the connection between poverty and illness. These reports are promoted by organizations like the World Health Organization (WHO), the World Bank, and *The Lancet*, and can be found on their websites. See also Habibov et al., "Poverty Does Make Us Sick."

3. Norman Daniels et al. speak of a cycle in which poverty causes bad health, which makes vulnerable people even poorer, resulting in an even lower health status for this population. Daniels et al., "Health and Inequality," 65–66.

the chapter by offering the key elements of a liberation approach to global health grounded on this foundation.

1. Biblical-Theological Foundations of the Catholic Mission in Global and Public Health

There is significant scholarship in the areas of biblical and pastoral studies related to the healing aspect of Jesus's historical mission, and on how the church has continued this mission throughout history. It is common to see Catholic health institutions state that their mission is to continue the healing ministry of Jesus. This is seen, for example, in the mission statement of Christus Health: "Our mission [is] to extend the healing ministry of Jesus Christ,"[4] and in that of the Catholic Health Association: "Catholic health care is a ministry of the Catholic Church continuing Jesus's mission of love and healing in the world today."[5]

Gospel passages describing Jesus caring for the sick are regularly referred to in order to illustrate the biblical foundation for the church's health care mission. There are many of these passages in all four gospels. Jesus healed people with skin diseases, a woman with a chronic hemorrhage, blind men, a child, and even brought back to life his dear friend Lazarus. Perhaps the most common action of Jesus in the gospels is related to his ministry to the sick, most of them poor and marginalized. In addition, Jesus told stories to show the importance of caring for those who are sick. These stories include the parable of the good Samaritan (Luke 10:29–37) and the allegory of the last judgment: "I was sick and you visited me" (Matt 25:36, RSVCE).

There is no doubt that the historical ministry of Jesus has care for the sick, particularly the impoverished and marginalized sick, at the center of his mission.[6] This care is in turn placed at the center of the mission of his followers. The connection between the sick and the poor was present in the ministry of Jesus, and most Catholic health institutions highlight this connection in their mission statements; for example, Ascension Health: "Rooted in the loving ministry of Jesus as healer, we commit ourselves to serving all persons with special attention to those who are poor and vulnerable."[7]

One can say that the option for the poor is clearly present in Jesus's ministry to the sick. Continuing this ministry means an option for the poor

---

4. Christus Health, "Our Mission, Values, and Vision."
5. Catholic Health Association of the United States, "About."
6. Vendrame, *A Cura dos Doentes na Bíblia*.
7. Ascension, "Our Mission."

in health care. We need to observe the actions of the historical Jesus in order to understand this option and its relevance for the ministry of the church.

Considering how Jesus conducted his ministry, the choices he made—going to where life was most threatened to help the poor, the sick, and the suffering—and his cry against all forms of injustice and oppression that hurt people's dignity, it is possible to know, in a very concrete way, that Jesus chose to promote all human lives, beginning with those who have been prevented from flourishing with dignity. Moreover, he was killed because of this choice of promoting the life of the oppressed and marginalized. It was a redemptive death, freely accepted, that united historical and eschatological salvation. Therefore, eschatological salvation is the continuation of a historical life with dignity sustained by justice. Where this has been broken by oppression, poverty, and marginalization, the mission of the church is to work to rebuild justice to sustain human dignity. Inspired by his deeds and teaching, the historical mission of Jesus's disciples includes the defense and promotion of life with dignity of those bearing the burden of oppression and its consequences, such as the impacts of health inequalities. Following Jesus means making his choices and going to where the poor and oppressed are crying out for help, health, and dignity.

The Beatitudes, narrated by Luke 6:20–23 (also Matt 5:1–12), show how blessed the poor, the hungry, and those who weep are. They will have the kingdom of God and will be satisfied and comforted. And happy are also those who are persecuted for Jesus's sake; that is, for being his disciples, following in his footsteps in proclaiming the good news to the poor as privileged recipients (Luke 4:16–19). Catholic health ministry must understand that its mission is to go to where the poor, the hungry, and the weeping sufferers are. This is a Samaritan solidarity (Luke 10:25–37) marked by a union between physical care (for example, medical assistance) and social care (for example, fighting against health inequalities). Solidarity is a social virtue, as was stated by Pope John Paul II.[8]

The Episcopal Conference of Latin American and Caribbean Bishops (CELAM) states that Jesus's actions communicate the church's mission of promoting life:

> Jesus, the Good Shepherd, wants to communicate his life to us and place himself at the service of life. We see him when he approaches the blind man on the road (cf. Mk 10:46–52), when

---

8. John Paul II affirms: "When interdependence becomes recognized in this way, the correlative response as a moral and social attitude, as a 'virtue,' is solidarity. This then is not a feeling of vague compassion or shallow distress at the misfortunes of so many people, both near and far. On the contrary, it is a firm and persevering determination to commit oneself to the common good." John Paul II, *Sollicitudo Rei Socialis*, 38.

he ennobles the Samaritan woman (cf. Jn 4:7–26), when he heals the sick (cf. Mt 11:2–6), when he feeds the people who are hungry (cf. Mk 6:30–44), when he frees the possessed (cf. Mk 5:1–20). Jesus includes all in his Kingdom of life: he eats and drinks with sinners (cf. Mk 2:16), unconcerned that he is regarded as a glutton and drunkard (cf. Mt 11:19); he touches lepers (cf. Lk 5:13), and he receives Nicodemus by night to invite him to be born again (cf. Jn 3:1–15). He likewise invites his disciples to reconciliation (cf. Mt 5:24), love for enemies (cf. Mt 5:44), and to opt for the poorest (cf. Lk 14:15–24).[9]

Although the gospels present Jesus discoursing about his ministry, it is through his actions that his teaching gains meaning and concrete relevance, pointing out the value of life and where his disciples should go to promote it.

Jesus had a posture of total gratuitousness characterized by an unconditional acceptance of the other. He was not afraid of criticism and made his life an expression of love in total self-giving to the other, to the point of offering his own life. Jesus's life reveals an authentic existence and rescues us from the slavery of an individualistic world so that we can experience the mystery of communion with God and our neighbor. This mystery is capable of leading, by the power of the Spirit, the Catholic health ministry to serve not only the sick person who is suffering because of an illness but also the impoverished sick person who cries for justice, revealing that his/her illness is the result of injustice and health inequalities. "In the face of exclusion, Jesus defends the rights of the weak and a decent life of every human being. From their Master, the disciples have learned to struggle against every form of contempt for life and exploitation of the human person."[10]

Jesus's ministry was marked by caring for the poor and the sick. This is clear in the gospels. Grounded in the gospel, Catholic health ministry has no choice but to make health care service a work for the poor, who are disproportionately vulnerable to fall ill and then are prevented from finding proper health assistance. This, in many cases, leads to premature death. Catholic health ministry can't pick and choose where and whom to serve, especially if the choice is playing in a health market for those patients who can pay. Guided by faith in Christ, Catholic health ministry is above all for the impoverished and marginalized sick. Thus, the option for the poor is at the center of this ministry.

---

9. Fifth General Conference of the Bishops of Latin America and the Caribbean, *Concluding Document: Aparecida*, 353.

10. Fifth General Conference of the Bishops of Latin America and the Caribbean, *Concluding Document: Aparecida*, 112.

In the Aparecida Document, the bishops of CELAM state that the preferential option for the poor is an option "implicit in the christological faith."[11] Pope Francis reaffirmed this in his encyclical *Evangelii Gaudium*[12] and added: "We need only look around us to see that, today, this option [for the poor] is in fact an ethical imperative essential for effectively attaining the common good."[13] The option for the poor is necessary in attaining the common good. The common good includes health care and well-being in addition to decent living conditions and access to opportunities that allow people to flourish. Therefore, care for the sick—which includes global health initiatives that promote social justice—embraces the preferential option for the poor as an ethical imperative that originated in our christological faith for the purpose of attaining the common good.

What does "attaining the common good" mean in this context of health and well-being? It means that continuing the healing ministry of Jesus is not simply providing health care for those who are sick. It is not simply a designation of health care resources to those who are poor as an act of charity, or as a humanitarian effort to help suffering, impoverished people. This is only a part of the ministry addressing a small piece of the problem and does not "effectively" lead impoverished and oppressed populations to "attaining the common good." The preferential option for the poor shows that continuing the healing ministry of Jesus is also fighting against the system and structures responsible for creating poverty and oppression. These are the very systems and structures that make people vulnerable to becoming ill and dying prematurely because of a lack of decent living conditions, opportunities, and access to health care.

Continuing the healing ministry of Jesus in history does not mean playing within the system, maintaining it in the way it is (sometimes even promoting it), and providing some sort of halfway care for the poor who are sick. The healing ministry of Jesus is prophetic because it provides a comprehensive perspective in caring for the sick. This includes the option for the poor and liberation from oppression for the "acceptable year of the Lord," a Jubilee Year when all can attain the common good. There is no care for the sick detached from a commitment to the liberation of the poor and oppressed. As stressed by CELAM and Pope Francis, this conclusion comes from our christological faith with biblical roots.

---

11. Fifth General Conference of the Bishops of Latin America and the Caribbean, *Concluding Document: Aparecida*, 392.

12. Francis, *Evangelii Gaudium*, 198.

13. Francis, *Laudato Si'*, 158.

2. The Integral Healing Ministry of Jesus in Luke 4:16–30

As previously stated, gospel narratives about Jesus's healing of the sick are frequently used to highlight his healing ministry and are often presented as a foundation for the church's mission in health care. However, there is sometimes a narrow understanding of these narratives that lacks consideration of the entire ministry of Jesus and the privileged recipients of the good news. This understanding fails to present the links between the healing ministry, the poor, liberation, and the common good. The healing ministry of Jesus is part of an integral program (in using the word integral, I am referring to the perspective of *integral development* as presented by Pope Paul VI) that is clearly present in the Gospel of Luke when Jesus launches his program of action in a synagogue in Nazareth, a program known as "The Galilean Ministry" (Luke 4:1–30). Let us hear the core of this pericope:

> He came to Nazareth, where he had been brought up, and went into the synagogue on the sabbath day as he usually did. He stood up to read, and they handed him the scroll of the prophet Isaiah. Unrolling the scroll, he found the place where it is written:
>
> "The spirit of the Lord is on me, for he has anointed me to bring the good news to the poor, to proclaim liberty to captives, and sight to the blind, to free the oppressed, to proclaim the acceptable year of the Lord." He then rolled up the scroll, gave it back to the assistant and sat down. And all eyes in the synagogue were fixed on him. Then he began to speak to them, "This text is being fulfilled today even while you are listening." And he won the approval of all, and they were astonished by the gracious words that came from his lips. They said, "This is Joseph's son, surely?" But he replied, "No doubt you will quote me the saying, 'Physician, heal yourself' and tell me, 'We have heard all that happened in Capernaum, do the same here in your own country.'" And he went on, "In truth I tell you, no prophet is ever accepted in his own country."[14] (Luke 4:16–24)

I would like to proceed with a detailed exegetical-hermeneutical analysis of this text. I will then move on to a theological understanding of Luke 4 and its christological value for our faith and for the ecclesiastical mission of Jesus's disciples. I don't have space for a very detailed analysis,[15] but I

---

14. Aland et al., *Greek New Testament*; my own translation from the Greek text into English.

15. For those interested in a quite detailed analysis of Luke 4 and its theological and christological implications, see Martins, *Introdução à Cristologia Latino-americana*.

will present some key christological elements of this text because they are foundations for our historical mission of continuing the healing ministry of Jesus.

Luke 4:16–30 is a pericope in the literary bloc of the gospel known Jesus's Galilean ministry (Luke 4:14—9:50). The author of this pericope is editing an authentic Lukan text. The parallel texts of Jesus in the synagogue presented by Mark 6:1–6 and Matt 13:53–58 are very objective and short. They don't have the drama and conflict described by Luke, nor the reading of the quote from Isaiah. Thus Luke 4:16–30 was either a creation of the author of this gospel with significant edits to include the reading of the verses from Isaiah, or he and his community had sources that the other synoptic gospels did not have. The way Luke 4:16–30 is built within the gospel signifies a clear objective. The opening address in the synagogue of Nazareth provides the tone and the plan of Jesus's ministry during this time in Galilee and probably for the entire gospel until the narrative of his Passion. It is not by chance that the author uses verses from the book of the prophet Isaiah (61:1–2 and 58:6) with some edits likely from the Septuagint. Therefore, the reading of these verses by Jesus clearly shows his ministerial program.

When comparing Isaiah quoted by Luke and the text in the Septuagint, one sees that Luke's quote from Isaiah is actually a montage. He omitted two sentences from Isa 61:1–2 and added one from Isa 58:6. Perhaps Luke excluded the harsh phrases "to soothe the broken-hearted" and "a day of vengeance for our God" because they would not fit well into his theological project. An objective of this project was to show a God concerned with the poor on the social level and not only spiritual poverty, a possible interpretation for the expression "broken-hearted." I suggest this based on the Beatitudes (Luke 6:20–23) and with the well accepted understanding that the Gospel of Luke exhibits a particular concern about social poverty.[16] Luke also presents God as a merciful Father (Luke 15:11–31) who seeks after the lost sheep (Luke 15:4-7) and demands that his Son's followers act out of compassion (Luke 10:29–37). When presenting a merciful God in this way, it seems incompatible to God's mercy to stress "a day of vengeance for our God."

The Lukan author added "to free the oppressed" (from Isa 58:6) before the conclusion "to proclaim the acceptable year of the Lord" (Isa 61:2). This

16. Some biblical scholars interpret Jesus's reading of Isaiah and his talking about liberation as not referring to an earthly, social, and material liberation, but rather to an interior liberation from the currents of sin, that is, a spiritual liberation. For this perspective, see Champlin, *Novo Testamento Interpretado*, 50. I think this interpretation as a spiritual liberation is appropriate, but it does not exclude an understanding of a more social perspective. The Gospel of Luke is clearly concerned with the poor and a rejection of wealth, because wealth prevents Jesus's followers from having a genuine evangelical experience. See Crossan and Reed, *Em busca de Jesus*.

addition corresponds to what was presented in the previous sentences from Isa 61:1–2 so that the readers of the gospel don't realize that there is a montage from two Isaiah texts. The term *aphései* (αφέσει)—"liberty" or "to free" in the text of Isa 58:6—corresponds to one of the actions of the Messiah, who comes to free the oppressed and those who are in captivity. This is a practice that occurs in the sabbatical year, a tradition certainly known by Luke and his community. Therefore, Jesus came to fulfill God's promises. The terms *aphésai* (αφέσαι)—"to free"—and *dektón* (δεκτόν)—"acceptable," referring to the Jubilee Year—are fundamental for the understanding of Luke's objective when he montages this quote. This is because behind these terms is the Jewish tradition of the seventh year (Sabbatical Year) and the Jubilee Year, also known as the year of justice of the Lord.

Finally, the meaning of the edited quote from Isaiah is better understood from verse 21 in Luke 4 when Jesus says, "This text is being fulfilled today." This "today" shows that Jesus is the true Messiah and is under the anointing of the Spirit revealed in the baptism in the Jordan River (Luke 3:22). A characteristic of Luke is that Jesus's actions are guided by "the power of the Spirit" (4:14–15), which acts as an introduction for this event in the synagogue; this pericope in chapter 4 shows the action of the Spirit in Jesus, who will now carry out his ministry from a plan developed by the prophet Isaiah centuries before. The "acceptable year of the Lord" begins the inauguration of the age of the Messiah announced by the prophets.[17] According to the prophet Isaiah, the core of Jesus's ministry is:

1. to bring the good news to the poor (the poor are the privileged recipients of the gospel);
2. to proclaim liberty to captives (give new opportunities and freedom for those who did something wrong, that is, offer them mercy);
3. to give sight to the blind (heal the sick and the disabled);
4. to free the oppressed (promoting liberation from oppression); and
5. to proclaim the acceptable year of the Lord (build a new time and new society based on God's justice).

According to Luke, Jesus's ministry is centered on these five core aspects in an internal equilibrium. This equilibrium matches the dynamism of human societies in which all aspects of their development are interconnected. Hence, Jesus's ministry reveals actions for an integral development as stressed by Catholic social teaching. This teaching suggests that the mission of the Catholic Church to continue the healing ministry of Jesus is not limited to caring for those who are sick. It also includes a prophetic praxis,

---

17. Champlin, *Novo Testamento Interpretado*, 50.

which includes the poor, toward attaining the common good and freeing the oppressed from structures of oppression and injustice that are responsible for the vicious cycle of poverty, vulnerability to illness, the absence of health care, and premature death. Bringing the good news to the poor and proclaiming the acceptable year of the Lord in health care includes caring for the sick *and* freeing the oppressed. That is liberation, a truth from our christological faith. Any care for the sick which ignores systemic structures responsible for creating poverty and oppression limits the healing mission to a palliative role. This facilitates keeping, and many times promoting, these structures of oppression. This partial ministry is not the healing ministry of Jesus's mission.

Moreover, Luke 4:16–30 goes beyond this practical teaching about Jesus's mission. It is also a source for a theological understanding of our faith in God from a christological account developed in the gospel. Luke 4 reveals the mystery of God and the mission of Jesus's disciples in a profound depth of interaction, with the concrete historical experience of a community and its struggles for liberation. This demonstrates a harmonic circular relationship between Scriptures and the experience of a community in history.

In Luke 4:16–30, Jesus is anointed by the Spirit to lead a mission entrusted to him by the Lord God, the Father. In this mission, the poor are presented as the privileged recipients of the gospel message. This New Testament pericope points to a search for understanding of the joint mission of the Word (Jesus) and the Spirit in communion with the Father, revealing the Trinitarian mystery of God. At the same time, the Lukan text suggests that the church's mission is to continue the work of Jesus in history under the guidance of the Holy Spirit. Thus, Luke 4 allows us to realize the actions of Jesus in history that were guided by the Spirit. The same Spirit empowers the church to continue the ministry of Jesus throughout history. Announcing the gospel of liberation (the good news) to the poor was a central part of Jesus's ministry. Within the liberating gospel, the healing of the sick occurs without contradiction to practices of medical care and justice in health care, but rather complementary to them. Thus, the earthly journey of the Catholic Church is to continue Jesus's mission of liberation and healing in history assisted by the Holy Spirit. The christological understanding of Luke 4 has Trinitarian implications (the Trinitarian mystery revealed by Jesus) and ecclesiological implications for the church's historical mission of integral development.

Luke 4:16–30 reveals the pivotal event that provides a Christology unifying all of the interconnected aspects of Christian life and the church's mission in history. This mission is to bring the good news to the poor, care for the sick, free the oppressed, and build a new reality for "effectively attaining the common good." Catholic health institutions and the church's actions in the sphere of global public health that aim at extending the healing ministry of Jesus cannot excuse themselves from their responsibility to promote justice and address health inequalities created by poverty and structures of oppression. The healing ministry of Jesus is a ministry of care for the sick *and* of liberation. It is a ministry in which the poor can attain the common good.

3. A Liberation Approach to Health Care

Being rooted in the christological faith that inspired the Catholic healing ministry as a historical continuation of Jesus's mission means embodying his actions and teachings in the practice of Catholic health care institutions. This includes a preferential option for the poor in health care. The journey of this chapter up to this point has shown the centrality of this option in the church's life and how a portion of this life—the ministry to the sick—is not exempted from operating with an option for the poor.

A liberation approach in health care inverts the most common way health issues are seen and addressed.[18] First, this common way involves a top-down approach; that is, from health "experts" and leaders distant from the reality of the people, which prevents them from engaging in an authentic and productive dialogue with the victims of health inequalities. Second, health contexts are dominated by a strongly competitive health market under neoliberal rule, such as in the US, where health care is reduced to a privilege accessed by particular social groups, mostly those who have access to health insurance and can afford medical services. Neoliberal health markets focus on offering medical services having the biggest potential for financial gain; it is profit-based health care.

Top-down approaches and neoliberal health markets work well together. The results of these markets, however, is that patients and communities are excluded from active participation in decision-making processes and the poor and historically marginalized groups are excluded from accessing health care. The focus on medical services with more potential for financial gain rejects a comprehensive view of health as something more than health care delivered by providers, but rather as a part of a wider societal system including, for example, the social determinants of health. Poverty and social

---

18. This liberation approach to health care is developed from a liberation ethics, which is "an exercise of the transcendental spirit in the midst of the historical praxis of the poor. It is a dialogical movement of listening to the poor and being open to learn from them. Far from a romantic vision of the poor, liberation ethics is the fruit of a practical engagement in the life, suffering, faith, hope, and struggle of the poor." Martins, *Cry of the Poor*, xxxiv.

injustice are determinants of health that cannot be addressed only by clinicians in hospitals.

Catholic health systems are not immune from top-down and neoliberal health care. Many times, these systems operate with a top-down approach, playing inside the health market. When this happens, they narrow the services they provide to the poor to mere health assistance without challenging structures responsible for health inequalities. This creates a separation between structural mechanisms—which create the vicious cycle described at the beginning of this text—and the care offered by a health system. In this scenario, caring for the impoverished sick becomes restricted to a mere act of philanthropy without a concrete commitment to justice and the participation of the poor in the common good, while maintaining the neoliberal health market and its way of health care delivery as a privilege rather than a right. In light of what was said above, it is clear that this was not Jesus's approach to caring for the sick and the poor.

Health care philanthropy that does not address the structural violence responsible for creating poverty and injustice, with their consequences for the lives of the poor and historically marginalized communities, does not challenge structural injustice nor create opportunities for people to attain the common good needed to flourish with independence and dignity. This approach that does not challenge unfair structures treats the poor as passive recipients of certain forms of assistance, only available to a few individuals lucky enough to find a clinic that delivers free medical care. In global health, this kind of assistance employing a top-down approach often functions to keep the poor within the reality of dependency, far from any kind of agency and socioeconomic development. This reproduces forms of colonialism using very sophisticated mechanisms. The poor are infantilized through a friendly form of poverty management creating dependency and a charity that prevents individual poor from dying but doesn't do anything to raise them from poverty into independence.

Any action that aims to help the poor and dismisses their contribution as agents of transformation reproduces oppression as part of a new and sophisticated form of colonialism. This is an evil, because it provides bread to the poor, so they don't die hungry and so that they love those who offer the bread. However, the poor and their historical agency are not recognized. They are prevented from realizing their own knowledge of the human condition and reality. Consequently, they don't become aware of the structural forces that create the poverty they live in or of paths to fight against these forces. For those who provide the bread, it is good that the poor are still there; otherwise, how could they be seen as good or even saints back home? Helping the poor in such a way that they realize they are agents of their own history, asking why they are poor, and what we can do together to change this reality, does not please people from the upper social classes who are beneficiaries of the current socioeconomic structures. This is very well depicted in a famous phrase of a Brazilian bishop, Dom Hélder Câmara, who was persecuted during the dictatorship in Brazil: "When I feed the poor, they call me a saint. But when I ask why they are poor, they call me a communist."[19]

Feeding the poor without asking why they are poor and struggling for their independence within their own reality is a contribution to what Paul Farmer calls the "management of poverty."[20] Managing this poverty provides benefits to many people, even to those who say they are working for the poor. According to Paulo Freire, it also imprints a false historical determinism in the minds of the oppressed, so they do not believe in their capacity to rebuild reality and make history. Freire understands this as a source of oppression inside everyone's mind.[21] For him, justice begins with a process of liberation of the mentality from this historical determinism that decides who is rich and who is poor. History is made by the human being who is always challenged to create and re-create the world. The poor have the creativity to re-create their world every day in order to survive in their impoverished reality and oppression. They are not and cannot be seen as passive recipients of our actions "for them," as part of a colonial paternalism that is already a fruit of this historical determinism.

The poor have a power in history that, once it is recognized and empowered, entails what Gustavo Gutiérrez calls "the irruption of the poor in history."[22] If we want to act to build justice for the poor, it must be made *with* and *from* the poor. We don't liberate them, but they liberate themselves and us among them. As Freire suggests in his book *Pedagogy of the Oppressed*, liberation and justice can only happen from the agency of the poor. The poor not only liberate themselves but also the oppressor, because the oppressing class does not liberate and cannot be liberated by its own actions.[23]

The christological option for the poor empowers Catholic health ministry, at home or abroad, to be a ministry of mutual learning and liberation in which the poor and their partners work together, learning from each other toward justice. The option for the poor leads us to join them in a process of learning from them and in the social *locus* where these victims

19. McDonagh, *Dom Hélder Câmara*, 11.
20. Farmer, *Pathologies of Power*, 127.
21. Freire, *Pedagogia do Oprimido*, 50–54.
22. Gutiérrez, "Irruption of the Poor," 107.
23. Freire, *Pedagogia do Oprimido*, 41.

of structural violence responsible for health inequalities are. The option for the poor is a perspective *from below*, from the experience of the poor, that places their voices at the center of the discussions and actions for the common good in global health through their participation in decision-making processes.

In this liberation approach, the preferential option for the poor is for the Catholic health ministry an *existential* and *operational* principle. First, this option is an existential commitment as a response to Jesus's call to be his disciple, to continue this historical mission as presented in the gospel. Leonardo Boff suggests that the historical reality of the poor is the *theological locus* of a new way of doing theology.[24] In this perspective, it is only in the midst of the poor that one can recognize the human condition and the historical situation that reveals the experience of suffering of those who are victims of injustice. At the same time, this is an encounter with the crucified Jesus, who died poor, also a victim of socioeconomic and political injustice. This double encounter, with the poor and with Jesus, guides the mission of the church. Consequently, it is an encounter that should guide the Catholic health ministry.

As noted above, Pope Francis stresses the option for the poor as "an ethical imperative for effectively attaining the common good."[25] In doing so, Francis points out the operational aspect of this Catholic social principle as necessary for leading us to the development of the common good in a way that all can participate in it. Francis believes that the forces of the market alone are not capable of promoting care that is able to answer to the cry of the earth and the poor.[26] Therefore, he argues for an integral perspective of development in which all participate, including the poor, who are not only recipients of actions, but active agents of transformation.[27] Their voices matter. They have a knowledge that counts.

As an ethical imperative, the preferential option for the poor means allowing ourselves to be poor (whether spiritual and/or material poverty) and to learn from the poor and their suffering, from their reality and their beauty. Quoting the Document of Aparecida, Francis stresses that "only the closeness that makes us friends can enable us to appreciate deeply the values of the poor today, their legitimate desires, and their own manner of living the faith. The option for the poor should lead us to friendship with the

---

24. Boff, *Jesus Cristo Libertador*, 13–14.
25. Francis, *Laudato Si'*, 158.
26. Francis, *Laudato Si'*, 49, 109, 190.
27. Francis, *Laudato Si'*, 179.

poor."[28] The preferential option for the poor suggests an ethic of personal commitment, friendship, and collective effort. It is an option for the poor against poverty in order to break the cycle of violence against the dignity of human beings who are vulnerable because of socioeconomic oppression.

Considering health care as a common good, the option for the poor becomes necessary to attain this good, something that any health system playing within the forces of the free market cannot achieve. Therefore, to be coherent with Jesus's mission, Catholic health ministry must embrace the preferential option for the poor as an ethical imperative originating in our christological faith in order to attain the common good, with prophetic praxis that includes promoting social justice for the health of the people.

Finally, this liberation approach is *from below* and grounded in the Catholic principle of a preferential option for the poor in health. Although a principle from a religious tradition, it is an inclusive concept with an operational aspect that creates encounters, encourages dialogue, promotes learning, and offers directions for global and public health strategies inside local realities. For this reason, this principle has also a secular value. Sociologically speaking, the preferential option for the poor leads us to where injustice occurs, to see the faces of the poor, listen to their voices, and learn from the stories of those who carry the burden of injustice and suffer its consequences, which often enough include premature death. In this reality, therefore, seeking the causes of injustice and death becomes a natural development. The preferential option for the poor is a perspective that creates partners who listen to one another and work together to address the roots of injustice in order to create independence, breaking the vicious cycle of violence and the structures that make people vulnerable to illness and premature death because of a lack of good living conditions, opportunities, and access to health care.

Conclusion

> The spirit of the Lord is on me,
> for he has anointed me.
> to bring the good news to the poor,
> to proclaim liberty to captives,
> and sight to the blind,
> to free the oppressed,
> to proclaim the acceptable year of the Lord. (Luke 4:18)

---

28. Francis, *Fratelli Tutti*, 234, quoting CELAM, *Concluding Document: Aparecida*, 398.

Jesus read this text from the prophet Isaiah in a synagogue in Nazareth, presenting it as a project of his public ministry. This narrative shows the centrality of the sick, the oppressed, and the poor in Jesus's mission led by the Holy Spirit. Therefore, care for the sick, the oppressed, and the poor is part of the mission of his followers, who are also guided by the Holy Spirit in a project of integral development. Promotion of health and well-being is an effort that needs to combine medical care for the sick with practices to build justice with the participation of the poor as agents of historical change. This is done by liberating the oppressed and raising the poor from their poverty, and it includes their active participation to attain the common good.

Bibliography

Aland, Kurt, et al., eds. *The Greek New Testament.* New York: American Bible Society, 1966.

Ascension. "Our Mission." https://about.ascension.org/our-mission/mission-vision-values-ethics.

Boff, Leonardo. *Jesus Cristo Libertador: Ensaio de Cristologia Crítica para o Nosso Tempo.* Petrópolis: Vozes, 2012.

Catholic Health Association of the United States. "About." https://www.chausa.org/about/about.

Champlin, Russel N. *O Novo Testamento Interpretado: Versículo por Versículo.* Vol. 2, Lucas e João. São Paulo: Hagnos, 2002.

Christus Health. "Our Mission, Values, and Vision." https://christushealth.org/about/our-mission-values-and-vision.

Crossan, John Dominic, and Jonathan L. Reed. *Em busca de Jesus.* São Paulo: Paulinas, 2007.

Daniels, Norman, et al. "Health and Inequality, or, Why Justice Is Good for Our Health." In *Public Health, Ethics, and Equity,* edited by Sudhir Anand et al., 63–92. New York: Oxford University Press, 2004.

Farmer, Paul. *Pathologies of Power: Health, Human Rights, and the New War on the Poor.* Berkeley: University of California Press, 2003.

Fifth General Conference of the Bishops of Latin America and the Caribbean (CELAM). *Concluding Document: Aparecida, 13–31 May, 2007.* Bogotá: CELAM, 2008. https://www.celam.org/aparecida/Ingles.pdf.

Francis, Pope. *Evangelii Gaudium: On the Proclamation of the Gospel in Today's World.* Vatican City: Libreria Editrice Vaticana, November 24, 2013. http://www.vatican.va/holy_father/francesco/apost_exhortations/documents/papa-francesco_esortazione-ap_20131124_evangelii-gaudium_en.html.

———. *Fratelli Tutti: On Social Fraternity and Friendship.* Vatican City: Libreria Editrice Vaticana, October 3, 2020. http://www.vatican.va/content/francesco/en/encyclicals/documents/papa-francesco_20201003_enciclica-fratelli-tutti.html.

———. *Laudato Si': On Care for Our Common Home.* Vatican City: Libreria Editrice Vaticana, May 25, 2015. http://w2.vatican.va/content/francesco/en/encyclicals/documents/papa-francesco_20150524_enciclica-laudato-si.html.

Freire, Paulo. *Pedagogia do Oprimido*. 59th ed. Rio de Janeiro: Paz e Terra, 2015.

Gutiérrez, Gustavo. "The Irruption of the Poor in Latin American and the Christian Communities of the Common People." In *The Challenge of Basic Christian Communities*, edited by Sergio Torres and John Eagleson, 107–23. Maryknoll, NY: Orbis, 1981.

Habibov, Nazim, et al. "Poverty Does Make Us Sick." *Annals of Global Health* 85.1 (2019) 1–12. https://annalsofglobalhealth.org/articles/10.5334/aogh.2357.

John Paul II, Pope. *Sollicitudo Rei Socialis: For the Twentieth Anniversary of Populorum Progressio*. Vatican City: Libreria Editrice Vaticana, December 30, 1987. https://www.vatican.va/content/john-paul-ii/en/encyclicals/documents/hf_jp-ii_enc_30121987_sollicitudo-rei-socialis.html.

Martins, Alexandre A. *The Cry of the Poor: Liberation Ethics and Justice in Health Care*. Lanham, MD: Lexington, 2020.

———. *Introdução à Cristologia Latino-americana: Cristologia No Encontro com a Realidade Pobre e Plural da América Latina*. São Paulo: Paulus, 2014.

McDonagh, Francis, ed. *Dom Hélder Câmara: Essential Writings*. Modern Spiritual Masters. Maryknoll, NY: Orbis, 2009.

Vendrame, Calisto. *A Cura dos Doentes na Bíblia*. São Paulo: Loyola, 2001.

2

"Rise Up and Walk": A Biblical Theology of Healing and Hope for the Sick

Stan Chu Ilo

Introduction

THIS CHAPTER SEEKS TO show why sickness, health, and healing are central to the mission of the church and to offer a biblical theology for the church's leadership in healing and pastoral care for the sick. It is an attempt to contribute to a biblical theology on health and healing for the ministry of churches and church agencies. Hopefully, it can offer some helpful theological justification and encouragement to Christians and men and women of good will who are involved in the ministry of healing the sick and serving the most vulnerable members of our society in times like these.

Healing and helping to lift those who are down with sickness and all kinds of ailments is the vocation of all Christians. Indeed, the Greek word for salvation, *soteria*, was not originally a term applied to religion. It was a medical term, meaning "to heal." The church exists to heal. All Christians, Christian communities, and Christian agencies should find the most effective means for living out this vocation. In the words of the United States Conference of Catholic Bishops (USCCB),

> In faithful imitation of Jesus Christ, the Church has served the sick, suffering, and dying in various ways throughout history.

The zealous service of individuals and communities has provided shelter for the traveler; infirmaries for the sick; and homes for children, adults, and the elderly. In the United States, the many religious communities as well as dioceses that sponsor and staff this country's Catholic health care institutions and services have established an effective Catholic presence in health care. Modeling their efforts on the gospel parable of the Good Samaritan, these communities of women and men have exemplified authentic neighborliness to those in need. (Lk 10:25–37)[1]

In this chapter, I have selected three miracles of healing in Luke-Acts to develop a theology of healing. Given the limitations of space, I will concentrate on three theological principles at work in these three miracles of healing in answering the following questions:

1. What does it mean to be sick?
2. What attitudes and approaches to sickness, health, and healing might be drawn from the three types of figures I will focus on in this chapter (i.e., Jesus, the healer; the crowd at the sites of these healing miracles; and the sick persons or those who were interceding with the Lord on their behalf)?
3. What does it mean to be healed of sickness?

Drawing our attention to the theme of this volume, "Rise Up and Walk," I will conclude by proposing three approaches to leadership for church leaders and agencies in providing optimal health care in order to bring hope to the wounded after the mind of Jesus. We can restate the task of this chapter this way: What did Jesus mean by saying to the paralyzed man, "rise up and walk," and how can the Christian community speak this word of healing and hope to the wounded and broken today through Catholic health care services?

Three Miracles of Healing

The three selected biblical narratives of healing that I will briefly explore are from Luke-Acts: the healing of the paralyzed man (Luke 5:17–26); the healing of the woman with the flow of blood (Luke 8:43–48); and the raising of Jairus's daughter (Luke 8:40–42, 49–56).[2] These miracles point to

---

1. USCCB, *Ethical and Religious Directives*, 6.

2. I acknowledge that this article draws from the brief interpretation of these three miracles by Teresa Okure in "The Will to Arise." I particularly appreciate the arguments she makes on pages 222–23 that Jesus meets the sick in the very depth of their

important theological themes that can help develop a theology of health and healing. Some of these theological themes are (1) the presence, pain, and tragedy of human suffering in the face of sickness and death; (2) the Christian community's interpretation/understanding/response to suffering, sickness, and death over against some false interpretations of sickness as a narrative of contamination and divine punishment for the sick person's sin; and (3) the Christian community's vocation to accompany the sick and dying in solidarity, sharing in their pain and suffering and proclaiming and enacting hope in the midst of human suffering. Our brothers and sisters who are sick cannot rise and walk unless they are helped by the community. To use an African proverb here to make this point: *Ummera ummera-sha,* or "Courage, find courage, and let us use your courage." This means that there are times in life when someone does not have the strength to carry on. In those times, the community carries the person, and the sick person uses the courage of the community. This is at the core of the principle of solidarity, and it is a theological principle found in the healing ministry of Jesus.

First, the Person and Attitude of Jesus in These Three Healing Miracles

Jesus is presented in these three miracles as a healer. His healing ministry had a personal touch; he connected with the person suffering at the personal level. By stepping into the pain of the sick, by immersing himself in their suffering, he was able to touch them at their pain points, and offered the right remedy to those who came to him.

In addition, it is worth noting that at the core of the healing ministry of Jesus was the affirmation and restoration of the human dignity of the person who is sick: respect for the person's agency and deep love and connection with the sick. His attitude was that of a compassionate, caring, comforting, and supportive healer who accompanied the sick who came to him.

Furthermore, he was concerned not simply with the healing of physical ailments; his healing was holistic. Jesus healed the whole person because he located sickness within the wider social, cultural, economic, and psychological determinants of health.

Finally, the healing of Jesus brought hope in the midst of human suffering and despair. Thus, his intervention was not simply a momentary response to human pain; it was an interruption of a cycle of decay, a reinsertion of the divine redemptive story into the story of human brokenness.

---

whole being and personhood and does not just engage in "an impersonal, unintentional crowd-conditioned touch" (223).

Through his healing miracles we can see the salvific irruption of God's power to roll back the hand of death and defeat the forces of sin, disease, and evil. In this way, his healing miracles are signs of God's kingdom and contain important christological keys for interpreting, understanding, and embracing the identity and the mission of the Son of God. These miracles are, therefore, signs that help us understand the power and prerogatives of Jesus, his total identification with our human condition, and how his presence in the face of the human condition brings something fundamentally new from what was there before.

Central to Jesus's healing ministry is the proclamation that we find in the programmatic logion in the synagogue at the beginning of Jesus's earthly ministry: "The Spirit of the Lord has been given to me, he has anointed me. He has sent me to bring good news to the poor, to proclaim liberty to the captives, and to the blind new sight, to set the downtrodden free, and to proclaim the Lord's year of favor" (Luke 4:18–19).[3] I propose that the healing ministry of Jesus was the concrete realization of the promise and purpose of the coming of the Messiah in history as God among us. His healing ministry was tied to his mission of saving the world. Through his healing ministry, he reveals his divine identity and models for the Christian community the proper interpretation of sickness and how to respond to the sick in the community that he was shaping into the church.

What follows is intended to show how some of these theological principles and general features of the healing ministry of Jesus are displayed in the three miracles of healing that I have chosen.

The Healing of the Paralytic

In the healing of the paralytic in Luke 5:17–26, Jesus first says to the man, "Your sins are forgiven." Later in dialogue—or rather contestation—with his opponents who questioned his authority to forgive sins, since only God can forgive sins, Jesus says to the paralytic, in the words that form the theme of this volume, "Rise up, take up your mat, and go home."

Without going into the rather complex exegesis of the dispute with the Pharisees and the doctors of the law from every village in Galilee, Judea, and Jerusalem, what stands out here is that Jesus recognized the wider determinants of health—he offered to the paralytic a holistic healing. In his

---

3. All Scripture quotations in this chapter are taken from *The New Greek/English Interlinear New Testament*, edited by J. D. Douglas and published by Tyndale; it includes the original Greek, a literal English translation, and the text of the New Revised Standard Version in parallel.

times, people thought of sickness as a curse from God for sin. He could have cured the sick man instantly without dealing with the root cause of the man's social and spiritual alienation—the perception that he could have been paralyzed because of his sin. This does not mean that Jesus accepted the general notion of the times that sickness is the consequence of or punishment for sin; rather, Jesus paid attention to the wider social and cultural determinants and perception of sickness and addressed them in a direct way. As Stuart Love writes in relation to Matthew's account of Jesus's healing ministry, there are two directions to the redaction of the healing miracles of Jesus. The first has to do with the *sitz im leben* of the evangelist's historical moment (which is different from the social-scientific and biomedical models of today), the second with the historical emergence of Jesus at this point "as an Israelite healer."[4]

We have much evidence of Jesus refuting the notion that it is people's sins that brought about their sickness, for example in John 9:2 when he met a blind man. The disciples of Jesus, embracing the common belief of the times, asked Jesus, "Who sinned, this man or his parents that he was born blind?" (see also Luke 13:1–5 about those killed by a collapsed tower). In forgiving the sin of the paralyzed man, Jesus was granting the man holistic health for both his soul and his body and restoring his social standing. Thus, this paralyzed man moved from a man who was dying because in the eyes of his own people he was a sinner, to a man who would now live—rise up—because his sins are forgiven, and his health is restored. Verse 18 of this text also points to why Jesus did what he did; it says simply, "And the power of the Lord was behind the words of healing."

This power will later be affirmed by the crowd and the healed man at the end of the account. The recovered man at the word of Jesus "rose up" and picked up his mat and was jumping and praising God. A similar reaction is found in Acts 3:1–10 at the healing by Peter of the lame man who was begging by the Beautiful Gate.

Already we see here a similar structure that, when placed side by side, tells us that Peter and the early church had already begun to do what Jesus did—heal the sick. The early church was already helping sick persons to rise from their paralysis, to live again and to serve God by being reintegrated into the community.

However, there is a slight difference between these two healings (the healing of the paralytic by Jesus in Luke, and the healing of the lame man by Peter at the Beautiful Gate) that I wish to note. In the healing of the paralyzed man, in Luke 5:24, Jesus commands him by the word: *hegeine* or "rise

---

4. Love, "Jesus Heals," 86–87.

up and walk." In Peter's case, the account says that Peter gave the lame man a hand and helped him to stand (*hegeiren*, Acts 3:7). Divine authority was at work in the healing of the paralytic in the presence of the Son of God; by the same token, divine authority from the Lord Jesus was at work in the healing of the lame man by Peter, who heals him in the name of Jesus: "In the Name of Jesus Christ the Nazarene, rise up and walk" (Acts 3:6). In this case Peter, representing the early church, "lent a hand and helped him up"—this act of solidarity should not be missed. In ministry to the sick, we need to touch them, walk with them, and help lift them up. Healing the sick requires the direct presence of the Christian communities in their lives. In both cases, the healing ends with the affirmation that the healing of the sick is what God does. Jesus, God with us, proved that he is the Son of God by healing the sick. On the other hand, the head of the early church, Peter, in the healing of the lame man by the Beautiful Gate, affirms that the same power through which Jesus healed, and the same priorities and practices that guided Jesus's healing, were also fully at work in the healing ministries of the early church as displayed by Peter. They continue the selfsame mission of Jesus.

The Healing of the Woman with the Flow of Blood

This same compassion and restoration of dignity to the sick, holistic healing, and accompanying the sick while addressing the wider determinants of health, is evident particularly in Jesus's healing of the woman with the flow of blood in Luke 8:43–48, the second healing miracle under consideration. This is a woman who was considered contaminated, a social outcast, a woman who lives in the shadows. What happened when she came to Jesus is remarkable and fundamental to the way sickness is interpreted then as well as today—in what Stuart Love calls "models of social domains," reflecting how socially marginalized individuals are stratified with different degrees of impurity.[5] However, in his ministry, Jesus moves away from objectifying people who are suffering or in need. Thus, Jesus reveals in this encounter a different outlook on how sickness should be interpreted and reveals a different way of looking at life, health, sickness, God, and community. When we touch God, we do not contaminate God. When we come into contact with God, God touches us deeply and heals what in human terms may be perceived as contaminated about us.[6] When Jesus felt power go out of him, he knew that, even though this woman came secretly to touch the tassels of his garment (*kraspedon*) from behind, a truly intimate and transformative

5. Love, "Jesus Heals," 97.
6. Okure, "Will to Arise," 223.

exchange had occurred between the divine power to heal and restore and this woman's human weakness and vulnerability.

There is a deep personal touch to this encounter. When this woman came trembling before the Lord, the Lord recognized her pain and her burden-filled history and addressed her no longer as a strange sick person but with a dignified affirmation that shows a continuity of pattern and intention between this miracle and the healing of the daughter of Jairus: "My daughter, your faith has restored you to health, go in peace" (Luke 8:48). Like the paralytic, there is an exchange here in the encounter: the woman moved from being an unknown woman without a name or a history, who was carrying a contagion, dirty, alienated, rejected, and abandoned by society, to being affirmed as "my daughter," a child of God, a member of God's family. Here, Jesus associates himself with her and confers on her a new identity as family, restores her dignity, and gives her a new mission when he says to her "go in peace." This affirmation—"my daughter, go in peace"—is a missionary mandate in Scripture, like the missionary mandate given to the Twelve in Matthew 28: "Go out to the whole world." It has been retained in the Catholic liturgy of the Mass with the mandate given to the faithful at the end of the Mass: "Go in peace!" This woman, now called the daughter of God, is not only integrated into the family of God, but also into the family of God's people, the church, and given a vocation to go and proclaim the mercies and blessings of God.

The Healing of Jairus's Daughter

Finally, the healing of the daughter of Jairus (Luke 8:40–42, 49–56) continues the same pattern: Jesus enters into the pain and suffering of people. He came into the house at the invitation of Jairus, who came to Jesus seeking healing for his daughter, but then while he was still presenting his case to the Lord, he heard the sad news that his daughter had died. The people who brought the news even advised him not to bother Jesus any further since all hope was lost. However, Jesus encourages him as he did the woman with the flow of blood to have faith. Here, there is also a personal touch. Jesus accompanies Jairus to his house. This, I will say, was a good pastoral approach. In a few instances, like the healing of the centurion's servant (Matt 8:5–13; Luke 7:1–10) and the healing of the son of the official of Capernaum (John 4:46–54), Jesus heals from a distance. Here, Jesus walks with Jairus to his house. We do not know exactly all that the Lord said to Jairus along the way to his house, but we hear of the reaction of the people who ridiculed Jesus when he said that the girl was sleeping, because they knew that she was dead. Their certainty about the death of the child presents a good scenario for the display of the Lord's miracle and the manifestation of the fruits of the certainty of faith, particularly present here in Jairus's unflagging faith in God.

Jesus's personal touch continues when he touches the girl by taking her by the hand and calling her forth into life again saying, "child, arise" (in Greek, *egeirō*, v. 54). The account has it, that in v. 55, "her breath returned and she immediately arose" (in Greek, *anistēmi*). Pablo Gadenz shows that these two words ("arise"/*egeirō* and "arose"/*anistēmi*) "are later used to describe Jesus's resurrection ([Luke] 24:6–7, 34, 46)" and that just as Jesus asked the people to give the girl something to eat after raising her to life, Jesus himself will ask for something to eat in his appearance to his disciples in Jerusalem (Luke 24:41).[7] Gadenz argues further that these miracles in Luke 8 "emphasize the importance of faith and show Jesus's great power over nature, evil, sickness, and death. His power over death looks ahead to his own resurrection. As he was sleeping but then arose to calm the storm, and as he raised the 'sleeping' girl, so too will he rise from the sleep of death, so that all those who have faith in him may be saved and share in his resurrection."[8]

Some Theological Principles

What are the theological principles that we can draw from these three miracles? The community of faith that continues the mission of Christ here on earth must commit herself to holistic healing. The church must be involved in the lives of the sick, in understanding the nature of people's sickness, and in entering into the world of the sick. In order to walk with the sick, the church must understand the wider determinants of health. The recognition of these determinants—like commercial interests that continue to promote tobacco, sugar-sweetened products, and industrial pollution, among others—requires a more social justice–oriented approach to health care. It also invites Christians to advocate for the sick and the poor, for the empowerment of communities, and for the prioritization of preventative health, health education, and health improvement.

In order to offer hope to the sick, there is, in addition, the need to properly interpret what is causing suboptimal health outcomes for many people, especially the poor. A good metaphor that is often used in health care to capture this point "depicts illness as a river that people find themselves 'pushed into' by adverse socioeconomic conditions. They then float

7. Gadenz, *Gospel of Luke*, 170.
8. Gadenz, *Gospel of Luke*, 170.

down the river until, if they are lucky, the health service intervenes and pulls them out. The health service clearly performs a vital role in this scene, but the public health response is to look further up the river and address those circumstances that make people fall in to begin with: prevention being preferred to cure."[9]

Viewed in this light, a theology of health and healing must also develop the suitable ethical responses and practices that will be driven by compassionate accompaniment, on the one hand, and the ability to disrupt the cumulative factors that are pushing people into the river, on the other. Furthermore, the need for accessible, available, acceptable, and coordinated health care systems run by Catholic agencies cannot be overemphasized, and the adequacy and safety of the care that is provided will be decisive for promoting the quality and dignity of people's lives.

Ethical and pastoral principles must also be operationalized in developing some performance measures for evaluating the adequacy of the church's health systems and health care services in bringing healing and hope through holistic health care. As the saying goes, what gets measured gets done. Simply enunciating ethical and pastoral principles does not suffice. What is needed are practical designs for developing and evaluating church health care systems that provide holistic health care. Church health system agencies must go beyond episodic biomedical approaches to health care delivery toward addressing why people get sick in the first place: the environment in which they live; water, sanitation, hygiene (WASH); social conditions; the quality of relationships among people; a country's political situation; etc. These factors are decisive in the pursuit of holistic health—a global effort to improve the quality of life and human well-being through multisectoral and collaborative efforts by all stakeholders in improving all of the aspects of health and wholeness—human, animal, and environmental—in equal measure.

In addition, Christian communities must seek to confront unhelpful interpretations of sickness, especially infectious diseases like COVID-19, Ebola, and HIV/AIDS, the prevalence and origin of which have led to the stigmatization and stereotyping of peoples, cultures, and races. Particularly with regard to gender issues, in Africa, for example, a lot of women are stigmatized (like the woman with the flow of blood) and condemned as witches or blamed for causing the deaths of their husbands or lovers, and they are subjected to all kinds of ritual and social ostracism. In many parts of the world, the blaming of the sick, particularly women, often leads to subjecting people to Pentecostal and charismatic exorcisms and violent

---

9. Egan, "Healthy Public Policy," 71.

healing sessions. All this requires greater theological penetration and a holistic interpretation of why people are sick, seeking causes in the quality of relationships among people, which often create fear and suspicion.

In most cases, what ails people is not just a virus, bacteria, or pathogen, or a single spiritual factor, but the environment and social contagions that create the conditions for sickness, death, and suffering. A more total approach to understanding sickness, health, and healing could be developed using the paradigm offered to us in the example of the Lord.

What Theological Principles Do We See at Work in the Attitude of the People We Encounter in These Miracles?

These three miracle stories have a very human quality and reflect the behavior or attitudes of people today toward those who are sick. How do we see sick people today? Do our brothers and sisters who suffer from HIV/AIDS or mental illness, and people who recover from COVID and diseases like Ebola, feel fully integrated into the community? For many sick people—no matter the sickness, whether communicable or noncommunicable—what they need is integration into communities of acceptance, inclusion, love, spiritual/pastoral accompaniment, and solidarity. We find in the miracles different attitudes that we can relate to today's context.

In the three healing miracles, we meet various people: the friends of the paralyzed man who had to make an opening in the roof to transport him down before Jesus and the crowds milling around Jesus, who saw a sick man and would not make way for him to be brought to the one who could heal him. We see also a similar attitude in the healing of the woman with the flow of blood: the crowd was preventing her from getting to Jesus, and she had to fight her way to him. We also see Jairus, the president of the synagogue; the messengers who brought the bad news to Jairus that his daughter had died; and the crowd who were mourning in Jairus's house following his daughter's death.

The Reality of Sickness

All three sick persons in the miracles had reached the end of their strength. The paralyzed man was so sick that he could not talk for himself or walk. In the healing miracle under consideration, his friends carried him and cared for him and brought him to Jesus. This is a core theological principle for the churches and Christians today to adopt. The church must be a place of healing, and all Christians are called to become friends to the sick, the poor, those who are dying, and those who are condemned to die because of sickness and disease. The prophetic witness of doing everything possible, even attempting what was nearly impossible, as the friends of the paralyzed man did to bring him healing, is a good model for us. We might interpret the action of these friends as desperation, but there is another hidden meaning to it: in the face of human suffering like chronic or terminal diseases, we cannot give up on the sick or treat them as disposable. The church that continues the mission of the Lord must be a place of healing where the sick are brought to receive health and be restored. The image Pope Francis uses of the church as a field hospital comes to mind here, in a metaphoric sense, but also in a proper sense.

The Attitude of the Crowd

We can contrast the attitude of the friends of the paralytic with that of the crowd, the Pharisees and the Scribes. The crowd around the paralytic, just as in the case of the woman with the flow of blood, was not moved by his suffering. For some in the crowd, the sickness of the paralytic was more a theological argument rather than a matter of finding out how to help him. They were more concerned about why Jesus would forgive his sins or even cure him, and they questioned by what authority he was doing what he was doing.

We see a slightly different but related attitude in the crowd around the synagogue official. This crowd had already given up hope for his daughter being healed. This is why they approached him and told him that "your daughter is dead, do not trouble the master any further" (v. 49). However, the official, even when messengers came from his house telling him that his daughter had died, did not lose hope. We see a relationship between his undying faith, the strong faith of the woman with the flow of blood, and the faith of the paralytic's friends. Jesus tells the official not to be afraid but rather to believe. His faith brought Jesus to his house. His faith brought healing to his daughter. His faith restored his joy, wiped away his tears, and brought him new hope and a new reality.

The message here for a theology of health and healing is that of hope. There are today in our world so many people who are giving up on the sick, the elderly, and the terminally ill. In a world driven by the myth of physical efficiency and productivity, the very ill are often expendable and disposable; for example, some think that many elderly COVID patients were abandoned by DNR (do not resuscitate) orders in many countries. They are considered in some settings to be a burden on health care services, especially in the individualist and libertarian model of health care that is opposed to more communal approaches. All kinds of moral issues confront us in the burgeoning and vocal right-to-die movements in many parts of the world. The theological principle favoring healing should highlight the dignity of every life, from conception to natural death, and the affirmation of the gift of life at every stage. Society must fight the collapse of compassion today, while the church and Christians are called to continue to be signs of hope in the shadows of sickness. The church's health care system and pastoral care for the sick should embody the quality of love that we are shown in the Last Supper account of John 13 that reflects loves for the sick to the end, just as Jesus loves us to the end. The sick must be loved until the end if we are to be faithful to the practices and priorities of the Lord.

The Pain and Burden of the Sick

The sick of our world need us. They are crying unto us today. As we see in these miracles, sickness touches each and every one of us. Social status and economic power do not matter. In this contingent world, the cycle of our years goes through sickness and recovery, life and death. Jairus's only daughter, who was twelve years old, was sick unto death. Jairus was a rich man. He must have tried everything possible to get the best medical intervention for his daughter, but all of his efforts failed, and his daughter was brought home to die.

No matter how much wealth or status we have, there is always something that comes upon us—a temptation, a sickness, an unfortunate event—that interrupts our normal routine to remind us that we are frail creatures and that we are not in control of things here on earth. This is important in the development of a theology of sickness, health, and healing because the acceptance of sickness as part and parcel of our human finality, and suffering as related to the reality of living, is part of what theology should offer today. As the US bishops noted,

> The mystery of Christ casts light on every facet of Catholic health care: to see Christian love as the animating principle of health care; to see healing and compassion as a continuation of Christ's mission; to see suffering as a participation in the redemptive power of Christ's passion, death, and resurrection; and to see death, transformed by the resurrection, as an opportunity for a final act of communion with Christ. For the Christian, our encounter with suffering and death can take on a positive and

distinctive meaning through the redemptive power of Jesus's suffering and death. As St. Paul says, we are "always carrying about in the body the dying of Jesus, so that the life of Jesus may also be manifested in our body." (2 Cor 4:10)[10]

A theology of healing is a theology of the in-between, one that affirms the healing of diseases but also points ultimately to our human finality and the possibility that someday, we will likely be afflicted with some sickness that will lead us home. However, dying from diseases and sicknesses that are preventable and treatable should not be a cost that society or churches impose on people, particularly the poor. This is particularly to be stressed in light of the false miracles of healing and exploitation of the sick by religious charlatans who claim all kinds of healing and in light of health care systems that exploit the people.

This aspect of exploitation of the sick and manipulation of the vulnerable was the case with the woman who had suffered from a hemorrhage for twelve years. In the Gospel of Mark (5:26), she is said to have spent all that she had seeking medical attention, but her condition, instead of then improving, was getting worse. She represents so many people who are being exploited by the health care system, but she also represents the isolation many people who are sick feel when no one cares about them or when they are simply a number, people who are as good as dead. She was probably a single woman, abandoned by her husband and her family because of her sickness, which made her ritually unclean according to the precepts laid down in Leviticus 15:25–30. We can see from these miracles that the woman who touched the hem of Jesus's garment, Jairus's daughter, and the paralyzed man were all in desperate situations and needed help.

However, there is also a display of courage born of hope and faith in all three stories. Unlike the prominent synagogue official, the woman had many obstacles, many odds stacked against her. She was a woman who was considered contaminated because of her flow of blood, a social and religious outcast. Again, she had suffered this ailment for twelve years—most people would simply resign themselves to their fate and wait to die. But not this woman. She had heard of Jesus, and she was not going to let any crowd or social norms of purity or exclusion stop her from encountering the one and only person who she believed would grant her healing and wholeness. Her faith empowered her to advocate for her health before the Lord. Bioethics and pastoral care must uphold the right and agency of the sick to decide how their health care should be handled. The sick should not be treated as

---

10. USCCB, *Ethical and Religious Directives*, 6.

nonpersons; they must be empowered to participate in decisions about their health, treatment, and end-of-life issues.[11]

How Can Churches Bring Healing and Hope to the Sick After the Mind of Jesus?

How does this biblical study apply to our context today? The three questions raised at the beginning are still facing us today:

1. What does it mean to be sick, e.g., someone who is fighting for his or her life in the ICU from COVID? Who is that person to me and to the church community?
2. What are the attitudes and approaches to sickness, health, and healing in today's church and society? In other words, how should church public health leaders translate biblical, theological principles into ethical guidelines, the pastoral care of accompaniment, and optimal health care delivery through church agencies? And what kind of leadership role should the church play in health care delivery today?
3. What does it mean to be healed?

I recently spoke with the administrator of the only Catholic hospital and the most important hospital in my home municipality in Nigeria (Achi Joint Hospital), who told me that the only department functioning in that hospital today is the morgue. A Catholic hospital meant to bring healing to the sick is now only useful as a place for storing dead bodies. I was told that this is actually very profitable, because there has been a sharp rise in the number of people who are dying as a result of the pandemic. So, this hospital has stopped seeking the best ways to provide primary health care and is now specializing in mortuary services, trying to be profitable in order to survive.

There are two aspects of leadership that I propose for the churches to help the poor and the sick to rise up and walk again. First, the church must fight the growing health inequity in local settings and globally and be a strong advocate for the sick, particularly in countries where there is no universal health coverage and where the poor are exposed to suboptimal health care and left to die from treatable and preventable diseases. On the continent of Africa, for instance, there has been no "epidemiological transition," leaving the majority of God's people vulnerable to the double tragedy of being exposed to preventable communicable diseases and treatable

---

11. On client participation, medical decision-making, and medical education, see Wildes, "Institutional Identity."

noncommunicable diseases.[12] This runs contrary to the universal consensus of the health community, as stated in the famous Alma Ata Declaration of 1978, in which the international community expanded the approach to improving health for all people from a focus on doctors, hospitals, and biomedical services to include human rights, community empowerment and participation, and combating health inequity.[13]

The WHO's Commission on Social Determinants of Health defines health equity as "the absence of unfair and avoidable or remediable differences in health among population groups defined socially, economically, demographically or geographically."[14] Health inequities are thus to be understood as health differences "that are socially produced, systematic in their distribution across the population, and unfair. Identifying a health difference as inequitable is not an objective description, but necessarily implies an appeal to ethical norms."[15] Health inequity has been called "an inverse care law," because it means that the poor who are most in need of health care locally, nationally, and globally are those who consistently have less access to health services than the rich.[16]

Health inequities are thus worse than diseases, because they make one's place of birth and social location the number one condition for whether that person lives to a glorious old age or dies from early childhood diseases; they are the greatest driver of unacceptable social reproduction, stubborn cultural habits, and intergenerational differentials in socioeconomic gradient in the remotest villages of Africa as well as in the big cities.

Before COVID-19, many people outside Brazil (ravaged by Zika) and parts of Africa (ravaged by Ebola) thought of themselves as isolated or immune from diseases like Ebola, malaria, or Zika. In their minds, these are sicknesses of Africa or Latin America. However, COVID-19 and new infectious diseases have shown us that the health of each person in the remotest parts of the world is consequential for the health of every other person in any part of the world. It is the same lesson that climate change has taught us. Protecting, promoting, and improving the health of all people, especially the poor and the forgotten, should be central to the mission of churches, just as it was for the mission of the Lord Jesus Christ.

---

12. On epidemiological transition, see Rose, "Sick Individuals." See also Wilkinson, "Epidemiological Transition."

13. Rifkin, "Alma Ata."

14. WHO, *Conceptual Framework*, 12.

15. WHO, *Conceptual Framework*, 12.

16. Guest et al., *Oxford Handbook of Public Health Practice*, 408.

The future is uncertain beyond this pandemic. The church must rethink her current model of health care, health intervention, and health systems from the charity model to a social justice model. The social justice model goes beyond prevention, treatment, and humanitarian response to a more proactive and integrated approach to health protection and health improvement. It also seeks to advocate for the rights of the poor in health system development and implementation; community empowerment through an asset-based approach to health and healing; advancing the agency of the poor; and courageously addressing some of the social, commercial, and religious determinants of health. This particularly calls for a new approach to leadership in the church's health care ministry to create resilient health care systems that can meet the challenges of emerging diseases.

Our Capacity for Shared Action to Heal the Sick

In addition to fighting health inequity and advocating strongly for the sick who are poor, the second aspect of leadership that I propose for the church is to work to address the root causes of health inequity. Hannah Arendt's definition of power seems to me a good way of capturing the kind of power that Foucault asserts "fosters life."[17] For Arendt, as Angus Stewart notes, "power is conceptually and *above all politically* distinguished, not by its implication in agency, but above all by its character as *collective* action."[18] As Arendt says herself, "Power corresponds to the human ability not just to act, but to act in concert. Power is never the property of an individual; it belongs to a group and remains in existence only so long as the group keeps together."[19] For Arendt, power is not a relation in which people are dominated, exploited, or manipulated, but rather one in which—through critical reflection on their world and experiences—they develop collective actions.

This capacity for "collective action" is what I identify in shared leadership and transformational servant leadership. Dugan defines shared leadership this way: "Sometimes referred to as distributive leadership, shared leadership differs from team leadership in its shift away from a singular leader attempting to shepherd group effectiveness and toward the simultaneous emergence of multiple leaders in a group process."[20] Relying on Wassenaar and Pearce, Dugan shows that shared leadership is adaptable to different environments; it recognizes the assets of all stakeholders and

---

17. See Foucault, *History of Sexuality*, 138.
18. Stewart, *Theories of Power*, 36; italics original.
19. Arendt, *Crises of the Republic*, 143.
20. Dugan, *Leadership Theory*, 169.

embraces a process of reciprocity, collective capacity, and healthy exchanges emerging dynamically from a group. In order to implement a whole-population approach to fighting malaria—to give an example of a disease that still kills more people in Africa than any other—the agency of community leaders at the grassroots is vital, as is cooperation and buy-in from religious leaders working in tandem with public health workers.

Following Dugan's proposal and the WHO's call for a greater involvement in providing for primary health care, churches must identify the interdependency and collective efficacy among all members of the community, including interfaith and church-state partnerships, while recognizing diverse levels of responsibility. This approach helps to avoid a command-and-control approach and favors the conscious and deliberate distribution of power and responsibility among the stakeholders, creating a respectful and collaborative space for each person to participate in the process that is mutually agreed on for improving and protecting people's health and the treatment of diseases. For example, in the fight against malaria in Africa, the churches can help introduce practices like cleaning people's compounds to avoid the creation of stagnant water sources that serve as breeding grounds for mosquitoes, helping to distribute mosquito nets and encouraging people to use them at home, aggressive fumigation of homes, hospitals, and other public spaces, and more.

Ultimately, Catholic agencies need transformational servant leadership in order to run effective, affordable, accessible, and coordinated health care systems. Transformational leadership, according to Burns, occurs "when one or more persons engage with others in such a way that leaders and followers raise one another to higher levels of motivation and morality. Their purposes, which might have started out as separate but related, as in the case of transactional leadership, become fused."[21]

Greenleaf's servant leadership concept proposes that the test of servant leadership is how the person who holds power inspires everyone to service. As Greenleaf puts it, "The best test, and difficult to administer, is this: Do those served grow as persons? Do they, while being served, become healthier, wiser, freer, more autonomous, more likely themselves to become servants? And what is the effect on the least privileged in society? Will they benefit or at least not be further deprived?"[22] How can both servant and transformational leadership be adapted to meet the challenges of healing the sick and improving the ministry of the church to the sick?

---

21. Burns, *Transforming Leadership*, 20.
22. Greenleaf, *Servant Leadership*, 27.

Using Greenleaf's framework and transformational leadership theories, I have adapted below some qualities and principles of public health leadership for churches: (a) servant leaders *cherish everyone's contribution to the community*, bringing politicians, frontline health care workers, public health practitioners, and local leaders together for community mobilization through a coordinated response; (b) servant leaders *place more emphasis on listening, empathy, and the unconditional acceptance of others*, especially those who are sick themselves, who should always be given a voice in the plan of care, and on being present where sick people are by having boots on the ground, reframing policy goals by leveraging local knowledge; and (c) servant leaders consistently *engage all of their followers*—they see themselves as part of the community and not above it. A key factor in choosing transformational and servant leadership and a shared leadership approach is that they were central to the practices and priorities of Jesus Christ as he made himself one with all the sick who came to him.

Conclusion

The central argument of this chapter is that a theology of healing and a pastoral care of accompaniment are central to the mission of the church today. This mission will grow more complex in this period of the pandemic and beyond. It will require that the Catholic Church and other Christian faith actors who are involved in the provision of health care develop new tools and approaches for understanding health and some of the social, commercial, and religious determinants of health. This will equip them to prioritize preventative health and health improvement on the one hand, and to advocate for optimal health care and the rights of the poor to universal health care, on the other. The health care services provided by churches through hospitals and international health missions, and the biomedical ethical reflections and prescriptions from church entities, scholars, and practitioners, must be oriented toward protecting and promoting the health of the poor. The churches are being invited to embrace a greater commitment in our times to the option for the poor in order to help remove the barriers that prevent God's people from enjoying the abundant life promised and offered to them by the Lord Jesus Christ. This is why improvement of the church's public health leadership today and innovative approaches to maintaining health systems that are accessible, affordable, and safe for the poor are both urgent missions today. These are credible ways of prophetically witnessing to the gospel in these times of great distress. In embracing this mission of global public health leadership with renewed urgency and commitment, churches will be helping many of our brothers and sisters who are down with sickness to rise up again and walk.

Bibliography

Arendt, Hannah. *Crises of the Republic: Lying in Politics; Civil Disobedience; On Violence; Thoughts on Politics and Revolution.* New York: Harvest, 1972.

Burns, James MacGregor. *Transforming Leadership.* 1st ed. New York: Grove, 2004.

Douglas, J. D., ed. *The New Greek/English Interlinear New Testament.* Carol Stream, IL: Tyndale, 1990.

Dugan, John P. *Leadership Theory: Cultivating Critical Perspectives.* San Francisco: Jossey-Bass, 2007.

Egan, Matt. "Healthy Public Policy." In *Health Promotion Practice*, edited by Will Nutland and Liza Cragg, 69–81. 2nd ed. New York: Open University, 2015.

Foucault, Michel. *The History of Sexuality, Volume I: An Introduction.* Translated by Robert Hurley. New York: Pantheon, 1978.

Gadenz, Pablo. *The Gospel of Luke.* Grand Rapids: Baker Academic, 2018.

Greenleaf, Robert K. *Servant Leadership: A Journey into the Nature of Legitimate Power and Greatness.* New York: Paulist, 2002.

Guest, Charles, et al. *Oxford Handbook of Public Health Practice.* Oxford: Oxford University Press, 2013.

Love, Stuart L. "Jesus Heals the Hemorrhaging Woman." In *The Social Setting of Jesus and the Gospels*, edited by Wolfgang Stegemann et al., 85–103. Minneapolis: Fortress, 2002.

Okure, Teresa. "The Will to Arise: Reflections on Luke 8:40–56." In *The Will to Arise: Women, Tradition, and the Church in Africa*, edited by Mercy Amba Oduyoye and Musimbi R. A. Kanyoro, 221–30. Maryknoll, NY: Orbis, 1997.

Rifkin, Susan. "Alma Ata after Forty Years: Primary Health Care and Health for All—From Consensus to Complexity." *BMJ Global Health* 3.3 (2018) e001188.

Rose, Geoffrey. "Sick Individuals and Sick Populations." *International Journal of Epidemiology* 30.3 (2001) 427–32.

Stewart, Angus. *Theories of Power and Domination: The Politics of Empowerment in Late Modernity.* London: SAGE, 2001.

United States Conference of Catholic Bishops (USCCB). *Ethical and Religious Directives for Catholic Health Care Services.* 6th ed. Washington, DC: USCCB, 2018.

Wildes, Kevin. "Institutional Identity and Conscience." In *Applying Theories and Principles to the Patient Encounter*, edited by Matt Weinberg, 472–78. Amherst, NY: Prometheus, 2001.

Wilkinson, Richard G. "The Epidemiological Transition: From Material Scarcity to Social Disadvantage?" *Daedalus* 123.4 (1994) 61–77.

World Health Organization (WHO). *A Conceptual Framework for Action on the Social Determinants of Health.* Geneva: World Health Organization, 2010.

PART TWO

Catholic Health Care Services and Strategies

3

Catholic Sisters in Health Care: Conflict, Entanglements, and Crossovers in Medicine, Nursing, and Religion[1]

BARBRA MANN WALL, RN, FAAN

ONE WAY TO THINK about the interconnected history of medicine, nursing, and Catholicism is by using Catholic sister nurses as a case study. Typically, storylines of conflict have persisted in the historiography of these topics, but further research has revealed a history of entanglement and crossovers between medicine, nursing, and religion.[2] My thinking on this topic has been shaped by years of research on Catholic sisters and hospitals, including interviews with sisters and studying in various archives. In my early reading of the historiography of hospitals, I realized that there was no analysis of the many Catholic hospitals that grew up across the United States and the world. In this chapter, I will begin by discussing sisters' hospital establish-

---

1. Wall, *American Catholic Hospitals: A Century of Changing Markets and Missions*. New Brunswick: Rutgers University Press, 2011. Copyright © 2011 by Barbra Mann Wall. Reprinted by permission of Rutgers University Press. Barbra Mann Wall, *Into Africa: A Transnational History of Catholic Medical Missions and Social Change*. New Brunswick: Rutgers University Press, 2015. Copyright © 2015 by Barbra Mann Wall. Reprinted by permission of Rutgers University Press.

2. Lightman, *Rethinking History*; Martucci, "Religion, Medicine, and Politics"; McCauley, *Who Shall Take Care of Our Sick?*; Kaufman, *Consuming Visions*; Ferngren, *Medicine and Religion*; Nelson, *Say Little*.

ment in the United States, then move to their work in sub-Saharan Africa, and then bring it back to the United States at the end.

In the eighteenth and nineteenth centuries, the few hospitals that developed in the United States were established by Protestants, mainly men. Yet it was Catholic sister nurses, the women of the church, who established and administered the Catholic hospital system in the entire country. They built institutions and created services for the poor long before the emergence of the modern hospital and scientific medicine. In fact, the woman-centered, nurse-based entrepreneurship of Catholic sisters had a distinctive effect on the character of today's American health care institutions.

The greatest number of these women were European immigrants, mainly Irish, who were nurses. The Alexian Brothers also were nurses and hospital administrators, but most Catholic hospital owners were sisters. They had no money when they first arrived in the United States; furthermore, the public face of Catholic authority undoubtedly has been male. Yet most Catholic hospitals in America were established and originally managed by women.[3] They could not count on the church for aid, yet these sisters did things that the rest of us urgently need to learn, particularly around questions of power, engagement, and change.

Historically, Catholic sister nurses have had a mission to care for the sick, the injured, the aged, and the dying. In the process, they found multiple connections between biomedicine and religion. In the seventeenth century, St. Vincent DePaul and St. Louise de Marillac's Daughters of Charity went into the streets of France to do nursing. By the early nineteenth century, sisters were establishing hospitals at a time of rapid economic development in Europe and elsewhere. Famine and religious persecution led many Europeans to emigrate to the United States, as the United States had available jobs and land. By the 1860s, with the influx of many Catholics, church leaders sensed that this growing population had only a few spiritual institutions, which included hospitals, and the sisters led in hospital establishment.[4]

Sisters in the United States

As sisters expanded their health care in the United States in the wake of immigration, they faced Protestant anxieties over Catholics' obedience to the pope, which Protestants thought was incompatible with republican citizenship and religious freedom. Catholic leaders counterattacked this nativism by attempting to demonstrate the church's compatibility with American

3. Wall, *Unlikely Entrepreneurs.*
4. Dolan, *American Catholic Experience.*

democracy. Because of the prevailing anti-Catholicism, Catholics formed strong attachments to their own institutions.[5]

While Protestant growth occurred particularly in the southern regions of the United States, Catholic European immigrants predominated in eastern cities such as New York, Boston, and Philadelphia, and in Midwestern cities such as St. Paul, St. Louis, and Chicago. The Catholic Church was in the minority in Texas and Utah, but these areas attracted many immigrant miners and railroad workers from Catholic countries who were potential American Catholics. And Texas had a large Catholic Hispanic population. Catholic sisters went to all these places.[6]

Wherever they went, sisters renegotiated dominant notions of what being a sister nurse meant as they navigated among an array of representations, from nurse to hospital administrator, to woman, to religious person, to professional practitioner of scientific medicine. They would never have succeeded in the American hospital marketplace had they not demonstrated the flexibility to adapt. This adaptation resulted from the standpoint of making connections: with religious and secular leaders and with people of other cultures.[7]

Sisters eventually established their own nurse training schools at the turn of the twentieth century. Before that, however, they received on-the-job instruction in the care of the sick from doctors and experienced nursing sisters. Their religious constitutions articulated how the sick were to be treated, what daily schedule sister-nurses should follow, how they should relate to physicians, how to care for the dying, and how they were to prepare food and medicines. They incorporated various healing practices associated with regular medicine while also carrying out devotions and rituals, such as devotions to the saints and the Virgin Mary.

In 1823, nuns first began staffing hospitals in the continental United States at the Baltimore Infirmary, where they charged a small fee for admission. University officials asked the Sisters of Charity from Emmitsburg, Maryland, founded by Saint Elizabeth Seton, to staff the infirmary. In the process, sisters had to construct a kind of nursing and hospital management that focused on accountability, skill, and flexibility. In the turmoil of immigration, sisters contributed greatly to the production of something new: the modern hospital and the modern nurse. Sisters' prayer life, their business

---

5. Dolan, *American Catholic Experience*.
6. Dolan, *American Catholic Experience*; Wall, *Unlikely Entrepreneurs*.
7. Dries, "American Catholic 'Woman's Work.'"

acumen, and their health care ministry intertwined as they worked in the hospital marketplace.[8]

Other scholars have made similar arguments; Sioban Nelson, Diane Batts Morrow, Carol Coburn and Martha Smith, Margaret McGuinness, Bernadette McCauley, and others have written about sisters in health care.[9] All dispel the notion that these sisters were separate from the world. Their work reveals conflicts but also adaptations in nursing and hospital development as secular society changed.

For example, the American Civil War from 1861 to 1865 was a defining event for the Catholic sisterhoods. Six hundred sisters from twenty-one different communities nursed in military hospitals, US Navy hospital ships, prisons, and improvised field hospitals. Other sisters converted their own hospitals into Army facilities.[10] Most women nurses were untrained, but some of the sisters were tutored in basic elements of nursing. The Sisters of Charity in Emmitsburg, Maryland, for example, had been educated by Mother Xavier Clark, who wrote "Instructions for the Care of the Sick" in 1841.[11]

Mother Xavier was superior of Saint Elizabeth Seton's Sisters of Charity in the United States from 1839 to 1845, and she wrote this booklet for sister nurses. Her "Instructions" were an addendum to a part written by a priest in 1796. Mother Xavier gave detailed instructions on prayer, but she also taught the sisters how to administer medicines. They were to keep them covered to prevent evaporation, avoid mixing them, know the correct doses, and use clean utensils and clean water in all the preparations.[12] Mother Xavier taught that the sisters would be "in charge" and should "know everything." The experienced sisters were to guide the less experienced ones and to supervise men who tended male patients. Significantly, Mother Xavier taught her sister-nurses to respect both bodies and souls; indeed, any selfish intentions opposed the calling of a religious sister.[13] While Florence Nightingale helped to legitimize nursing as a respectable field for middle-class women, Catholic sisters' nursing became the model for the modern nurse, long before Nightingale came on the scene.

---

8. Wall and Nelson, "Our Heels Are Praying;" Nelson, *Say Little*.

9. Nelson, *Say Little*; Morrow, *Persons of Color*; McGuinness, *Called to Serve*; McCauley, *Who Shall Take Care of Our Sick?*; Coburn and Smith, *Spirited Lives*.

10. Maher, *To Bind Up the Wounds*; Wall, "Called to a Mission;" Wall, "Grace Under Pressure;" McNeil, *Balm of Hope*.

11. Wall, *Unlikely Entrepreneurs*; Wall, "Textual Analysis;" Clark, "Instructions."

12. Clark, "Instructions," 4, 5, 6, 8.

13. Clark, "Instructions," 10, 13.

Sisters worked with the government in ways that became innovative models of church and state working together. For example, in 1864, the Sisters of St. Joseph in Wheeling, West Virginia, contracted with the Union government for six hundred dollars a year for the sister nurses to care for soldiers at their hospital. The superior, Mother de Chantal Keating, was a young Irish immigrant who had come to the United States during the Irish famine years in the 1850s, and she strongly believed in financial stability. On February 8, 1865, she traveled to the War Department in Washington, DC, to demand that the Army pay the overdue rent to the sisters for the use of their hospital in Wheeling. She had her data, consisting of all accounts and certificates, and stayed for two weeks until she received the money due her. She and her sisters had a strong religious commitment to their work, but their entrepreneurship led them to expect the government to uphold its end of their deal as well. Mother de Chantal's perseverance was significant: wartime was an especially important time for sisters to demonstrate their skilled nursing care, and their work helped enhance the general public's perceptions of Catholics.[14]

After the American Civil War, Catholic hospitals in the United States grew alongside other hospitals during a period of scientific expansion. Few Catholic donors existed at the time, and sisters had to charge patients for hospital admissions from the very beginning. The sisters did not dwell on the need for Catholic doctors in their hospitals, because they partnered with as many physicians as possible who brought in paying patients. Both Protestant and Catholic doctors and sisters depended on each other to maintain medical accreditation, financial viability, and religious authority.

Also, by the early twentieth century, the germ theory had been accepted, and doctors became more disease-oriented. While they could more skillfully diagnose a problem, they could not cure most diseases until the Second World War and the arrival of antibiotics and other wonder drugs. Doctors could bring relief, but they increasingly focused on a narrower scientific orientation and institutional structure of modern medicine.[15]

By contrast, from the beginning of their hospital establishments, sisters had an expanded idea about illness and its treatment. They accepted the values and orientations of modern American medicine, but they also believed in supernatural causes and treatments based on a long-standing Catholic devotional culture. They developed a space in the United States where "a specific, socially beneficial type of care could be provided and purchased." These sisters brought into being new hospitals with different

---

14. Wall, "Called to a Mission."
15. Rosenberg, *Care of Strangers.*

economic models, those in which authority depended not on male physicians or church leaders or state support but on the ability of women religious, who convinced other people to have confidence in the Catholic hospital that they created. In the process, sisters assumed full financial responsibility of their institutions. They were members of the board of directors, administrators, nurses, X-ray workers, and leaders of schools of nursing, while building collaborative networks with influential sponsors, many of whom were non-Catholic.[16]

As nursing and medical standards increased and science and technology expanded over the course of the twentieth century, sisters' schools of nursing and hospitals kept pace. This included requiring the newest equipment, more intensive coursework for nursing students, higher admissions standards, and licensure examinations. At the same time, Catholic hospitals became both medical and religious spaces as sisters integrated both spiritual and scientific care.[17]

In 1915, sisters and priests formed the Catholic Hospital Association to work toward greater standardization in their hospitals. The American College of Surgeons had adopted certain standards for hospitals to obtain approval, and other hospitals were doing the same thing.[18] Yet, by the 1930s sisters faced new challenges. The Great Depression created emergencies that caused a flood of federal legislation that affected all members of society, including hospitals.[19] The poor economy and expanding demands for free care led different hospital associations and administrators to work together for health policy in the political arena. They became avid proponents of the value of private hospitals as equal partners with government institutions.

Resolutions asking for government aid were passed at the 1934 Catholic Hospital Association Convention, but money could be accepted only under one condition: even though federal relief to hospitals was desired, this did not mean federal control. Implicit in the association's resolution was the fear that the government might challenge hospital leaders' authority by becoming more involved in management issues. Eventually, Catholic and Protestant leaders secured a ruling to allow government employees to be admitted to private hospitals, with reimbursement from the federal government but without significant government regulation.[20]

16. Wall, *Unlikely Entrepreneurs*, 3.
17. Wall, "Science and Ritual."
18. Wall, *Unlikely Entrepreneurs*.
19. Wall, *American Catholic Hospitals*; and Shanahan, *History of the Catholic Hospital Association*.
20. "US Aid in Care of Indigents," 34; Shanahan, *History of the Catholic Hospital Association*, 119, 121.

But real success in health reform did not come until the mid-1940s, and by then, Father Alphonse Schwitalla was the Catholic Hospital Association president. In 1945, he and representatives from the Protestant Hospital Association and the American Hospital Association joined together for the first time to sponsor a bill that they themselves helped develop, culminating in the Hospital Survey and Construction Act, or the Hill-Burton Act, which provided federal grants to states for the construction of hospitals and health centers. In return, hospitals agreed to provide a reasonable number of free services to people unable to pay.[21] Significantly, the bill restricted the government's role in determining how funds would be distributed to states, which meant "no strings attached," and the Hill-Burton Act was signed into law in August 1946. This was a great example of church and state working together to solve a problem. Unfortunately, the Hill-Burton Act maintained "separate but equal" hospitals. It did not demand desegregation of hospitals as a prerequisite for getting federal dollars. After World War II, Catholic leaders did not yet embrace the view that everyone had a basic human right to health care, even via the government if necessary.

Sisters in Sub-Saharan Africa

As the secular scene in the United States was changing and Catholic hospital leaders were becoming more involved in politics, so the world was changing. Following World War II, national identities and international alliances were shifting rapidly, and many colonized nations found courage and opportunities to move toward independence. In sub-Saharan Africa, as the voices of independence grew louder, British and other colonizers reacted by moving out in droves. Consequently, indigenous populations struggled to realign their countries and begin the arduous process of self-rule. Catholic women's religious congregations, whose work in Africa had been hampered by the war, now saw themselves playing a supportive role in this transition process by expanding their medical missions.[22] They did so in the context of an accelerating Catholic missionary movement: in the 1950s, there were more foreign missionaries in Africa than ever before.[23]

Under the leadership of Austrian-born Anna Dengel, foundress of the Society of Catholic Medical Missionaries, or the Medical Mission Sisters, sisters established a new position for themselves that combined religious commitment and medical science. By the mid-twentieth century, Catholic

21. Schwitalla, "19th Resolution"; Schwitalla, "Hospital Construction Act."
22. Dries, *Missionary Movement*.
23. Hastings, *African Catholicism*, 122; Bender, *Rethinking American History*.

sisters were being educated to be scientific practitioners, and they were convinced that they could bring established biomedical knowledge and therapeutics to the missions. They could provide greater health care access as one answer to an uneven distribution of hospitals. Indeed, the Catholic Church provided a structure for women in religious congregations as vowed, celibate women to obtain a medical education and, eventually, to cross national borders as they developed care networks all over the world.[24]

Mother Anna and others had worked with the pope to change a centuries-old policy that prohibited Catholic sisters from practicing medicine. They could practice nursing, but after 1936, they were able to become surgeons, midwives, and obstetricians in the missions. This was new. They worked alongside nurses in new initiatives and, for the most part, embraced the power structure of the Catholic Church and what it could provide them. Their personal negotiations of their religious and gendered identities in secular medical schools and later in their mission hospitals reveal the possibilities of professional roles for Catholic sister doctors, nurses, and midwives to bridge international boundaries.

While the sisters could study nursing in both the United States and Europe, American sisters had to go to Europe for midwifery training due to restrictions on that practice in the United States. Some sisters from colonized areas such as Nigeria were able to go to Europe, including Ireland, to qualify as nurses and midwives. Others trained in different mission congregations' schools of nursing and midwifery in the colonies.[25]

In her 1945 publication, *Mission for Samaritans*, Mother Anna outlined a particular framework for mission work that combined religious commitment, medical science, and politics. She saw it as a "branch of missionary work through which skilled medical care is given to the sick and poor of mission countries, as a means of relieving their physical suffering and bringing to them a knowledge and appreciation of our Faith. . . ."[26] Yet one of the reasons she gave for medical missions was as an act of "restitution as well as of charity"; she wrote, "[i]t is the tremendous debt which we, the white race, owe to the peoples subjected and exploited by our forefathers."[27] Furthermore, the sisters would care for "all whom we see sick and suffering, even if we know that they will not therefore accept our Faith."[28] Although Mother

24. Wall, *Into Africa*.

25. O'Hogartaigh, *Quiet Revolutionaries*; Kelly, "'Fascinating Scalper-Wielders'"; Hogan, *Irish Missionary Movement*.

26. Dengel, *Mission for Samaritans*, 1.

27. Dengel, *Mission for Samaritans*, 3.

28. Dengel, *Mission for Samaritans*, 5.

Anna recognized that missionary priests and sisters had worked for centuries in relieving the sick, what was new for her religious community was "organized, systematic medical care by people . . . who have been trained in the medical field as doctors, nurses, or technicians."[29] She was convinced of the superiority of scientific knowledge, and she wanted to make it available to others. Mother Anna's congregation, the Medical Mission Sisters, was one of the first groups of its kind in the medical field to be both professional and religious and to work as physicians, surgeons, and obstetricians.[30]

Disagreements, however, on the nature of mission legacies are central to historians today. Many see missionaries as agents of British imperialism, and indeed, when they first went to Africa, sisters did align with British colonial authorities to get their foot in the door. Although it took a period of soul-searching and of questioning the very idea of mission, the social and economic realities of the people with whom sisters worked became part of the mission focus, as did a greater respect for African cultural practices.[31]

From the beginning of their work in sub-Saharan Africa, Catholic sisters focused not only on acute care but also on public health. This brought with it many challenges as they worked in environments that were different from their own backgrounds in Europe or the United States. Although sister nurses, physicians, and midwives were well trained in colleges and universities, when working in the bush or holding clinics during wartime or other periods of violence, they faced new challenges. Because physicians were in short supply, sister nurses often took on roles that physicians carried out in Europe or the United States.[32]

Just as in the United States, Catholic sisters' medical practices in Africa incorporated both science and religion. Even though they performed surgery in sterile operating rooms, sisters also included religious feasts, processions, and rituals in their hospitals, and they celebrated holy days. Mission hospitals were sites where one could witness a variety of healing practices. One hospital administered by the American Maryknoll Sisters in Tanzania was such a space. In 1949, a sister delivered a premature baby who did not thrive, and after performing life-saving measures, she eventually gave up and baptized the infant. Yet, she had also allowed an indigenous practitioner into the delivery room. According to the sister, this person beat "some sort of a cooking pot which she held over the baby's head, and chant[ed] a

---

29. Dengel, *Mission for Samaritans*, 1.
30. Dries, *Missionary Movement*.
31. Wall, *Into Africa*.
32. Wall, *Into Africa*.

'pagan' song to ward off the evil spirits." Soon, the baby started breathing.[33] Blending of cultural practices was not common in Africa in the 1940s and 1950s, though, and sisters strongly believed in the superiority of their scientific medical practices. They also believed in miracles. In this case, the sister attributed the baby's survival to the baptism rather than the work of the indigenous healer.[34]

Nigerian Civil War

Sisters also faced ethical challenges as their work intertwined with political movements. As medical missionaries in sub-Saharan Africa, sister doctors, nurses, and midwives had a major role to play in health care delivery in war-torn areas. The Nigerian Civil War lasted from 1967 to 1970, and one million people—mostly unarmed civilians including women and children—lost their lives. Irish missionary doctors, nurses, and midwives, sponsored by the Roman Catholic Church, provided wide-ranging humanitarian relief and medical care.

The Medical Missionaries of Mary had come to Nigeria from Ireland in 1937 to do both missionary and medical work. In the 1960s, however, they shifted their understanding of mission away from conversion of souls toward humanitarian relief.[35] Catholic sisters had come to Nigeria during the colonial era when Christianity was the religion of the colonial powers, and the missions had a privileged position.[36] Irish priests and sisters aligned with British colonialists, and the sisters were hardly ecumenical. Over time, however, sisters learned the local language and acculturated to their surroundings, and this resulted in many tensions that were exacerbated during periods of revolution or civil war.

The Nigerian Civil War led to a public health emergency when a segment of the Nigerian population became displaced in an area renamed Biafra, and food was cut off to them.[37] The Catholic Church was one of the private agencies that played a significant role in the war. Although they had made little impact in the northern part of Nigeria, with its Muslim majority, Catholic missionaries were more successful in the southeastern region, particularly among the Ibo (Igbo) population. For the Irish, Nigeria

33. Diary Digest.
34. Wall, *Into Africa*.
35. Velho, "Missionization," 36; Casanova, "Religion."
36. Stanley, "Missions, Nationalism."
37. Obiaga, *Politics of Humanitarian Organizations*; Ojeleye, *Politics of Post-War Demobilization*.

was the centerpiece of their "religious empire," with more Irish missionaries concentrated there than elsewhere in the entire world.[38] By 1965, the southeastern area had over two million conversions.[39] The Irish also made great inroads in education and health care, where the British colonial state had not played a large role.

Nigeria was formed in 1914 when Britain joined the two northern and southern protectorates, and it received full independence in 1960. Yet, the ideological and social differences between the Muslim north and Christian east were huge. The civil war that began in 1967 was between the eastern region of Nigeria, renamed Biafra, and the rest of the country. Biafra declared itself an independent state, which the Federal Military Government of Nigeria regarded as an act of illegal secession, and the federals fought the war to reunite the country. One million people had fled to the East, and by April 1968, Biafrans had flooded into a landlocked enclave surrounded by federal forces who blockaded all the roads. Western nations were unwilling to violate Nigeria's national sovereignty and channel assistance across the border. While most Protestant organizations fled, the sisters and many Irish priests made the crucial decision to stay in Biafra. The thirty-month war ended in 1970 when the revolt collapsed.[40]

One important document from this time is a diary by Sister Doctor Pauline Dean, a Medical Missionary of Mary, who worked at St. Mary's Hospital in Urua Akpan during the war. Sister Pauline wrote her diary from January to September 1968.[41] It was during this period that her hospital was in the middle of the conflict. St. Mary's had begun in 1952, and at the time of the Civil War, it boasted one hundred and fifty beds, a large surgical clinic, and a training school for midwifery.

In her diary, Sister Pauline gave eyewitness accounts of aerial bombardments of her hospital, people being killed, roadblocks established by soldiers, and the disease situation in the refugee camps. The diary provides a vivid account of the most severe health and nutritional problems resulting from the war. Her first entry on January 23 was an acknowledgment of the food problem. She said, "Food was scarce, so we started to farm. Planted pumpkin, melon, and okra." On January 28, she noted the turmoil of the region: "Plane and two thuds in OPD [outpatient department]. I did not hear because of screaming children."[42] On February 19, she wrote, "Bad day

38. Staunton, "Case of Biafra," 513.
39. Wiseberg, "Christian Churches."
40. Staunton, "Case of Biafra;" Ojeleye, *Politics of Post-War Demobilization*.
41. Dean, *Biafra War Diary*.
42. Dean, *Biafra War Diary*, entries for January 23, 28, 30, 1968.

trying to do Male Ward, Children's Ward, and 2 clinics. Head just doesn't work after 1:30 when working at such a pace." February 20 was another "bad day," and on the twenty-first, she was "up at night 2–5 am" and the next day faced 108 patients as the only doctor.[43]

In the eastern region where military operations were the most active, farming could not take place, and famine resulted. Thus, an international ecumenical airlift began operating in violation of Nigerian airspace and without Nigerian authority. This airlift defied the federal blockade, often under gunfire, and flew in medicines and food to Biafra, even though the Nigerian government had banned outside aid flights. The airlifts were the only remaining lifelines for those in the eastern enclave. While the public face of the Nigerian Civil War was of starving children and of priests who ran the airlift, women also played critical roles in relieving suffering. And the sisters had a key resource on their side: Nigerian sisters in their congregations who could maintain the hospitals after the expatriates left. For example, Sister Joseph Theresa Agbasiere, a Biafran Holy Rosary Sister, cared for many patients at a feeding station, revealing the local response of Nigerians caring for themselves.[44]

Still, the role of Christian churches during the war was ambivalent, and churches supported both sides. In the process, the Catholic Church's role in the conflict caused considerable political controversy. The Nigerian government was hostile to the priests, sister nurses, and physicians, and other relief agencies in Biafra, arguing that they prolonged the war by feeding the enemy.[45] To the government, this work was illegal, and the Catholic Church was meddling and aiding rebellion. The federal government eventually expelled three hundred priests and two hundred sister nurses and physicians from the country. Only a few were invited back later in the 1970s.[46]

Yet, as much as the Irish sisters tried to project an objective image, in reading their documents it is not difficult to see where their loyalties lay. As they saw their people dying, their voices became more critical. To the extent that their humanitarianism reflected their identification with vulnerable Biafrans, it then became political.[47] For the Irish sisters, who thought the suffering would be greater if they did nothing, the consequences of their involvement in the political struggles were tremendous, because they lost their hospitals.

43. Dean, *Biafra War Diary*, February 19, 20, 21, 22, 1968.
44. Wall, *Into Africa*.
45. Wiseberg, "Christian Churches."
46. Sundkler and Steed, *History of the Church in Africa*.
47. Obiaga, *Politics*; Wiseberg, "Humanitarian Intervention."

When the Irish Medical Missionaries of Mary were expelled from Nigeria, what was lost for them became an opportunity for Nigerians. The Catholic Church had been slow to indigenize its institutions. With fewer white expatriates in the church after the war, more Nigerians were ordained as priests, and Nigerian sister nurses, physicians, and midwives also continued to work. Africanization of church institutions did, in fact, increase after the war.[48]

Work with African Indigenous Healers

The Nigerian story is a conflict narrative, but an example of an "entangled" history and one of crossovers can be seen in the sisters' work with African indigenous healers. When sisters first came to Africa in the 1930s and 1940s, they were very critical of indigenous healers, but by the 1970s, sisters and other healers began mutually exchanging knowledge. This occurred in the context of expanded primary health care endeavors, with preventive nursing and medical strategies increasing.[49] The sisters also began allying with national organizations such as local and state ministries of health and global actors such as the Christian Medical Commission and the World Health Organization.[50]

As early as 1962, Sister Doctor Margaret Mary Nolan, a Medical Missionary of Mary who worked in Nigeria, wrote about indigenous healers:

> The native doctors have many useful, powerful leaves and herbs at their disposal. In many cases, native treatment will save a life, through controlling haemorrhage, or relieving pain and preventing shock. The ill effects seen from these raw drugs, we presume, arise simply because the dosages have never been studied. All this leaves plenty of scope for research workers.[51]

In addition, Sister Rose Kerschbaumer, a Medical Mission Sister and nurse midwife in several countries in sub-Saharan Africa, recalled that, as the years progressed, "We would have groups of traditional healers get together . . . as the countries then began to recognize that there is some good in traditional medicine. And what you have to do is try to eliminate what isn't good and support what is good."[52]

48. Hastings, "Ministry of the Catholic Church," 26–42.
49. Ranger, "Godly Medicine."
50. Akerele et al., "New Role for Medical Missionaries."
51. Nolan, *Medical Missionaries of Mary*, 147.
52. Johnson and Wall, oral interview.

By the mid-1960s, sister nurses were incorporating some indigenous healing measures into their own practice. The Maryknoll sisters in Tanzania ran a clinic that had a "snake stone," as one of the sisters called it. They had learned about this treatment from another local doctor. Poisonous snake bites were common, and when a patient came with the problem, the sister nurse incised the bite to get it to bleed and then pressed the small black stone into the blood for an hour until it fell off. The therapeutic effect was that it absorbed the poison, and the sisters marveled at how patients' pain was relieved soon after. It also proved effective for spider bites and bee and wasp stings.[53]

More crossovers occurred in Ghana in the 1980s, when the Medical Mission Sisters worked extensively with public health workers in primary health care. The sisters realized that indigenous healers did better work on fractures and with psychiatric illnesses, so sisters referred patients with these conditions to the healers. In turn, the healers referred other illnesses to the sisters. Indeed, through the partnerships negotiated on the ground, Catholic sisters and local healers played a key role in shaping the international agenda for primary health care.[54]

It is significant to understand that, after the 1960s, Vatican II proved extremely important in influencing changes in the sisters' mission, because it reversed many long-standing and uncompromising doctrinal policies. It supported the idea of "church" as the people of God, and it also brought about a renewed focus on social justice. But as early as 1945, Mother Anna Dengel wrote that sisters' endeavors to heal would be of little help unless they were accompanied by an attendance upon "basic social and economic structures."[55] Sisters' growing attention to social and economic factors foreshadowed ideas of social determinants of health that are prominent in discourse today.

Sisters in the United States, Post-1960s

The 1960s, 1970s, and 1980s brought other changes in the United States. Not only was hospital management changing, but the sisters were leaving their congregations after Vatican II. As one sister noted, "Sisters in habits were replaced by men in suits." Some sisters went on to get master's degrees in hospital management, while others left to pursue theology or pastoral care rather than nursing. And of course, Medicare and Medicaid came in

53. "Birth of Tanzania, Africa."
54. Wall, *Into Africa*.
55. Dengel, *Mission for Samaritans*, 5.

1965, changing everything in terms of financial support and hospitals' operating margins.[56]

How much charity care could be provided was certainly being contested at that time due to increased hospital costs and growing insurance programs. Acrimonious debates among Catholics grew as large health care institutions were expanding. This is when some sisters chose to get out of the business altogether, because they could not meet their historic response to the poor. But others stayed. Today, the Catholic Church sponsors the largest not-for-profit health care system in the country.[57]

The health care reform debates of 2009 and 2010 show how religious issues, power conflicts, and crossover interests continued to permeate the health care system. On March 3, 2010, Sister Carol Keehan, president of the Catholic Health Association, was invited to the White House to hear President Barack Obama speak about his health reform plan. The Catholic Health Association viewed the legislation as going far toward covering more than thirty million uninsured people in the country. To the association, the bill was about access to care. On March 17, fifty-nine thousand more sisters joined with the Catholic Health Association to support the legislation. Asserting that it would "make historic new investments in support of pregnant women," the sisters declared: "This is the *real* pro-life stance, and we as Catholics are all for it."[58]

It is not surprising that sisters would take such a stand, because they offered a different way of seeing the poor and oppressed. They witnessed the problems that developed when poor women could not get prenatal care, and the tragic misfortunes that often resulted when the sick were left alone to care for themselves. The sisters' actions gave a degree of inspiration and political cover to some congressional members who then came out in support of the bill.[59] On March 23, 2010, President Obama signed the Patient Protection and Affordable Care Act, the first health care legislation passed in fifty years. The sisters' actions did not go uncontested, though, by the laity and by priests.

In conclusion, historically, conflict, cooperation, entanglements, and crossovers have long lurked in the background of sisters' work. In all of their hospitals in different countries, sisters had to adapt to diverse political, medical, social, religious, and professional circumstances to remain financially

---

56. Wall, *Into Africa*.

57. Catholic Health Association, "U.S. Catholic Health Care," 1–2. It consists of six hundred hospitals and 1,600 long-term care and other health facilities in all fifty states.

58. Alonso-Zaldivar and Fram, "Obama's Health Care," para. 1.

59. Wall, *American Catholic Hospitals*.

viable and ethically compliant to church directives. Tensions erupted among the clergy, sisters, the government, and lay public that persist to the present. But sisters' successes in finding common ground and building coalitions among disparate entities have provided valuable working models for how to blend the sacred and the secular.

In November 2013, Pope Francis issued his apostolic exhortation, *Evangelii Gaudium: The Joy of the Gospel*, in which he stated, "I prefer a Church which is bruised, hurting, and dirty because it has been out on the streets, rather than a Church which is unhealthy from being confined and from clinging to its own security."[60] The sisters must have smiled broadly when they heard this exhortation, as it lent credence and approval for what they have been doing since the sixteenth century.

Bibliography

Akerele, Olayiwola, et al. "A New Role for Medical Missionaries in Africa." *WHO Chronicle* 30 (1976) 175–80.

Alonso-Zaldivar, Ricardo, and Alan Fram. "Obama's Health Care Plan Picks Up Support." *The Oakland Press*, March 17, 2010. https://www.theoaklandpress.com/2010/03/17/obamas-health-care-plan-picks-up-support/.

Bender, Thomas, ed. *Rethinking American History in a Global Age*. Berkeley: University of California Press, 2002.

"Birth of Tanzania, Africa," 1966. Africa History, Box 2, Maryknoll Sisters Archives, Ossining, NY.

Burke, Daniel. "Pope Francis Calls for Big Changes in Roman Catholic Church." CNN, November 26, 2013. https://www.cnn.com/2013/11/26/world/pope-church-reforms/.

Casanova, Jose. "Religion, the New Millennium, and Globalization." *Sociology of Religion* 62.4 (2001) 415–41.

Catholic Health Association. "U.S. Catholic Health Care." CHAUSA, 2023. https://www.chausa.org/docs/default-source/default-document-library/the-strategic-profile.pdf.

Clark, Mother Xavier. "Instructions on the Care of the Sick," 1841; Marillac Provincial House Archives, Daughters of Charity of St. Vincent de Paul, St. Louis, MO.

Coburn, Carol K., and Martha Smith. *Spirited Lives: How Nuns Shaped Catholic Culture and American Life, 1836–1920*. Chapel Hill: University of North Carolina Press, 1999.

Dean, Sister Doctor Pauline. *Biafra War Diary*, Urua Akpan 1968. Archives of the Medical Missionaries of Mary, Drogheda, Ireland.

Dengel, Anna. *Mission for Samaritans*. Milwaukee, WI: Bruce, 1945.

Diary Digest, October 18, 1949. Diaries, Africa, Mauritius, and Tanganyika, Box 1. Maryknoll Sisters Archives, Ossining, NY.

---

60. Burke, "Pope Francis," para. 2.

Dolan, Jay P. *American Catholic Experience: A History from Colonial Times to the Present*. Notre Dame: University of Notre Dame Press, 1992.

Dries, Angelyn. "American Catholic 'Woman's Work for Woman' in the Twentieth Century." In *Gospel Bearers, Gender Barriers: Missionary Women in the Twentieth Century*, edited by Dana Robert, 127–42. Maryknoll, NY: Orbis, 2002.

———. *The Missionary Movement in American Catholic History*. Maryknoll, NY: Orbis, 1998.

Ferngren, Gary B. *Medicine and Religion: A Historical Introduction*. Baltimore: Johns Hopkins University Press, 2014.

Hastings, Adrian. *African Catholicism: Essays in Discovery*. London: SCM, 1989.

———. "The Ministry of the Catholic Church in Africa, 1960–1975." In *Christianity in Independent Africa*, edited by Edward Fashole-Luke et al., 26–42. London: R. Collings, 1978.

Hogan, Edmund M. *The Irish Missionary Movement*. Dublin: Gill and Macmillan, 1990.

Johnson, Lauren, and Barbra Mann Wall. Oral interview with Sister Rose Kershbaumer, May 10, 2012, Philadelphia, PA.

Kaufman, Suzanne. *Consuming Visions: Mass Culture and the Lourdes Shrine*. Ithaca, NY: Cornell University Press, 2005.

Kelly, Laura. "'Fascinating Scalper-Wielders and Fair Dissectors': Women's Experience of Irish Medical Education, c 1880s–1920s." *Medical History* 54 (2010) 495–516.

Lightman, Bernard, ed. *Rethinking History, Science, and Religion: An Exploration of Conflict and the Complexity Principle*. Pittsburgh: University of Pittsburgh Press, 2019.

Maher, Mary Denis. *To Bind Up the Wounds: Catholic Sister Nurses in the U.S. Civil War*. New York: Greenwood, 1989.

Martucci, Jessica. "Religion, Medicine, and Politics: Catholic Physicians' Guilds in America, 1909–32." *Bulletin of the History of Medicine* 92 (2018) 287–316.

McCauley, Bernadette. *Who Shall Take Care of Our Sick"? Roman Catholic Sisters and the Development of Catholic Hospitals in New York City*. Baltimore: Johns Hopkins University Press, 2005.

McGuinness, Margaret M. *Called to Serve: A History of Nuns in America*. New York: New York University Press, 2013.

McNeil, Betty Ann, ed. *Balm of Hope: Charity Afire Impels Daughters of Charity to Civil War Nursing*. Chicago: DePaul University Vincentian Studies Institute, 2015.

Morrow, Diane Batts. *Persons of Color and Religious at the Same Time: The Oblate Sisters of Providence, 1828–1860*. Chapel Hill: University of North Carolina Press, 2002.

Nelson, Sioban. *Say Little, Do Much: Nursing, Nuns, and Hospitals in the Nineteenth Century*. Philadelphia: University of Pennsylvania Press, 2001.

Nolan, Margaret Mary. *Medical Missionaries of Mary, Covering the First Twenty-Five Years of the Medical Missionaries of Mary, 1937–1962*. Dublin: Medical Missionaries of Mary, 1962.

Obiaga, Ndubisi. *The Politics of Humanitarian Organizations*. Dallas: University Press of America, 2004.

O'Hogartaigh, Margaret. *Quiet Revolutionaries: Irish Women in Education, Medicine, and Sport, 1861–1964*. Dublin: History Press Ireland, 2011.

Ojeleye, Olukunle. *The Politics of Post-War Demobilization and Reintegration in Nigeria*. Burlington, VT: Ashgate, 2010.

Ranger, Terence O. "Godly Medicine: The Ambiguities of Medical Mission in Southeastern Tanzania, 1900–1945." *Social Science and Medicine* 15.3 (1981) 261–77.

Rosenberg, Charles E. *Care of Strangers: The Rise of America's Hospital System*. Baltimore: Johns Hopkins University Press, 1987.

Schwitalla, Alphonse. "19th Resolution, 1942 CHA Convention." *Hospital Progress* XXIII (October 1942) 306–7.

———. "The Hospital Construction Act." *Hospital Progress* XXVI (January 1945) 27–31.

Shanahan, Robert J. *History of the Catholic Hospital Association, 1915–1965: Fifty Years of Progress*. St. Louis: Catholic Hospital Association, 1965.

Stanley, Brian. "Missions, Nationalism, and the End of Empire: Report on a Conference Organized by the Currents in World Christianity Project, Queens College, Cambridge, UK, September 6–9, 2000." *Journal of Religion in Africa* 31, fasc. 1 (February 2001) 115–17.

Staunton, Enda. "The Case of Biafra: Ireland and the Nigerian Civil War." *Irish Historical Studies* 31.124 (1999) 513–35.

Sundkler, Bengt, and Christopher Steed. *A History of the Church in Africa*. Cambridge, UK: Press Syndicate of the University of Cambridge, 2000.

"US Aid in Care of Indigents Asked by Catholic Group." *Hospital Management* 38.1 (July 1934) 34–5, 43.

Velho, Otávio. "Missionization in the Post-Colonial World: A View from Brazil and Elsewhere." *Anthropological Theory* 7.3 (September 2007) 259–367. https://journals.sagepub.com/doi/10.1177/1463499607080190.

Wall, Barbra Mann. *American Catholic Hospitals: A Century of Changing Markets and Missions*. New Brunswick: Rutgers University Press, 2011.

———. "Called to a Mission of Charity: The Sisters of St. Joseph in the Civil War." *Nursing History Review* 6 (1998) 85–113.

———. "Grace Under Pressure: The Nursing Sisters of the Holy Cross, 1861–1865." *Nursing History Review* 1 (1993) 71–87.

———. *Into Africa: A Transnational History of Catholic Medical Missions and Social Change*. New Brunswick: Rutgers University Press, 2015.

———. "Science and Ritual: The Hospital as Medical and Sacred Space, 1865–1920." *Nursing History Review* 11 (2003) 51–68.

———. "Textual Analysis as a Method for Historians of Nursing." *Nursing History Review* 14 (2006) 227–42.

———. *Unlikely Entrepreneurs: Catholic Sisters and the Hospital Marketplace, 1865–1925*. Columbus: Ohio State University Press, 2005.

Wall, Barbra Mann, and Sioban Nelson. "Our Heels Are Praying Very Hard All Day: The Working Prayer of the Nineteenth-Century Religious Nurse." *Holistic Nursing Practice* 17.6 (2003) 320–28.

Wiseberg, Laurie S. "Christian Churches and the Nigerian Civil War." *Journal of African Studies* 2 (1972) 297–331.

———. "Humanitarian Intervention: Lessons from the Nigerian Civil War." *Human Rights Journal* 7.1 (1974) 61–98.

4

Catholic Health Care in the Global South: Does the Giant Matter? A Perspective from Africa

SAM OROCHI ORACH, MD

I. Introduction

A HEALTH SYSTEM IS AN arrangement of institutions, the people therein, other resources, and the actual service delivery for the purpose of meeting the health needs of the targeted population. While this reflection is on Africa in general, much of this paper is drawn from my experience in Uganda. Quite often the health system focuses on health care. In the context of universal health coverage, within the larger UN Sustainable Development Goal 3, health care is only a contributor to health. This concern for overall health, which manifests "universality," inclusivity, and preferential concern for the vulnerable, is reflected in the mission of the Catholic health services in Uganda.

The participation of the Catholic Church in protecting and maintaining health is not an option but rather a scriptural demand and a moment for evangelism. In most of Africa, the Catholic Church and other religious bodies started providing health care that formed the foundation for the eventual national health systems. But the contribution by faith-based or religious organizations, including the Catholic Church, varies across the continent.

This paper endeavors to bring out the contribution of faith-based health care as well as the specific contribution made by the Catholic Church to national health systems today, especially in Africa. These contributions are to the institutional structure, policies, health care delivery, and the six World Health Organization (WHO) building blocks for health systems strengthening. But balancing faithfulness to the mission of Christ's healing ministry with services sustainability has become a big challenge. These challenges are both internal and external to the Catholic Church itself. Some are related to structures and corporate governance as well as to the perception, both in the population and within the institution of the church, that Catholic health services must be "free" or available at a minimal cost regardless of actual cost and sustainability.

This chapter looks at what is Catholic about "Catholic health services" and the threats posed to the sustainability of true Catholic health services. There is a need for an understanding, both within and outside the church, of the reality and sustainability of Catholic health services and its relevance not just to the population but also to its mission.

II. Health Care in the Global South

This chapter is written under the theme "rise up and walk." The call to "rise up and walk" is found in the Holy Bible in Acts 3:6; Acts 14:8–11; Matthew 9:5; Mark 2:9–12; and John 5:8. In this paper, these readings call the global South, the faith-based communities, and the Catholic Church in particular to rise up and overcome the challenges it faces in carrying out the healing ministry of Christ within the respective health systems. It is a call to hold hands, unite, and move together in contributing toward achievement of universal health coverage. The Catholic Church, which is a giant in the health sector but not visible enough, has to make itself visible and relevant.

The "global South" is a term often used to denote regions outside Europe and North America, mostly (though not all) characterized by low-income, low total expenditure on health and, in particular, low government expenditure on health, and often politically unstable or culturally marginalized. Africa, especially sub-Saharan Africa (SSA), scores poorly on many global rankings of health and health systems indicators. Sub-Saharan Africa is characterized by a low sociodemographic index, which impacts negatively on the burden of disease and health systems on the continent. The sociodemographic index combines the economy, education, and fertility rate and is used as a representation of social and economic development.[1]

The role religious or faith-based bodies play in health in the global South is within the general context of health systems in the region. Despite

---

1. "Global Burden," 1.

the stiffer challenge faith-based health providers get in the above context, they make relatively large contributions to national health outputs and outcomes.

According to 2018 data, only five countries on the entire African continent have less than 5 percent of the population living in abject poverty. Most of the others have levels well over 25 percent.[2] At the same time, Africa has the highest burden of disease, dominated largely by preventable communicable diseases. However, a transition is taking place, with increasing numbers of noncommunicable diseases due partly to demographic changes.

a. Health Systems

While there is no uniform definition of what a health system is, it may be defined as an arrangement of institutions, the people therein, the other resources, and the arrangement of the actual service delivery for the purpose of meeting the health needs of the targeted population, and not just the individual. It is a combination of "all organizations, people and actions whose primary intent is to promote, restore or maintain health."[3] This includes efforts to influence social determinants of health as well as more direct health-improving activities. The World Bank therefore correctly observes that "what sets apart a health system is that its purpose is concerned with people's health. It has many parts, being the interconnection of roles and functions played by patients, families, and communities, Ministries of Health, health providers, health services organizations, pharmaceutical companies, health financing bodies, and other organizations."[4]

At every level, the health system is comprised of the six WHO health system "building blocks," namely (i) leadership/governance/management, (ii) human resources, (iii) health financing, (iv) information and informatics, (v) medicines and medical technologies, and (vi) service delivery structure.[5] These building blocks interlink, although financing has a crosscutting relationship with all the others. For example, the level of political commitment or support of the national policy or the inadequacy of its implementation thereof has an impact on health through the level of funding of the other building blocks—e.g., quality and retention of human resources for health, strength of the medical supply chain, etc.

2. "World Poverty Map."
3. World Health Organization, *World Health Report 2003*, 105.
4. World Bank, *Healthy Development*, 173.
5. World Health Organization, *Monitoring the Building Blocks*, 7.

Health systems in the global South are generally weak, not because the experts in these countries do not know what to do, but because health is politically lower in priority, resulting in heavy reliance on donor funding, often rendering the systems vulnerable to distortions by the donors. There is often also inequity, and systems are easily overburdened by preventable diseases. For the purpose of illustration, this chapter highlights mainly health financing and some of the human resources for health (HRH) building blocks.

b. Health Financing in the Global South

Globally, there has been slow growth in health expenditures, but this is worst in the low- to lower-middle income countries.[6] In 2018, most African countries spent less than US $100 per capita per year. The share of government spending on health is lowest in low-income and lower-middle income countries. The situation is worse in the sub-Saharan region of Africa, which covers forty-eight (89 percent) of the fifty-four African countries. Algeria, Djibouti, Egypt, Libya, Morocco, Somalia, Sudan, and Tunisia are classified as "North African" countries. Somalia and Djibouti are actually sub-Saharan African countries but are sometimes called "North African" by the World Bank, because it oversees these two countries from its Middle East office. That reduces the number of sub-Saharan African countries to forty-six.

In the sub-Saharan region, there has generally been a downward trend in the current health expenditure (CHE) as a percent of the gross domestic product (GDP), with a plateauing from 2016 to 2018. Although Uganda is above the regional average, it has also registered a steep downward trend from 6.46 percent in 2006 to 4.96 percent in 2016, plateauing from the 2015 value of 5.08 percent.[7]

Consequent to low government expenditure on health, the poor countries register high out-of-pocket expenditures (OOPs). This is likely to be catastrophic, sending poor people deeper into poverty and ill-health. The WHO's 2013 report from its Regional Office for Africa indicates that, with acknowledgment of inter-country variations, the higher the national GDP per capita, the lower the OOP expenditure. The report shows that the majority of African countries congregate around low per capita GDP with high OOP.

However, the WHO cautions that those countries that have low per capita GDP but low OOP may have poor access to good quality services, "meaning that the levels of out-of-pocket payments simply reflect low levels

---

6. World Health Organization, *Global Spending on Health*, 7.
7. World Bank, "Current Health Expenditure."

of service use"[8] and adding that "data are needed on both service use and out-of-pocket payments for a valid assessment."[9] The report states that "in about half of African countries, 40 percent or more of the total health expenditure is constituted of household out-of-pocket payments, which is the most regressive way of funding health care."[10] It then went on to say, "These weaknesses in the health financing systems have been identified as the main underlying reasons for the limited progress towards achieving the health MDGs [Millennium Development Goals] in Africa."[11]

This trend of increasing OOP with decreasing government contributions to the CHE is demonstrated in the specific case of Uganda. Five years down the road, the picture has not changed much from what was seen in 2015, as shown in the 2019–20 Uganda health sector annual performance report.

There is a rise in the proportion of external funding to health as the government expenditure on health, compared to total government expenditure (TGE), drops. But the proportional rise in external funding does not cause a reduction in the out-of-pocket expenditure. This is, first of all, because the biggest part of the external funding—e.g., 64.3 percent in 2014–15 and 75.1 percent in 2015–16—goes to "preventive services" and not health care where the patients make out-of-pocket payments, which, in principle, is a good thing. The external funding was largely taken up by epidemiological surveillance and risk and disease control programs, these adding up to 78 percent in 2014 and 86.5 percent in 2015. However, in large part, these programs are related to HIV/AIDS, tuberculosis (TB), and malaria vertical programs[12] (even where part of the funding is for clinical services).[13] Based on data obtained from Catholic-founded hospitals, vertical funding for HIV/AIDS, TB, and malaria accounts for 60–80 percent of the donor funds for recurrent costs.[14] This means that the rest of primary health care needs,

---

8. WHO Regional Office for Africa, *State of Health Financing*, 24.
9. WHO Regional Office for Africa, *State of Health Financing*, 24.
10. WHO Regional Office for Africa, *State of Health Financing*, 6.
11. WHO Regional Office for Africa, *State of Health Financing*, 6. (Note: The MDGs were replaced by the Sustainable Development Goals (SDGs) when the UN's member nations adopted them in 2015. For more information, see International Monetary Fund, "IMF."
12. "The vertical delivery of health services implies a selective targeting of specific interventions not fully integrated in health systems, often linked with particular interests of the funding entity." Sakala et al., "Integration of Vertical and Horizontal Programs," 1.
13. Uganda Ministry of Health, *Uganda Health Accounts*, 36–39.
14. Uganda Catholic Medical Bureau (UCMB) database, December 2020.

underfunded by government, can only be privately financed, hence the still high out-of-pocket expenditure.

Although TGE has increased a lot over the last ten years, health care has not received the highest allocative priority. In 2010–11, the TGE was UGS 7.377 trillion. The government expenditure budget on health was 8.9 percent. In 2019–20, the TGE budget was UGS 36.113 trillion with health taking a paltry 7.2 percent.[15]

c. Human Resources for Health

As it is for health financing on the African continent, and especially the SSA, the situation of human resources for health is best understood when it is numerically compared and related to the burden of disease it must handle compared to other parts of the world. In 2006, the WHO reported that "the WHO Region of the Americas, with 10 percent of the global burden of disease, has 37 percent of the world's health workers, spending more than 50 percent of the world's health financing, whereas the African Region has 24 percent of the burden but only 3 percent of health workers commanding less than 1 percent of world health expenditure."[16] Since 2006, the situation has, to date, not changed much.

The Role and Contribution of Religious or Faith-Based Health Services[17]

Governments all over the world finance services from various domestic taxes, voluntary and compulsory prepayments, donations, etc. Religious bodies do not collect such taxes and therefore do not have access to such large sums of money to put toward social services, including health care. When they operate in countries that are economically constrained or poor, the challenge of raising resources is even worse. So, why do religious bodies continue to provide health services in such situations as is the case in the SSA?

First, for religious bodies, involvement in health and health systems is a matter of compliance with Scripture. The Lord God said to Moses, "It is I who deal death and life; when I have struck it is I who heal" (Deut 32:39 JB). Jesus combined passing on the Word with the practical healing

---

15. Uganda Ministry of Health, *Annual Health Sector Performance*, 51.
16. World Health Organization, *Working Together for Health*, xviii–xix.
17. In this chapter, the term "faith-based" is used synonymously or interchangeably with "religious."

of disease and sickness (Matt 4:23). Among those he healed were Simon's mother-in-law, a leper in one of the towns he visited (Luke 5:12–15), and many others brought to him (Luke 4:38–40). He also charged his apostles in explicit terms to heal the sick (Luke 10:9) "and gave them authority over unclean spirits to drive them out and to cure every disease and sickness" (Matt 10:1 JB); he promised to those who should believe in him that they would have power over disease (Mark 16:18). Then, he commissioned them: "And as you go, make this proclamation 'the kingdom of heaven is at hand,' cure the sick, raise the dead, cleanse the lepers, drive out the demons" (Matt 10:7–8 JB).

Christian charity has always included the obligation and practice of hospitality (Rom 12:13; Heb 13:2; 1 Pet 4:9). The word "hospital" originally meant a place where strangers or visitors were received; it was eventually restricted to institutions for the care of the sick,[18] gradually leading to construction of buildings specifically meant for the sick, called hospitals. Evidence of such buildings devoted to health care are only found beginning with the Christian era.[19] This may suggest that Christianity started playing a role in health in the early centuries (AD).

In Africa, churches played a pioneer role in introducing Western types of medicine from the late nineteenth century ahead of, or as part of, colonialism. In Uganda, for example, construction of the first hospital started in February 1897 (Mengo Hospital, built by the Anglican Church) and the second in 1899 (Lubaga Hospital, built by the Catholic Church).[20] In South Africa, the first hospital may have been the government-owned Somerset Hospital built in 1818, while the first faith-based hospital may have been the Bremersdorp, now Manzini Hospital, built in July 1927 as the first medical mission in colonial Swaziland.[21]

In some countries like South Africa and Mali, health care is largely nationalized, i.e., provided by the government. In other countries, the contribution of religious bodies is much bigger. However, there is no single proxy indicator that measures the contribution in one piece. In fact, although many people talk of "high quality," "greatly compassionate care," "large coverage," and "highly appreciated," in comparison to government services, faith-based services in Africa largely remain "invisible" in terms of systematic documentation. Besides the visible infrastructures, still not enough is known, in statistical data, about the quantities and qualities of the performance, collectively

18. Walsh, "Hospitals," 480.
19. Koenig et al., *Handbook*, 31.
20. Orach, "Is Religion Relevant," 2.
21. Dlamini, "Introduction of Western Medicine," 557–72.

for the continent, in a documented form. As former World Bank President James Wolfensohn is quoted to have said in 2002, "half the work in education and health in sub-Saharan Africa is done by the church . . . but they don't talk to each other, and they don't talk to us."[22]

An African Religious Health Assets Program study quoted a USAID report of 2007, stating that contributions of religious or faith-based organizations to the national outputs ranged from 30–70 percent.[23] However, this depends on which indicator one looks at (infrastructure, health workforce, general units of output, specific outputs like patients undergoing antiretroviral therapy, surgery, etc.). Because these contributions are measured using varying indicators, there is inconsistency in the chain of what is reported, hence describing the story of the contribution of faith-based health services as the children's game of "broken telephone."[24]

a. Who Is the Giant in Africa—the Catholic Church, Its Health Services, or Both?

This question is to be asked from both the perspectives of population and of proportion of health services provided. The Catholic Church is fast-growing in Africa, especially SSA. Overall, it is a minority, but it is the majority in a number of countries. Among the religious bodies, it is clearly in the lead when it comes to the provision of health services.

The Vatican reports that, in 2017, the Catholics comprised only 17.7 percent of the world's population, with a continental distribution of 48.5 percent being in the Americas, 21.8 percent in Europe, 17.8 percent in Africa, 11.1 percent in Asia, and 0.8 percent in Oceania.[25] However, Catholics make up a large portion of the world Christian population, and the Catholic Church is a growing giant in Africa, both in terms of its size and influence, in the overall national arena and, specifically, the health sector.

In 1910, Catholics made up 48 percent of the world's Christian population and 17 percent of the world's total population. A century later, they constituted 50 percent of all Christians worldwide and still 16 percent of the world's total population.[26] This implies that all Christians together in 2010 comprised only 32 percent of the world's population, hence 68 percent being non-Christian. But the 32 percent is a significant figure for a single block.

22. Quoted in Olivier and Wodon, "Playing Broken Telephone," 822.
23. Schmid et al., *Contribution of Religious Entities*, 50.
24. Olivier and Wodon, "Playing Broken Telephone," 820–21.
25. Holy See Press Office, "Presentation of the Pontifical Yearbook."
26. "Global Catholic Population."

The Pew Research Center's analysis of data from the World Christian Database further shows that Catholics were less than 1 percent of the sub-Saharan population in 1910 but grew to 21 percent in 2010. And whereas less than 1 percent of the world's Catholics lived in SSA in 1910, by 2010, the region had 171 million Catholics—16 percent of the world's Catholic population[27]—and by late 2022, more than 256 million Catholics resided in Africa.[28]

Therefore, the Catholic population is making tremendous strides in Africa. However, while there is rapid growth of the Catholic Church overall in Africa, in some countries, it is registering a reduction or stagnation, compared to other religions. Uganda is one such country. Although Catholics are still the largest single religious group in Uganda, the national census[29] shows that, whereas there was an increase in the total Catholic population between 2002 and 2014—as was true for all other religions—the Catholic numbers dropped from 41.6 percent to 39.3 percent of the total national population. The Anglicans (Church of Uganda) experienced an even bigger drop, from 36.7 percent to 32 percent of the total population. These translate into a 6 percent and a 13 percent decrease, respectively. In contrast, the population of Pentecostal/evangelical/born-again Christians grew 136 percent, up from 4.7 to 11.1 percent of the national population. Nonetheless, Catholics still remained the single largest religious group in Uganda.

b. Does the Rapid Growth of the Catholic Church in Africa or Its Majority Population in Some African Countries Matter?

First, does it matter that Catholics are the single largest majority in any country? Does that make them the giant in the health sector? For something to matter, its importance, significance, and relevance need to be felt by the assessor. In the case of health services, the assessors are the service users, policy makers, and financiers. The importance of any health service or health system lies in its quantity and quality, scope of services, and level of expressed satisfaction with the quality (perceived or real) on the part of the above assessors.

In terms of numbers, the Pentecostals/evangelical/born-again Christians are clearly eroding both the Anglican and the Catholic churches but more so the former. It is much easier for them to recruit from the Anglicans with whom they may share more similarities and who, like them, are already

27. "Global Catholic Population."
28. "Vatican—Catholics and Pastoral Workers."
29. Uganda Bureau of Statistics, *National Population and Housing*, 19.

protesting the Catholic Church. Secondly, in countries where the Catholic population is showing rapid growth in both numbers and in proportion to the total population, does that growth matter?

What matters about a number is what that number is seen and understood to be doing or what influence it wields. Otherwise, without visibility and influence, Catholics who are the single majority in these countries simply remain overall minorities against a large non-Catholic block. For example, Catholics making up 39.3 percent of the population in Uganda simply means they are "up against" a 60.7-percent non-Catholic population who can, and quite often do, unite to challenge the growing "common enemy" or "common opposition" of the Catholic Church.

c. The Specific Contribution of the Catholic Church to the Health Sectors

So, what role is this rapidly growing church playing in the health sector on the African continent? Worldwide, the Catholic Church remains the largest nongovernmental provider of health care services: "Sixty-five percent of these [faith-based clinics] are in developing countries (global South). A significant fraction of those is in Africa."[30] But it is not easy to get continent-wide data about them. Some Episcopal Conference health offices do not readily share information. During the writing of this paper, an attempt was made to get such information through the Africa Christian Health Associations Platform (ACHAP), and it was not possible.

Therefore, besides the visible infrastructure and anecdotal evidence, there is still not enough documented about the quantities and qualities of the performance of faith-based health services, including Catholic health facilities. It is largely not the practice of Catholic health systems to make publicly visible their performance despite all the data they have. Catholics seem to "overextend" what Jesus said after he healed the leper: "'Mind you say nothing to anyone, but go and show yourself to the priest, and make the offering for your healing prescribed by Moses as evidence of your recovery'" (Mark 1:41–44 JB), and also when he healed the little girl and "her parents were astonished but he ordered them not to tell anyone what had happened" (Luke 8:56 JB). There seems to be a feeling that, when you create awareness about the services you provide, it means you are advertising. Instead, there is a common feeling that works in the healing ministry of Christ must "speak for themselves."

---

30. Loy, "Role of Faith-Based Clinics," 17–18.

Much more so than the huge contribution the Catholic Church makes to health care in general, the first thing that "speaks for itself" and becomes much more audible and visible about the church is its opposition to abortion, contraception, and euthanasia. It has long been quite common to hear statements like "The Catholic Church does a lot in health care, and everybody can see it," or "The Catholic Church is the largest provider of health care among all the non-state providers in Africa." These statements come from ministries of health, donors, resource partners, development partners, other religious groups, etc. Users and other stakeholders recognize Catholic health care services for relatively better services and better corporate governance. However, it is rare that someone tries to provide evidence for these claims. Perhaps, one way to assess the centrality of the Catholic Church to the life of the community and, particularly, its important contribution to the national health sectors, is to answer the question, "What would happen if the Catholic Church's health services or facilities were to close in any African country?"

d. Some Evidence on the Level of Faith-Based Health Services, Including Catholic Health Services

The contribution may be measured in terms of the number of health facilities, human resources, or outputs. The Catholic Church, the world over, was reportedly managing 26 percent of the world's health care facilities in 2010.[31] In the same year, it reportedly had around 18,000 clinics, 16,000 homes for the elderly and those with special needs, and 5,500 hospitals.[32] Sixty-five percent of all of these were reported to be in developing countries.

But the actual performance or contribution includes the comparative extent to which the population feels satisfied with the services of these facilities; thus, we must look beyond numbers at the quality of care received and beyond the health facilities to home care and the church's support for people's socioeconomic livelihood that impact their health. In Uganda, for example, some HIV/AIDS programs help those living with HIV/AIDS to form savings and internal lending communities (SILCs). This improves their quality of life and treatment retention, hence contributing to faster viral suppression.

For a very long time, the Catholic Church's approach has been an integrated one that today matches with the strategies of the UN Sustainable Development Goal 3, creating links between health care and the social

31. "Catholic Hospitals."
32. Calderisi, *Earthly Mission*, 40.

determinants of health. Catholic missions and today's parishes provide a continuum of spiritual care, health care, education, and other social services that are quite often geographically placed around the church.

In some African countries, the Christian health associations (or medical bureaus, as they are called in Uganda) also contribute to national health policy, health sector development planning, and the monitoring of the health sector's performance. However, quite often non-facility-based services are invisible because they are not measured. A report on the contribution of religious entities to health in sub-Saharan Africa observed that "while visible structures such as hospitals and clinics can be counted, the multitude of smaller faith-based programs and initiatives are rarely visible, especially to decision-makers at a national or international level."[33] It further states that "ARHAP mapping undertaken in Lesotho and Zambia in 2006 revealed that while the larger, facility-based entities such as hospitals are (sometimes) visible on public health maps, the mass of smaller non-facility based programs and initiatives are rarely visible to public health systems."[34]

The contribution that religious bodies, or even the Catholic Church alone, make to national health care varies across the continent. Therefore, in terms of numbers, their significance would better be measured in proportion to the respective national totals. However, the specific contribution of the Catholic Church is often blurred into the more general category of "faith-based or "non-state" actors, or the "private" health sector. One challenge lies in the definition of "faith-based" and the further question, "Faith in what?" Even spiritual healers have "faith" in spirit. It isn't always clear—and this can be problematic—if health services are labeled "faith-based" simply because the facilities are owned by organizations that promote faith or because the services provided in those facilities are actually inspired by faith—i.e., faith is manifest in the delivery of those services. The lack of well-disaggregated national data leaves room for wrong or unclear attributions or classification. It also takes advantage of Catholics who do not take visibility seriously. However, challenged by the above questions, the Uganda Catholic Medical Bureau (UCMB) took the lead around 2001 to make the data "speak" by strengthening the generation and utilization of health services data right from the point of care. By 2006, while it was not easy for the Ministry of Health to tease out data attributable to Catholic health services, the UCMB was already able to show the collective contribution of the church. So, what makes the Catholic Church a giant in the health sector is

---

33. Schmid et al., *Contribution of Religious Entities*, 50.
34. Schmid et al., *Contribution of Religious Entities*, 50.

not only its population, or the number of its health facilities, but the totality of all of these and what and how it provides the services.

1. Ghana (West Africa)

In 2010, Catholics made up 13.1 percent of Ghana's population.[35] However, in 2020, this small fraction of the population had the largest number of faith-based health facilities within the Christian Health Association of Ghana (CHAG) with 41 percent of CHAG hospitals being Catholic owned. CHAG also reported that 48.5 percent of outpatient services, 63.4 percent of major surgeries, 78.7 percent of minor surgeries, 64.4 percent of in-patient admissions, and 53.7 percent of deliveries occurred in Catholic health facilities (see Figure 1).

Figure 1: Catholic contribution to health care in Ghana, 2020[36]

Indicator	National Total	CHAG Total	Catholic Health Service (HS) Total	Catholic HS as % of National Total	Catholic HS as % of CHAG Total
Number of hospitals	1,757	95	39	2.2%	41.1%
Hospital beds	23,829	11,902	4,922	20.7%	41.4%
Other admission bed (clinics, HCs, PHCs)	10,962	3,948	1,046	9.5%	26.5%
Health centers (Clinics, HCs, PHCs)	7,423	231	79	1.1%	34.2%
Total workforce	70,103	27,581	11,500	16.4%	41.7%
Outpatients	30,849,769	6,785,233	3,288,897	10.7%	48.5%
Admissions	1,688,050	542,689	349,356	20.7%	64.4%
Deliveries	695,647	143,242	76,916	11.1%	53.7%
Minor operations	116,949	44,309	34,882	29.8%	78.7%
Major operations	128,912	46,896	29,724	23.1%	63.4%

2. Uganda (East Africa)

In Uganda, local health care was reportedly practiced long before the introduction of Western health care. A British traveler, R. W. Felkin, is reported to have witnessed a cesarean section performed by Ugandans in Kahura (Western Uganda) in 1879.[37] However, the first hospital in the country,

---

35. Ghana Statistical Service, *2010 Population and Housing,* 63.

36. Author's personal correspondence with Dr. Peter Yeboah, executive secretary of CHAG and executive director of ACHAP.

37. Dunn, "Robert Felkin, MD," F250.

Mengo Hospital in Kampala, formally opened in February 1897.[38] Two years later, in 1899, the Roman Catholic Church formally opened what is now Lubaga Hospital.[39] Today, the Catholic Church, whose members comprise 39.3 percent of Uganda's population, has over 50 percent of the faith-based or religious health facilities in the country.

Figure 2: Proportion of UCMB health facilities to the national total and to the total for faith-based, private not-for-profit networks (PNFPs) in 2021[40]

Type of Facility	PNFP as % of National Total	UCMB as % of National Total	UCMB as % of Faith-Based PNFP	UCMB as % of Total PNFP (incl. non-religious-founded)
Hospitals	36 percent	21 percent	59 percent	52 percent
Health center level IV	8 percent	4 percent	57 percent	57 percent
Health center level III	19 percent	17 percent	86 percent	86 percent
Health center level II	17 percent	3 percent	17 percent	17 percent

As Figure 2 shows, among both the faith-based, private not-for-profits (PNFPs) and all PNFPs put together, Catholic health facilities are the majority, especially in terms of facilities that have in-patient care (Level III and upwards). The other faith-based PNFPs run more of the smaller ambulatory service (outpatient) facilities if compared to UCMB. Similarly, as shown in Figure 3, more health care services are provided by Catholic/UCMB facilities than by any other faith-based PNFP; in fact, they provide more services than all PNFPs (including non-faith-based) combined.

---

38. Billington, "Albert Cook," 738.
39. Uganda Catholic Medical Bureau, "Uganda Martyrs' Hospital–Lubaga."
40. Derived from Ministry of Health, District Health Information System (DHIS2), 2021.

Figure 3: Selected output performance of Catholic/UCMB health facilities as proportion of national totals and as proportion of PNFPs in 2020[41]

Service provided	PNFP as % of National Total	UCMB as % of National Total	UCMB as % of Faith-Based PNFP	UCMB as % of Total PNFP
Bed capacity	31 percent	21 percent	68 percent	63 percent
Total new outpatients	10 percent	6 percent	58 percent	45 percent
Total admissions	24 percent	16 percent	68 percent	65 percent
Major surgeries	27 percent	17 percent	61 percent	59 percent
Deliveries	17 percent	11 percent	64 percent	58 percent
Antiretroviral therapy (ART) currently	16 percent	10 percent	63 percent	45 percent
TB treatment currently	26 percent	21 percent	84 percent	26 percent

3. Some Other Countries

In Rwanda, church-based organizations owned and operated 30 percent of the health care facilities in 2015 under the umbrella of faith-based organizations, covering Catholics (who account for 44 percent of the total population), Protestants (38 percent), Adventists (12 percent), Jehovah's Witnesses (1 percent), and Muslims (2 percent). Those with no religious affiliations are 2 percent of the country's population.[42]

In Cameroon, Delphine Boulenger and Bart Criel noted that the PNFP sector in 2012 held 40 percent of the overall health care provisions, consisting mainly of faith-based providers linked to three main organizations: Organisation Catholique pour la Sante au Cameroun (OCASC), Federation of Protestant Churches and Missions in Cameroon (CEPCA), and Foundation ad Lucem (FALC). In Tanzania, they observed that the faith-based sector was the second biggest provider after the government. Meanwhile in Chad, although Christian churches were still young, their facilities accounted for about 20 percent of the national health services provided, and half of them were Catholic hospitals or health centers.[43]

41. Derived from UCMB data compared to total PNFP and total "National" data on Ministry of Health's District Health Information System (DHIS2).
42. Maurice, "Faith-Based Organizations," 123–34.
43. Boulenger and Criel, *Difficult Relationship*.

e. Financing Catholic Health Facilities

It has not been possible to get financial figures for all faith-based health services, including that of Catholic health facilities for the whole of Africa, including Uganda. However, Figure 4 shows the four main sources of funding that finance the recurrent costs of Ugandan Catholic health facilities. Overall cost keeps increasing annually, yet user fees or out-of-pocket financing remains the main funding source, quite often accounting for over 50 percent of the income spent on operations. This high dependence on out-of-pocket payments constrains the efforts to make services financially affordable to the least privileged. But "there is no free lunch," and the facilities must charge in order to raise the money needed to provide the services. External funding is increasing in both proportion and absolute terms. But as mentioned earlier, 60 to 70 percent of this funding is for vertical programs for HIV/AIDS control. "Other sources" include income-generating activities like farming, animal husbandry, canteens; funds brought forward from past savings; and occasionally bank loans.

Figure 4: Sources of funds to finance recurrent costs of Catholic/UCMB health facilities in Uganda, 2010–11 to 2019–20[44]

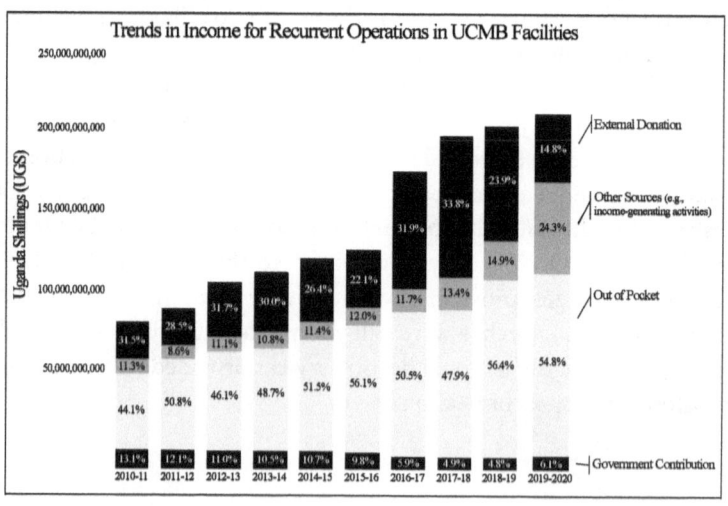

44. Uganda Catholic Medical Bureau (UCMB) database, from health facilities reports.

f. Contribution to the Medical Supply Chain

While this might not be common among faith-based health bodies in many African countries, in Uganda, the UCMB and the Protestant Medical Bureau (UPMB) co-own the Joint Medical Store (JMS), which is the second largest medical supply chain after the government's National Medical Store. JMS is now progressing into production, specifically of an immune booster called Replenish+, which is now being supplied to many countries. The government of Uganda is also using it as a supportive treatment for the "nodding disease"[45] due to its high content of seleno-excel (selenium). During the COVID-19 pandemic, JMS became one of the producers and suppliers of hand sanitizer. With other initiatives also in the pipeline, it has started producing medical oxygen.

Similarly, in Kenya, the Kenya Conference of Catholic Bishops (KCCB) and the Protestant Christian Health Association (CHAK) jointly own the Mission for Essential Drugs and Supplies (MEDS), which is also the nation's second largest medical supply chain after the government.

g. Bringing Holistic Care to the Table

Although this has begun to erode in some cases, Catholic health services still stand apart for their efforts to provide holistic health care. They are appreciated for being compassionate, pro-poor, "hard working," and offering better quality. For many years, health workers in these facilities seemed to silently be asking themselves the questions, "What is Jesus's way of doing things? How would Jesus have liked me to do this if I could see him physically right now?" Answers to these questions are what make Catholic health services Catholic. At the center of this is value-based discernment in dealing with a patient, in planning, and in choosing what to do and with whom, thus integrating faith and professionalism.

III. Challenges

The Catholic Church is growing in size and proportion, particularly in Africa. In some countries, it is the largest of the non-state health service providers, hence a giant, especially among the faith-based providers. However, little is done to make the giant visible and attract more partnerships and support. This giant, with relatively stronger systems, can surely do more

---

45. Pollanen et al., "Spectrum of Disease," 954.

to stand tall as a very important player in the health sector. Health systems in the global South, however, are generally weak due to underfunding, and faith-based providers like the church also face these challenges of health financing. Operating in the same poor economic environments, as well as the same policy environments, as the government, the church faces a number of challenges including the following:

1. The very poor economy poses cross-cutting effects. Serving a poor population who cannot meet the true cost of service affects the balancing of the rising cost of services on the one hand and sustainability and quality of services on the other hand. There is "no free lunch," but the "not-for-profit" concept is widely misunderstood—there is, in fact, a cost to everything that must be recovered or covered in order to serve the next person or improve on the services. There is generally a perception that Catholic health services are a charity and receive funds from the Vatican, but this is not the case.

2. There is a high turnover of the workforce due to lower pay, as compared with that of government and nongovernmental organizations, especially those funded by the U.S. President's Emergency Plan for AIDS Relief (PEPFAR) to provide HIV/AIDS-related programs.

3. In many faith-based organizations, the focus is more on providing services and less on the quality of leadership; therefore, corporate governance is not often a priority. This unseen challenge gradually breaks down the organization and fails service provision. The UCMB stands out for having made its focus, over the last twenty years, the strengthening of health systems, including corporate governance, within Catholic health institutions. The result is that, often, when these facilities are assessed alongside others for various reasons—including project funding—they emerge stronger.

4. Fearing misinterpretation as "advertisement," the failure to create awareness about the services provided is often compounded by the failure to use available data to generate information for advocacy.

5. The financial challenges affect technological growth, often manifested in obsolete equipment and delays in the digitalization of systems, especially in rural health facilities.

6. The reluctance to partner with bodies whose practices conflict with Catholic teachings is on the one hand, proper, to keep the Catholic Church from appearing to "support" or market what it does not support. On the other hand, there are some missed opportunities for collaboration limited to areas of common interest—e.g., strengthening

systems. The church collaborates with the national governments' Ministries of Health in areas of common interest, but these Ministries of Health also support certain things that the Catholic Church does not agree with—for example, contraceptives and, in some countries, abortion. Should the Catholic Church stop collaborating with the Ministries of Health? It can be difficult to discern which is "the lesser evil."

7. Some financial donors are also slow to work with health departments that are not corporate entities, separate from the church and its respective Conferences of Catholic Bishops. Some fear their money may be used for works of proselytization. Others fear dealing with church leaders, because they don't understand the line between faith leadership and leadership of technical programs. These potential partners think it will be difficult to follow up with church leaders on issues of funds in cases of mismanagement.

8. Increased funding for vertical disease programs often projects the targeted illnesses as "monsters" that are killing people, while obscuring the attention of governments and other funding partners to general health care. This can result in decreased funds for general health systems and services.

9. To varying degrees, there is mutual mistrust and competition between the church and state. Some people in government think church health facilities receive undisclosed money from organizations abroad. And some church leaders fear that, while it is good to receive funds from the state, this could lead to the government's takeover of church-founded health facilities. In such countries, this fear stems from past experiences of the nationalization of educational institutions, as in Uganda, or of health institutions, as in South Africa. There is also the fear that the state could use its financial support of church health institutions to require the church to accept policies like contraceptive family planning and legalization of abortion.

All of these challenges threaten the sustainability of Catholic health systems and services.

III. Conclusion: A Call to the Worldwide Catholic Church, Particularly in Africa

It is important that the Catholic Church quickly turn its growing size in the global South, especially in Africa, into an opportunity to do more healing ministry. The giant must rise up to be seen and appreciated and become a preferred partner in health systems and services. This can be done by strategically investing in strengthening systems and by making better use of the massive data the church has, including the evidence available of its huge contribution to the health sector. By doing so, it will be able to influence national policies even more.

There is also a need to explore alternative health financing mechanisms—for example, community health financing schemes. Both the sources of funding and the scope of services need to be diversified, so that, rather than replicate what many others are doing, the church can rediscover its role in non-facility-based services or other niches.

Bibliography

Billington, W. R. "Albert Cook 1870–1951: Uganda Pioneer." *The British Medical Journal* 4.5737 (December 19, 1970) 738–40. https://www.ncbi.nlm.nih.gov/pmc/articles/PMC1820337/pdf/brmedj02167-0060.pdf.

Boulenger, Delphine, and Bart Criel. *The Difficult Relationship between Faith-Based Health Care Organisations and the Public Sector in Sub-Saharan Africa: The Case of Contracting Experiences in Cameroon, Tanzania, Chad, and Uganda*. Studies in Health Services Organisation and Policy 29. Antwerp, Belgium: ITG, 2012. https://research.itg.be/en/publications/the-difficult-relationship-between-faith-based-health-care-organi.

Calderisi, Robert. *Earthly Mission: The Catholic Church and World Development*. New Haven: Yale University Press, 2016.

"Catholic Hospitals Comprise One Quarter of World's Healthcare, Council Reports." *Catholic News Agency*, February 10, 2010. https://www.catholicnewsagency.com/news/18624/catholic-hospitals-comprise-one-quarter-of-worlds-healthcare-council-reports.

Dlamini, Shokahle R. "The Introduction of Western Medicine in Southern Africa: The Case of Ainsworth Dickson Nursing Training School in Bremersdorp, Swaziland, 1927–1949." *South African Historical Journal* 68.4 (2016) 557–72.

Dunn, Peter M. "Robert Felkin, MD (1853–1926) and Caesarean Delivery in Central Africa (1879)." *Archives of Disease in Childhood: Fetal and Neonatal Edition* 80.3 (1999) F250–F251. https://fn.bmj.com/content/80/3/F250.

Ghana Statistical Service. *2010 Population and Housing Census: National Analytical Report*. Accra, May 2013. https://statsghana.gov.gh/gssmain/fileUpload/pressrelease/2010_PHC_National_Analytical_Report.pdf.

"Global Burden of Disease 2019." *The Lancet*, October 15, 2020. https://www.thelancet.com/infographics-do/gbd-2019.

"The Global Catholic Population." Pew Research Center, February 22, 2013. https://www.pewforum.org/2013/02/13/the-global-catholic-population.

Holy See Press Office. "Presentation of the Pontifical Yearbook 2019 and the Annuarium Statisticum Ecclesiae Sala Stampa della Santa Sede 2017, 06.03.2019." *Summary of Bulletin* (March 2019). https://press.vatican.va/content/salastampa/en/bollettino/pubblico/2019/03/06/190306b.html.

International Monetary Fund. "The IMF and the Sustainable Development Goals." IMF, March 2023. https://www.imf.org/en/About/Factsheets/Sheets/2023/IMF-Sustainable-development-goals-SDGs.

Koenig, Harold G., et al. *Handbook of Religion and Health.* Oxford: Oxford University Press, 2001.

Loy, Parker Jennings. "The Role of Faith-Based Clinics in America's Healthcare System." Chancellor's Honors Program Projects, University of Tennessee Knoxville, May 7, 2014. https://trace.tennessee.edu/cgi/viewcontent.cgi?article=2771&context=utk_chanhonoproj.

Maurice, John. "Faith-Based Organizations Bolster Health Care in Rwanda." *The Lancet* 386.9989 (July 11, 2015) 123–24. https://www.thelancet.com/journals/lancet/issue/vol386no9989/PIIS0140-6736(15)X6150-2.

Olivier, Jill, and Quentin Wodon. "Playing Broken Telephone: Assessing Faith-Inspired Health Care Provision in Africa." *Development in Practice* 22.5–6 (July 5, 2012) 819–34. https://www.jstor.org/stable/41723141.

Orach, Sam Orochi. "Is Religion Relevant in Health Care in Africa in the Twenty-First Century? The Uganda Experience." Paper presented at African Religious Health Assets Programme (ARHAP) Conference, Cape Town, South Africa, July 13–17, 2009. https://www.ucmb.co.ug/?smd_process_download=1&download_id=1602.

Pollanen, Michael S., et al. "The Spectrum of Disease and Tau Pathology of Nodding Syndrome in Uganda." *Brain* 146.3 (March 2023) 954–67. https://academic.oup.com/brain/article/146/3/954/6566797.

Sakala, Joseph J., et al. "The Integration of Vertical and Horizontal Programmes for Health Systems Strengthening in Malawi: A Case Study." *Malawi Medical Journal* 34.3 (September 2022) 206–12. https://www.ajol.info/index.php/mmj/article/view/233657.

Schmid, Barbara, et al. *The Contribution of Religious Entities to Health in Sub-Saharan Africa: An ARHAP Report.* Cape Town: African Religious Health Assets Programme (ARHAP), 2008. https://s3.amazonaws.com/berkley-center/08ARHAPGatesContributionReligiousSubsaharanAfrica.pdf.

Uganda Bureau of Statistics (UBOS). *The National Population and Housing Census 2014: Main Report.* Kampala: UBOS, 2016. https://unstats.un.org/unsd/demographic/sources/census/wphc/Uganda/UGA-2016-05-23.pdf.

Uganda Catholic Medical Bureau. "Uganda Martyrs' Hospital–Lubaga." https://www.ucmb.co.ug/hospital/uganda-martyrs-hospital-lubaga.

Uganda Ministry of Health. *Annual Health Sector Performance Report: Financial Year 2019/20.* Kampala: Ministry of Health, 2020.

———. *Uganda Health Accounts: National Health Expenditure, Financial Years 2014/15 and 2015/16.* Kampala: Ministry of Health, 2016. http://library.health.go.ug/sites/default/files/resources/NHA_FINAL%20-UGANDA-1%20FY%202016-17_2017-18%20final%20%20%202018-1.pdf.

"Vatican—Catholics and Pastoral Workers Increase in Africa." *Agenzia Fides,* October 21, 2022. http://www.fides.org/en/news/72958-VATICAN_Catholics_and_pastoral_workers_increase_in_Africa.

Walsh, James Joseph. "Hospitals." In vol. 7 of *The Catholic Encyclopedia*, edited by Charles G. Herbermann et al., 480–99. New York: Robert Appleton, 1910. http://www.newadvent.org/cathen/07480a.htm.

WHO Regional Office for Africa. *State of Health Financing in the African Region.* Brazzaville, Republic of Congo: WHO Regional Office for Africa, 2013. https://www.afro.who.int/sites/default/files/2017-06/state-of-health-financing-afro.pdf.

The World Bank. "Current Health Expenditure (Percent of GDP): Sub-Saharan Africa, Uganda." January 30, 2022. https://data.worldbank.org/indicator/SH.XPD.CHEX.GD.ZS?end=2018&locations=ZG-UG&name_desc=true&start=2000&view=chart.

———. *Healthy Development: The World Bank Strategy for Health, Nutrition, and Population Results.* Washington, DC: The World Bank, 2007. https://documents1.worldbank.org/curated/en/102281468140385647/pdf/409280PAPER0He101OFFICIAL0USE0ONLY1.pdf.

World Health Organization. *Global Spending on Health: Weathering the Storm—Global Report 2020.* Geneva: WHO, 2020. https://www.who.int/publications/i/item/9789240017788.

———. *Monitoring the Building Blocks of Health Systems: A Handbook of Indicators and Their Measurement Strategies.* Geneva: WHO, 2010. https://apps.who.int/iris/bitstream/handle/10665/258734/9789241564052-eng.pdf.

———. *Working Together for Health: The World Health Report 2006.* Geneva: WHO, 2006. https://apps.who.int/iris/bitstream/handle/10665/43432/9241563176_eng.pdf?sequence=1&isAllowed=y.

———. *The World Health Report 2003: Shaping the Future.* Geneva: WHO, 2003. http://apps.who.int/iris/bitstream/handle/10665/42789/9241562439.pdf?sequence=1.

"World Poverty Map: How Many People Live in Extreme Poverty by Country." HowMuch.net, October 30, 2018. https://howmuch.net/articles/people-living-in-extreme-poverty-2018.

5

The History and Mission of Korea's Catholic Medical Center

Soojung Kim and Pyeong Man Kim

The Origin of the Catholic Church's Medical Mission

THE ORIGIN OF THE Catholic Church's medical mission is Jesus's healing as recorded in the four gospels. The episodes of Jesus's healing appear forty-one times in the gospels, amounting to 20 percent of their volume. Jesus roamed throughout Israel, proclaiming the good news of the kingdom of God and healing those who suffered from sickness. "Jesus went around to all the towns and villages, teaching in their synagogues, proclaiming the gospel of the kingdom, and curing every disease and illness. At the sight of the crowds, his heart was moved with pity for them because they were troubled and abandoned, like sheep without a shepherd" (Matt 9:35–36).[1]

Pope John Paul II explained the implications of Jesus's healing of the sick in the encyclical *Redemptoris Missio* as follows: "The liberation and salvation brought by the kingdom of God come to the human person both in his physical and spiritual dimensions. Two gestures are characteristic of Jesus's mission: healing and forgiving. Jesus's many healings clearly show his great compassion in the face of human distress, but they also signify that in the kingdom, there will no longer be sickness or suffering, and that

---

1. Biblical citations herein are taken from the New American Bible, 1970.

his mission, from the very beginning, is meant to free people from these evils. In Jesus's eyes, healings are also a sign of spiritual salvation, namely liberation from sin."[2]

Many of Jesus's healings reveal the fullness of God's love. For example, Jesus came "to bring glad tidings to the poor . . . to proclaim liberty to captives and recovery of sight to the blind" (Luke 4:18) and "to seek and to save what was lost" (Luke 19:10). "Jesus as a role model of holistic health care provider is well described in the Gospel. During his life as a human, Jesus always reached out for the sick to cure them with love and compassion."[3] Jesus, who is sent from the Heavenly Father, dispatched his disciples to carry on these works. As a sign of the approach of God, he went through all the towns and villages, healing both the sick and the feeble, commanding his disciples to do the same.[4]

Jesus also teaches that the greatest commandment of all is "love your neighbors" through the parable of the good Samaritan (Luke 10:29–37) and says that we all should become neighbors to the sufferer, the marginalized, the sinners, and the sick. "Like the Good Samaritan, we should be compassionate for those who suffer from the pain and share God's love. With the talent given by God, health care providers should treat the patient as a person, share their pain, and show respect so patients do not feel abandoned and isolated. At the same time, health care providers should approach the patients with love and compassion and encourage them to believe in God's healing."[5] At the end of the parable, Jesus said, "Go and do likewise" (Luke 10:37). That is the essential mission that he has entrusted to his disciples, and the church is called to do it.[6]

In order to carry out this mission, the church has cared for and healed the sick from the time of its beginnings and has continuously supported medical missionary activities. The church has healed the suffering of the sick, led them to realize the meaning of suffering in accordance with the cross of Christ, and communicated God's love to them. The medical institutions of the Catholic Church have made significant contributions to the development of health care and have experienced both quantitative and qualitative growth so that more people can receive the benefits they provide. These institutions embrace all of the poor and suffering with the love of

---

2. John Paul II, *Redemptoris Missio*, para. 14.

3. Noh, "Healthcare Provider's Spiritual Care," 100.

4. "As you go, make this proclamation: 'The kingdom of heaven is at hand.' Cure the sick, raise the dead, cleanse lepers, drive out demons" (Matt 10:7–8).

5. Noh, "Healthcare Provider's Spiritual Care," 103.

6. Second Vatican Council, *Lumen Gentium*, 8.

Christ. They are organized to protect human life at every level, and thus are a precious asset of the church.[7]

History of the Catholic Medical Centre in Korea

The Beginnings

When the Catholic Church was introduced into Korea in 1784, its medical activities were limited to the personal level as a practice engaged in by loving neighbors. Medical missionary activities at the church level in Korea began in the 1850s when Father Maistre, a member of the Paris Foreign Missions Society, supported by the Congregation of the Holy Spirit, a child relief organization in France, began to care for the hungry and raise orphans in 1859.[8] He also carried out medical activities, including the installation of reagent stations.[9] The church's medical activities were suspended as part of a persecution of the church for twenty years but resumed in 1886 after the signing of the Korea-France Treaty. These activities started with charitable pharmacies in orphanages and nursing homes and then expanded to charitable clinics.

When the Korean Catholic diocese celebrated its one hundredth anniversary in 1931, the Catholic Diocesan Youth Union in the capital reached the consensus that the first and most appropriate project was to establish a medical institution.[10] The opening of St. Mary's Hospital in 1936, after five years of preparation, was a historic moment for the medical missionary work of the Catholic Church in Korea. St. Mary's Hospital began with fifteen medical professionals and twenty-four hospital beds; in 1962, it became the Catholic Medical Center (hereafter referred to as CMC), which has nine affiliated institutions, including a medical college and a nursing college. It is currently one of the largest medical centers in terms of scale and income in Korea.

Its Achievements

Since its opening in 1936, the achievements of St. Mary's Hospital can be understood as falling within four categories relating to its (1) contribution

---

7. Benedict XVI, *Message of His Holiness*.
8. Cho, 세계 의료사와 [Introduction to World Medical History], 29–31.
9. Kim, *Medical History of Korea*, 493.
10. Cho, 세계 의료사와 [Introduction to World Medical History], 169.

to the nation's medical care, (2) provision of quality medical care and innovative medical research, (3) social concern and charitable activities, and (4) pastoral care and hospice.

Contribution to the Nation's Medical Care

CMC currently has 5,800 beds and 13,000 staff members. It trains about 10 percent of the nation's health practitioners every year and has produced about eight thousand interns and seven thousand residents. CMC takes care of 6.4 million outpatients and 1.9 million inpatients annually, which amounts to 5 percent of the Korean population.

St. Mary's Hospital has always paid attention to marginalized and less well known areas of medicine. The Catholic Industrial Medical Center (CIMC) was established in 1962 as a subsidiary of the College of Medicine of the Catholic University of Korea. It was created to meet the growing needs of industry, which was experiencing a growth in work-related diseases and injuries and required a way to educate the public on the subject. It has operated inpatient and outpatient clinics to treat and prevent pneumoconiosis since 1962. It provides an occupational management service for small/medium-sized enterprises in collaboration with the Korea Occupational Safety and Health Agency—KOSHA (WHO-CC KOR-86)—and concentrates on potentially vulnerable and/or informal sector workers.[11] CIMC conducts research on occupational diseases, disseminates information and data to researchers and the general population, and cooperates with international and domestic researchers to enhance the academic exchange related to occupational and environmental diseases. CIMC includes the departments of Occupational and Environmental Medicine, Occupational and Environmental Hygiene/Toxicology, Health Management, and Ergonomics.

---

11. "As the WHO-Collaborating Center in Occupational Health, the Catholic Industrial Medical Center (KOR-9) collaborates with WHO-WPRO [Western Pacific Region Office] to support 1) technical assistance and support provided to Member States for strengthening national occupational and environmental health risk management systems, functions, and services; 2) guidance, tools, and initiatives created in order to support the health sector in influencing policies in other sectors to allow policies that improve health, the environment, and safety to be identified and adopted; and 3) health-sector leadership enhanced for creating a healthier environment and changing policies in all sectors to tackle the root causes of environmental threats to health, through means such as responding to emerging and re-emerging consequences of development on environmental health and altered patterns of consumption and production and to the damaging effect of evolving technologies." Catholic Industrial Medical Center, introduction brochure.

The Hansen's Disease Research Center at St. Mary's Hospital was founded in 1961 with the financial help of Fr. Joseph A. Sweeny, MM, of Maryknoll of America, and the Catholic Leprosy Service of the Korean Catholic Church. It has been dedicated to the treatment of the disease and identification of its underlying causes. Furthermore, it has focused on protecting the human rights of people who suffer from Hansen's disease against social discrimination and stereotyping due to a misunderstanding of the disease. The stereotyping, stigmatization, and oppression of people suffering from certain illnesses or handicaps have caused human rights violations. It is necessary to build an integrated community in which people live harmoniously with mutual respect regardless of the presence of any disease or handicap. The Hansen's Disease Research Center includes the medical department, which houses an outpatient treatment room and a mobile clinic, and the research department, in which an immunology laboratory and a chemotherapy laboratory are located. The Department of Medical Treatment deals with early detection and treatment of Hansen's disease and offers plastic surgery, correction and rehabilitation, and care of patients who have suffered from the disease in the past and visited settlement villages. For more than forty years, it has been dedicated to the physical, mental, and economic rehabilitation of patients with Hansen's disease. The research department is concerned with the development of an experimental model for Hansen's disease and the effective use of drugs for treating it. It is comprised of the Microresection Development Department, the Microarray Production Department, and the Bioinformatics Department.

The major activities of the Hansen's Disease Research Center are medical treatment, research, education, and public promotion. The medical service cares for patients (currently negative for leprosy) in seven settlement villages located north of the Han River in Gyeonggi-do and nine public health centers in four cities, and together with the Catholic Leprosy Service, operates an outpatient clinic and visits St. Najaro village. As part of the research project, with the support of the Center for Disease Control in the Ministry of Health and Welfare, lepromin reagents are being produced to maintain leprosy colonies using nude mice and to measure cell-mediated immunity in patients with the disease. Basic research includes research on drug resistance to leprosy and the regeneration of damaged nerves and tissues using stem cells. With regard to educational activity, the Hansen's Disease Research Center provides a short-term course once a year for clinical medicine and basic medical education on leprosy for medical students and nursing students nationwide and sponsors seminars by volunteer organizations related to leprosy. Education and training of medical staff have also been provided from abroad.[12] As a promotional project, it endeavors to inform the public about Hansen's disease through its website and to reduce prejudice toward people who have suffered from the disease.[13]

Provision of Quality Medical Care and Innovative Medical Research

St. Mary's Hospital was Korea's first hospital to successfully accomplish the following: corneal transplantation in 1966, kidney transplantation in 1969, pediatric cerebrovascular anastomosis in 1977, inguinal microvascular surgery in 1978, allogeneic bone marrow transplantation between siblings in 1983 for a leukemia patient, liver transplantation in 1993, mini hematopoietic stem cell transplantation in 2002, small intestine transplantation in 2004, and small intestine transplantation for a child in 2005. Hematopoietic stem cell transplantation was performed in more than three hundred cases per year, and six hundred liver transplants and two thousand kidney transplants were provided in 2011. St. Mary's Hospital has promoted quality medical care through innovative medical research.

Social Concern and Charity Activities

National health insurance was established in Korea in the 1980s, and medical benefits for the poor are now systematically provided by the government. St. Mary's Hospital currently provides support for basic benefits for the poor based on an evaluation of individuals' ability to pay for medical expenses, including counseling on medical treatments before admission and coordination of medical insurance. Last year, CMC provided KRW 10.3 billion in medical expenses to more than 33,500 patients who were unable to receive adequate medical treatment due to economic difficulties.

Pastoral Care and Hospice

Scientific developments pertaining to medical specialization have isolated patients from their bodies and illness experiences. Modern medicine tends to regard patients as subjects of medical technology rather than of

12. From October 1–31, 2005, Dr. Le Huyen My, a dermatologist at the Vietnam National Dermatology Hospital, visited the Hansen's Disease Research Center to offer basic training on tests related to the disease.
13. See the Catholic University College of Medicine's homepage at https://medicine.catholic.ac.kr/html/research/hansen.jsp.

medical actions. Patients alienated during personal encounters with medical professionals are typically no longer able to deal with the anxiety and suffering caused by their illnesses. Furthermore, the commercialization and conglomeration of hospitals discourage Catholic medical institutions from maintaining their identity in the healing community.

In this difficult situation, the core identity of the healing community of CMC is maintained by the combination of pastoral and hospice care. Pastoral care deals with the spiritual needs of people who suffer from mental and physical illness, regardless of their religion. It provides liturgical activities, such as Mass, sacraments, and other blessings through which people can encounter the healer Christ. In addition, faith education and counseling for the staff as part of pastoral work leads to their sanctification and evangelization.

Hospice provides for the physical, emotional, social, and spiritual care of terminally ill patients and their families. It allows the patients to enjoy the last moments of their lives in peace while maintaining their human dignity. It also helps families overcome their pain and sorrow during bereavement. In 1981, medical and nursing students worked with nurses and nuns to conduct research and carry out volunteer services to promote hospice care. Their efforts contributed to the establishment of the first hospice care unit at St. Mary's Hospital in 1988. The people at the university continued to work for hospice, resulting in the designation of the College of Nursing as a WHO Collaborating Center (WHO-CC) in 1995. To implement the work it took on as part of this designation, the College of Nursing founded the Research Institute for Hospice and Palliative Care in 1996. The Research Institute launched the first hospice and palliative care training in that year, and this course of training continues to this day.

Pastoral care and hospice allow CMC to maintain the core values of the healing community and fulfill the mission of holistic care, which tries to reach and embrace physical, social, and spiritual suffering. Its mission is to improve quality of life by respecting human dignity and providing holistic care. Hospice helps patients at the end of their lives and their families maintain their dignity and increase their life satisfaction by means of physical, psychological, and spiritual care. Cardinal Souhwan Stephen Kim said that "hospice care, which helps those at the end of life to keep the dignity of their soul and body as human, is the noblest care."[14] As a WHO Collaborating Center, the Hospice Center delivered the First International Hospice and Palliative Care Workforce Training on April 10–20, 2017. The trainees included two nurses from Mongolia, two from Vietnam, and one from

---

14. Kim, 하나님의 사랑을 믿고 [Best Preparation], 2–3.

Benin. Hospice Center staff also traveled to Lomé, Togo, to deliver the Second International Hospice and Palliative Care Workforce Training on December 11–22, 2017. A total of twenty trainees from Benin, Burkina Faso, Chad, Côte d'Ivoire, and Togo participated in the program.

Sr. Jinsun (Julianna) Yong, professor and director of The Catholic University of Korea College of Nursing WHO Collaborating Center for Training in Hospice and Palliative Care, led the conference in Togo and reflected on her experience as follows:

> Suffering stemming from a life-threatening illness forces patients and families to confront the finitude and mortality of human existence. One may say that this is one of the greatest hardships that one comes across in his/her lifetime. But paradoxically, it is this immense suffering that can act as a source of strength which enables one to restore the original essence of the human person. Such suffering also guides healthcare professionals to purify themselves and become humble, fostering the compassion that lives in their hearts. What is compassion? It is deeply empathizing with the suffering of others and taking altruistic action to alleviate their suffering. Indeed, compassion is at the core of spiritual care. And it was the strength flowing from our compassionate hearts that had propelled our WHO-CC to head to West Africa.[15]

Challenges and Agendas

The Identity and Mission of Church Hospitals

The first challenge was criticism of and reflection on whether the expansion of the church hospital was necessary. As the hospital expanded and became more commercialized, it resulted in a decrease in the involvement of religious staff in its management, and personal encounters with the patients seemed to be devalued. Of course, it is not a problem for church medical institutions to be equipped with high-tech facilities and then to expand them. Since accurate diagnosis and treatment are indispensable to medical activities, modernizing church medical institutions to maintain the superiority of treatment technology is desirable. However, this process can lead to an inability to treat the patient as a whole and result in neglect of medical activities in marginalized rural areas.[16] Since the 1980s, CMC has pondered

15. Yong, "Reflection Two," 3.
16. Meng, 한국 천주교회의 어제 [Yesterday, Today, and Tomorrow], 16.

whether the church really needs to run a big and extravagant hospital[17] or if instead, it needs to concentrate on caring for the underprivileged. Furthermore, the government regards the medical industry as one of the nation's new growth engines and has set up a so-called advancement of medical service plan. The project recognizes health care as a commodity and utilizes it as an investment opportunity. In particular, the opening of the medical market due to the emergence of the market economy and neoliberalism and the advent of infinite competition have allowed Catholicism to gradually take a backseat and have encouraged an unintended competition for survival. To rediscover the mission of CMC as a church medical institution, it was necessary to overcome both internal conflicts and external challenges.[18]

CMC launched a committee to address these concerns in 1985 and proclaimed its philosophy of care with the approval of Cardinal Kim Souhwan in the following year. It was decided that the philosophy of CMC as a healing community needs to be implemented in care, research, education, training, and management. Furthermore, it was necessary for all members of CMC to share in and affirm its mission as a healing community through education and collaborative practice. CMC developed an educational program through which its staff could share core values and identify with working in a Catholic institution. "Window of Communication" was the name of the project that aimed to acknowledge the unique values of CMC and implement its mission as a truly healing community through interprofessional education and collaboration. It was agreed that the employees should affirm the mission and vision of the institution in a reasonable and timely manner. The Task Force Team (hereafter referred to as TFT) was comprised of fifteen medical professors, twenty-five medical staff, and twelve priests and religious leaders from eight institutions within CMC. Its aim was to develop educational modules and train in-house instructors.

The purpose of the educational program was to affirm CMC's values and ethics, empower roles and responsibilities, improve communication among members, and promote team and teamwork. The domain of values and ethics was embodied by discovering the identity and talents of CMC

17. Kim, 한일 가톨릭의료기술협 [Reflections on the Twenty-Fifth Anniversary], 31–33.

18. The late Cardinal Joseph Bernardin of the Archdiocese of Chicago said that it is not a small challenge for church hospitals to practice Catholic medicine while competing with other hospitals having state-of-the-art medical facilities but that doing so could present challenges with opportunities for spiritual renewal. The core of crisis management in church hospitals is to affirm that the ultimate goal of church medical care is to maintain and develop an identity as a church hospital. All members of the institution need to share in this affirmation. See Bernardin, *Celebrating the Ministry of Healing*.

and understanding the meaning and implications of its mission. The domain of roles and responsibilities was established so that employees could affirm their own roles and sense of responsibility as seen in practically relevant cases. It was recognized that interprofessional communication would naturally arise from building the framework and contents of educational programs together. Finally, it was expected that the domain of team and teamwork would achieve its goals naturally by continuing education offered by in-house instructors.

As a result, five educational modules (identity, education, treatment, research, and management) were developed and eighty-five educational sessions were provided to various professionals who had worked at CMC for more than five years.[19] The TFT prepared training and formed a team from January to March 2011, shared tasks and philosophy, and identified core values with five groups from April to June of that year. From August to December, an educational program was created based on everyday cases from the clinical field, and in-house instructors were recruited. Its training contents were developed and concretized through twenty-four planning team meetings, five group workshops, and seven general workshops. Finally, in December 2011, an educational demonstration was conducted. The in-house instructors were trained to acquire and strengthen their competencies so that they could deliver the contents effectively. The educational content organized by the TFT was structured according to CMC's mission and specific goals. CMC's mission is "to embody Jesus Christ as a healer in us to care for those who suffer from disease." In order to do this, the CMC strives "to train medical professionals with a noble sense of mission, to research and develop medicine, and to provide loving medical services."[20] CMC's core values are as follows:

- respect for life and medical mission
- patient-first holistic care
- creative research based on Catholic ethics
- nurturing mature and competent professionals
- mutual trust and ethical management[21]

As of May 27, 2016, Window of Communication had been conducted eighty-seven times for employees who had worked for CMC for at least five years.

19. Kim et al., "Education Program Development."
20. "CMC Spirituality."
21. "Core Value."

In sum, Window of Communication aimed at internalizing the core values of CMC among its members, a goal that was concretely embodied in the questions of "why," "how," and "what." In other words, CMC declares the identity of why it exists and implements its core values (mission). CMC members are also expected to be ready to practice the spirit of CMC in their work. The five educational modules were designed on the themes of mission, service, education, research, and management. After finishing the program, employees are expected to appreciate the importance of their roles and responsibilities, respect the roles of colleagues, and ultimately decide to make CMC a better medical institution.

First, the respect for life and medical mission module deals with the main events that reveal the identity of CMC and the particular cases that have concretized the value of human dignity in its history. In particular, role models like Seon Woo Gyeong-sik, who built and ran Joseph House for the homeless, were presented. Second, the patient-first holistic care module allowed time for self-reflection. Third, the module for nurturing mature and competent professionals presented role models and provided time for self-assessment of maturity and competency. Fourth, as part of the module related to creative research based on Catholic ethics, cases of unethical research were presented. Time was allowed for staff to identify the problems with such research, and various options for performing ethical creative and innovative research were discussed. Fifth, the mutual trust and ethical management module pictured what it would be like to achieve the best goals through work efficiency and competitiveness within a framework of sustainable management. Each two-hour module was comprised of educational materials and followed the order of understanding, reflection, and exercise. The TFT members who designed the training modules and participated as in-house instructors said that, in the process of discussing each other's roles and responsibilities, they more greatly appreciated other people's work and professions. It was said that this project allowed the educator and the trainee to share the educational content at the same level, regardless of their knowledge and expertise.

CMC also has awards for the teams that best implement CMC's mission every year, so that employees can affirm their core values as a healing community and are proud of working at CMC.

Ethical Treatments and Research

In today's medical practice, are we providing holistic care based on an understanding of human beings as a whole? Although health care providers are aware of the basic principles of the Geneva Convention, which prescribe the respect and dignity of the human being, it is not easy for them to follow these principles in reality. With the development of science, medical practice has focused on treating disease instead of seeking out the needs of patients. This attitude creates a lack of humanity in the treatment of patients.[22] Ethical issues arise from the application of some advanced medical technologies. Church tradition has continually reminded us that the ultimate purpose of Catholic medical activity is the service of human life and has firmly rejected any attempt to resist this purpose. Science and technology exist only for human beings, and every new medical discovery or marvelous technology reveals its true value in its service to human beings. The prevalence of anti-life activities like suicide, abortion, euthanasia, and environmental destruction threatens the dignity and sanctity of human life. In addition, biomedical engineering, such as embryonic stem cell research and genetic engineering, regard human life as a commodity and the object of manipulation.

In early 2000, the Archdiocese of Seoul endeavored to turn away from a disregard for human life, including embryonic stem cell research, life cloning, and abortion. On October 5, 2005, it established a Committee for Life under the governance of Nicholas Cardinal Cheong in order to protect human life and promote the fundamental values of the Catholic Church.[23] The Committee for Life has supported activities promoting life and medical research.[24] In particular, the Committee for Life founded the Catholic Institute of Cell Therapy, which shuns research or treatments that participate in the destruction of human embryos and promotes research and treatments that protect the dignity of human life. The Catholic Institute of Cell Therapy promotes basic research and clinical studies on adult stem cells. It is also equipped with a good manufacturing product (GMP) facility for cell therapy and promotes the industrialization of stem cell technologies.[25]

Human life is a gift of God's love and should be respected at every level. The lives of those who are weakest and least able to protect themselves need greater acceptance, love, and care. To prevent any attempt to disregard and destroy fragile lives, CMC actively carries out—along with strengthening education on biomedical ethics—various social activities and

22. Noh, "Healthcare Provider's Spiritual Care."

23. "Campaign of Prayer."

24. For more details, see the Archdiocese of Seoul's Committee for Life website at http://www.forlife.or.kr.

25. For more details, see the English version of the Catholic Institute of Cell Therapy's website at https://www.cic.re.kr/eng/introduction/summary.jsp.

research, including the following: adult stem cell research and treatment,[26] the Natural Procreative Technology (NaPro) method, incurable disease treatment and research, hospice, blood donations, bone marrow donations, suicide prevention, etc. NaPro is a reproductive science that is designed to cooperate with the menstrual and fertility cycle.[27] It is a service program for making natural procreative choices and monitoring, maintaining, and evaluating a woman's procreative and gynecological health. It takes women's natural fertility into account and empowers women to appreciate this fertility. A NaPro Technology approach for the infertile couple has the goals of working toward finding the underlying causes of reproductive abnormality, allowing treatment of these underlying causes, and assists the couple in achieving pregnancy while engaging in natural acts of intercourse. If the treatment program is unsuccessful, research into unknown causes is undertaken; in addition, the program will assist with successful family-building by supporting adoption.[28] Catholic medical institutions must also resist the temptation to participate in euthanasia by providing holistic care for terminally ill patients, such as hospice care.

In 2002, the Catholic Institute of Bioethics and the Nicholas Cardinal Cheong Graduate School for Life were established at the Catholic University of Korea to disseminate the teachings of the Catholic Church on human life and promote a culture of life.[29] Both aim to provide interdisciplinary education related to human life, provide opportunities to reflect on the influences of biomedical technology, and encourage workers who will promote a culture of life by exploring the mystery of life. Although remarkable advances in modern medicine and biotechnology have provided many opportunities and benefits to humans, their improper use may endanger human relationships and ecosystems, and even threaten human survival. Therefore, it is necessary to critically evaluate the activities arising from science and medicine and to think about what contributes to human survival and flourishing. To this end, the Graduate School for Life conducts multilateral reflection and research with faculty members in science, medicine, philosophy,

26. The Catholic Institute of Cell Therapy was launched in 2005 after a scandal involving Woo Suk Hwang's embryonic stem cell research. For details on the scandal, see Hong, "Hwang Scandal."

27. In 1980, Thomas Hilgers, MD, designed standardized instruction for couples using this system, and it became officially known as the Creighton Model Fertility Care System. See Hilgers, "Natural Methods," 52–53, and also the Creighton Model website at https://creightonmodel.com.

28. "What Is NaPro Technology?"

29. See the timeline under "History" on the Nicholas Cardinal Cheong Graduate School for Life home page at https://songeui.catholic.ac.kr/gslife/html/about/history.jsp.

theology, anthropology, and ethics. It recruits twenty-five students every year, who choose their majors from among bioethics, life culture, and clinical research ethics.

To address the ethical issues and concerns raised by biomedicine, CMC has published various Catholic ethical guides related to medical ethics, including the *Catholic Clinical Medical Ethics Guidebook*. In addition, the Medical Ethics Committee was established to ensure that all medical personnel in the institution comply and to police those who do not. In order to lead in the area of ethical research and to ensure the protection of research subjects, in 2010, St. Mary's Hospital acquired AAHRPP certification[30] for international clinical research, a joint project of eight CMC hospitals.

Care for the Underprivileged and Marginalized

With the introduction of the national health insurance system, today basic medical services for the whole nation are theoretically possible. Under this system, how can we maintain traditional charitable care, such as that provided by church medical institutions? It will be necessary for Catholic medical institutions to maintain their identity in this period, when the government's policies, laws, and systems are applied uniformly to all medical institutions. By the 1970s, most Catholic medical institutions were largely focused on charitable work for the poor. Since the mid-1970s, however, the improvement of the national economy and the government's active participation in health care have changed the charitable nature of Catholic medicine. Despite this and regardless of the prosperity of the Korean economy, it is inevitable that the underprivileged are excluded from access to health care. The number of patients who are unable to pay for expensive medical care is higher than ever, and from the point of view of the church medical institution, the financial burden of charitable care is greater than ever.

In Korea, hospital-based home care, which was created to reduce medical insurance deficits and increase hospital utilization in tertiary hospitals when patients are discharged early did not benefit the poor in the community. Since 1996, CMC has operated the family nursing team, in which hospitals and churches have connected with one another to reach out to the poor and sick in the church community. Nurses care for elderly people

---

30. AAHRPP is the acronym for the Association for the Accreditation of Human Research Protection Programs, Inc. As stated on its home page, https://www.aahrpp.org, it is "an independent, non-profit accrediting body . . . [that] uses a voluntary, peer-driven, educational model to ensure that HRPPs [human research protection programs] meet rigorous standards for quality and protection."

living alone or chronically ill patients suffering from long-term illnesses in their homes. Since health involves restoring physical, psychological, and spiritual integrity, pastoral care should be strengthened for patients as well as health care workers.

Catholic medical missionary activities should not be limited to Korea but should extend beyond particular states and religions. Asia is home to 60 percent of the world's population, a population that experiences a variety of inequalities and sharp contrasts. Hundreds of millions of people struggle against poverty to survive, and many are alienated by extreme social inequality. The mission of CMC in Asia is to overcome social, cultural, religious, and ethnic boundaries and to provide physical and spiritual healing through an encounter with Christ, both for the patients who are suffering and the people who help them and convey Christ's love and gospel. Since 1987, CMC has continued to spread the love of Jesus Christ to medically disadvantaged and underprivileged areas around the world, such as Ecuador (1987–91), Kenya (1992–95), Mongolia (1997–present), and Colombia (2003–5). St. Mary's Hospital has been active in cooperation with Catholic schools, corporations, and peacemakers in Asia, including Nepal, the Philippines, and the Cambodian Mobile Clinic Project.

Mission and Tasks of the New Age

If the medical missionaries of Korea's Catholic Church in the 1950s and 1960s had a strong philanthropic proposal, it might be said that today, they have the evangelical answer to the dehumanization and secularization of modern medicine. Because all human beings are created in the likeness of God, we have the dignity that requires us to receive maximum respect. Providing medical care is an important and necessary task for protecting human dignity and sustaining the full growth of humanity. The church's medical care should address all of the problems that harm people's health and life in the community, including political, social, and economic problems. The goal of Catholic medical missionary work, as expressed in its long tradition, is not just to cure patients' illnesses. Rather, it is to restore humanity to its fullest by healing physical pain and disease and to achieve the development of all human resources. Therefore, the Catholic Church's missionary work should go beyond disease treatment, expanding its activities by contributing to a culture of life that respects human life, protects the sanctity of all people, and promotes humanity.

In the future, medical institutions in the Catholic Church should also engage in activities that are conducive to the well-being of the international community, focusing on the following activities:

1. Provide data and evidence for the contribution of the church's medical institutions toward the achievement of the UN's sustainable development goals.
2. Empower community-based church medical institutions to strengthen their impact on health care indicators.
3. Strengthen monitoring and cooperation activities so the budgets of government agencies can be properly used to achieve sustainable development.
4. Carry out their activities in close connection with the goal of achieving the common good, as well as sustainable development goals.[31]

The medical missionary work of the Catholic Church is to embody the spirit of Christ the healer and proclaim God's love in the gospel. As Jesus said, "Heal the sick and raise the dead. Cleanse the lepers and cast out the demons" (Matt 10:8). Caring for those who are sick and suffering from disease is an important duty of the Catholic Church.[32]

In closing, I would like to call to mind Pope Benedict XVI's words of comfort and encouragement to health care workers in 2012 on the World Day of the Sick: "To all those who work in the field of health, and to the families who see in their relatives the suffering face of the Lord Jesus, I renew my thanks and that of the Church, because, in their professional expertise and in silence, often without even mentioning the name of Christ, they manifest him in a concrete way."[33]

Bibliography

Benedict XVI, Pope. *Message of His Holiness Benedict XVI for the Seventeenth World Day of the Sick*. Vatican City: Libreria Editrice Vaticana, February 2, 2009. https://www.vatican.va/content/benedict-xvi/en/messages/sick/documents/hf_ben-xvi_mes_20090202_world-day-of-the-sick-2009.html.

———. *Message of the Holy Father on the Occasion of the Twentieth World Day of the Sick*. Vatican City: Libreria Editrice Vaticana, February 11, 2012. https://www.vatican.va/content/benedict-xvi/en/messages/sick/documents/hf_ben-xvi_mes_20111120_world-day-of-the-sick-2012.html.

31. Duff and Manguerra, "Dignity of the Human Person."
32. Noh, "Healthcare Provider's Spiritual Care."
33. Benedict XVI, *Message of the Holy Father*.

Bernardin, Joseph Cardinal. *Celebrating the Ministry of Healing: Joseph Cardinal Bernardin's Reflections on Healthcare.* Washington, DC: Catholic Health Association of the United States, 1999.

"Campaign of Prayer for Life, Raising Awareness to Avoid Abortion." *Agenzia Fides,* October 1, 2022. http://www.fides.org/en/news/72873-ASIA_SOUTH_KOREA_Campaign_of_prayer_for_life_raising_awareness_to_avoid_abortion.

Catholic Industrial Medical Center. Introduction brochure stored in the center. June 2023.

Cho, Kyu Sang. 세계 의료사와 한국 가톨릭 의료사 개관 [An Introduction to World Medical History and the Contribution of Catholic Church in Korea]. Seoul: Korean Catholic Medical Association, 2008.

"CMC Spirituality." Catholic Medical Center, 2017. https://www.cmc.or.kr/vision.index.sp.

"Core Value." Catholic Medical Center, 2017. https://www.cmc.or.kr/vision.index.sp.

Duff, Jean F., and Helena Manguerra. "Dignity of the Human Person is Central to UN Sustainable Goals." *Health Progress, Journal of the Catholic Health Association of the United States* 97.5 (September–October 2016) 7–13. https://www.chausa.org/publications/health-progress/archives/issues/september-october-2016/dignity-of-the-human-person-is-central-to-un-sustainable-goals.

Hilgers, Thomas W. "The Natural Methods for the Regulation of Fertility: The Authentic Alternative." *The Linacre Quarterly* 62.1 (1995) 52–59.

Hong, Sungook. "The Hwang Scandal that 'Shook the World of Science.'" *East Asian Science, Technology, and Society* 2.1 (2008) 1–7. https://doi.org/10.1215/s12280-008-9041-x.

John Paul, Pope, II. *Redemptoris Missio.* Vatican City: Libreria Editrice Vaticana, December 7, 1990. https://www.vatican.va/content/john-paul-ii/en/encyclicals/documents/hf_jp-ii_enc_07121990_redemptoris-missio.html.

Kim, Cardinal Souhwan Stephen. 하나님의 사랑을 믿고 그리스도를 본받아 이웃을 사랑하는 것이 가장 좋은 죽음의 준비 [The Best Preparation for Death Is to Believe in God's Love, Follow Christ, and Love Our Neighbors]. In *Life and Death,* vol. 10. Seoul: Gakdang Welfare Foundation, 1993.

Kim, Dae Gyun. "한일 가톨릭의료기술협력협정 25주년 합의문에 대한 성찰 [Reflections on the Twenty-Fifth Anniversary of the Korea-Japan Catholic Medical Technology Cooperation Agreement]." *Health and Mission* 33 (2014) 31–33.

Kim, Doo Jeong. *The Medical History of Korea.* Seoul: Tamgudang, 1966.

Kim, Pyeong Man, et al. "Education Program Development for Interprofessional Collaboration." *Journal of the Korea Service Management Society* 19.4 (2018) 293–310.

Kim, Pyeong Man, et al. "NOh Development for Interprofessional Collaboration." *Journal of the Korea Service Management Society* 19.4 (2018) 293–310.

Meng, Kwang Ho. "한국 천주교회의 어제 오늘 내일 35-VI 한국 가톨릭교회 사회개발 및 복지 사업 4 [Yesterday, Today, and Tomorrow 35-VI, Social Development and Welfare Work of the Catholic Church in Korea 4]." *Catholic Times* 2007 (June 16, 1996) 16. https://m.catholictimes.org/mobile/article_view.php?aid=240102.

Noh, Hyunki. "Healthcare Provider's Spiritual Care for Holistic Healing." *Personalist Bioethics* 5 (2015) 87–123.

Second Vatican Council. *Lumen Gentium: Dogmatic Constitution on the Church.* Vatican City: Libreria Editrice Vaticana, November 21, 1964. https://www.vatican.va/archive/hist_councils/ii_vatican_council/documents/vat-ii_const_19641121_lumen-gentium_en.html.

"What Is NaPro Technology?" Fertility Care Center of America, 2023. https://fertilitycare.org/what-is-naprotechnology.

Yong, Jinsun. "Reflection Two: Bringing the Compassionate Presence of Healing to Suffering Patients in West Africa." *Research Institute for Hospice and Palliative Care Newsletter* 18 (2017) 2–3.

PART THREE

Western and Non-Western Traditions of Medicine

6

Medical Nemesis Revisited

DAVID CAYLEY

MY PURPOSE IN THIS talk is to bring the work of Ivan Illich to bear on the present moment. But since the book from which my title is taken was written nearly fifty years ago and its author has been largely forgotten, even in Catholic circles, I'll begin with some introductions—first of Illich and then of the book. I hope those already familiar with Illich will bear with me.

Ivan Illich was born in 1926 in Vienna. His mother's family were wealthy converted Jews, and his father's people were merchant aristocracy from Split on the Adriatic Coast in present-day Croatia. In the early years of World War II, his family fled Vienna for Florence after being reclassified as Jews. In 1950 Illich was ordained a priest. The future Pope Paul VI, among others, tried to persuade him to remain in Rome. They saw in Illich a future prince of the church, a role for which his intellectual brilliance and facility with languages made him apt in every way. But he instead left Rome for New York and became an assistant priest in upper Manhattan in a parish that was then receiving a lot of Puerto Rican migrants. The strain of Catholicism they had brought with them from their Caribbean island was very different than the established varieties in the New York church, and their reception was sometimes hostile. Illich became their champion and, in 1956, was appointed vice-rector of the Catholic University at Ponce in Puerto Rico. There he established the first of a series of intercultural institutes devoted to propagating a new philosophy of mission. In 1961 Illich moved to Mexico. His institute in Cuernavaca—eventually called the Center for Intercultural

Documentation, or CIDOC—became a center of missionary training but also of radical critique of the neocolonial dimension in the relations between the American church and Latin America. CIDOC eventually grew into a major center of radical thought right across the board. Opposition to Illich on the right swelled throughout the 1960s—a dramatic story I haven't time for here—and, in 1968, he was summoned to Rome by the Holy Office and subjected to formal inquisition. The following year a ban was placed on his center, and priests and religious were forbidden to attend there. Illich, without renouncing his priesthood, resigned from service to the church.

During the next seven years before CIDOC closed its doors in 1976, Illich wrote prolifically, publishing five books, and lecturing throughout the world. When I hosted one such lecture in Toronto in 1970, we had to turn people away from the 600-seat auditorium that we had expected would be more than ample. His books promoted what he called "institutional revolution."[1] Political revolution, he said, was premised on either an expanded supply or a more equal distribution of the same old things—staples like education, health, transportation, and so on—which meanwhile went unexamined and unchallenged. What he wanted was to query the basic institutions of modern society rather than improve their distribution. These institutions, he argued, were just then reaching a watershed at which they would become counterproductive and begin to defeat their own ostensible purposes—education would begin to stupefy, medicine to sicken, transportation to immobilize, etc. What Francis Bacon had called "the relief of man's estate" would turn into its replacement by what Illich called "an artificial creation"—a service economy so total than no human act, from birth to death, love to mourning, play to celebration, would go untutored, unimproved, or unmanaged.

Medical Nemesis: The Expropriation of Health—to come at last to my theme—belonged to this genre of prophetic sociology. (In its final expanded edition, the book gained the title *Limits to Medicine*, but I will refer to it here as *Medical Nemesis*, which remained its subtitle.) It was the last, the most thorough, and the most scholarly of a series of institutional critiques that had begun with *Deschooling Society*. All of these books sought a point of balance, "a virtue of enoughness," as one of Illich's friends called it, "a roof of technological characteristics," Illich said, "under which people can live and be happy."[2] I call it "a constitution of limits" in order to highlight the fact that Illich was at all times making a political and a constitutional proposal. Modern professions had established what he called "radical monopolies"—they

---

1. "A call for institutional revolution" was the subtitle of Illich, *Celebration of Awareness*.
2. Sachs, "Virtue of Enoughness"; Illich, *Powerless Church*, 165.

had made their services compulsory, as is the case, for example, when only an educational certificate rather than proven competence qualifies you for a job.[3] His solution, in a word, was "disestablishment."[4] The echo of religion in the term was quite intentional. He believed that the Roman church was the mold from which all our institutions were stamped, and that all these institutions in some way promised the ersatz of salvation.

Medical Nemesis begins with the claim that "the medical establishment has become a major threat to health." He called this threat "iatrogenesis," a little known and then little used word for what originates with the physician. Iatrogenesis, he said, has three branches—clinical, social, and cultural. The first, clinical iatrogenesis, is the most familiar and its existence is probably better accepted and less controversial today than when Illich wrote. It refers to direct and immediate harms caused by medicine—getting the wrong diagnosis, prescribing the wrong drug, performing the wrong operation, and so on. How extensive is this damage? Ralph Nader, writing in *Harper's Magazine* a few years ago, suggested that the number of people in the United States who die annually as a result of preventable medical errors may be as high as 400,000—more than two-thirds of the registered COVID-19 mortality to date.[5] This is probably a high estimate but even half that number would be sobering.

However, clinical iatrogenesis was not Illich's primary concern. The effects of medicine on society and culture were, in his view, much more serious. He defined social iatrogenesis as "socioeconomic transformations" that had been made "attractive, possible or necessary by the institutional shape health care has taken," and continued:

> Social iatrogenesis . . . obtains when medical bureaucracy creates ill-health by increasing stress, by multiplying disabling dependence, by generating painful new needs, by lowering the levels of tolerance for discomfort and pain, by reducing the leeway that people are wont to concede to an individual when he suffers, and by abolishing even the right to self-care. . . . Social iatrogenesis is at work when health care is turned into a standardized item, a staple, when home becomes inhospitable to birth, sickness and death, when the language in which people can experience their bodies is turned into bureaucratic gobbledygook; or

---

3. Illich, *Tools for Conviviality*, 57.

4. "Why We Must Disestablish School" is one of the chapter titles in Illich, *Deschooling Society*.

5. Nader, "Suing for Justice," 61. Nader cites a story in the *Washington Post* but gives no date. The likely source of Nader's claim was an article in the *Journal of Patient Safety* 9.3 (September 2013) 122–28, which sets 400,000 as the upper limit of what is possible.

when suffering, mourning, and healing outside the patient role are labeled a form of deviance.[6]

Illich's final category was cultural iatrogenesis. "It sets in," he writes, "when the medical enterprise saps the will of people to suffer their reality."[7] This will, he wrote, is rooted in a culture that, in its religious aspect, offers "a rationale, a style, and a community setting in which suffering can become a dignified performance."[8] Contemporary medicine, on the other hand, makes suffering an abomination, even while sometimes increasing it. Suffering is a sign of failure or of a problem not yet solved. The constantly reiterated figure of people "battling" diseases evinces the same attitude. Death, likewise, loses its significance as something that belongs to me as my last act. Indeed, it cannot be understood as an act at all when it is undergone by a *patient*, someone who, as the word implies, is acted upon. Death cannot retain its meaning as life's complement and completion when it is seen only as the loss of a battle or the termination of treatment. And this is all the more true when death at the time of my choosing becomes a constitutional right, as is now the case here in Canada, and doctors are asked to administer death as their final professional benediction. Culture withers in the face of this degree of professional power, Illich says.

I cannot hope to digest a three-hundred-page book for you in a nineteen-page chapter, but there are two other points I would like to emphasize. The first is the way in which medicine's scientific character undercuts its moral character. Medicine is scientific in several senses. First, its diagnostic categories have the character of objective facts—I have x, y, or z, one simply says—and this entails an immense power to capture, reify, and slot experience into a set of stereotypes. Second, technoscientific capabilities often determine treatment: decisions are made on the basis of what can be done, not what ought to be done. And finally, there is the fact that "as a member of the medical profession the individual physician is an inextricable part of a scientific team."[9] The method of science is experiment, and, therefore, whatever the attitude of the individual physician, "each treatment [will be] one more repetition of an experiment with a statistically known probability of success." Two consequences follow, according to Illich. First, the experimenter will want to control the variables bearing on the outcome of the experiment, including "that elusive variable which is the patient himself." And, second, the exigencies of the ongoing experiment will tend to become

---

6. Illich, *Medical Nemesis*, 49.
7. Illich, *Medical Nemesis*, 133.
8. Illich, *Medical Nemesis*, 116.
9. Illich, *Medical Nemesis*, 253. The following quotes are on the same page.

the medical practitioner's main concern. As a result, Illich says, "only a high level of tolerance for cognitive dissonance will allow him to carry on in the divergent roles of healer and scientist."

That the physician is, or ought to be, a healer testifies to medicine's moral character. "In every society," Illich wrote,

> medicine, like law and religion, defines what is normal, proper, or desirable. Medicine has the authority to label one man's complaint a legitimate illness, to declare a second man sick though he does not complain, and to refuse a third social recognition of his pain, his disability, and even his death. The physician . . . is a moral entrepreneur, charged with inquisitorial powers to discover certain wrongs to be righted. Medicine, like all crusades, creates a new group of outsiders each time it makes a new diagnosis stick. Morality is as implicit in sickness as it is in crime or in sin.[10]

This brings me to the second point that I want to briefly highlight for you. Illich uses the term moral here in a sense that is closely akin to political—the sense in which what we now call political science was once called moral science. The "health occupations," he says, exercise a power that derives ultimately from the political sphere and that has been, in his word, "delegated" to them. He gives a striking example of professional power as political power in *Medical Nemesis* where he writes of the extraordinary prerogatives conferred on "the medical functionary" by "the ritualization of crisis." "It provides him," Illich goes on, "with a license that usually only the military can claim. Under the stress of crisis, the professional who is believed to be in command can easily presume immunity from the ordinary rules of justice and decency. He who is assigned control over death ceases to be an ordinary human. . . . Because they form a charmed borderland not quite of this world, the time-span and the community space claimed by the medical enterprise are as sacred as their religious and military counterparts."[11]

In a footnote to this passage Illich adds that "he who successfully claims power in an emergency suspends and can destroy rational evaluation. The insistence of the physician on his exclusive capacity to evaluate and solve individual crises moves him symbolically into the neighborhood of the White House."[12] Rereading these sentences recently I heard an echo of the German jurist Carl Schmitt's claim in his book *Political Theology* that

---

10. Illich, *Medical Nemesis*, 53–54.
11. Illich, *Medical Nemesis*, 107.
12. Illich, *Medical Nemesis*, 107.

the hallmark of true sovereignty is the power to "decide on the exception."[13] Schmitt's point is that sovereignty stands above law because in an emergency the sovereign can suspend the law—declare an exception—and rule in its place as the very source of law. This is precisely the power that Illich says the physician "claims ... in an emergency." Exceptional circumstances make him/her "immune" to the "ordinary rules" and able to make new ones as the case dictates.

But there is an interesting and, to me, telling difference between Schmitt and Illich, and this brings me to the final point I want to make about Illich's work of the 1970s. Schmitt, writing in the 1920s, is transfixed by what he calls "the political." Illich, fifty years later, argues that much of what Schmitt calls "sovereignty" has escaped, or been usurped from the political realm and reinvested in various professional hegemonies. And this was Illich's great point in all of his writings about what he called, in a book of that name, "disabling professions." In modern liberal states, with what British parliamentary tradition calls mixed constitutions—checks and balances, as Americans say—it is often assumed that political power resides within the executive, legislative, or judicial branches of government. Illich argued that the preponderance of political power was now held, unacknowledged and unaccounted for, in professional hands and that as a result politics had "withered."[14]

Medical Nemesis enjoyed a considerable *success de scandale,* but—it would appear—not much influence. When Illich revisited the book about a decade later,[15] he said that he was "not dissatisfied with my text, as far as it goes." "But I am distressed," he went on, "that I was blind to a much more profound symbolic iatrogenic effect: the iatrogenesis of the body itself. I overlooked the degree to which, at mid-century, the experience of 'our bodies and our selves' had become the result of medical concepts and cares."[16] By this he meant first that he had not sufficiently recognized the historicity of the body itself. He had taken it for a natural object standing outside history, whereas now he recognized that "each historical moment is incarnated in an epoch-specific body."[17] And, second, he meant that self-perception was being medicalized as never before. In the mid-seventies, in the famous opening sentence of *Medical Nemesis,* he had claimed that "the medical

13. Schmitt, *Political Theology,* 5.
14. Illich et al., *Disabling Professions,* 12.
15. Illich, *Mirror of the Past,* 213. Illich first revisited the book in a 1985 talk he gave at Pennsylvania State University, and this was later reprinted in *Mirror of the Past.*
16. Illich, *Mirror of the Past,* 213.
17. Illich, *Mirror of the Past,* 214.

establishment has become a major threat to health." Now he said the major threat to health had become "the pathogenic pursuit of health"[18] itself.

In the period before he wrote this reappraisal of *Medical Nemesis*, Illich had come to the conclusion that his world had changed in a fundamental and unexpected way. "I believe," he told me in 1988, "that . . . there [has been] a change in the mental space in which many people live. Some kind of a catastrophic breakdown of one way of seeing things has led to the emergence of a different way of seeing things. The subject of my writing has been the perception of sense in the way we live; and, in this respect, we are, in my opinion, at this moment, passing over a watershed. I had not expected in my lifetime to observe this passage."[19] He called what lay on the far side of this unexpected watershed "The Age of Systems," and he came to the conclusion that it had entirely engulfed medicine, just as it had everything else. In *Medical Nemesis*, he had seen himself, along with the political majority he had hoped to mobilize, as standing outside and above something that could be imagined as "the medical establishment," something that could, in effect, be taken in hand and changed. Now he saw people as having been, as he said, "swallowed by the system,"[20] or as living in "an ontology of systems."[21] This new state is exemplified in talk of "my system" or of its surrounding world as an ecosystem. Health, he thought, now measured the state of such a system, rather than the integrity of a person. He began to speak of contemporary persons as having undergone disembodiment, as a unique, fleshy, and personal mode of being was replaced by a collage of risks, averages, and probabilities. People were becoming—you might say—more hypothetical.

This changed everything for Illich. There was no longer any definite medical establishment at which to take aim. The "health care system" as a whole had assumed the protagonist's role; doctors had become its functionaries. A paradigm of this new condition is the concept of risk. A person treated according to their "risk," for example, is being treated not as an embodied person but as an item of statistical information. Risks don't refer to individuals; they refer to probabilities distributed across a population. My "risk" reveals nothing about me as a discrete being—it describes only the frequency with which something is apt to happen in the category to which I have been assigned. So, insofar as I am a subject of risk, I have been disembodied and disconnected from my person. My experience has been subsumed into a system in which I appear only as an informational

---

18. Illich, *Mirror of the Past*, 212.
19. Cayley, *Ivan Illich in Conversation*, 169–70.
20. Cayley, *Rivers North of the Future*, 63.
21. Illich, "Brave New Biocracy," 9.

abstract—a set of risks and imperatives bearing on the class in which I have been enrolled. This was the new "epoch-specific" body, according to Illich.

Illich was a man who liked to move on, to live in the moment, and to offer analysis that was of the moment. Now and then, he carried this liking to a fault, treating his earlier work as no more—he once said—than "dead written stuff of that time."[22] I find *Medical Nemesis* to be much more than dead written stuff, and I hope you can see the continuing pertinence of the ideas I outlined earlier—from the socially and culturally disabling effect of too much medicine, to the tension between the moral and the scientific sides of medical practice, to the inherently political character of medical power. But these ideas do need to be supplemented with those Illich developed in the last twenty years of his life—about risk and allied concepts as, in his words, a "religiously celebrated ideology,"[23] about the antithesis between systems and persons, and about the way in which the body itself is now an iatrogenic construct.

There's one more theme that I can't avoid introducing before coming to our present circumstances, and that is the complex of meanings that have come to surround the word *life*. In 1989 in Chicago, the city where I wish I were standing in front of you right now, Illich told a convocation of the Lutheran church in America that *life* had become "the most powerful idol that the church has had to face in the course of her history."[24] Life, he said, had become a stuff, a substance, a palpable resource that institutions count, conserve, manage, and advertise as their raison d'être. Whether one speaks of "life on earth," *my* life, or the *lives* saved and lost that one encounters in the news media, one refers to something that belongs to us as our concern, our possession, and our justification. In the New Testament, life is said to be "in Christ." He *is* life. This life is given to us, but never on our terms. According to Illich, the aura that now radiates from the word "life" in the discourses of law, medicine, politics, ecology, and ethics would be unthinkable without the Incarnation, but at the same time it perverts and parodies the Incarnation by making life the work of human hands—an idol. This is the essential ambiguity of the word in Illich's view. It invokes what is out of our hands and what is in our hands at the same time. These meanings are easily elided, and the slide from one to the other often goes unremarked and unaccounted for in contemporary discourses.

I believe that the COVID-19 pandemic has marked the arrival and full manifestation of the type of society that Illich saw coming. One of the

---

22. Cayley, *Ivan Illich in Conversation*, 120.
23. Cayley, *Rivers North of the Future*, 210.
24. Illich, *Mirror of the Past*, 220.

proofs that this is so is the way in which the pandemic has been received, construed, and countered. To establish this point, I will need to digress from Illich for a little in order to explain what I mean in speaking of the way in which the pandemic has been received. After I have done this, I will return to the ways in which it consummates the social order Illich foresaw.

There seems to be a class of great historical events to which people respond with a kind of unconscious unanimity, as if all had been foreordained. The occurrence of these events seems destined, their meaning and implications obvious to all. Within living memory, 9/11 was like that. The dust and ashes of the fallen towers had barely settled before the meaning of the event was plain to all: history had spoken, the world had changed forever, a "new normal" was imminent. One newspaper columnist where I live even discerned the end of "the age of irony" in the still-smoldering wreckage. In an earlier time, the First World War began with the same collective acceptance of a doom foretold. Economic historian Karl Polanyi who fought and suffered in that war remembered afterwards how Europe had "sleep-walked" to its destruction. The pandemic too had this quality. Its appearance was answered by an extraordinary and unprecedented policy whose novelty no one seemed to notice. This readiness and sense of inevitability can only be accounted for on the hypothesis that a long period of unconscious practice had preceded the actual event. The new habits of heart and mind that the pandemic evinced had been slowly matured.

This was why the pandemic arrived with its meaning already legible, and the policy response it demanded already prescribed. "Lockdowns" were the order of the day, and, among Western countries, all but Sweden implemented this policy, more or less immediately, in some form. Those who delayed, like the United Kingdom, were soon mocked and bullied into line. How such a word as *lockdown*—borrowed from prisons, used occasionally with reference to large public high schools, and still resonant with these associations—could suddenly slide so smoothly into the common tongue is a study in itself. What I want to draw attention to here is how dramatically this policy broke with what had up until then been conventional wisdom in public health. Quarantine had been something imposed on the sick, not on the healthy. Public health had been, at least ideally, a comprehensive idea referring to a common good, and taking account of the diverse and sometimes contradictory determinants that bear on this common good. Now, almost overnight, public health policy became entirely one-dimensional. The novel coronavirus filled the entire sky, panic was actively fostered by what appeared to be a seamless consortium of media, politicians, and public health officials, and nobody seemed to care who got hurt so long as the "war" against the virus was won. When seasoned public health professionals warned that lockdown was an untried and possibly counterproductive policy, they were ignored.

This was so egregious and so little noticed that it's worth dwelling on for a moment. In Canada, on March 16, 2020, a former chief officer of public health in Manitoba, Dr. Joel Kettner, called the Canadian Broadcasting Corporation's national radio phone-in show *Cross-Country Checkup* to warn against overreaction and to point out that "social distancing" was a largely unproven technique. "We actually do not have that much good evidence," Dr. Kettner said. "It . . . might work, [but] we really don't know to what degree and the evidence is pretty weak."[25] He was treated with strained courtesy by the program's host and never consulted again, so far as I know, by Canada's public broadcaster. Later that summer, Dr. Kettner was one of a large group of public health professionals who warned that quarantining the entire eligible population of the country was a radical departure from previous public health practice and might well backfire, doing more harm than good. In their open letter to Canada's political leaders, this group pleaded for "a balanced response" to the pandemic, arguing that the "current approach" posed serious threats to both "population health" and "equity."[26] The signers of this letter included two former chief public health officers for Canada, two former provincial public health chiefs, three former deputy ministers of health, three present or former deans of medicine at Canadian universities, and various other academic luminaries—a virtual who's who of public health in Canada. Their statement was ignored by the politicians to whom it was addressed and went virtually unreported in Canadian print and broadcast media. It remains completely unknown, so far as I can tell, to the Canadian public.

This pattern was repeated elsewhere. In the first days of the pandemic, John Ioannidis of the Stanford School of Medicine, a recognized expert in the fields of epidemiology, population health, and biomedical data science, warned of "a fiasco in the making" if draconian political decisions were taken in the absence of evidence as to the actual danger posed by the disease.[27] A number of other equally qualified doctors and medical scientists followed suit. Epidemiologist Kurt Wittkowski, an emeritus professor at New York's Rockefeller University, recommended that the disease be allowed to spread through the healthy part of the population as rapidly as possible.[28]

25. "Listen: CBC Radio Cuts Off," para. 12.
26. Bell, "Dealing with COVID-19."
27. Ioannidis, "Fiasco in the Making?"
28. The video of Dr. Wittkowski that I originally intended to cite has since been removed from YouTube, which has selectively censored "misinformation," i.e., dissident opinions, throughout the pandemic. For another, so-far-uncensored conversation with Dr. Wittkowski, see Wittkowski, "PandaCast."

Virologist John Oxford, a professor at Queen Mary University London, warned that what we were experiencing was "a media epidemic."[29] Toward the end of 2020, on October 4, three eminent epidemiologists, accredited at Oxford, Harvard, and Stanford, authored and signed what they called the Great Barrington Declaration.[30] In their statement, Sunetra Gupta, Martin Kulldorff, and Jayanta Bhattacharya called for a policy of "focused protection" for the vulnerable and a return to normality for the majority. This statement too was either ignored or treated with derision in the organs of polite opinion. In Ontario, on April 30, 2021, the College of Physicians and Surgeons warned the doctors whom they regulate, by statute, that these doctors would face discipline should they "communicate anti-vaccine, anti-masking, anti-distancing and anti-lockdown statements" or promote "unsupported, unproven treatments for COVID-19."[31] Such a threat was necessary, the College said, to counteract the spreading, by some doctors, of "blatant misinformation." This term has been widely used, along with *dis*information, to exclude unwanted opinions from journalistic media. In Australia, Dr. Paul Oosterhuis, an anesthetist who has been practicing for more than thirty years, was ordered to appear before his medical board in New South Wales for "endangering the health and safety of the public," because he questioned vaccination and counseled alternative treatment in social media posts.[32]

Paradoxically, the marginalization and, at times, outright suppression of dissident opinion has been accompanied by the universal claim that governments, with the great obedient majority of their citizens in train, are "following science." This too is extraordinary. Many of the policies governments pursued were novel, and so had no warranting evidence by definition. The virus too was novel, which meant that most of its features were unknown, most notably its virulence and mortality rate in different segments of the population. In short, there was little or no science to follow. But the claims that were made for science, along with the attempt to ostracize and discredit discordant opinions had two crucial effects. First, they served to disguise the moral and political character of the policy being followed. Lockdown

---

29. NOVUS Communications, "View from the HVivo."

30. The declaration is published online at https://gbdeclaration.org. It was initially signed by Sunetra Gupta, Martin Kulldorff, and Jayanta Bhattacharya. Many scientists, doctors, and public health professionals subsequently co-signed, as did nearly a million members of the public.

31. Ontario College of Physicians and Surgeons, "Statement on Public Health Misinformation," para. 2.

32. Doctors for COVID Ethics, "Supporting Dr. Paul Oosterhuis."

and its concomitants—masking, distancing, isolation, anxiety about infection—had profound social and economic consequences.

Even a short and very partial list would have to include unprecedented debt, deaths from diseases that have gone undiagnosed and untreated during the COVID mobilization, lost jobs, stalled careers, failed businesses, decimation of the performing arts, troubles occurring behind closed doors among distraught and isolated people, and untold injuries to habits of sociability and conviviality. Economists who have tried estimate the mortality associated with these harms have often come up with totals that far exceed the mortality ascribed to the virus.[33] A recent study done for the Ontario Civil Liberties Association, for example, examined mortality from all causes in Canada between January 2010 and March 2021. It found that while there was "no extraordinary surge in yearly or seasonal mortality which can be ascribed to a COVID-19 pandemic," there was a startling jump in what they called "response-caused deaths"; that is, deaths attributable to measures taken against the pandemic among young males and the elderly.[34]

All of these consequences of COVID lockdowns and other countermeasures have followed from political decisions. But these decisions (according to those who made them) were not decisions at all. They were merely entailments of "science"—logical and necessary corollaries to what "the science" said. "I gotta do what the docs tell me," as I once heard Doug Ford, Ontario's folksy premier, say. What else could he do but "follow science"? In this way, moral choice was hidden and moral responsibility abdicated.

The second profound consequence of the discourse about science that has prevailed during the pandemic is the support it has given to the reactionary myth that science is a compact, consistent, and unitary entity that addresses the public as an unequivocal and unquestionable oracle. The phrase "following the science" sums up this view. More than thirty-five years ago Steven Shapin and Simon Schaffer published an influential book called *Leviathan and the Air-Pump: Hobbes, Boyle, and the Experimental Life*. The book showed, in brief, that at the very beginning of the seventeenth century's "scientific revolution" there stood a profound disagreement. Robert Boyle, a pioneering experimentalist, held that experiment was a method capable of producing unassailable "matters of fact," and thus could provide a secure basis on which to found social order. His antagonist, Thomas Hobbes, who was just as much an exponent of the new "mechanical philosophy" as Boyle, believed that knowledge must have an axiomatic foundation, like Euclid's geometry. According to Hobbes, experiments such as Boyle was conducting

---

33. A number of studies to this effect are referenced in Yang, "Lockdowns."
34. Rancourt et al., "All-Cause Mortality," 16–21.

before a handful of witnesses at a private house in London could never provide such a foundation. They could be too easily challenged and swept up in contests of opinion, as our age of "alternative facts" now attests. Shapin and Schaffer's book, by showing science as divided and plural at its very inception, announced a revolution in the history of science. This revolution had many precursors, stretching back to Thomas Kuhn's *The Structure of Scientific Revolutions*, and, before that, to Kuhn's acknowledged ancestor, Ludwik Fleck, in the latter's *Genesis and Development of a Scientific Fact*. It has also had many sequels, as this revolution has continued to ramify widely through the history, philosophy, and anthropology of science in the years since.

What this movement has produced, in my estimation, is a new image of the sciences—a much chastened image when compared to the hieratic cult that gradually usurped the place of the Christian church in the modern West.[35] For brevity's sake, since my main purpose here is to show how the pandemic response has restored and reinforced the old image, let me quickly summarize the understandings that I think comprise this new image: 1) there is no such thing as "science" in the sense of a single entity with a unique method; there are sciences, each using the method that suits its subject matter; 2) all scientific knowledge rests on prior philosophical grounds; and 3) scientific findings are partial, fallible, and interested since they are produced by people who also have that character and possess no infallible method or transcendent guarantee.

None of this should be taken as a depreciation of the value of the sciences or their ability to produce, on the terrain on which they operate, the surest knowledge available to us. In my view, it deprives science only of its mystique. It does not deprecate any of the sciences' real virtues. So long as this mystique prevailed, science held a trump card by which it could, as philosopher Bruno Latour says, "silence politics."[36] What I have called the new image of science allows politics to revive. The sciences, as Latour says, must be brought "into democracy" with no ace up their sleeve.

In his 1973 book *Tools for Conviviality*, Illich argued that science, as commonly understood, had become "a spectral production agency," possessing such ineffable authority that, under its sway, "people . . . cease to trust their own judgment." "Political discussion," he said, had been "stunned by a delusion about science," and the regeneration of communities of people able to think and speak for themselves would depend on their first overcoming

---

35. British biologist Rupert Sheldrake captures this religious character nicely in his book, *The Science Delusion*. Sheldrake, having long been persecuted by the Church of Science, knows whereof he speaks.

36. Latour, *Politics of Nature*, 10.

this delusion.[37] For many years, I entertained the hope that the new image of science of which I have spoken was the beginning of this overcoming. The pandemic has provided an opportunity for journalists, politicians, and the medical-industrial complex to restore the image I had thought obsolete to its full high-modern luster. This particular aspect of the pandemic response preoccupies me, and so I have dwelt on it here. But this is far from the whole catastrophe that the pandemic has authorized. Given more space, I could also have emphasized the boost it has given to technocracy—government by experts—centralization of power, biosurveillance, and the virtualization of social relations. Societies have grown more polarized, and more unequal, as the work-from-home class have consolidated their privileges, and the economically redundant have been pushed to the margins.

Acquiescence in this new order has depended, in my view, on a complex of interrelated ideas concerning health, safety, risk, and life. This is where Illich comes back into the picture. In his book of the first half of the 1970s—the series that culminated in *Medical Nemesis*—Illich posed a stark choice. Guided by his idea that there are ascertainable thresholds at which institutions become counterproductive and begin to frustrate their own purposes, he claimed that contemporary societies must either write a constitution of limits or face becoming "totally enclosed [in an] artificial creation with no exit."[38] Predictions of a similar tenor appear in all of his books of the time. *Medical Nemesis* ends with the promise of "compulsory survival in a planned and engineered hell," should "limits to medicine" not be instituted.[39] I believe he was in earnest. He did think, in later years, that many of his contemporaries had entirely lost the points of orientation once provided by the human condition. "Only smoke remains," he wrote in a letter to his friend Hellmut Becker in 1992, "from the world-dwindling we have experienced. . . . Exciting, soul-capturing abstractions have extended themselves over the perception of world and self like plastic pillowcases."[40]

Illich explored the new, artificial human condition in the writings I discussed earlier—his reconsideration of *Medical Nemesis*, his reflections on risk and the loss of embodied personhood in the Age of Systems,[41] and his denunciation of commodified life as an "institutional fetish."[42] It's my

37. Illich, *Tools for Conviviality*, 92.
38. Illich, *Tools for Conviviality*, 54.
39. Illich, *Medical Nemesis*, 272.

40. A translation of this letter by Barbara Duden and Muska Nagel was read at Illich's funeral in Bremen in December of 2002, and I am quoting from the unpublished text that was made for that occasion.

41. Cayley, *Rivers North of the Future*, 210–11.

42. This is a reference to Illich's text titled "The Institutional Construction of a New Fetish: Human Life" in Illich, *Mirror of the Past*, 211–31.

contention that gradual acclimatization to this new condition explains how people have so easily accepted the idea that the current pandemic fully justifies the institution of what amounts to a new, and potentially permanent, biosecurity state. Like the apocryphal but still compelling figure of the frog that doesn't know it's being boiled because the temperature of the initially tepid water in which it is immersed has increased so slowly, people have gradually accepted a set of axiomatic ideas that have now sunk so deep that they are imperceptible and therefore unquestionable. Illich called such axiomatic convictions "certainties." They are the ideas we think with, not about, because they lie, as Illich says, "beyond the horizon of our attention."[43] A prime instance is risk, which Illich, as I mentioned earlier, dared to call "the most important religiously celebrated ideology today."[44] Every time the word "risk" is spoken, it says two crucial things, but, as it were, under its breath: first, that the reality I am to live has a hidden mathematical structure which is imperceptible to me, and second, that what is important about me is not my unique being but the type, class, or category in which risk enrolls me.

Here, a short digression is in order. All of Illich's early work depended on the idea of balance. What he tried to discern was the thresholds at which things that might be good in moderation turn bad and become counterproductive. A continuum is always implied. *Medical Nemesis*, for example, presents the great public health innovations of the nineteenth and twentieth centuries—clean water, fresh air, public sanitation, etc.—as unalloyed blessings. The book likewise praises the benefits of a basic toolkit of "demonstrably effective technical health devices." What is sought, as I mentioned earlier, is what Illich's friend Wolfgang Sachs called "the virtue of enoughness" and what Illich himself called "the roof of technological characteristics under which a society wants to live and be happy."[45] Risk, likewise, describes a continuum. Illich is not denouncing practical appraisals of danger or denying sociology's founding insight that societies exhibit stable and predictable regularities. He is talking about what happens when risk monopolizes thinking and people begin to engage in what he called "intensive self-algorithmization," as if they actually were mere probabilities on a statistician's curve.

Risk cultivates the habit of hypothetical thinking. Personal decisions begin to be made on the basis of *what might happen to someone like me* rather than on the basis of my personal situation. People become, in Illich's terms, disembodied—not, obviously, because they cease to have bodies; in

---

43. Cayley, *Ivan Illich in Conversation*, 124.
44. Cayley, *Rivers North of the Future*, 210.
45. Sachs, "Virtue of Enoughness," 16; Illich, *Powerless Church*, 165.

fact, they tend to be more preoccupied with their bodies than ever before—but because they have lost the "unique . . . now" which is "the only time the Lord is present to us."[46] This loss occurs, as I've been emphasizing, through "the introjection and self-ascription of statistical entities"—people mistake themselves for the statistical doppelgängers that represent them on this or that risk curve. This disposition to live in a hypothetical rather than an actual space shows up in the pandemic response in various ways. The first is in the sheer blizzard of imaginary numbers. It began, on March 16, 2020, when a hastily assembled "COVID-19 Response Team" from London's Imperial College released a speculative model which predicted catastrophe—2.2 million deaths in the US alone—without drastic intervention. Their statistical nightmare took the world by storm. The former chief medical officer for Sweden, Julian Giesecke, astonished, stated categorically that, in his experience, "no study has ever made such an impression on the world."[47] It seems fair to say that models have driven policy ever since. Trust in models seems unimpaired by the failure of their predictions. New "modeling" is always at hand to erase the memory of the old model. Illich's favorite figure for such rituals was the rain dance: "The idea that the rain dance will bring rain eclipses the social cost of organizing the rain dance and makes the dancers feel that if rain doesn't come then they ought to dance all the harder."[48]

Models, scenarios, and expert speculations tend to erase any stable sense of reality among a naïve public. Take "asymptomatic transmission"—the possibility that people who don't feel sick may still transmit the virus. The evidence as to how frequently this happens is quite mixed, but the idea took hold and then reproduced itself without reference to this evidence—everyone is potentially dangerous to everyone else. Another result of the constant repetition of case counts, death tolls, etc., was to quickly place the pandemic outside of all historical perspective—Canada's prime minister Justin Trudeau went so far as to call the pandemic "the worst health care crisis in our history," a claim that ought to have evoked derision in anyone who knows anything of the devastating effect of smallpox on indigenous people during the first centuries of colonization. Instead, it passed unremarked amidst all the hyperbole about the new normal, and how "unprecedented" it all was.[49]

---

46. Cayley, *Rivers North of the Future*, 222; Illich, *Powerless Church*, 159.
47. Giesecke, "Why Lockdowns," 7:48.
48. Cayley, *Rivers North of the Future*, 140.
49. CPAC, "PM Justin Trudeau," 10:30; his statement in French, subtitled in English, was "La plus grande crise de santé publique de son histoire."

I have emphasized risk. I could as well have mentioned other certainties—like safety, systems, or management—that have taken root alongside risk and played a comparable role in normalizing and naturalizing destructive and disorienting elements in the pandemic response. One in particular deserves reemphasis before I conclude: *life*. Illich claimed that life, in its contemporary usage, is the lynchpin of "a new phase of religiosity."[50] To save and secure life, almost anything may now be done, including the overturning of fundamental cultural and moral norms. Consider: a coroner's inquest in the province of Quebec has recently heard that, during the early days of the pandemic, residents of the Herron Nursing Home in Montreal died of hunger and of thirst, while others were left unattended in horrible conditions, following a government directive banning visitors.[51] Everywhere old people died alone, cut off from their families. Funeral rites were prohibited. This is paradoxical—life sacrificed to life—but revealing. Elementary cultural decencies and personal loyalties can now be swept aside as long as the goal is to save life. Persons may be injured, but the resource is conserved, the new god placated.

Illich warned of "the pathogenic pursuit of health." The pandemic has revealed a society in an advanced state of "cultural iatrogenesis"—a society that may be about to tip into a permanent state of mutual fear and bio-surveillance more closely resembling a giant immune system than a liberal social order. If this dark prediction comes to pass, it will be scant comfort to know that somebody foresaw it. But one can hope that the panic will abate and a sober reckoning of the injuries inflicted by the pandemic response will become possible. The very extremity of this response may then help to identify it as a form of "medical nemesis." Even if this doesn't happen, some will continue to try and live outside the sway of the health security state, and, for them, Illich will continue to offer a way to begin to discover "the limits to medicine."

Bibliography

Bell, Robert. "Dealing with COVID-19: An Open Letter to Canada's Prime Minister and Provincial and Territorial Premiers." *HealthyDebate*, July 9, 2020. https://healthydebate.ca/2020/n07/topic/an-open-letter-to-pm-covid19/.

Cayley, David. *Ivan Illich: An Intellectual Journey*. University Park: Pennsylvania State University Press, 2021.

———. *Ivan Illich in Conversation*. Toronto: House of Anansi, 1992.

---

50. Cayley, *Ivan Illich in Conversation*, 276.
51. Ha, "Herron Residents."

---. *The Rivers North of the Future: The Testament of Ivan Illich.* Toronto: House of Anansi, 2005.
CPAC, Cable Public Affairs Channel. "PM Justin Trudeau Provides Update on Federal Response to COVID-19." YouTube video, 27:51. March 25, 2020. https://www.youtube.com/watch?v=NzRw-AIeNuY.
Doctors for COVID Ethics. "Supporting Dr. Paul Oosterhuis." Doctors for COVID Ethics. https://doctors4covidethics.org/supporting-dr-oosterhuis/.
Fleck, Ludwik. *Genesis and Development of a Scientific Fact.* Edited by Thaddeus J. Trenn and Edward K. Merton. Translated by Fred Bradley and Thaddeus J. Trenn. Chicago: University of Chicago Press, 1979.
Giesecke, Johan. "Why Lockdowns Are the Wrong Policy: Swedish Expert Prof. Johan Giesecke." Interview by Freddie Sayers. YouTube video, 34:53. UnHerd, April 17, 2020. https://www.youtube.com/watch?v=bfN2JWifLCY&t=28s.
Ha, Tu Thanh. "Herron Residents Died of Thirst, Malnourishment, Quebec Coroner's Inquest Told." *Globe and Mail*, September 14, 2021. https://www.theglobeandmail.com/canada/article-herron-long-term-care-residents-died-of-thirst-malnourishment-quebec.
Illich, Ivan. "Brave New Biocracy: Health Care from Womb to Tomb." *NPQ: New Perspectives Quarterly* 11.1 (Winter 1994) 4–12.
---. *Celebration of Awareness: A Call for Institutional Reform.* New York: Doubleday, 1970.
---. *Deschooling Society.* New York: Harper and Row, 1971.
---. *In the Mirror of the Past: Lectures and Addresses 1978–1990.* London: Marion Boyars, 1992.
---. *Limits to Medicine: Medical Nemesis: The Expropriation of Health.* Harmondsworth, UK: Penguin, 1976.
---. *The Powerless Church and Other Selected Writings, 1955–1985.* University Park: Pennsylvania State University Press, 2018.
---. *Tools for Conviviality.* New York: Harper and Row, 1973.
Illich, Ivan, et al. *Disabling Professions.* London: Marion Boyars, 1977.
Ioannidis, John P. A. "A Fiasco in the Making? As the Coronavirus Pandemic Takes Hold, We Are Making Decisions Without Reliable Data." *STAT*, March 17, 2020. https://www.statnews.com/2020/03/17/a-fiasco-in-the-making-as-the-coronavirus-pandemic-takes-hold-we-are-making-decisions-without-reliable-data/.
Kuhn, Thomas. *The Structure of Scientific Revolutions.* Chicago: University of Chicago Press, 1962.
Latour, Bruno. *Politics of Nature: How to Bring the Sciences into Democracy.* Translated by Catherine Porter. Cambridge: Harvard University Press, 2004.
"Listen: CBC Radio Cuts Off Expert When He Questions COVID19 Narrative." *OffGuardian*, March 17, 2020. https://off-guardian.org/2020/03/17/listen-cbc-radio-cuts-off-expert-when-he-questions-covid19-narrative/.
Nader, Ralph. "Suing for Justice." *Harper's Magazine*, April 2016. https://harpers.org/archive/2016/04/suing-for-justice/.
NOVUS Communications. "A View from the HVivo/OpenOrphan #Orph Laboratory—Professor John Oxford." *Open Orphan (Orph)*, March 31, 2020. https://novuscomms.com/2020/03/31/a-view-from-the-hvivo-open-orphan-orph-laboratory-professor-john-oxford/.

Ontario College of Physicians and Surgeons. "Statement on Public Health Misinformation." April 30, 2021. https://cpsodev.cpso.on.ca/en/News/News-Articles/COVID-misinformation.

Rancourt, Denis G., et al. "Analysis of All-Cause Mortality by Week in Canada 2010–2021, by Province, Sex, and Age." Global Research: Centre for Research on Globalization website, August 6, 2021. https://www.globalresearch.ca/analysis-all-cause-mortality-week-canada-2010-2021-province-age-sex-no-covid-19-pandemic-strong-evidence-response-caused-deaths-most-elderly-young-males/5754402.

Sachs, Wolfgang. "The Virtue of Enoughness." *NPQ: New Perspectives Quarterly* 6 (Spring 1989) 16–19.

Schmitt, Carl. *Political Theology: Four Chapters on the Concept of Sovereignty.* Cambridge: MIT Press, 1985.

Shapin, Steven, and Simon Shaffer. *Leviathan and the Air-Pump: Hobbes, Boyle, and the Experimental Life.* Princeton: Princeton University Press, 1985.

Sheldrake, Rupert. *The Science Delusion: Freeing the Spirit of Enquiry.* London: Coronet, 2012.

Wittkowski, Knut. "PandaCast: A Conversation with Knut Wittkowski." Interview by Nick Hudson. YouTube video, 53:56. PANDA, February 17, 2021. https://www.youtube.com/watch?v=H4onjXeT8og.

Yang, Ethan. "Lockdowns Need to Be Intellectually Discredited Once and for All." American Institute of Economic Research website, May 26, 2021, https://www.aier.org/article/lockdowns-need-to-be-intellectually-discredited-once-and-for-all.

7

Concepts of Health: Challenges to the Healing Ministry from a Zambian Perspective

BERNHARD UDELHOVEN, MAFR

AFRICA HAS TO SHOULDER a very large share of the global disease burden.[1] Given the chronic underfunding of most of the continent's national health sectors, it is obvious that faith-based health interventions provide very important contributions in the fight against disease. Among the Catholic health initiatives, one could mention hospitals and clinics, nursing schools, educational programs, youth and women's ministries, home-based care, behavior change and other health awareness programs, homes and services for the disabled, sanitation and hygiene programs, and, of course, outreach ministries to the sick in all parishes. The church is widely associated with health care. When people praise Catholic health institutions in Zambia, they refer usually to the administrative side of biomedical interventions: the presence of international doctors in Catholic hospitals, the medical apparatus available, well-stocked pharmacies, supervision of the work force, and linkages to other health institutions. Catholic health care is often lauded as a competent service provider.

But what about spiritual healing? I believe that the Catholic charism of spiritual healing is less visible and relevant in Zambia than what the church would like it to be! Hospitals, including Catholic ones, operate largely on the biomedical paradigm, which has been extremely successful in combating

---

1. See, for example, Roser et al., "Burden of Disease," § "The global distribution of the disease burden"; or Haddad, *Potential and Perils*, 30.

acute and infectious disease. Its success on this level has overshadowed the local, African healing paradigms. The church often identified with the biomedical successes as proof of Christian superiority over local beliefs. But the modern health care sector did not gain a monopoly on healing, because African health care needs were never limited to biomedical concerns. Even today, the number of traditional healers outweighs that of registered nurses and doctors in Zambia. In addition to traditional and modern healing practices, people also frequent countless Pentecostal, Zion, and other Christian ministries in a quest for faith healing. It may be tempting to conclude that traditional healers and faith healing only fill a gap that is left by the underfunded modern health sector. But more fundamentally, they answer questions and needs that are eclipsed by biomedical approaches. In Zambia, especially in times of crisis, we notice that patients and their families hold very different ideas about sickness, health, and the human body from those of the medical establishment. Their own paradigm and notions root them better into an awareness of family and belonging than modern medical interventions.

"Catholic" translates as "universal" or "according to the whole." Consequently, Catholic health care cannot be fixed exclusively to the health categories of the Western, industrialized world. Catholic healing needs to be attentive to the concerns that are met by persuasive African traditions of medicine. At the same time, we are also aware that the different models of health that people use are not always compatible with each other. This poses the need for clarity and focus in the healing ministry.

Healing and Trust

I have been living and working in Zambia for twenty-five years as a priest. The parish in which I presently work is located in a rural area, in the Luangwa Valley. People greatly value modern health facilities. But the COVID-19 crisis also revealed, like everywhere else in the world, a lack of trust in the official health care narratives. Take the following incident in our parish:

As part of a new malaria elimination program, the Ministry of Health, together with its international partners, rolled out a mass drug administration in the village of Chifunda. Local health workers went from door to door to educate people about the drug. Wide participation was crucial for the success of the health initiative. When the health workers tried to disseminate the pills in the school, the children panicked and jumped out of the windows to escape. Word had gone round that international institutions were secretly testing a suspicious COVID vaccine on African populations.

Others linked the malaria drug to a conspiracy of Satanism. During the following days, the school remained closed, because pupils, supported by their parents, no longer came. In addition, many households dumped the pills that they had received into the toilets.[2]

Such events are, of course, out of the usual run of things. People generally trust the modern health sector with regards to established, routine interventions. But trust cannot be taken for granted. For example, since colonial times, persistent rumors have linked the modern health sector to conspiracy theories in which international organizations use human blood extracted from Africans for sinister, magical purposes in order to obtain power, wealth, and health.[3] Health workers in Zambia are well aware that their work is often misunderstood. In 2020, the Ministry of Health halted a large-scale HIV assessment project during a highly volatile situation, because health workers going through the compounds taking blood samples were easily subject to sinister rumors and violence.[4]

Trust is, however, fundamental when we come to Christian healing. In its institutions, Catholic healing wants to radiate hope and create a safe space where the patient and caring community can reach out to God, the ultimate source of life and health. The quality of biomedical interventions is very important in the process of building up trust. But the biomedical discourse on its own is not able to deal with many of the questions that sickness throws out.[5] Sickness is disturbing—and should be allowed to be disturbing—both for the patient and the caregiver. Despair, loneliness,

---

2. Adama et al., *Lumimba Diary 2021*, February 20 entry.

3. Musambachime, "Impact of Rumour," 201–15; White, *Speaking with Vampires*, 208–41.

4. The volatile situation was caused by mysterious events of ritual killings and gassing that had stunned Zambia and that resulted in innumerable incidents of mob justice. See "Door to Door Collection"—Released on February 20, 2020, the public statement of the MQHZ (Medical for Quality Healthcare in Zambia) read: "Continuing with the door-to-door collection of blood from people in various communities would have directly put innocent health workers in great danger of being attacked, owing to the volatile security situation in Zambia. While this project has good health objectives, we strongly feel that the timing was suicidal and could not clearly sit well with the mood in the country. The current widespread gassing of citizens and suspicions of ritual killings cannot allow a project of drawing blood from citizens coming from tensed up compounds."

5. When I speak in this chapter about biomedicine, I am well aware that the biopsychosocial model (Engel, "Need for a New Medical Model," 129–36; and Engel, "Clinical Application," 535–44) has long been adopted in the mission statements of many Catholic health institutions. However, in my experience in Africa, the biopsychosocial model has, apart from lip service, not replaced—in practice—the biomedical model in health institutions.

anger, blame, a feeling of alienation from one's body, and fundamental questions of belonging and identity all feed into the spiritual experiences of the sick and also of the caregivers.

Caregiver–Patient Relationships in Modern Health Facilities

For most sicknesses—for example, malaria, diarrhea, worms, tuberculosis, or HIV—and also for prenatal care, people in Zambia usually opt for a modern clinic or a hospital, even if these are understaffed, underequipped, and undersupplied. Avoiding the clinic is often frowned upon, also in the rural areas, even when people suspect that a sickness has resulted from the violation of cultural taboos or from witchcraft. Different systems of healing are not viewed as exclusive in Zambia; people may visit a hospital and, hidden from the doctors, also consult a traditional healer.

Health care touches the core of human life. Sometimes, the modern doctor and health worker in a white coat become idealized as angelic heroes who think about saving lives all the time. The scientific procedures that underscore the medical equipment can also become easily idolized in Zambia's imagination: they are developed by overly intelligent people of international origins who dedicate their lonely lives to new achievements in the medical laboratory. Modern medical machinery easily obtains quasi magical associations. In Africa, the modern health sector can greatly impress people, but it can also alienate such that the interventions fail to reach the intended conclusions. The idealized hero-image of modern medical doctors can mutate into that of cold-hearted agents—maybe with a secret agenda that serves international organizations, far removed from the patient's world—who leave the patient helpless and powerless. People's experiences in Zambia's health facilities are not always positive. With reference to Zambia, Uganda, and Mali, a study concludes:

> Just over half of the respondents (51 percent) reported having a problem with health services. These problems ranged from long waiting times (nearly three quarters of respondents), shortage of medicine (66 percent), absence of doctors (54 percent), fees too high (52 percent), as well as other quality of care issues such as lack of respect (53 percent), dirty facilities (35 percent), and demand for bribes (26 percent). The study found that problems with health services were greater in rural areas.[6]

---

6. Haddad et al., *Potential and Perils*, 32.

In practice, we know that doctors and nurses can be overwhelmed, irritated, short on time to spend with patients; they can misdiagnose, make wrong decisions, and can also fail in their duties—and even more so in rural Africa where there is very little supervision and control.

In the developing world, medical knowledge and position become social power. In my own situation, the next medical doctor lives one hundred and twenty kilometers away on very bad roads, inaccessible during any major downpour in the rainy reason. The local clinic, ten kilometers away and chronically out of essential medicines, is staffed by caregivers whose dedication and medical knowledge rarely match that of the angelic hero. And not all clients live up to the role of the ideal patient! Some bully caregivers into special privileges. Also, the accompanying family members who stay with the patient at the clinic do not always settle into a passive mode of submission; they dish out comments and unsolicited advice. Caregivers need to learn how to balance official rules and local demands.

However, the time of face-to-face interaction between patient and health worker often shortens to a minimum, or below a minimum. It may be marked by frustrations and by a strained emotional chemistry. For example, many patients are not able to describe the symptoms of their illness in accordance with the body parts and frequencies represented in the textbooks. Pain seems to be everywhere! Much treatment is given on the basis of presumptions. For example, malaria is very common in our area and can be fatal. Hence, if a person has a fever, he/she is given malaria treatment anyway, even when a malaria test comes out negative. Maybe the test did not work (tests *do* fail), and tests for other sicknesses may not be available anyway. If a person lives near the clinic, a wrong diagnosis may not be a big deal—one can always go back for a second treatment option. But for people living farther away, coming back is often not an option at all.[7]

Before people come to a health facility, they will often try curing themselves. Pharmacies and drugstores are popular in Zambia, and even in remote villages, antibiotics are easily available (notwithstanding that some may be expired). Most adults also know traditional remedies for common sicknesses. People use medicines in the way that makes sense to them, and that does not always correspond with the small print on the package. Self-help is guided by the images that a person associates with sickness. Not all sicknesses can be talked about. The HIV/AIDS crisis revealed that existential sickness may even be concealed from a spouse for as long as possible. Secrecy plays itself out within the dynamics of social and domestic power.

7. See especially Farmer, *Pathologies of Power*; and Farmer et al., *Reimagining Global Health*, about different dynamics in the modern health sector that implicitly tend to exclude the poor.

If the family discerns witchcraft to be the cause of the illness, an alternative treatment with traditional healers may evolve in absolute secrecy, to outwit the witch. Doctors or health workers (and the same point can be made about priests or pastors) are often in the dark about what people have gone through (or are still going through) in the healing process. Interactions are based on a lot of guesswork on all sides.

If sickness incapacitates the patient, the patient relies on the time and economic resources of family members for care, being present at the hospital bed, bringing food, and paying for treatment. The burden of illness in Africa is shared across many shoulders. This also means that the patient cannot decide alone on the treatment options.[8] Often, he/she has little to say about where to look for help. Those who shoulder the costs of treatment (money, time, taking over household and work chores, etc.) have to be brought on board. Health interventions must make sense to the wider family. When the family weighs treatment options, convenience, economic costs, and social costs play decisive roles.

People also understand sickness and healing in their own ways. They put their own theories to work. It always takes time for a health worker to explain different options and possibilities and build up a relationship of trust. It also takes time for a patient to embrace the theory of the doctor. With the chronic financial strains on the health sector, this positive interaction is often presumed to be there, but it is rarely evaluated. Breakdowns in communication are simply ignored. Many regard investing in medical knowledge and biomedical machinery to be more important than investing in the quality of human relations and interactions. But when patients and their families fail to understand and trust the healing process, health care cannot reach a spiritual or mystical dimension of healing, not even in a Catholic hospital. The space of interaction among all persons involved in the healing process should be the most crucial point to address on the path toward spiritual healing, not the last one in an already long list of unfulfilled needs.

Making Sense of an Illness in the Healing Ministry

When we speak of spiritual healing, we imply that the patient's awareness of the body gains a new perspective that is marked by trust in God and in life. Most people in Zambia are not trained in biomedical vocabulary and models. But that does not mean that they lack medical theories or that they fail to

---

8. Janzen, "Therapy Management," 68–84. Feierman, "Struggles for Control," 73–147.

compare the situation and symptoms with those of other patients who were treated successfully or unsuccessfully in one way or another. Many patients adapt simultaneously to traditional, biomedical, or Pentecostal "languages of health," depending on the situation. Concepts of medicine and healing can become hybrid in the process and give rise to contradictions. It becomes important to know the diverse discourses on illness, apart from the modern health sector, through which people process their experiences. I want to introduce three of them: family traditions, those of traditional healers, and those of Christian faith healers.

1. Cultural Traditions Invoked by Family

In Zambia, people know that many forms of illness result from violating cultural traditions and family morality. For example, family members may scrutinize each other about violations regarding sexual taboos. A husband who commits adultery when his wife is pregnant is widely believed to cause the death of the unborn child and/or of the mother during childbirth. According to the underlying theory, husband and wife have become "one blood." Unfaithfulness means that "blood mixes," which causes the death of the unborn child and also of the innocent spouse. According to our indigenous medical theory, sexual activity makes a couple—ritually speaking—hot. Small children and elderly people are ritually cold. The fire on which food is cooked for them needs to be protected from the emanating heat of the sexually active people, lest they catch a serious or even fatal coughing disease. Menstrual blood needs to be handled with the utmost care, because it can bring medical disaster upon the whole family. A woman who has had a miscarriage or who aborted a child may bring mysterious sicknesses to the people she greets. She is expected to sit numb, and her husband to stay around the house, until they are ritually released from this burden.[9]

My list of important cultural beliefs could go on and on. Such beliefs are largely dismissed by the biomedical discourse as superstitious, but they are linked to an extensive system that safeguards family morality, which in turn holds the extended family together. When people evoke these beliefs, or when they scrutinize each other along the lines of such beliefs, they acknowledge the presence of mysterious forces that affect their health. But they also want to make a point about morals, identity, tradition, and belonging. If Christian healing ignores such questions, then it may touch the body but will fail to reach the soul.

9. For more examples and their impact on individuals and families, see Udelhoven, "Domestic Morality."

Very often, our modern health institutions are insensitive and even hostile to local cultural models of sickness and healing. Some nurses call local people "ignorant," but this evaluation is mutual. Locals often consider doctors and nurses—and also us priests—to be ignorant and incompetent about the moral issues and family situations that people determine as the root cause of their illnesses.

If the Catholic healing ministry wants to reach the soul together with the body, some meaningful and respectful engagement with cultural notions with respect, humility, and empathy seems absolutely necessary. I am not advocating here that cultural theories should override biomedical knowledge in Africa or elsewhere, though it is obvious that the modern health sector has much to learn from Africa's traditional ways of healing, also on the biomedical sphere. What I want to do is draw attention to using cultural traditions as a way of pointing out the moral questions and concerns of belonging and identity that people struggle with during their sickness—questions which cannot be answered by the biomedical discourse.

Let me take the example of a difficult childbirth, which people in Zambia easily link to the adultery of the husband. The husband is then often called and encouraged to confess his misadventures to the midwives, in order to save the lives of his wife and child. In the meantime, the wife's family prepares the required medicines, which consist in our area of warm water in which they have soaked the roots of a local plant called *musutula*. The name of the plant is very symbolic and translates as "opening up, untie." To facilitate the "untying" of the baby, all other women present in the room also untie any knots in their own clothes, wraps, and headgear; this is a common procedure in our area among women to facilitate birth. Medical doctors, however, have little sympathy for traditional medicine and these rituals of "untying." They opt for a cesarean operation (which requires a referral to a faraway hospital) and may succeed in saving mother and child from the precarious situation if they manage the race against time. But even then, the task of healing is hardly completed if the husband has indeed gone out with another woman, or if the wife suspects this to such a degree that the alleged adultery symbolizes itself in memories of the breech presentation of the unborn child. For the wife and her family, such suspicions remain to be addressed, and all the more so if the man's relationship with another woman and his carelessness show itself in other signs as well. When pastors do not believe in the cultural theory behind people's reasoning, they can opt for ignoring such beliefs and proceed as if nothing happened. Hence, there is also nothing to pray about. But they can also use the same beliefs as stepping stones toward spiritual healing in a marriage crisis. Maybe prayers can seek to reestablish honesty and trust between husband and wife—or forgiveness.

Instead of condemning the use of the *musutula* plant, can we not bless it and allow it to become a symbol in prayer, in order to facilitate a greater opening up between husband and wife and "untie" the unresolved issues? And can the wife's memory of the breech presentation be allowed to symbolize a call for greater mutual commitment in marriage or for becoming clearer about their common vocation as a couple? Or for developing a sense of gratitude for the gift of life that needs to be protected?[10] With the help of some cultural and theological intelligence, pastors can often succeed in finding ways of prayer that help people to link their own awareness and experiences with their Christian faith.

2. Concepts of Traditional Healers

In Zambia, people value modern health facilities and bemoan the lack thereof. At the same time, for many conditions, they prefer African traditional healers over the hospital. In our area in the Luangwa Valley, this is the case for many chronic diseases (swollen legs, migraines, back pain) for which people do not expect to receive much help in a hospital. The same is true of mental disorders, both short-term and chronic. Mostly, it applies to cultural and spiritual notions of sickness with which people struggle—and to the question of guilt and blame. Traditional healers have managed to develop their own arsenal of healing methods. They use a much wider concept of health that includes biological issues but also questions of bad luck, failure to find a marriage partner, or failure to obtain a promotion at work. Healers know of medicines that make the co-wives of a man love each other, prevent a husband from performing with another woman, make a thief go mad, or influence the judge in order to obtain a favorable judgement in a court case. They know of sicknesses that result from witchcraft or spells, from the ghost of a former marriage partner, or from the world of the ancestors. Hospitals cannot deal with these issues.

Traditional healers are often viewed as the antithesis of modern medicinal practice. Many medical doctors hold a very low opinion of traditional medicine. They see its failures, the many cases in which local treatment delayed a visit to the hospital, or in which it even exacerbated a medical condition. But they may not see its successes. Allow me to give an example from my own experience, which I recorded in our parish diary:

---

10. I have described elsewhere (Udelhoven, "Domestic Morality") the cultural implications of this example on a concrete example.

> In Zewe, I visited a group headman who was dying. He was stretched out on a mat in his yard, surrounded by his wives and family who attended to him. Some had already started to silently weep because of the immanent death. His limbs were cold and unresponsive. His problem, I was told, was anemia, a serious lack of blood. I suggested that I take him to the nearest clinic, around ten kilometers away. "Not the clinic!" the man replied, as if speaking with his last breath. Another one explained to me (I seemed to be the only ignorant person on the scene) in a low but firm voice, "Ncha ku ŵanthu!" ("It comes from people!"), which means witchcraft.

The local healer, Doctor Chipyera, then approached the yard. He asked for a clean razor blade. Then he made the sick man sit up, asked him whether he recognized him—the sick man nodded—and started to cut deep tattoos below the ears, into his forehead, neck, back and chest, into which he then wrapped his medicines that he had come with. No blood was pouring out of the cuts, which confirmed to people that his blood was already finished, together with his life. Again, a few women started to wail but were asked to be quiet. The healer then ordered the man to lie down and sleep. After half an hour, the dying man got up, to the surprise of everybody. He was weak but started to walk, looking very much alive. After the miracle cure, I asked the healer about the medicines. "I will show you later," he replied.

> In the evening, he visited me, visibly happy about his success, and asked if I had noticed that everybody was expecting the man to die and how fast his treatment achieved the cure. He showed me the roots that he used and also how he prepared the medicines. "I could not show you this in the presence of people, because not all of them are innocent. I neutralized what they used against him." "Witchcraft?" I asked. "Of course! Here we don't die of common sicknesses. Sicknesses that kill are those that come from people [witchcraft]."[11]

The said man is still alive today. I guessed that he was cured not so much as a result of the biomedical properties of the roots, but because the healer managed to bring his mind—and the mind of his family—on board with the healing process. For them, his procedures were apt and potent to counteract the witchcraft attack.

The success of traditional healers does not necessarily come from their ability to explain sicknesses to people in a way they can understand, though this can, of course, also be the case. Some healers explain to the patient very

---

11. O'Shea et al., *Lumimba Diary 2018*, January 7, 2018.

little: "We don't want to scare the patient about the gravity of the condition." By bringing the mind on board, what I mean is this: the patient is forced, by the procedures of the healer, to engage with his/her body and sickness, also on a mental and spiritual or mystical level. The patient may be requested to collect certain herbs at certain times all by him/herself. Or to subject him/herself to special baths, steam baths, or other cleansing procedures. Or to follow a specific diet. Or to undergo certain rituals. Or to dance with others throughout the night as part of a healing cult. In many ways, the procedures of the local healers are much more demanding and engaging on the side of the patient—something that the simple procedure of swallowing red and yellow pills does not require. The mind is forced to engage in the healing process. In contrast, the biomedical discourse of our hospitals tends to cure the body in isolation of the person's soul, beliefs, and relationships. Maybe Christian rituals of healing need to be equally demanding in bringing the heart and mind of the sick, and their families, on board.

3. Faith Healing

Zambia has been declared a Christian nation, and ideas of sickness and healing have also been shaped by the quest for faith healing, especially in Pentecostal but also in Zion and African Initiated Churches. Many Christian ministries respond to prayer requests by bringing people's afflictions before God. Within the Catholic church in Zambia, we must especially mention the charismatic renewal movement that has taken up the Pentecostal experience and that readily offers prayers for healing and deliverance. Many ministries counteract sickness on the spiritual level: not with the help of the ancestors, charms, or local roots, but by invoking the Holy Spirit. Going a step further, prayer warriors also address the spiritual condition that they divine as the root cause for affliction. A demon or the force of witchcraft may lurk behind a biomedical condition; it will not show up in the microscope of the doctor but in the dream of the pastor. Sickness is driven out like a demon.

In some churches, faith healing may not look very demanding for the patient. The sick person comes up front, utters a prayer request into the pastor's ear, waits for the pastor to lay on hands, tries to be open to the Holy Spirit, and after a short time goes back to his/her seat in church. But at other times, the demands of faith healing are extensive and go much beyond the expectations of the biomedical discourse. The patient may have to pay a tithe. He/she may be required to fast for extensive periods, follow common prayers for weeks, spend a whole day on top of a holy mountain, or spend whole nights in singing and prayer together with other congregants. Again, such lengthy procedures force the patient to engage with sickness on a mental and also on a spiritual level. One of the attractions of Catholicism in Africa is its ritual dimension that we encounter in the liturgy, processions, pilgrimages, songs, or litanies that some parishes manage to link more clearly to the healing ministry. For the church to be catholic, she will be open also to other Christian traditions that enable people to engage mystically with their own bodily awareness of their afflictions, including those traditions that have grown in Africa.

Dealing with Preternatural Realities

All three cultural traditions that I have described (of families, of traditional healers, and of Christian prophets) refer to mysterious forces that cannot be captured by modern science. Patients, their families, and healers share an intersubjective reality in which supernatural forces mingle in natural affairs. God, demons, spiritual agents, or witchcraft are known by both patient and healer to be part of both the problem and the solution. They consider them and speak about them as objective realities. In the biomedical discourse, they are dealt with in categories such as psychosomatic illnesses or placebo/nocebo effects, as realities that exist through the power of the imagination. The newer biopsychosocial model does not accord them recognition as spiritual powers, unless they are translated into social and psychological categories. But in the Catholic healing ministry in Zambia, we cannot dodge the question of how we should deal with such realities, because they are important for the people who come to us for help. Would we subscribe to an idea that reduces the entire spiritual world to the power of the imagination? How, then, can we negotiate through such realities in our healing ministry?

Many postmodern writers argue that an African view of healing, which builds on premises such as spirits and witchcraft, has as much access to the truth about human life as Western biomedical thought. They see the rejection of such notions to be part of a postcolonial mentality of Africa's oppression by the West.[12] Also, an approach to witchcraft that is based on a Western human rights discourse and protects the victims of witchcraft accusations without acknowledging the crimes of the witches has been portrayed as counterintuitive to African populations.[13] Many of us may

12. For example, Hund, "Witchcraft and Accusations," 366–89.
13. Ashforth, "Witchcraft, Justice, and Human Rights." Note, however, that witchcraft discourses are often dehumanizing in nature and therefore do give rise to violence; see Udelhoven, *Unseen Worlds,* 208.

share with them a pessimism about the human ability to understand reality independent of our language and concepts, which in turn are rooted in our specific ways of life, while we also acknowledge that there are nonlinguistic ways of reaching out to reality—ritual is one of them. But a postmodern approach in which we simply acknowledge that spirits exist for some people but not for others—as if we were living in different worlds—drives a wedge between different ways to healing that needs to be overcome if we want to gain clarity in the healing ministry. Believers and nonbelievers need to find ways to understand each other. People who care for the sick come from all walks of life, but we live in the same world.

On the biological level, the truth claims and precisions of modern biomedicine about the functioning of the human body are based on an international and institutionalized consensus of a large part of the scientific community that was established through controlled observations, statistically established correlations, and persistent evaluation over and against other alternatives and challenges. Notwithstanding that the scientific status of some medical theories can rightly be disputed, modern medicine does seek validation by appeals to common and well-defined standards; it subjects its theories to methods of verification and falsification that are, in principle, open to all who study medicine, also in Zambia. In contrast, African healers often fail to agree, even among themselves, about the details of their knowledge and concepts; secrecy is part and parcel of many healing traditions. The same applies to Christian faith healers in Africa. While all agree, in general terms, about the existence of demons and their role in conferring sickness, we quickly reach disagreements when we attempt to nail the workings of the demonic world down to its details: Satanism, spiritual husbands, mermaids, ocean spirits, and spirits from the mountain attain idiosyncratic meanings depending on church and context. The Catholic healing ministry does well to rely on modern biomedical paradigms for the understanding of biological concepts. How then can we also meaningfully deal with spirits and witchcraft?

Not as alternatives to the processes of biology. When we mix biological, theological, and spiritual notions, we also mix up the contexts that establish the system of reference for the specific terms. We then start to speak nonsense (in Wittgenstein's technical sense) by violating the standards that establish the shared meaning of a concept.[14]

Can the scholastic differentiation of the natural, the preternatural, and the supernatural—often invoked in official Catholic exorcisms—be of any help? I regard it as problematic, if we understand these concepts as referring

---

14. See Ricketts, "Pictures, Logic, and the Limits of Sense."

to clearly demarcated and exclusive realities, because the distinction does not correspond to the fluid realities of spirits that people deal with. In Africa, the spiritual and material worlds are not only intertwined, but spiritual notions, as well as the notions of the self and of the soul, are also rooted in specific relationships.[15] Nevertheless, I have argued elsewhere that the Thomistic distinction can be positively used in the pastoral setting if it is part of a person-centered approach (in contrast to a demon-centered approach that classifies spiritual realities according to their inherent characteristics).

It can give rise to explorative questions, which can help to disentangle experiences of affliction: Were you created with the forces that you experience and that affect you so negatively? Are they part of your own inner life (natural)? Or do you experience them as coming from outside (preternatural)? How do they affect you? And where do you experience God's direct intervention (supernatural) in your struggle with these forces? The answers to such questions can provide the vocabulary for prayer. But we have to accept that they don't lead us to objective certainty, nor do they dissolve the need to look at the concrete relationships in which the spiritual realities play themselves out.[16]

The Wittgensteinian philosopher Hermen Kroesbergen proposed some helpful clarifications.[17] The meanings of "African tradition," "witchcraft," or "demon," come not from the words themselves but from the usage of these words. Only in the life contexts in which people understand each other and in which their communication succeeds can we draw out the implicit meanings of these terms. On the one hand, it is true that many people in southern Africa believe that spirits and witchcraft intervene in the laws of biology, as does also God. On the other hand, we misunderstand people if we conjecture that their models of spirits or witchcraft simply fulfill the quest of explanation, prediction, and control, much like Western science, as Robin Horton (in the footsteps of Edward Tylor) famously postulated.[18] It would be quite wrong to say that people in Zambia live with spirits and witchcraft in the same way as they live with radio waves and GPS signals. Even when people regard religious concepts and ideas as unproblematic affirmations of visible or invisible aspects of outside reality (as in an ostensive definition), their religious language always conveys more than this: namely, a personal and, when accepted, also a communal truth claim and response

---

15. Udelhoven, *Unseen Worlds*, 234–75.
16. Udelhoven, *Unseen Worlds*, 33–4.
17. I am referring here to Kroesbergen's article, "Beyond Realism and Non-Realism," and to his book, *Language of Faith*.
18. Kroesbergen, *Language of Faith*, versus Horton, *Patterns of Thought*.

to sickness or misfortune, a challenge that demands a reaction. As such, religious language is tied to a personal perspective and response to the world.

I have been engaged in the healing ministry for many years. Even when I consider myself a skeptic, I do try to find a way of dealing with the broken relationships and questions of belonging that witchcraft beliefs and demons raise. I have described elsewhere such an approach in detail.[19] Here, I just want to point to the important pastoral distinction between the interior and external forum. In the former, we can deal with supernatural realities in the way the patient experiences them and knows them (I call this the "inner world"), while we reserve the exterior forum only for those public truth claims that prove themselves in communication between different belief systems (I call this the "outer world" or the "common world"). The distinction between inner and outer worlds has nothing to do with an objective evaluation of truth claims but with the appropriate pastoral response. The concepts of the patient can guide the pastor in the interior forum to the intersubjective and relational realities that stand in need of healing as much as the biological body of the patient. We address these issues not on the grounds of preternatural or supernatural evidence but on that of observable behavior that causes conflict. Thereby, it is often possible to remain respectful of other people's experiences and beliefs and yet reach a common consensus about the relational issues that are associated with the vocabulary of the supernatural world and that need to be addressed.

Dealing with the Problem of Culpability

The success of traditional healers in Zambia has much to do with their ability and courage to address the problem of culpability—of the patient (by disregarding cultural obligations and taboos) or of others (for example, through witchcraft). Who is to blame for a grave sickness? The discernment of witchcraft leads to the search for human culprits, often within the family, who are then easily portrayed as no longer human. In contrast, when demons are discerned, people absolve humans from guilt and blame. Nevertheless, in Zambia, demons too are embedded within concrete relationships and life contexts.[20] When things go well, traditional healers facilitate confession by the guilty party, the making of amends, and the reordering of social relationships through the treatment. When things do not go well—and unfortunately, this is also often the case—the assignment of guilt and blame leads to witch hunts and even witch killings that divide a community in the healing process. As a

---

19. Udelhoven, *Unseen Worlds*.
20. Udelhoven, *Unseen Worlds*, 157–67.

church, we have always condemned traditional healers when they engage in witch-finding. But we have not managed to make witch-finding redundant. For this to happen, we need to stay very close to people's concepts of health and sickness, especially the moral dimension, and engage with these in a meaningful way. The biomedical discourse sidelines the question of guilt and blame in the process of curing illnesses. But these questions are not easily sidelined in the minds of the patients and their families! A Catholic approach to healing, I believe, does not eclipse the moral questions that are attached to sickness. But it seeks to transform them:

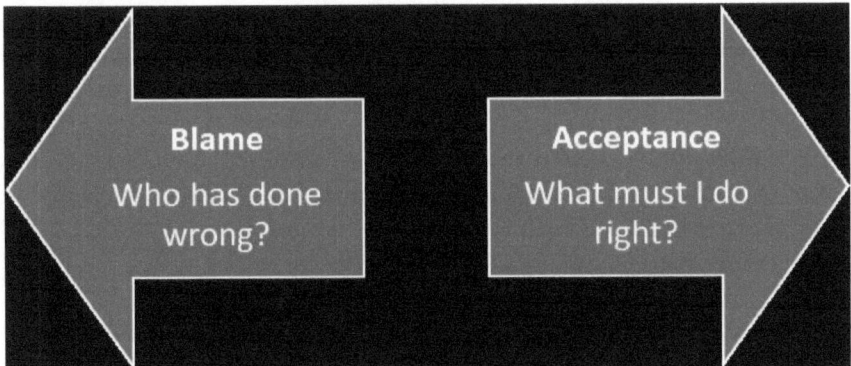

The question about whom to blame shifts to another moral question about reacting from the awareness of the person's Christian life vocation.

This question brings me to the last part of my presentation. While we respond to the different ideas of sickness and healing, we also need clarity about our own aims in the Catholic healing discourse. If our approach to healing is Catholic, it will be open to all fundamental aspects of experiences of illness. But it will also seek to imprint its own Christian dynamics on the processes.

The Catholic Healing Ministry

In the explanations of healing in the *Catechism of the Catholic Church* (§1500—§1510), we find a consensus on elements that should be part of any paradigm that the church employs in the healing ministry: a faith response to God, a fundamental orientation toward eternal life, the invitation to the sick person to unite himself/herself with Christ on the cross, and a renewed sense of community and reconciliation that healing establishes.

(1) Any Catholic approach will look at healing in relation to God. We implore God for healing. Health in Catholic thought is not a human right

that a person can demand. Health is a gift that links me to my creator in the most amazing ways. Catholics have no problem entrusting themselves to the best qualified doctor while at the same time turning to God—out of an acknowledgement that all true healing comes from God. Grace means that, even in the face of pain, a person can still develop a sense of gratitude and trust before God. In Zambia, people often make a distinction and say that a certain condition can only be cured by prayer while another condition is cured by biomedical interventions. As a methodological distinction (where can I find help for my condition?), this is, of course, understandable. But when it becomes a conceptual distinction that introduces a dualism, the Catholic idea of healing tries to overcome it. Catholic thought knows many applications of the principle of multicausality. It is not wrong to say that a sickness is cured by the correct biological treatment and also by the grace of God.

(2) Health in Catholic thought is not an absolute. Health is subordinate to a higher good: eternal life. The ultimate aim of Catholic healing is not the restoration of health in a narrow sense, but salvation.[21] Jesus said that it is better to enter the kingdom of heaven with one leg, or one eye, than to have two but lose the prospect of eternal life.

But what does it mean to speak today about eternal life in the healing ministry? Many commentators say that people in Africa look much more towards help in their daily concerns of this present life than in the life to come![22] If salvation looks and feels remote, vague, distant, futuristic, and unrealistic, it will be irrelevant to a person's present needs and remain outside of the person's own horizon.

In Africa, the prosperity gospel has opened up a way that regards eternal life as the fullness or abundance of life, which must start here and now. Healing means to grant a person access to God's Shalom, which includes health, prosperity, peace, bodily well-being, victory in one's struggles, success in business, marriage, and on all levels of life. Whoever has been in Africa cannot remain unmoved by the success of the prosperity gospel, which has also entered the Catholic Church. It also comes, however, with the danger of denying the reality of death and pain. In Zambia, we die, and we die often very young. As a priest, I am often at a funeral where God did not heal, even though we all prayed.

A Catholic approach to healing cannot eclipse death. When a person is seriously sick, we need to be able to look at death and accept death as part

---

21. Note, however, that Salus was a Roman goddess of health and well-being and that the Latin *salus* from which we derive the word *salvation* translates also as health. Salvation, therefore, cannot be totally isolated from the concept of health.

22. See, for example, the discussion in Uzukwu, *God, Spirit*, chapter 3.

of each and every life, even when we pray for healing. So much so that death should even mark my life once I am cured. This brings me to another way of linking eternal life to the present moment. Instead of asking, "What can God do for me?," I ask, "How do I want to live my short life in the presence of God? What am I living for, and what am I ready to die for?" Sacrifice, in Catholic thought, goes beyond the calculated giving experience of tithing (I give to God so that God gives much more to me) that we find in some versions of the prosperity gospel. The Catholic healing ministry wants to present an existential challenge to the sick: to unite oneself with Jesus on the cross. There exists something in my relationship with God that goes beyond my present life as I know it. Death puts limits on what life can give. It forces us to make choices. The prospect of embracing a life-vocation comes only for a person who is able to embrace the reality of death. No death, no vocation.

(3) The cross is a physical bodily experience. When the church encourages the sick to connect themselves to the body of Christ on the cross, it also asks the patient to reconnect with his/her own body, to allow the body and one's pain to become the sacrament of a relationship with God, with others, and with a broken world. In the biomedical discourse, pain should be avoided at all costs. Patients are flooded with painkillers and anesthesia. I am not advocating here that we should engage in some form of masochism. I certainly want painkillers when I am in pain. What I am saying is: Where the patient becomes alienated from his/her own body and feelings, healing should help the person to reconnect with his/her own bodily awareness—however painful and uncomfortable. Catholic theology does not allow a dualist separation of body and soul. We reach the soul through the body. A bodily condition, therefore, is allowed to express what is wrong in the world, in relationships with other people, or with God. We can learn, in this regard, from African experiences of healing. Healers have developed the art of reflecting on relationships through the pain that the person experiences. This can go terribly wrong where people remain on the level of blame, but it does not need to go wrong if we turn the moral question about guilt and blame into the question about accepting a life vocation (Christian agency).

(4) Finally, Jesus was not satisfied with restoring lepers to their former health. He also wanted to bring them back into a community and, at the same time, challenge the community with the healing. When he told them, "Show yourselves to the priests!" (Luke 17:14), the healing was to constitute a challenge to the establishment.

The Catholic idea of healing is more about transformation than about restoration. The latter notion means going back to a previous condition; the former acknowledges that the healed is becoming something new. Also, the community that is touched by the experience of healing is called to change. Healing, therefore, has always a political dimension. Again, here we can learn a lot from African traditions of healing, because they have never lost sight of the sick person's relationships, family, identity, morality, and sense of belonging.

The Catholic healing ministry has clear procedures that are laid out in its rituals and guidelines. At the same time, the gift of healing is a grace, and the accompaniment of the sick is not a science but an art and a faith experience, in which we struggle as much with the condition of the patient as with ourselves and with God. Whatever way we choose, it always starts with being present to the sick person and to his/her caring family. If we are allowed to become part of their journey of suffering, we will also find the grace that helps us find a way of meaningful prayer.

Bibliography

Adama, Basile, et al. *Lumimba Diary 2021*. Lusaka: Archives of the Missionaries of Africa, FENZA, 2021.

Ashforth, Adam. "Witchcraft, Justice, and Human Rights in Africa: Cases from Malawi." *African Studies Review* 58.1 (2015) 5–38.

Catechism of the Catholic Church. Vatican City: Libreria Editrice Vaticana, 2012.

"Door to Door Collection of Blood Would Have Directly Put Innocent Health Workers in Great Danger—MQHZ." *Lusaka Times*, February 23, 2020. https://www.lusakatimes.com/2020/02/23/door-to-door-collection-of-blood-would-have-directly-put-innocent-health-workers-in-great-danger-mqhz.

Engel, George L. "The Clinical Application of the Biopsychosocial Model." *American Journal of Psychiatry* 137 (1980) 535–44.

———. "The Need for a New Medical Model: A Challenge for Biomedicine." *Science* 129 (1977) 129–36.

Farmer, Paul. *Pathologies of Power: Health, Human Rights, and the New War on the Poor*. Berkeley: University of California Press, 2003.

Farmer, Paul, et al. *Reimagining Global Health: An Introduction*. Berkeley: University of California Press, 2013.

Feierman, Steven. "Struggles for Control: The Social Roots of Health and Healing in Modern Africa." *African Studies Review* 28 (1985) 73–147.

Haddad, B., et al. *The Potential and Perils of Partnership: Christian Religious Entities and Collaborative Stakeholders Responding to HIV and AIDS in Kenya, Malawi, and the DRC*. Cape Town, South Africa: African Religious Health Assets Programme (ARHAP), 2008.

Horton, Robin. *Patterns of Thought in Africa and the West: Essays on Magic, Religion, and Science*. Cambridge: Cambridge University Press, 1997.

Hund, John. "Witchcraft and Accusations of Witchcraft in South Africa: Ontological Denial and the Suppression of African Justice." *Comparative and International Law Journal of Southern Africa* 33 (2000) 366–89.

Janzen, John M. "Therapy Management: Concept, Reality, Process." *Medical Anthropology Quarterly* 1 (1987) 68–84.

Kagawa, Rose Calnin, et al. "The Scale of Faith Based Organization Participation in Health Service Delivery in Developing Countries: Systematic [Corrected] Review and Meta-analysis." *PLOS ONE* 7.11 (2012) e48457. https://journals.plos.org/plosone/article?id=10.1371/journal.pone.0048457.

Kroesbergen, Hermen. "Beyond Realism and Non-Realism: Religious Language-Games and Reality." *NGTT Ned Geref Teologiese Tydskrif* 55.1–2 (2014) 189–204. https://ngtt.journals.ac.za/pub/article/view/521.

———. *The Language of Faith in Southern Africa: Spirit World, Power, Community, Holism*. HTS Religion and Society 6. Cape Town, South Africa: AOSIS, 2020.

Musambachime, Mwelwa C. "The Impact of Rumor: The Case of the Banyama (Vampire Men) Scare in Northern Rhodesia, 1930–1964." *The International Journal of African Historical Studies* 21.2 (1988) 201–15.

O'Shea, Brendan, et al. *Lumimba Diary 2018*. Lusaka: Archives of the Missionaries of Africa, FENZA, 2018.

Ricketts, Thomas. "Pictures, Logic, and the Limits of Sense in Wittgenstein's *Tractatus*." In *The Cambridge Companion to Wiitgenstein*, edited by Hans Sluga and David Stern, 54–95. 2nd ed. Cambridge: Cambridge University Press, 2018.

Roser, Max, et al. "Burden of Disease." OurWorldinData.org, 2016. https://ourworldindata.org/burden-of-disease/.

Udelhoven, Bernhard. "Domestic Morality, 'Traditional Dogma', and Christianity in a Rural Zambian Community." *Zambia Social Science Journal* 8.1 (2022) https://scholarship.law.cornell.edu/zssj/vol8/iss1/2.

———. *Unseen Worlds: Dealing with Spirits, Witchcraft, and Satanism*. 3rd ed. Lusaka: FENZA, 2021.

Uzukwu, Elochukwu E. *God, Spirit, and Human Wholeness: Appropriating Faith and Culture in West African Style*. Eugene, OR: Pickwick, 2012.

White, Louise. *Speaking with Vampires: Rumor and History in Colonial Africa*. Berkeley: University of California Press, 2000.

8

Western Medicine and Ethnomedicine: How Culture and Cost Affect Access to Quality Care in Chiapas, Mexico

Abraham Castañeda-Chávez, MD, MPH, and Carolina Martínez Haro, MD, with Karen M. Kraft[1]

I. The Conquest of the New World and the Extermination of the Native Peoples

THE EXTERMINATION OF THE native peoples began with the accidental encounter of the "New World" by Christopher Columbus in 1492 (he was looking for a commercial route to the Indies, and that is why they mistakenly call us Indians), in Mexico; it was started by Spain in 1519. The Spanish mercenaries sought gold, precious stones, new land, and new slave subjects for the crown of King Carlos the Fifth. Mercenaries exterminated more than 80 percent of the entire native population on the continent, murdering astronomers, mathematicians, botanists, religious leaders, and protectors of the Earth. They called us dirty savages, devilish pagans, uneducated, sinful, animals, filling us with shame.

---

1. All translations from Spanish to English are by this chapter's authors.

On the Caribbean islands, the natives were all murdered. On the continent, they remain hidden from slavery and extermination. They were forced to take shelter in the worst geographical, economic, and social conditions. Nowadays, indigenous people are in reservations, resilient and ignored by all current governments of the American Continent. On January 1, 1994, the Zapatista Army of National Liberation (EZLN, Ejército Zapatista de Liberación Nacional) began an armed movement against the government, simultaneous with the start of the free trade agreement between the United States, Canada, and Mexico. EZLN supported the innumerable peaceful demands for justice and dignity made by other native communities of Mexico. They were against systemic cultural extermination, demanding respect for their customs, autonomy, and their right to better opportunities for education, health, housing, and citizenship. As a consequence of social pressure, the armed conflict between the EZLN and the army lasted sixteen days. In response to society's demands, peace talks were organized, with civil society as the mediator, both at national and international levels. In 1996, the peace talks broke down, and although there were no longer armed confrontations between the two sides, indigenous paramilitary groups emerged with a dirty, or "low intensity," war in which their targets were EZLN leaders and groups sympathetic to it. The paramilitary groups were allegedly created by political power groups within the government and later by drug trafficking cartels.

On December 23, 1994, the UN General Assembly decided to celebrate August 9 as International Indigenous Peoples Day. It wasn't until the end of the 1990s and into the first decade of the 2000s that the Organization of American States (OAS) and the UN consolidated human rights for native people of the Americas by finally recognizing their customs and lifestyles. It only took them five hundred years.[2] However, according to the National Institute of Statistics and Geography (INEGI, Instituto Nacional de Estadística y Geografía) in 2015, marginalization and poverty data show us that international declarations are meaningless—they are nothing but words on paper. Native peoples continue to live in the worst economic and social conditions,[3] and their human rights are constantly violated.[4] National statistics show a decreasing trend in both the native population of Mexico and their languages: in just the five years between 2015 and 2020, the indigenous population dropped from 10.1 percent[5] to 9.4 percent[6] of the nation's

2. See, generally, Organization of American States, *American Declaration*.
3. INEGI, *Encuesta Intercensal 2015*, 79–84.
4. Arellano, "Organización Documenta la Violación."
5. INPI, "Niñas, Niños y Adolescentes."
6. INEGI, "En México Somos," 1.

total, and between 2006 and 2020, the number of native languages fell from eighty-five[7] to sixty-eight.[8]

II. The Mexican Native Population Today

For historical reference purposes, Mexicans are mostly considered mestizo (a colonial term). However, as of 2020, Mexico is home to about 12 million indigenous people.[9] Amid an economic crisis, the Mexican health system faces the challenge of achieving 100 percent universal coverage, but service quality and care, in both the public and private sectors, never measure up to these high aspirations. By law, health care in Mexico *must* be free to the entire population.[10]

The cultural history of postcolonial indigenous peoples in the Americas has been described as a state of resistance due to surviving extermination and ongoing racial, linguistic, economic, and religious discrimination. Today, seven out of ten indigenous people are victims of poverty, and extreme poverty affects three out of ten,[11] while the life expectancy of the poor and indigenous person is seven years shorter than the average.[12]

Mexico's indigenous population also experiences some of the *worst* conditions of social inequity. In terms of health, the main causes of mortality among indigenous adults are malnutrition and chronic diseases,[13] especially heart disease and diabetes.[14] Between 2008 and 2018, when compared to the rest of the country, the native population had the worst level of *access to food*.[15] In terms of housing quality, a significant number of the poor indigenous live in houses with *dirt floors* (nearly 44 percent) with no plumbing (almost 17 percent), or electricity, and more than 60 percent use firewood for cooking.[16] The same situation *repeats itself* in education. The indigenous population also has a lower level of education and a higher rate of illiteracy in those over the age of fifteen.[17] Likewise, regarding health care, nearly 84

7. INMUJERES, *Población Indígena Mexicana*, 4.
8. INEGI, "Estadísticas," 3.
9. INEGI, "En México Somos," 2.
10. Political Constitution, Art. 4, 12.
11. García, "7 de Cada 10."
12. Zolla, "Salud de los Pueblos," 14.
13. Juárez-Ramírez et al., "Desigualdad en Salud," 285.
14. CEVECE, "Mujer Indígena y Salud," 2.
15. CONEVAL, "Población Indígena," 1.
16. Zolla, "Salud de los Pueblos," 10.
17. INEGI, "Estadísticas," 2–3.

percent of the native community is more dependent on the deficient health services of the state (but actually have less access to government health services due to labor laws), and only 0.4 percent have access to private health care services.[18]

III. Health Care in Mexico

In Mexico, there are three health systems: (1) the biomedical model (Western medicine); (2) traditional medicine or ethnomedicine; and (3) self-attention. Each system has a broad concept of therapeutic knowledge, skills, resources, and different specialties.[19]

1. Biomedical Model

Part of the public and private health systems, the biomedical model is recognized for being scientific, academic, legal, and representative of Western culture; it has been the global medical model since the end of the eighteenth century. Imposed on different societies and cultures, it rejects non-Western healing options, which are said to be informal, deceptive, obscure, and ignorant. Under this model, health workers are mostly trained to heal, rather than *prevent* illness, and services are not free. Language is neither easy nor intuitive, for the patient or society. Although health care may be a *worker's* right, it is not considered a basic *human* right.[20]

To expand the reach of national health services, the Mexican Constitution requires students completing their medical studies to serve as a *pasante*, completing one year of mandatory social service in rural communities in order to receive their professional degree as doctors. In general, many graduating students wish to avoid this requirement, fearful of being sent to isolated, often indigenous areas—located far from hospitals where they would refer complicated cases—where they would need to deliver care with limited support, materials, or medicines. The following are comments from indigenous people about their encounters with the biomedical model:

> The doctors are concentrated in the cities and never go out into the countryside; they don't know the Tzotzil language, they do not know our customs, and they hold great contempt for the indigenous.

18. INMUJERES, "Población Indígena," 2.
19. "Biomedicina, Dominante."
20. Menéndez, "Modelo Médico Hegemónico," 1–25.

In health centers, they treat us badly; there is no possible communication with the doctor, and so, even if he is a good doctor, he cannot cure us. That is why we do not trust them [the health centers]. The nurses treat us as if we were things. For this reason, for us, it's as if the doctor's medicine doesn't exist.

The health programs are not realistic; they do not know our customs and never take herbal medicine into account. A well-thought-out program that isn't carried out by the staff is useless. Neither the doctors nor the nurses are prepared to deal with us. If we get sick, we are second-rate.

Additionally, medicine is very expensive. It is a business. Sometimes, we have only enough money to pay the clinic fee but not the medicine. They sell us bad, expired medicine that's ineffective. That's why we do not trust the doctors' medicine.[21]

2. Traditional Medicine, or Ethnomedicine

In the traditional medical system, disease is perceived as a break in the natural and social order. A person becomes ill because they have transgressed some established norm in the biopsychosocial balance. Traditional doctors reestablish this balance through spiritual healing processes, including dream interpretation, prayers, herbal baths, massages, and spiritual/healing chants. Herbalism in Mexico has been documented for centuries. For example, in the 1500s, Hernán Cortés said that "there is a street of herbalists, where there is every root and medicinal herb found on earth. There are apothecary-like houses where freshly-made medicines are sold, such as ointments and poultices."[22] And the work of Mexican herbalists has been recorded extensively in many colonial-era publications, including

- *Historia General de las Cosas de Nueva España [The General History of the Things of New Spain: The Florentine Codex]*, an encyclopedic work completed by Fray Bernardino de Sahagún in 1577[23]

21. Almaguer González et al., *Interculturalidad en Salud*, 88–89.

22. Cortés and Sánchez-Barba, *Cartas y Documentos*, 72–73. The original Spanish reads: "Hay calle de herbolarios, donde hay todas las raíces y hierbas medicinales que en la tierra se hallan. Hay casas como de boticarios donde se venden las medicinas hechas, así potables como ungüentos y emplastos."

23. "Florentine Codex." This page of the Dumbarton Oaks's website states the fascinating fact that "[e]mpirical analysis has found 60 percent of the plants listed in the

- *Libellus de Medicinalibus Indorum Herbis [The Cruz-Badiano Codex]*, written by Aztec healer Martín de la Cruz and translated into Latin by Juan Badiano in 1552
- *Historia Natural de Nueva España [The Natural History of New Spain]*, completed by Dr. Francisco Hernández in 1577
- *La Real Expedición Botánica a Nueva España [The Royal Botanical Expedition to New Spain]*, a twelve-volume collection published in 2010 by the National Autonomous University of Mexico (UNAM), bringing together three manuscripts written in the late 1700s by Martín de Sessé and José Mariano Mociño as a result of the nearly twenty-year survey of flora and fauna they undertook in Mexico on order of the Spanish Crown[24]

Today, in the twenty-first century, courses on both ethnobotany (*etnobotánica*) and medicinal plants (*plantas medicinales*) are taught in master's degree programs in Mexico's largest universities, such as the Universidad Autónoma Chapingo (UACH) in Texcoco.[25]

Traditional or ethnomedicine is holistic and considers disease an imbalance of spirit, mind, body, *and environment*.[26] The origin and detection of diseases are identified by whether they come from cold or heat and by the type of pulse the person has (fast, slow, strong, or weak). The raw material of traditional medicines comes from forests, oceans, deserts . . . animals, insects, eggs, plants, fruits . . . and is made into extracts, juices, infusions, herbal baths, creams, etc. These can be used separately or combined with candles, incense, liquor, stones, and the power of prayer to heal, which serve to remove "bad airs" and alleviate the spirit-soul-mind.

In native communities, the *ticiti, xamanes,* or *iloles* ("healers" in the Nahua, Yucatec Mayan, and Tzotzil Mayan cultures, respectively) are still present, and in force, to solve many health issues. We have been surprised to see them treat many health problems successfully, including

- controlling fever by wrapping the feet with oil and banana leaves;
- treating parasites by using absinthe;

Florentine Codex to be medically effective, a striking efficacy, especially considering that empirical methods are unable to evaluate the magical and supernatural aspects of Nahua medicine."

24. Montemayor Aceves, "Publicación de la Obra."

25. UACH Departamento de Fitnotecnia, "Plan de Estudios," 5–6; courses on *etnobotánica avanzada* and *plantas medicinales* are listed here in UACH's 2023 degree plan for its master's in horticultural sciences.

26. Aparicio Mena, "Medicina Tradicional," §3 and 5.

- heating the pulp of green tomatoes in a *comal* (griddle used to make tortillas) and gently applying to the throat to cure tonsillitis;
- using powdered coffee to control the bleeding resulting from machete accidents;
- treating abdominal pain with external heat;
- using the skins of avocado as an antiworm treatment;
- incorporating the power of prayer and spiritual words to relieve stress, anxiety attacks, and to improve mood, and to help terminally ill patients;
- giving massages and a *temazcal* bath (a ritualistic steam bath) to pregnant women in order to change the baby's position before delivery from the breech to the cephalic position;
- treating heartburn and indigestion with pumpkin seeds;
- controlling hyperglycemia by using prickly pear cactus; and
- using the chia plant to treat tuberculosis.

Traditional medicine prepared at home is the first choice of native people, using inexpensive ingredients and not requiring laboratory tests, drugs, hospital procedures, and other expensive treatments.

3. Self-Attention

The native community exercises self-attention the most to diagnose, treat, control, prevent, and cure diseases. Western doctors or alternative professional healers do not intervene. This model, historically, is the basis of the previous ones and is based on its curative-preventive and economic functions. Grandmothers and mothers have passed down this knowledge from generation to generation.[27] Self-care is the most recurrent among poor urban and rural native communities, due to the marginalization and cultural and linguistic barriers they face. Additionally, *healing at home saves more money* than any other external therapeutic resource.

IV. Health Care in the State of Chiapas

Chiapas is located on the southeastern Pacific coast of Mexico. Bordering Central America, it is home to various ethnic groups such as the Zoques, Tzotziles, Tzeltales, Tojolabales, Ch'oles, Lacandón-Caribes, Mámes,

27. Menéndez, "Autoatención," 106–7.

Mochos, and Kakchikeles. According to Chiapas's 2020 census, nearly one and a half million native people lived there.[28] Chiapas boasts highlands, rainforests, the long Pacific coast, and abundant natural resources such as uranium, oil, gas, fresh water, and the ancient Mayan culture; however, during the last three decades, neoliberal policies and corruption have *plunged* its population into sustained poverty, with terrible indicators of the quality of life.[29]

Annually, hundreds of young doctors are sent to the heart of indigenous territories to work in health centers, rural medical units, and hospitals. As doctors in Chiapas offering Western medicine to remote communities, we have learned great respect for the role of traditional medicine. Despite the fact that the Spanish destroyed all of the original people's medical treatments (because they considered them diabolical or pagan), that knowledge has been passed down within the indigenous community for generations. Today, those who possess healing abilities from birth are considered divine. When traditional remedies do not work and disease persists, people seek solutions from doctors and the health care industry (paying a high price for those services). Our arrival as doctors in indigenous rural communities notably displaced the local shamans, *iloles*, or sorcerers. But for many other problems of the soul or spirit such as fear of the "evil eye," prayers and botanical remedies remain the first choice of native people. Western medicine is well received or even preferred by native communities, but their trust in the *caxlan pox tawanweg* ("foreign doctor" in the Tzotzil Mayan language) depends a lot on the transparency of the doctor to help, the resources offered, the cost, and the continuity of their activities.

V. Hospital San Carlos as an Example of Intercultural Health Care: Two Personal Accounts

Dr. Abraham Castañeda-Chávez's Story

Founded in 1976 and still managed today by the Daughters of Charity through the St. Vincent Social Work Foundation (Fundación de Obras Sociales de San Vicente), Hospital San Carlos is located in Altamirano, Chiapas, a predominantly rural indigenous area.[30] There, I was charged with establishing the directly observed therapy (DOT) program to control and

28. López, "Se Incrementa Población Indígena."
29. See, generally, Aguilar Ortega, "Desigualdad y Marginación en Chiapas," 143–59.
30. For more information about Hospital San Carlos (in Spanish), see its website, https://fossvi.org.mx/hospital-san-carlos/, as well as Martínez, "Hospital de Chiapas."

cure pulmonary tuberculosis. And my other great mission was to create a community health care system for the municipality, which included the bilingual training of more than fifteen native health worker volunteers. Activities were coordinated with government programs for immunization, TB-DOT, and nutrition, and the successful TB-DOT results were presented at various scientific congresses. In addition, we also support traditional medicine by working with OMIECH, the Organization of Indigenous Doctors of the State of Chiapas (Organización de Médicos Indígenas del Estado de Chiapas).

At San Carlos, the Daughters of Charity taught me the values of brotherhood, action for humanity, and bioethics, and I supplemented my medical learning and spiritual growth. There, helping my indigenous brothers and sisters, the Daughters also taught me to feel pride in belonging to the Nahuatl community. San Carlos is not a cold, impersonal, bureaucratic place like government and private hospitals. It is a place for all who ask for help and for those who want to help.

Dr. Carolina Martínez Haro's Story

At the edge of the jungle, two hours away from San Cristobal de las Casas in the southern state of Chiapas, Mexico, you will find a small town called Altamirano, where Hospital San Carlos is located. This missionary hospital founded by the Daughters of Charity in 1976 provides health care services for the indigenous population of the area. The main ethnic groups are the Tzeltal, Tojolabal, Tzotzil, Chol, and Zoque. Some patients travel as long as an entire day to get to us, due to the lack of other service options near their homes and also due to a sense of trust in the hospital from the years of good experiences others have had.

During my five years of practice at the hospital, I witnessed the impact on health outcomes of actively working to incorporate intercultural care. The hospital offers general outpatient consultations as well as inpatient care with fifty-two beds for adults and children, including isolated areas for tuberculosis patients. During the height of the COVID-19 pandemic, there was a special area to see potential COVID-19 patients. There are also two operating rooms and one emergency care area. In terms of auxiliary services, the hospital has the only X-ray machine in town, a point-of-care (POC) ultrasound machine, and a basic laboratory with connections to other labs in nearby cities for specialty blood tests. It also has its own pharmacy.

In addition to its regular services, Hospital San Carlos also offers special programs that focus on important health and social issues such as child malnutrition, tuberculosis, and mental health. Each of these serves otherwise forgotten patients. Unfortunately, due to the COVID-19 pandemic and having to relocate resources, the malnutrition program had to close in May 2020; the other programs, however, continue to operate with some modifications.

Volunteers are a big part of this institution, and surgical and medical campaigns help provide specialty care to those who would never be able to access it otherwise. Specialists in urology, gynecology, dermatology, rheumatology, internal, and family medicine visit the hospital for a couple of weeks or months, providing not only care but also important knowledge to the local doctors and the *pasantes*. In most cases, there is a remote follow-up. The hospital also participates in a program with the University of California, Los Angeles (UCLA) that provides basic POC ultrasound training on a yearly basis, something which has become an invaluable tool for patient care here.

The beauty of Hospital San Carlos is that it strives to provide health care with quality and warmth through an intercultural approach, and this mission is at work in different ways:

- Architecture—Surrounded by nature, the hospital was designed with big open spaces and gardens so patients could feel more at home.
- Staff—Most of the nurses are local women and men who have been trained by the hospital and can also act as translators during consultations. All doctors receive a course in Tzeltal, the main language spoken in the area, so they have a basic knowledge of the language and culture.
- Respect for traditional practices and spirituality—Patients and their families are allowed to bring their pastor, shaman, or *curandero* to perform any ritual appropriate for the condition. Sometimes, temporary hospital leave is granted to patients in order to avoid discharge against medical advice and losing patient trust. Patients and their families are also allowed to sleep on the floor with a few blankets since that feels more natural to them than beds, and there is always a family member with the patient on the ward, which is greatly appreciated and not an option in other hospitals. Local Catholic festivities are also celebrated at the hospital, always bringing joy and hope to the patients.

Even with all these positive points in its favor, the hospital faces a number of challenges in providing the quality care patients deserve and in adapting to every particular patient's unique needs. We know we cannot just give out a prescription and call it a day. We must consider a number of factors in every consult, including the following:

- With multiple languages and cultures interacting, there is always the possibility of not having a translator available for the less common languages.
- Patients come from many municipalities in the surrounding area, and usually, a large part of the family comes along. Consequently, the hospital offers a *posada*, accommodations providing patients and their family a place to sleep and have cooked meals.
- Due to a broken health system at the national level and even more so in the state of Chiapas (one of the poorest in Mexico), the government is unable to provide for the health care needs of its population.
- There is an increasing number of patients arriving that require specialty care for illnesses such as end-stage cancer, rare diseases as Kartagener syndrome, severe psoriasis, rheumatoid arthritis, multidrug-resistant TB (TB-MDR), etc.
- Discrimination, poverty, racism, and fear can keep patients from traveling to other cities for the medical services that Hospital San Carlos is unable to provide; many patients prefer to die at home with dignity rather than submit themselves to the horrors and costs of such an endeavor.

In response to these challenges, Hospital San Carlos provides assistance through flexibility, advocacy, empowerment, and partnerships. The social workers, doctors, and nurses who work here end up having to fight for their patients on many fronts and, as a result, they form amazing teams. Some examples are the partnerships made through the ultrasound course and the international specialists who come on surgical campaigns. Locally, the hospital does a lot of advocacy through the tuberculosis program, working with the local health department to make sure patients are accepted and receive their treatments at their local clinics as required by law. We established a similar partnership following a surge of HIV cases that started in December 2018.

However, the COVID-19 pandemic took a huge toll, as it did all over the world—patients no longer left their homes, many communities decided to isolate themselves, and there was an increasing mistrust of health professionals due to the spread of misinformation and fear. Slowly, patients began to need care and return, but now with fewer resources, all this work will be harder to continue.

Conclusions

Western or biomedical medicine continually demonstrates progress and documents the efficacy of its results. Epidemiological studies demonstrate its impact and benefits. However, Western medicine is often cold, technical, dehumanized, and strongly commercialized. Although it is globally recognized, neither its quality of care nor its user satisfaction is well measured.

In many places, Western medicine also does not achieve universal coverage. It is the world's poor who commonly experience the worst health conditions, but acute, chronic, and degenerative diseases require expensive procedures that they simply cannot afford. And among Mexico's poor, native communities—especially in rural regions—*still* do not receive full, quality, and compassionate care. New public health policies are needed to stimulate the equitable distribution of health personnel, especially to rural areas, accompanied by technical and cultural advisors.

One excellent example of accessible, humanitarian care for the indigenous poor is Hospital San Carlos, where health care is indeed a human right. The hospital offers compassion, quality, and dignity for those who deserve and need it most, and it combines Western biomedicine with a genuine respect for the traditional health and cultural practices of the indigenous community.

To achieve a more humanized health system, Western and traditional medicine should both be taught as part of the curricula in medical schools. Increasingly, people today are looking for alternatives to biomedicine and are interested in natural treatments, nontoxic medications, and lower costs. Slowly, companies have started to offer alternative healing options, mixing Western and traditional medicine products and procedures.

Since ancient times, indigenous communities have understood health as a balance of mind, body, spirit, as well as our surroundings. And for the continuity of our species, we cannot be oblivious to the environment in which we subsist. But for many people today, money is more important than our environment, more important than humanity, more important than God. If you do not have money, you do not have an education, a house, food, clothing, and you cannot pay for health care. Without money, you are nothing—*nada!* Why so much inequality? Something is not right; we are doing something wrong. We are annihilating ourselves.

The COVID-19 pandemic has shown us how fragile and vulnerable we are, especially in disadvantaged communities. We need to learn from this experience and change our health care systems, making them more inclusive and resilient. Catholics must fight for hope and act now; there is no time to waste thinking about the darkness and the final judgment. For more than five hundred years, the native peoples have not given up. We won't give up either. The native peoples have found the good God, the son of God who walks with the oppressed, with the poor: the God of hope.

Wokol a walik ta pisilik. (Mayan Tzeltal)

Tlazothkamati wel miak. (Aztec Nahuatl)
Gracias a todos.
Thank you all.

Bibliography

Aguilar Ortega, Teodoro. "Desigualdad y Marginación en Chiapas." *Peninsula* 11.2 (2016) 143–59. https://www.scielo.org.mx/scielo.php?script=sci_arttext&pid=S1870-5766 2016000200143.

Almaguer González, José Alejandro, et al. *Interculturalidad en Salud: Experiencias y Aportes para el Fortalecimiento de los Servicios de Salud.* Mexico City: Secretaría de Salud, 2014.

Aparicio Mena, Alfonso Julio. "La Medicina Tradicional como Medicina Ecocultural." *Gazeta de Antropología* 21 (2005) http://hdl.handle.net/10481/7181.

Arellano, Astrid. "Organización Documenta la Violación de Derechos Humanos contra Pueblos Indígenas detrás de 16 Casos en México." *Mongabay*, July 6, 2022. https://es.mongabay.com/2022/07/violacion-de-derechos-humanos-pueblos-indigenas-en-mexico/.

"La Biomedicina, Dominante en el Sistema de Salud." *Gaceta UNAM,* April 7, 2020. https://www.gaceta.unam.mx/la-biomedicina-dominante-en-el-sistema-de-salud/.

CEVECE (Centro Estatal de Vigilancia Epidemiológica y Control de Enfermedades). "Mujer Indígena y Salud." *VisiónCEVECE* (2019) Semana 36. https://cevece.edomex.gob.mx/sites/cevece.edomex.gob.mx/files/files/docs/tripticos/2019/Semana36.pdf.

CONEVAL (Consejo Nacional de Evaluación de la Política de Desarrollo Social). "La Población Indígena es el Grupo que Presenta la Mayor Carencia por Acceso a la Alimentación." October 16, 2019. https://www.coneval.org.mx/SalaPrensa/Comunicadosprensa/Documents/2019/NOTA_INFORMATIVA_DIA_MUNDIAL_DE_LA_ALIMENTACION.pdf.

Cortés, Hernán, and Mario Hernández Sánchez-Barba. *Cartas y Documentos.* Mexico City: Porrúa, 1963.

Encuesta Nacional sobre Discriminación (ENADIS) 2017: Principales Resultados. Mexico City: UNAM, CONACYT, INEGI, CNDH, and CONAPRED, 2017. https://en.www.inegi.org.mx/contenidos/programas/enadis/2017/doc/enadis2017_resultados.pdf.

"Florentine Codex." Dumbarton Oaks. https://www.doaks.org/resources/online-exhibits/epidemics/epidemics-english/crumbling-manuscripts/florentine-codex.

García, Ana Karen. "7 de Cada 10 Indígenas en México Son Pobres." *El Economista,* September 16, 2018. https://www.eleconomista.com.mx/economia/7-de-cada-10-indigenas-en-Mexico-son-pobres-20180916-0007.html.

INEGI (Instituto Nacional de Estadística y Geografía). "Comunicado de Prensa Núm 24/21: En México Somos 126,014,024 Habitantes: Censo de Población y Vivienda 2020." January 25, 2021. https://www.inegi.org.mx/contenidos/saladeprensa/boletines/2021/ EstSociodemo/ResultCenso2020_Nal.pdf.

———. "Comunicado de Prensa Núm 430/22: Estadísticas a Propósito del Día Internacional de los Pueblos Indígenas." August 8, 2022. https://www.inegi.org.mx/contenidos/saladeprensa/aproposito/2022/EAP_PueblosInd22.pdf.

———. *Encuesta Intercensal 2015: Principales Resultados.* Aguascalientes, Mexico: 2015. https://www.inegi.org.mx/contenidos/programas/intercensal/2015/doc/eic_2015_presentacion.pdf.
INMUJERES (Instituto Nacional de las Mujeres). "La Población Indígena." May 2021. http://estadistica.inmujeres.gob.mx/formas/tarjetas/Poblacion_indigena.pdf.
———. *La Población Indígena Mexicana.* Mexico City: INMUJERES, 2006. http://cedoc.inmujeres.gob.mx/documentos_download/100782.pdf.
INPI (Instituto Nacional de los Pueblos Indígenas). "Niñas, Niños y Adolescentes Indígenas. Datos de la Encuesta Intercensal 2015." April 28, 2017. https://www.gob.mx/inpi/articulos/ninas-ninos-y-adolescentes-indigenas-datos-de-la-encuesta-intercensal-2015.
Juárez-Ramírez, Clara, et al. "La Desigualdad en Salud de Grupos Vulnerables de México: Adultos Mayores, Indígenas y Migrantes." *Revista Panamaericana Salud Pública* 35.4 (2014) 284–90. https://www.minsal.cl/wp-content/uploads/2015/09/BP08Juarez-Ramirez-Mexico-Equidad-en-Salud-2014.pdf.
López, Isaí. "Se Incrementa Población Indígena en Chiapas: INEGI." *Diario del Sur,* March 7, 2021. https://www.diariodelsur.com.mx/local/comunidades-mujer-genero-poblaciones-lenguaje-se-incrementa-poblacion-indigena-en-chiapas-inegi-6444352.html.
Marcos, Subcomadante Insurgente, and Žiga Vodovnik, ed. *¡Ya Basta!: Ten Years of the Zapatista Uprising.* Oakland, CA: AK, 2004.
Martínez, Jessica. "El Hospital de Chiapas donde los Indígenas Pagan con Naranjas, Café y Maíz." *Forbes México,* August 26, 2018. https://www.forbes.com.mx/hospital-de-chiapas-indigenas-pagan-con-naranjas-cafe-maiz/.
Menéndez, Eduardo L. "Autoatención de los Padecimientos y Algunos Imaginarios Antropológicos." *Desacatos* 58 (September–December 2018) 104–13. https://www.scielo.org.mx/pdf/desacatos/n58/2448-5144-desacatos-58-104.pdf.
———. "Modelo Médico Hegemónico: Tendencias Posibles y Tendencias Más o Menos Imaginarias." *Salud Colectiva* 16 (2020). https://revistas.unla.edu.ar/saludcolectiva/article/view/2615/1591.
Montemayor Aceves, Martha Elena. "Publicación de la Obra La Real Expedición Botánica a Nueva España." *Nova Tellus* 28.2 (December 2010) 313–16. https://revistas-filologicas.unam.mx/nouatellus/index.php/nt/article/view/366.
Organization of American States (OAS). *American Declaration on the Rights of Indigenous Peoples.* Washington, DC: Organization of American States, 2016. https://www.oas.org/en/sare/documents/DecAmIND.pdf.
Political Constitution of the United Mexican States. Article 4. https://www.oas.org/ext/Portals/33/Files/Member-States/Mex_intro_txtfun_eng.pdf.
Universidad Autónoma Chapingo (UACH) Departamento de Fitnotecnia. "Plan de Estudios del Programa de Maestría en Ciencias en Horticultura: 2023." https://fitotecnia.posgrado.chapingo.edu.mx/wp-content/uploads/2023/07/PlanEstudiosMCH.pdf.
Zolla, Carlos. "La Salud de los Pueblos Indígenas de México." Permanent Seminar, Universidad Nacional Autónoma de México (UNAM), Programa Universitario de Estudios de la Diversidad Cultural y la Interculturalidad, 2007. https://www.nacionmulticultural.unam.mx/portal/pdf/proyectos_academicos/salud_pueblos_indigenas.pdf.

9

Connecting Western and Eastern Medicine from a Rural and Christian Perspective in India

Maria Vasantha, SCC, MD

1. Introduction

Non-Western medicines have gained popularity and acceptability worldwide over the last decade, owing to the belief that herbal therapy will improve one's quality of life and is also a balanced and moderate approach to treatment. Another argument is that, for lifestyle-related and noncommunicable diseases, which lead to death indirectly, lifestyle changes and changes in health-related behaviors are required, and many of non-Western medicine's therapeutic approaches focus on dietary and lifestyle modifications and target health-related behaviors. According to World Health Organization (WHO) in 2023, noncommunicable diseases accounted for 74 percent of all expected deaths worldwide—i.e., an estimated forty-one million people.[1]

As is widely documented, traditional systems of medicine have always played a significant part in providing for global health care needs. Traditional and complementary medicine of proven quality, safety, and efficacy contributes to the goal of ensuring that all people have access to care. Many countries now recognize the need to develop a cohesive and integrative

---

1. World Health Organization, "Noncommunicable Diseases."

approach to health care that allows governments, health care practitioners, and, most importantly, those who use health care services to access non-Western medicine in a safe, respectful, cost-efficient, and effective manner. A global strategy to foster its appropriate integration, regulation, and supervision will be useful to countries wishing to develop a proactive policy towards this important and often vibrant and expanding part of health care.[2]

It has also been observed in developing countries that, to meet their health care demands, non-Western medicine and its practitioners are a useful resource for public health, particularly in rural areas. In the communities where it operates, it is seen as more cost-effective, accessible, and acceptable than modern medicine.

Given that India is a developing country, there is a huge discrepancy in medical treatment quality and coverage between rural and urban areas. In rural areas, where 70 percent of the population live, conventional Western medicine has become secondary to non-Western (Eastern) treatment. This is due to inadequate (or nonexistent) conventional treatment, the poor financial resources of health care facilities, and the lack of awareness of health care needs and cultural beliefs.

In this chapter, I will study the role of non-Western treatment as complementary to conventional medicine to achieve optimal health, and I will also analyze the efficacy and the objective outcome of non-Western (Eastern) treatment with Western treatment in the rural areas of India. Through some case studies, I will illustrate the positive impact of complementing Western and non-Western medicine. From a Christian perspective, Jesus honored the physicians yet, at the same time, he applied some traditional healing methods to heal people. He responded to the faith of the people who were ill. As a divine healer, Jesus is a model for connecting conventional and nonconventional medicine.

2. History of Western and Non-Western Medicine in India

To understand Western and non-Western medicine from an Indian perspective, one must first comprehend their histories in India, which can be traced back through India's history in the precolonial, colonial, and postcolonial periods.

---

2. World Health Organization, *WHO Traditional Medicine*, 7.

2.1 The Precolonial Period

During the precolonial period, beginning in 600 BCE, India had no contact with the rest of the globe. At that time, traditional Indian medicine was the only system available. In this area, India has the distinction of having six recognized medical systems: Ayurveda, Siddha, Unani, yoga, naturopathy, and homoeopathy. Though homoeopathy arrived in India in the eighteenth century, it quickly merged into Indian culture and became enriched like any other traditional system, earning a place among Indian medical systems. (Aside from these six systems, there are a huge number of healers in the folklore stream who have not been classified.) The most ancient of the six recognized systems are Ayurveda, Unani, and Siddha, which are reported to be five thousand years old. Ayurveda, Siddha, and Unani are all based on the same principles—i.e., that there are five basic elements that make up the entire cosmos. The body has a perfect balance of these elements, and when that equilibrium is disrupted, an undesirable state called disease arises.

2.1.1 Ayurveda

Ayurveda means "science of life" in its entirety, and its origins can be traced back to Vedic culture.[3] The science of Ayurveda is based on the *Atharva Veda,* a sacred Hindu scripture from the early Iron Age and one of the earliest Indian literatures on medicine. The universe, according to Ayurveda, is made up of five elements: *vayu* (air), *jala* (water), *aakash* (space or ether), *prithvi* (earth), and *teja* (fire). It is thought that, by following the principles of divine wisdom, a perfect balance between these elements and the human body "should be maintained for a healthy condition of living."[4] Ayurvedic medicine is based on herbs, and to release their full potential, trees, flowers, roots, stems, and leaves are processed into numerous forms. Ayurveda is the most ancient, widely acknowledged, practiced, and thriving Indian traditional system of medicine. It is regarded not just as an ethnomedicine but also as a comprehensive medical system that considers humankind's physical, psychological, philosophical, ethical, and spiritual well-being.

---

3. Sharma, "Ayurveda," 87.
4. Jaiswal and Williams, "Glimpse of Ayurveda," 51.

2.1.2 Siddha

The Siddha medical system is regarded as a remarkable achievement and an emblem of Tamil culture, which originated in India's south during the Indus Valley Civilization. Siddha alchemy draws its inspiration mostly from Chinese alchemy and Taoism, especially Taoist patrology. Though the Siddha system of treatment shares many characteristics with Ayurveda, it has its own philosophy, as well as a holistic approach and lifestyle-oriented methods. The technique is thought to have been devised by eighteen Siddhars (a class of Tamil sages) in ancient times.[5] The Siddhars' knowledge, first passed down verbally, was eventually written down on palm leaf scrolls.[6]

2.1.3 Unani

Unani, like Ayurveda, is based on the theory of the presence of elements in the human body. It was introduced in India by the Arabs and Persians sometime during the eighth century, and soon after its introduction, the system took root in the country as an indigenous system of medicine. According to Unani medicine, maintaining health depends on six essential factors: (1) air; (2) food and drink; (3) bodily movement and rest; (4) mental movement and rest; (5) sleep and wakefulness; and (6) excretion and retention. Balancing these factors maintains health, while imbalance results in disease.[7] Regimental therapy, diet, medication, and surgery are among the treatment options.

Indian traditional medicine was at its peak during the precolonial period. The evolution of numerous formulations occurred during this period because most of the effort was linked to core concepts and the enunciation of different principles.

2.2 The Colonial Period

The history of Western medicine in India begins around 1800, when the first medical officers arrived in India with the British East India Company to provide medical care to the company's troops and servants.[8] They were trained in current medical techniques in Europe at the time and took care of

---

5. Sen and Chakraborty, "Revival, Modernization, and Integration," 235.
6. Rajkumar et al., "Survey of Tamil Siddha Manuscripts," 68–69.
7. Hashir, "Research Opportunities in Unani," 152–53.
8. Mushtaq, "Public Health in British India," 6–14.

the medical needs of the company's soldiers and officials. They are credited with bringing the Western medical system to India.

In the early years of their collaboration, Western medicine, Ayurveda, and Unani had similar views about the humoral structure of the human body and humoral imbalance as the major cause of disease. There was reciprocal respect, and European doctors were eager to learn from Indian doctors, particularly about tropical disease treatments. Botanical gardens were established to nurture and study indigenous species that could be exported or utilized as medicines.[9]

With the advent of rational thought in Europe, and a greater emphasis on observation and scientific technique over tradition and wisdom, British surgeons began to rely mostly on European remedies but frequently modified their curative regimens to fit Indian constitutions and environments. They were able to duplicate some highly efficient Indian treatments. They objected, however, to the dearth of texts on specific disorders, the unchanging duplication of traditional medicines across generations, and the absence of significant surgeries performed by Indian practitioners.

After 1820, Western medical research advanced at a breakneck pace, further separating European and Indian physicians. Modern Western devices such as thermometers, stethoscopes, and microscopes improved physicians' diagnostic powers. Once germ theory became fully established, vaccination arose as a revolutionary preventive method, which would eradicate many infectious illnesses in the future. And with the debut of chloroform in India in 1849, there were significant breakthroughs in obstetrics, amputations, fracture therapy, and various other procedures.[10]

As a result of Western medicine's invasion, traditional Indian medical systems and their physicians gradually lost the esteem of their Western counterparts. Some indigenous practitioners entirely abandoned Indian methods in favor of the Western system, which they believed to be the sole reasonable science. Others were staunch opponents of Western medicine; they defended indigenous systems, promoting them in their purest forms, and opposing the incorporation of Western notions into medical education. A few indigenous practitioners combined Ayurveda, Unani, and Western medicine, believing in the scientific superiority of Western medicine while also supporting local medical systems. By the end of the nineteenth century, Western medicine had a strong presence in India's major cities and towns, and Indian medicine faded into the background but, despite losing British sponsorship, remained popular in rural areas.

9. Saini, "Physicians of Colonial India," 529–31.
10. Saini, "Physicians of Colonial India," 528–32.

During the two hundred years of British rule, the health care system in India was completely transformed. Western medicine, as well as a vast network of hospitals, dispensaries, medical colleges, nursing, and paramedical institutions, revolutionized primary and tertiary medical treatment. Of course, the Western system's performance in treating the majority of the country's medical demands is commendable for a country of such continental scale in terms of area and population.

Medical services responded effectively to devastating diseases such as the plague and cholera. Almost all of the diseases that were widespread in India at that period, such as smallpox, leprosy, and malaria, were successfully managed. In the following years, there were few epidemics, and several diseases were nearly eradicated. Officers and researchers from the Indian Medical Services had made significant contributions to illness research and prevention.[11]

2.3 The Postcolonial Period

Under the influence of the British during the nineteenth and first part of the twentieth centuries, traditional systems were gradually displaced by modern medicine. Throughout the twentieth and twenty-first centuries in India, the Western system had a significant impact on the quality of life and lifespan of millions of people; its treatments and techniques have enhanced health outcomes and lifespans in ways that no one could have predicted. Western medicine was a significant factor in preventing mortality from acute emergencies and communicable diseases in India. While the importance and benefits of Western medicine were recognized, from the 1920s to the mid-1940s, there were also initiatives by provincial governments and popular leaders such as Mahatma Gandhi to revive Indian traditional medicine.[12]

Colleges and other institutions were established to revitalize the practice of indigenous medical sciences and integrate them with the country's main health care system. While Western medicine was pushed into a defensive position, there were several voices of reason calling for cooperation and synthesis between the two systems. The June 1928 issue of *The Journal of Ayurveda or the Hindu System of Medicine* advocated that medical education in India should be designed in such a way to incorporate not only current medical information but also historical medical knowledge.[13]

---

11. Mushtaq, "Public Health in British India," 6–14.
12. Joshi and Kumar, "Role of Traditional Medicine," 592–95.
13. Anshu and Supe, "Evolution of Medical Education," 255–59.

Various leaders and physicians of Indian traditional medicine held opposing viewpoints, and healers from India believed that, while Indian traditional medicine could not progress in an old way, it could move forward in a new way. They believed that Western medicine should not be accepted in toto for India, that we should learn about the pathology of diseases' seed from the Western system but entrust the pathology of diseases' soil to non-Western medicine. The two perspectives are still currently at odds, but they should be reconciled.

In 1946, when India's first national health care policy was outlined by the Bhore Committee, traditional practices were completely ignored.[14] But the first health ministers' conference that year brought the subject again prominently to the forefront; it passed a strongly worded resolution to allow provisions for training and research in indigenous systems of medicine and to absorb practitioners of Ayurveda and Unani into state health organizations. As a result of this, in 1946, the government of India appointed a committee chaired by Lt. Col R. N. Chopra, which did a thorough evaluation and made far-reaching recommendations. Their report was published in 1948 and included the following recommendations:

- To provide medical relief, the Western and indigenous systems should be harmonized.
- Though time-consuming and difficult, it is both possible and practicable to synthesize indigenous and Western medicines, and this process should begin immediately.
- Medical students should receive adequate instruction in indigenous medicine as well as the essentials of the Western system, especially in those areas where the indigenous system is lacking.[15]

Unfortunately, by the time this report was published, modern Western medicine was already deeply implanted throughout the country. Given the great benefits of the Western system in critical care and epidemics, it was futile to reverse this trend, and thus, its coexistence with indigenous medicine in India, with each having its benefits. The supremacy of Western medicine remained largely intact, as many Indians had entered its domain for treatment and medical education.

---

14. Srinivasan, "National Health Policy," 190–93.

15. Government of India's Ministry of Health, *Report of the Udupa K. N. Committee*, 3.

3. The Rural Perspective

India's colonial history had supplanted its five-thousand-year-old legacy of traditional medicine. In postcolonial times, despite the availability of both the traditional and new Western medical systems, access to Western medicine was limited in rural areas. Even today, the rural population of India faces difficulties obtaining Western treatment of their primary health care needs. The variables that lead to such conditions are contentious. A quick examination of the Indian health care system, particularly in rural regions, is necessary to provide new impetus for understanding the rural perspective on the use of non-Western medicine. India has a mixed health care system, including both public and private providers. However, most of the private providers are in urban India, providing secondary and tertiary health care services: 75 percent of the private health care infrastructure is concentrated in urban areas where only 27 percent of the total Indian population is living. The remaining 73 percent of the country's population—in rural areas—lacks proper primary health care facilities.

The public health care infrastructure in rural areas has been developed as a three-tier system.[16] Funded by the government, public health care is charged with maintaining the primary health requirements in rural and urban areas. Private health care and its services are paid out-of-pocket. Due to the low quality of public health services, most people go to the private sector for their health care needs. Though India's constitution guarantees free health care to all its citizens, in reality, most health care expenses are paid directly out-of-pocket by patients and their families.

The biggest concern for the rural health care system is the lack of adequate infrastructure. The existing health care centers in rural areas are underfinanced, use below-quality equipment, have a low supply of medicines, and lack qualified and dedicated human resources. On top of this, underdeveloped roads and railway systems, as well as a poor power supply, make it difficult to set up a rural health care facility. Villagers have to travel a long distance to the nearest hospital in case of emergencies, and their only viable transportation is private transport, which many cannot afford. Sixty-six percent of rural Indians do not have access to critical care medicines, and the majority of deaths result from preventable and curable diseases such as diarrhea, measles, and typhoid.

Due to the poor financial and human resources of conventional health care facilities, more than 70 percent of India's 1.1 billion population still use non-Western systems of medicine and prefer traditional healing medicine

---

16. Chokshi et al., "Health Systems in India," 36.

and indigenous plants for their basic health care needs.[17] Indians use traditional medicine not only for normal care but also for more serious health problems such as bone fractures, snake bites, gastrointestinal pain, and diarrhea. This pattern of use can be linked to a number of factors, including strong cultural beliefs, a desire to resuscitate a rich tradition, and this tradition's accessibility and affordability. The practice of traditional medicine in India ranges from recognized alternative systems to noncodified traditional healers that need to be regularized.

Regionally, there is also a trend in the use of certain types of traditional medicine, reflecting the regional elements of that system's history.[18] Tamil Nādu, for example, is known for its use of Siddha medication. The southern state of Kerala is famous for its Ayurvedic hospitals and treatment centers, where Ayurvedic doctors treat patients from all over the world. In north India, Ayurveda medicine is used more frequently than any other Indian school of medicine. More than five hundred tribal clans exist in India, with tribal people accounting for 8.2 percent of the country's overall population, and each tribe has its unique set of healing customs. Tribal medicine is not a formalized system; rather, conditions are diagnosed and treated via experience; even the rudimentary procedures people undertake at home are their own creations.[19]

It isn't uncommon for people to use both types of treatment for a particular disease simultaneously. For example, a patient with bronchial asthma may use a bronchodilator and also herbal medicine known as adhatoda (*Justicia adhatoda*), while a patient with a common cold may use antihistamines as well as turmeric milk or herbal tea made of basil, ginger, and pepper, a very common home remedy in India.

4. Cultural Beliefs

Each community has its own medical system, which is deeply grounded in its culture and driven by its philosophy of life. In rural places, cultural beliefs play an important role in the use of non-Western medicine. Traditional medicine has been a part of the community health care system since ancient times. In rural households, home cures, food and nutrition, midwifery, bone setting, ethnoveterinary techniques, and other unique local health practices have all played an essential role in meeting the primary health care requirements.

17. Vaidya and Devasagayam, "Current Status of Herbal Drugs," 1–11.
18. Srinivasan and Sugumar, "Spread of Traditional Medicines," 194–204.
19. Ayyanar, "Traditional Herbal Medicines."

A study conducted in the United States to understand the role of culture in the health-related behaviors of older Asian Indian immigrants[20] presents a clear picture of Indians' cultural ideas concerning Western and non-Western medicine. Their cultural ideas about non-Western remedies are based on personal experiences and inherited traditions.[21] Indians are a collective community that values a hierarchical organization, traditional medical systems, and links between the mind, body, and spirit. During a medical treatment process, there is a high level of family engagement, and at times, Indians defer decision-making to other family members. As a result, if the family believes in alternative medicine, it becomes the first treatment option. Because of our knowledge and faith in traditional healing systems, non-Western medicine is a realistic alternative for Indians.

When it comes to treating illness, Indians use both Western and Eastern medicinal techniques. Traditional healing methods are believed to be effective, making non-Western medicine a viable and enticing option for Indians when they are sick. Some individuals begin treatment using traditional remedies such as ginger, turmeric, lemon, and homemade brews because they have a strong belief in Eastern medicine. When Western treatment fails to help them, some Indians turn to Ayurvedic and homoeopathic medicine. Finally, in addition to honoring traditional medical systems, Indians also employ strategies that assist them in maintaining mental, bodily, and spiritual balance. Yoga, particularly Hatha yoga, is one of the most popular ways to achieve this. Hatha yoga is traditionally thought to be a full yogic path, consisting of 103 moral disciplines, physical exercises (such as postures and breath control), and meditation. Besides the physical benefits, Hatha yoga also highlights the mental and spiritual advantages of the exercises.

5. The Indian Government's Role in Promoting the Indian System of Medicine

The National Rural Health Mission (NRHM) of the government of India attempts to improve health care access in the country's rural regions. In response to the inequities of health care in rural areas, it has adopted as one of its key mandates the mainstreaming of these indigenous systems, known collectively as AYUSH[22] [an acronym that stands for Ayurveda, yoga and naturopathy, Unani, Siddha, and homoeopathy]. The rationale behind this mainstreaming was to strengthen the existing public health system across

20. Thaker, "Sacred Cow," 366–71.
21. Thaker, "Sacred Cow," 366–71.
22. Shankar and Patwardhan, "AYUSH for New India," 137.

the country at all levels by engaging alternative medicine practitioners, as they are a positive presence and are culturally accepted, especially in rural communities.

At the primary level, training is provided to AYUSH practitioners on primary care and national health programs. At the secondary level, AYUSH departments are established in district- and *taluka*[23]-level hospitals, and at the tertiary level, AYUSH centers of excellence are founded as referral centers, as well as places for research, development, and supervision. Some of the practical challenges that are faced include significant variations in basic practice philosophy, discrepancies in approaches to specific clinical diseases, differences in normative approaches to decision-making, unclear policies for cross-referral, and potential cross-practice concerns.

Mainstreaming AYUSH into the existing public health system can result in a number of problems, including the following:

- failing to focus on community value judgments about AYUSH;
- creating a confusing plurality of approaches and a segregation of practices without healthy dialogue between practitioners of either system;
- failing to disclose which type of practitioners (AYUSH or allopathy) the patient is seeing;
- and failing to implement proper public accountability mechanisms.

The mainstreaming of AYUSH is met with fierce opposition from Western medical practitioners, and as a result, it is up for discussion.[24]

6. The Christian Perspective

6.1 Jesus, a Holistic Healer

Jesus is the holistic healer *par excellence*. As the Gospels portray, healing the sick and restoring them to good health and acceptance in their communities played a pivotal role in his life and mission. As Arul J. Robin points out, Jesus "was a healer totally different from Jewish holy men as well as Gentile miracle worker [sic] like Apollonius of Tyana. We can highlight at least three differences: 1) for Jesus, healing was typical of his ministry; 2) his special emphasis on the component of faith . . . and 3) his unmediated exercise of the saving power of God. Jesus did not ask God to heal; rather, he healed

---

23. As defined in Merriam-Webster, a *taluka* is "a collectorate or administrative subdivision comprising an Indian revenue district" (https://www.merriam-webster.com/dictionary/taluk).

24. Gopichandran and Kumar, "Mainstreaming AYUSH," 272–77.

directly with authority. The healing work of Jesus is also different from his followers as well; they pronounced healing in the name of Jesus. . . ."[25] Besides the Gospel writers, contemporaries like the Jewish-Roman historian Josephus also refer to Jesus as a healer doing astounding deeds.

Among the synoptic Gospel writers, Matthew narrates nineteen healing miracles, while Mark has eighteen, and Luke has twenty healing stories. There is considerable overlap among the healing miracle stories in the Synoptic Gospels. Still, the number of healings narrated is impressive—six episodes of exorcisms and seventeen accounts of healing, including that of three persons being raised to life (resuscitation). The Gospel of John presents five episodes of healing, including one resuscitation. According to Arul J. Robin, "We find in the Gospels two types of healing: healings which demonstrate Jesus's power over sickness and exorcisms that manifest Jesus's power over Satanic forces. We should include also here Resuscitation which unveil Jesus's command over death."[26]

One of the factors that stands out in Jesus's ministry of healing is that many of the beneficiaries of these healings are those on the periphery of the society—lepers, the slave of a non-Jewish army officer, persons possessed by demons, a paralytic, and a woman with menstrual irregularities considered unclean by society. Jesus healed them in a holistic way from the category of unclean—physically, socially, and emotionally—leading them to acceptance in society and, in this way, restoring meaning to their lives. As John Pilch points out, when Jesus healed a person in a domestic setting, the healed person returns to performing her usual role in her household, as Peter's mother-in-law did.[27] Thus, concerned with the healing of the whole person and restoring him/her into society, Jesus was a true holistic healer.

6.2 The Church in India Reaches Out to the Peripheries

Following Jesus, the holistic healer, and inspired by his compassionate care for the sick, the church in India focuses on accessible, affordable, and holistic health care for all, especially the vulnerable and those on the periphery of the society. Its health care services are provided by sister and priest doctors and nurses, as well as lay collaborators.

As already discussed, the qualitative and quantitative availability of primary health care facilities in India's rural area is far less than the norms defined by the World Health Organization. Rural regions lack basic health

25. Robin, "Healing Ministry of Jesus," 212–13.
26. Robin, "Healing Ministry of Jesus," 214.
27. See Pilch, "Healing in the New Testament," in Fox, *Disability and the Way*, 31.

and sanitation facilities and, thus, there is a heavy burden of preventable diseases in these areas.

To address this reality, the Catholic Church in India took an important step. In 1963, in order to prepare people to serve the medical needs of poor, rural areas and reach the unreached, the Catholic Bishops' Conference of India (CBCI) founded St. John's Medical College in Bangalore, India. It was the first medical college to train Catholic nuns and Catholic lay men and women who promised to serve in the rural regions of our country. St. John's "was founded to provide relief for the suffering, to promote and preserve the health of the community and to give an example of enlightened training in dedicated service, which is characteristic of Christian educational and social welfare institutions."[28]

6.2.1 *The Catholic Health Association of India*

From its humble beginnings in July 1943, the Catholic Health Association of India (CHAI) has been serving the nation in reaching the unreached.[29] It is a network of 3,572 institutions across the country, including health and social service centers, hospitals, and nursing schools. This network employs more than seventy-six thousand health professionals, operating within all branches of health care, including medicine, surgery, dentistry, midwifery, pharmacy, psychology, nursing, and the allied health professions. Serving 21 million people every year, most of whom are poor and live in remote areas, CHAI plays a vital role in India's health care through its national reach, grassroots presence, and the unstinted commitment of its volunteers. Its members translate the core values of compassion, affordability, and quality of care into their daily work. In addition, CHAI has been successful in implementing a wide variety of projects related to community health, communicable and noncommunicable diseases, palliative care, disability, disaster intervention, and strengthening of the health care system. There are also five medical colleges run by CHAI member institutions, which impart medical education guided by the principles of Catholic ethics.

6.2.2 *Sister Doctors Forum of India (SDFI)*

The mission of the Sister Doctors Forum of India (SDFI) is to give fullness of life through holistic healing services, bringing the love and compassion

---

28. See Pilch, "Healing in the New Testament," in Fox, *Disability and the Way*, 31.
29. Catholic Health Association of India (CHAI), *Annual Report 2018*, 3.

of Jesus Christ to His people in need, irrespective of caste, creed, religion, age, and gender. Founded in 1993 during the CHAI national convention, SDFI currently has about one thousand members, and the majority of these sister doctors have dedicated their lives to the service of the unreached and less-reached of our country. Their medical specialties include cardiology, general medicine, surgery, pediatrics, obstetrics and gynecology, radiology, psychiatry, pathology, family medicine, and public health. Providing preventive, curative, promotive, and palliative care services, the sister doctors contribute greatly to the restoration of health and wholeness in India's rural, tribal, and remote areas.

Presently, SDFI organizes various activities at the regional and national level such as the "Save the Girl Child" campaign, the "Cancer Prevention in Women through Screening and Awareness Creation" program, as well as programs for anemia control and treatment, mother and child welfare, and the prevention of lifestyle-associated diseases. Some sister doctors are also actively participating in national health programs like the Revised National Tuberculosis Control Programme (RNTCP) and National AIDS Control Programme (NACO). They also organize continuing medical education (CME) programs at regional and national levels. In addition, SDFI has been at the forefront during natural calamities like earthquakes, floods, and tsunamis. It works in collaboration with other organizations such as CHAI, the CBCI Health Commission, the Catholic Medical Mission Board (CMMB), Catholic Relief Services (CRS), and Caritas India.[30]

6.3 The Church's Role in Promoting Alternative Medicine

Besides reaching out to those on the peripheries through its health care institutions, India's Catholic Church has made the choice to promote Indian traditional medicine. Some religious congregations have been supporting this alternative medicine for many years, through operating traditional medicine health centers. As an example, the Congregation of Servants of Mary has trained sister doctors in Siddha medicine, and they now run Siddha health clinics throughout Tamil Nādu. Despite their Western medical clinic, the Medical Mission Sisters run the Ayushya Centre for Healing and Integration, a wellness center in Kottayam, Kerala, that integrates the Indian system of medicine of AYUSH. Since 1985, it has been a pioneer in holistic health and complementary and alternative medicine (CAM). At Ayushya, there are workshops on health, healing, and wholeness as well as nutritional psychology "cure camps" that address chronic and psychosomatic illnesses

30. Sister Doctors Forum of India, "About Us."

through psychotherapy, emotional body work, health exercises, and nutrition therapy. There are also residential programs that offer treatment to those suffering with chronic ailments and rest and relaxation for those who are in crisis or conflict.[31]

In Mokoma, about sixty kilometers from Patna, capital of the state of Bihar, there is a group of Nazareth nuns who run an Indian traditional medicine center with the goal of providing psychological well-being. It has modern equipment and offers services that include yoga, aromatic herbal massages, hydrotherapy, mud therapy, and Ayurvedic treatments with oils. Dietary advice as well as spine and joint pain care and personalized counseling are also available.[32] In Tamil Nādu, on the banks of the Kaveri River in Perugamani, near Tiruchirappalli, the Capuchin friars operate a nature cure center called Sangamam, which offers complete naturopathy treatment.[33] Well-known across India is the Father Muller Homeopathic Medical College Hospital in Deralakatta, Karnataka. Part of its mission is to be progressive in offering comprehensive health care services that are sensitive to society's demands through homoeopathy. It trains young men and women in homoeopathic medicine, developing in them the skills they need to provide "effective health care to the suffering humanity."[34]

Also worth mentioning are the following Catholic initiatives that provide psychospiritual healing and wellness to the sick: Indian Christian yoga by Fr. Francis Vineeth Vadakethala, CMI (Carmelite of Mary Immaculate)[35]; Indian Christian vipassana meditations by Catholic nuns[36]; and Indian Christian Zen meditation by Fr. Ama Samy and Fr. Mathew Cyril, Jesuit priests who are also Zen masters at Bodhi Zendo, a Zen training and meditation center in Perumalmalai, Tamil Nādu.[37]

---

31. Ayushya Centre for Healing and Integration, "About."

32. "First Alternative Medicine Hospital," para 3.

33. To learn more about this naturopathy center, see Capuchin JPIC, "0001 Interview with Fr. Jacob."

34. See Father Muller Homeopathic Medical College, "Vision and Mission."

35. Fr. Vineeth passed away in 2021, but Vidyanan Ashram, the interfaith Christian ashram that he founded in 1996, is still in operation in Bengaluru, Bangalore, and its offerings include yoga retreats. See Fr. Francis Vineeth Vadakethala CMI, "About Fr. Vineeth," as well as the Vidyanan Ashram's website, https://vidyavanam.net.

36. See, for example, Mandapati, "My Journey."

37. Bodhi Zendo, "Zen Teachers."

6.3.1 The Amala Institute of Medical Sciences

In Thrissur, Kerala, CMI priests founded the Amala Institute of Medical Sciences, a one-of-a-kind institution that offers both modern medical facilities with advanced diagnostic and treatment procedures as well as holistic Ayurvedic and homoeopathic medical services.[38] Its campus includes a modern "super specialty" hospital with one thousand beds, as well as a medical college, research center, homoeopathic hospital, and the Amala Ayurvedic Hospital with over eighty beds.[39] Its Ayurvedic hospital is currently conducting research and providing treatment for cancer and HIV/AIDS,[40] and along with its research center, also offers various types of Ayurvedic packages for relaxation, rejuvenation, and detoxification.

6.3.2 Holistic Health Centre (HHC)

In 1997, the Medical Mission Sisters opened the Holistic Health Centre (HHC) in Pune offering training programs, a clinic, and outreach, all centered on the use of alternative systems of medicine. The HHC's holistic approach integrates the body, mind, spirit, and emotions; it studies how healing occurs in a person and how to create balance within the human person as well as with our ecological and cosmic relationships. The goal of holistic medicine is wellness in the fullest sense, and the HHC works to help people achieve a dynamic, ever expanding, purposeful, and vibrant lifestyle.[41]

6.3.3 CHAI's Role in Promoting Non-Western Medicine

Considering health to be a whole condition of physical, mental, social, and spiritual well-being, rather than simply the absence of disease, CHAI maintains its commitment to "health for all." As a result, it envisions an India in which people have access to clean air, water, and environment. CHAI endeavors to promote community health, understood as the process of enabling the people—especially the poor and the marginalized—to be responsible collectively for attaining and maintaining their health and

---

38. For more information on the Amala Institute of Medical Sciences, see their website at https://www.amalaims.org/hospital.
39. Amala Ayurvedic Hospital and Research Centre, "Why Amala?"
40. Niruja HealthTech, "Amala Ayurvedic Hospital"; "Anti-AIDS Treatment."
41. Medical Mission Sisters North India, "Holistic Health Centre (HHC)."

demanding health as a right, ensuring the availability of quality health care at a reasonable cost.[42]

To achieve this vision, CHAI also promotes traditional Indian medicine. For example, it publishes the *Health Action* monthly journal, devoted to the promotion of Indian traditional medicine and advice on how to avoid lifestyle-related ailments. For sister nurses who are serving in rural areas, CHAI also conducts a six-week training program on community health nursing with a special emphasis on Indian traditional medicine. Whether through certain religious congregations or national organizations, the church in India follows the example of Jesus the healer in promoting holistic healing to the people of this nation.

7. My Personal Experience of Complementing Western Medicine with Flower Remedies in Rural India

For the past fifteen years, I have been working in rural south India. Currently, I serve as director, consultant, and surgeon in the Department of Obstetrics and Gynecology at Lenoard Hospital, in the town of Batlagundu in Tamil Nadu. In my clinical practice, I follow an integrative approach, using a balance of Western science and alternative and spiritual therapies of Eastern science, such as Zen meditation, Bach flower medicine, reflexology, and yoga. I most typically use Indian traditional remedies with patients who have chronic disorders such as liver illnesses, arthritis, low back pain, gall stones, kidney stones, and dermatological ailments like psoriasis, etc. I have seen some of them get better, especially those with kidney stones who became completely asymptomatic, which I validated with an ultrasonogram. And I've seen Indian traditional medicine fail to cure thyroid-related illnesses and tumors. Patients who have strong confidence in alternative medicine improved more often than others.

7.1 Bach Flower Remedies

One form of complementary medicine that I have used often, and which has had positive outcomes in combination with Western treatments, is Bach flower remedies (BFRs). These are a widely available and popular type of complementary and alternative medicine created by British physician Dr. Edward Bach in the 1930s. Bach devoted his life to the development of thirty-eight medicines that correlate to thirty-eight different types of negative

---

42. Catholic Health Association of India (CHAI), *Annual Report 2018*, 3.

emotions. For example, the impatiens flower is used to address impatience and irritability; the mimulus flower treats fear of known things, shyness, and timidity; and the olive flower helps those who are drained of energy. In addition, some flower remedies are categorized as "type" remedies and are specific to a certain character trait or disposition. BFRs are thought to aid the body in healing itself by providing "a positive emotional state that is conducive to the restoration of a healthy equilibrium and by acting to catalyze an individual's own internal resources for maintaining balance."[43]

The negative emotional states addressed by BFRs include anxiety, uncertainty, lack of interest in current circumstances, loneliness, oversensitivity to influences and ideas, depression or despair, and excessive care for others' well-being. Based on the acute condition at hand, an individual patient is prescribed particular treatments that are carefully created and altered over the course of therapy, which often lasts weeks to months. Physical healing is enabled through decreasing negative sentiments and addressing the patient's underlying emotional and psychological difficulties. The potential for BFRs as a therapeutic agent for relieving pain does exist and is worthy of further qualitative and quantitative investigation. This must be done through robust, purpose-designed studies to replicate and progress the results shown here, according to a critical analysis investigating therapeutic value beyond the placebo effect and the potential of BFRs as a psychological method of pain relief.[44]

In my own experience, I cannot prove the effectiveness of flower remedies, since they address the emotional state of the person, which is subjective and experiential. However, I assessed the effectiveness through the feedback I received from patients about their wellness and symptom-free intervals, as well as through evidence of conception in two patients who had previously failed to conceive. The following are specific examples of my own personal experience treating patients successfully with different forms of Indian traditional medicine, including flower remedies.

7.1.1 Case No. 1

Mrs. X was a twenty-seven-year-old married woman who had been unable to conceive for six years and was anxious to do so. Her husband's medical evaluation was normal, and she was evaluated for the same polycystic ovarian disorder (PCOD) that was detected as the cause of her inability to conceive. For six months, she was treated for PCOD and infertility but did

---

43. Thaler et al., "Bach Flower Remedies," 16.
44. Howard, "Do Bach Flower Remedies Have a Role," 174–83.

not respond in any way. She was exceedingly concerned, hopeless, and impatient to conceive in the following months. As a complement to Western treatments, I offered flower remedies—specifically, the impatiens flower—to help her with the emotional issues, and she became pregnant after only thirty days of the flower remedies.

7.1.2 Case No. 2

Mrs. S. was a twenty-year-old female diagnosed with rheumatoid arthritis and prescribed high doses of steroids and hydroxychloroquine. Unable to tolerate this medicine, she was suffering from severe gastritis and vomiting, and she did not want to continue allopathic medicine. I referred her to an Ayurveda practitioner, and she began treatment within that system of medicine. Gradually, she was relieved of her symptoms and is doing well as of today.

7.1.3 Case No. 3

Married for six years, Mrs. Y presented with a history of primary infertility. She was evaluated and diagnosed with PCOD and treated for this for a year. When she did not conceive, her emotional status was addressed, as she was anxious and extremely devastated. Continuing the allopathic medicine, I also offered flower medicine and recommended meditation and Nama Japa[45] for her, and during the following month, she conceived.

On the whole, my experience with Indian traditional medicine is that it is effective in curing chronic diseases like arthritis, asthma, sinusitis, low back pain, and dermatological conditions. One of the most reported conditions leading to the use of non-Western medicine is chronic musculoskeletal pain caused by musculoskeletal disorders, a common cause of chronic pain and physical disability. Understanding how and why patients choose traditional medicine methods is important for chronic disease management.[46]

Several studies show that patients with specific chronic conditions use traditional medicine services more often, and in clinical practice, there are a number of conditions for which we find the allopathic system of treatment to be insufficient. A few of these include back problems, irritable bowel

---

45. Nama Japa is the meditative repetition of a divine name while performing other activities or as part of formal worship in group settings. The mantra or name may be spoken softly, loud enough for the practitioner to hear it, or it may be recited silently within the practitioner's mind.

46. Kavadar et al., "Use of Traditional and Complementary Medicine," 1509–71.

syndrome (IBS), asthma, postviral or chronic fatigue syndrome, skin illnesses, hepatitis, cancer, stress, and psychosomatic disorders. Alternative medicine may aid in the management of chronic conditions for which allopathic medicine has no cure.

8. The Effectiveness of Non-Western Medicine

Practitioners of Indian traditional medicine are frequently chastised for failing to conduct enough research to back up their claims of success. Rather than a corpus of proof as understood by Western medicine practitioners, the knowledge basis of the Indian medical system is primarily drawn from ancient wisdom. Unlike Western medicine, traditional Indian medicine and other non-Western systems are generally unsupported by scientific evidence. Because these practitioners use a holistic approach to treating sick people, they address physical, emotional, mental, spiritual, and environmental disorders all at the same time, rather than focusing on the disease as conventional allopathic medicine does. According to a comprehensive evaluation of thirty-four articles describing patient views of clinical treatment, complementary medicine consultations offered patients empathy, empowerment, and patient-centeredness.[47] However, when it comes to establishing evidence of efficacy, this holistic approach is problematic, because it is, by definition, at odds with the goal of the gold-standard clinical trial methodology, which is to reduce the treatment effect to a single, measurable metric.

9. The Central Council of Research

To close the evidence gap, in 1971, the Indian government established the Central Council of Research. There are four research councils that continue to initiate, guide, develop, and coordinate scientific research in different aspects of the respective systems, both fundamental and allied. Fully financed by the government of India, these councils are the apex bodies for research in the concerned systems of medicine. Their research activities have been reviewed to ensure that they have undertaken meaningful research under fixed parameters within the specified time period and have disseminated research findings for the benefit of educators, researchers, physicians, manufacturers, and the average person.

Because traditional medicine concentrates on the customized treatment of a person, an N-of-1 (or single-subject) trial may be a superior option

---

47. Foley and Steel, "Patient Perceptions of Clinical Care," 212–23.

for research. In this type of trial, a solitary patient is the lone unit of observation in assessing the efficacy or side effect profiles of various therapies.[48] A 2020 study on practice-based research in complementary medicine compares the randomized control trial (RCT) with single-case experimental designs (SCEDs), allowing non-Western medical practitioners to advance in the field of evidence-based medicine and exploring whether N-of-1 trials can become the new gold standard.[49] An N-of-1 randomized controlled trial is one in which random allocation is employed to decide the sequence in which an experimental and a control intervention are administered to a patient. The researcher can also change the order of the experimental and control interventions.

N-of-1 trials, along with the larger family of single-case experimental designs (SCEDs), are adaptable and may be well-suited to practitioners looking for the best therapy interventions for the full person, including those who aren't often included in clinical trials. While the development of an evidence base for non-Western medicine is fraught with difficulties, the N-of-1 trial design and the various versions of SCEDs may provide a mechanism to address many of these concerns. These study design families are ideal for holistic therapeutic practitioners who want to record proof of their practice's effectiveness.

As modern medicine progresses toward patient-centered care and an emphasis on personalized therapy, the N-of-1 study design is gaining popularity. According to the Oxford Centre for Evidence-Based Practice, Level One evidence is a systematic review of randomized trials or N-of-1 trials, and Level Two evidence is a randomized trial or observational research with dramatic effects. This elevation of the N-of-1 trial design is a significant step forward in favor of the therapeutic necessity of tailored patient care and in the shift away from statistical significance and population impact sizes provided by data obtained from mean differences between groups.[50]

10. Conclusion

Jesus cared for the sick, cured them of their illnesses, and thus gained for them human dignity and acceptance in their communities. And the whole Christian Church is called to this caring and curing ministry. As Pope Francis said in his message for the World Day of the Sick in 2018, "Jesus bestowed upon the Church his *healing* power. . . . The Church's mission is

---

48. Lillie et al., "N-of-1 Clinical Trial," 161–73.
49. Bradbury et al., "Practice-Based Research," 15.
50. Bradbury et al., "Practice-Based Research," 15.

a response to Jesus's gift, for she knows that she must bring to the sick the Lord's own gaze, full of tenderness and compassion. Health care ministry will always be a necessary and fundamental task, to be carried out with renewed enthusiasm by all, from parish communities to the . . . largest health care institutions."[51]

Following in the footsteps of Jesus, the holistic healer, Christians in India—doctors, nurses, and others involved in health care ministry—continue to undertake many new initiatives to make it possible for people who are suffering—especially for those on the fringes of the society—to be restored to physical, mental, and social well-being. This holistic well-being is in keeping with the WHO definition of health as involving the whole person—"a state of complete physical, mental, and social well-being and not merely the absence of disease or infirmity."[52]

Focusing on pathology and curing disease, Western medicine offers quick relief of symptoms and is highly effective in acute emergencies, but it is also reactive care that treats the disease and other ailments as the symptoms arise. Indian or alternative medicine, on the other hand, provides more preventative care. Connecting the body, mind, and spirit, it offers holistic healing.

Although it was Christianity that introduced India to Western medicine, in the recent past, the Catholic Church here has embraced both systems of medicine, promoting a combination of the two for common ailments and chronic illnesses. The factors that have influenced this integration include the inadequacy of the health care system in rural areas, the rich heritage of Indian traditional medicine, and strong cultural beliefs in Indian traditional medicine, as well as the experiences of empathy, empowerment, and patient-centeredness it offers during the treatment process. This holistic healing is part of Christ's mission, and the initiatives I've discussed in this chapter show how the Catholic Church in India is participating in that mission.

Bibliography

Amala Ayurvedic Hospital and Research Centre. "Why Amala?" https://www.amalaayurveda.org/about/why-amala.
Anshu, Arundhati, and Avinash N. Supe. "Evolution of Medical Education in India: The Impact of Colonialism." *Journal of Postgraduate Medicine* 62.4 (2016) 255–59. https://doi.org/10.4103%2F0022-3859.191011.

---

51. Francis, "Mater Ecclesiae," para. 6.
52. World Health Organization, "Constitution."

"Anti-AIDS Treatment Aims at Tolerating Virus." Down to Earth, August 15, 1993. https://www.downtoearth.org.in/coverage/antiaids-treatment-aims-at-tolerating-virus-31289.

Ayushya Centre for Healing and Integration. "About." https://www.ayushyamms.org/about-us.

Ayyanar, Muniappan. "Traditional Herbal Medicines for Primary Healthcare among Indigenous People in Tamil Nadu, India." *Journal of Homeopathy and Ayurvedic Medicine* 2.5 (2013). https://www.omicsonline.org/open-access-pdfs/traditional-herbal-medicines-for-primary-healthcare-among-indigenous-people-in-tamil-nadu-india-2167-1206.1000140.pdf.

Bodhi Zendo. "Zen Teachers." https://www.bodhisangha.net/index.php/en/zen-teachers.

Bradbury, Joanne, et al. "Practice-Based Research in Complementary Medicine Could N-of-1 Trials Become the New Gold Standard?" *Healthcare* 8.1 (2020) 15. https://www.mdpi.com/2227-9032/8/1/15.

Brockhaus, Hannah. "Pope Francis: Health Care Is Part of the Church's Mission." *Crux*, December 11, 2017. https://cruxnow.com/vatican/2017/12/pope-francis-health-care-part-churchs-mission.

Capuchin JPIC. "0001 Interview with Fr. Jacob, Sangamam Nature Cure Center, Trichy, India." YouTube video, 14:09, January 5, 2022. https://www.youtube.com/watch?v=MsXCK7C6C8E.

Catholic Health Association of India (CHAI). *Annual Report 2018*. Secunderabad, India: CHAI, 2018. https://chai-india.org/wp-content/uploads/2020/03/annual_report_2018.pdf.

Chokshi, Maulik, et al. "Health Systems in India." *Journal of Perinatology* 36 (2016) S9–S12. https://doi.org/10.1038/jp.2016.184.

Father Muller Homeopathic Medical College. "Vision and Mission." https://fathermuller.edu.in/homeopathic-college/vision-mission.php.

"First Alternative Medicine Hospital Run by the Sisters of Nazareth Opens in Bihar." *PIME AsiaNews*, April 22, 2016. https://www.asianews.it/news-en/First-alternative-medicine-hospital-run-by-the-Sisters-of-Nazareth-opens-in-Bihar-37304.html.

Foley, Hope, and Amie Steel. "Patient Perceptions of Clinical Care in Complementary Medicine: A Systematic Review of the Consultation Experience." *Patient Education and Counseling* 100.2 (2017) 212–23. https://www.sciencedirect.com/science/article/pii/S0738399116304438?via%3Dihub.

Fox, Bethany M. *Disability and the Way of Jesus: Holistic Healing in the Gospels and the Church*. Downers Grove, IL: IVP Academic, 2019.

Francis, Pope. "Mater Ecclesiae: 'Behold, your son . . . Behold, your mother. And from that hour, the disciple took her into his home.' (John 19:26–27)—Message of His Holiness Pope Francis for the Twenty-Sixth World Day of the Sick 2018." November 26, 2017. https://www.vatican.va/content/francesco/en/messages/sick/documents/papa-francesco_20171126_giornata-malato.html.

Fr. Francis Vineeth Vadakethala CMI. "About Fr. Vineeth." http://vineethcmi.in.

Gopichandran, Vijayaprasad, and Ch Satish Kumar. "Mainstreaming AYUSH: An Ethical Analysis." *Indian Journal of Medical Ethics* 4 (2012) 272–77. https://pubmed.ncbi.nlm.nih.gov/23099604.

Government of India's Ministry of Health. *Report of the Udupa K. N. Committee on Ayurveda Research Evaluation, 1958*. New Delhi: Ministry of Health, Government

of India, 1959. https://ruralindiaonline.org/en/library/resource/report-of-the-udupa-kn-committee-on-ayurveda-research-evaluation.
Hashir, Mohammad. "Research Opportunities in Unani/Greco-Arabian Medicine." *Journal of Drug Delivery and Therapeutics* 11.1 (2021) 152–55. https://jddtonline.info/index.php/jddt/article/view/4634.
Howard, Judy. "Do Bach Flower Remedies Have a Role to Play in Pain Control? A Critical Analysis Investigating Therapeutic Value Beyond the Placebo Effect, and the Potential of Bach Flower Remedies as a Psychological Method of Pain Relief." *Complementary Therapies in Clinical Practice* 3 (2007) 174–83. https://pubmed.ncbi.nlm.nih.gov/17631260.
Jacob, K. S. "NRHM, Addressing the Challenges." *The Hindu*, December 29, 2010. https://www.thehindu.com/opinion/lead/NRHM-addressing-the-challenges/article15612964.ece.
Jaiswal, Yogini S., and Leonard L. Williams. "A Glimpse of Ayurveda—The Forgotten History and Principles of Indian Traditional Medicine." *Journal of Traditional and Complementary Medicine* 7.1 (2017) 50–53. https://doi.org/10.1016/j.jtcme.2016.02.002.
Joshi, Kamakshi, and Subhash Kumar. "Role of Traditional Medicine in Improving the Socio-Economic Status of Rural and Urban India." *International Ayurvedic Medical Journal* 2.4 (2014) 591–95. https://iamj.in/posts/images/upload/591_604.pdf.
Kavadar, Gülis, et al. "Use of Traditional and Complementary Medicine for Musculoskeletal Diseases." *Turkish Journal of Medical Sciences* 49.3 (2019) 1509–71. https://journals.tubitak.gov.tr/medical/vol49/iss3/16/.
Lillie, Elizabeth O., et al. "The N-of-1 Clinical Trial: The Ultimate Strategy for Individualizing Medicine?" *Personalized Medicine* 8.2 (2011) 161–73. https://doi.org/10.2217/pme.11.7.
Mandapati, Prasanthi. "My Journey into the Divine." Sisters of Charity of Nazareth, November 30, 2023. https://nazareth.org/my-journey-into-the-divine.
Medical Mission Sisters North India. "Holistic Health Centre (HHC)." January 18, 2020. http://medicalmissionsistersnorthindia.in/holistic-health-centre/.
Mushtaq, Muhammad Umair. "Public Health in British India: A Brief Account of the History of Medical Services and Disease Prevention in Colonial India." *Indian Journal of Community Medicine* 34.1 (2009) 6–14. https://journals.lww.com/ijcm/fulltext/2009/34010/public_health_in_british_india__a_brief_account_of.3.aspx.
Niruja HealthTech. "Amala Ayurvedic Hospital, Kerala." https://www.nirujahealthtech.com/amala-ayurvedic-hospital-kerala/.
Rajkumar, Sahu, et al. "Survey of Tamil Siddha Manuscripts in Possession of Traditional Healers in Northern Tamil Nadu." *International Journal of Pharmacology and Clinical Sciences* 1.3 (September 2012) 68–73. https://www.ijphs.org/sites/default/files/IntJPharmacolClinSci_1_3_68.pdf.
Ravishankar, Basavaiah, and V. J. Shukla. "Indian Systems of Medicine: A Brief Profile." *African Journal of Traditional, Complementary, and Alternative Medicines* 4.3 (2007) 319–37. https://www.ajol.info/index.php/ajtcam/article/view/31226.
Robin, Arul Jesu. "The Healing Ministry of Jesus and Its Relevance for Consecrated Life." *Sanyasa Journal of Consecrated Life* 15.2 (2020) 207–29. https://sanyasa.com/wp-content/uploads/2022/10/5.-Sanyasa-Journal-July-2020.pdf.

Saini, Anu. "Physicians of Colonial India (1757–1900)." *Journal of Family Medicine and Primary Care* 5.3 (2016) 528–32. https://journals.lww.com/jfmpc/fulltext/2016/05030/physicians_of_colonial_india__1757_1900_.4.aspx.

Sen, Saikat, and Raja Chakraborty. "Revival, Modernization, and Integration of Indian Traditional Herbal Medicine in Clinical Practice: Importance, Challenges, and Future." *Journal of Traditional and Complementary Medicine* 7.2 (2016) 234–44. https://doi.org/10.1016/j.jtcme.2016.05.006.

Shankar, Darshan, and Bhushan Patwardhan. "AYUSH for New India: Vision and Strategy." *Journal of Ayurveda and Integrative Medicine* 8.3 (2017) 137–39. https://www.sciencedirect.com/science/article/pii/S0975947617305442?via%3Dihub.

Sharma, Hari. "Ayurveda: Science of Life, Genetics, and Epigenetics." *AYU* 37.2 (2016) 87–91. https://journals.lww.com/aayu/fulltext/2016/37020/ayurveda__science_of_life,_genetics,_and.2.aspx.

Sister Doctors Forum of India. "About Us." https://www.sisterdoctorsindia.org/about-us/.

Srinivasan, P. "National Health Policy for Traditional Medicine in India." *World Health Forum* 16.2 (1995) 190–93.

Srinivasan, Ramachandran, and V. Raji Sugumar. "Spread of Traditional Medicines in India: Results of National Sample Survey Organization's Perception Survey on Use of AYUSH." *Journal of Evidence-Based Complementary and Alternative Medicine* 22.2 (2017) 194–204. https://journals.sagepub.com/doi/10.1177/2156587215607673.

St. John's National Academy of Health Science. "Aim." https://www.cbci.in/st-johns.aspx.

Thaker, Swathi Nath. "The Sacred Cow: Understanding the Role of Culture in the Health-Related Behaviors of Older Asian Indian Immigrants." Presentation at the 50th Annual Adult Education Research Conference, Chicago, May 28–30, 2009. https://newprairiepress.org/aerc/2009/papers/64.

Thaler, Kylie, et al. "Bach Flower Remedies for Psychological Problems and Pain: A Systematic Review." *BMC Complementary and Alternative Medicine* 9 (2009) 16. https://bmccomplementmedtherapies.biomedcentral.com/articles/10.1186/1472-6882-9-16.

Vaidya, Ashok D. B., and Thomas P. A. Devasagayam. "Current Status of Herbal Drugs in India: An Overview." *Journal of Clinical Biochemistry and Nutrition* 41.1 (2007) 1–11. https://doi.org/10.3164/jcbn.2007001.

World Health Organization (WHO). "Constitution." 2023. https://www.who.int/about/governance/constitution.

———. "Noncommunicable Diseases" Fact Sheet. September 23, 2023. https://www.who.int/news-room/fact-sheets/detail/noncommunicable-diseases.

———. *WHO Traditional Medicine Strategy, 2014–2023*. Geneva: WHO, 2013. https://www.who.int/publications/i/item/9789241506096.

PART FOUR

Catholic Partnerships Between the Global North and Global South

10

Responding to the Call to Go Forth: Embracing Accompaniment in the Catholic Medical Mission Model

Susan Nedza, MD

Introduction

I AM HONORED TO have the opportunity in this chapter to share my perspective on how it was possible for a Catholic, laity-led, charitable entity to move from offering a traditional short-term medical mission model to one of accompaniment. It also must be asked: Why might such a conversion be necessary?

Each year, thousands of Catholics of all ages set out to experience the provision of health care in low-income countries. These short-term trips go by many names—solidarity trips, medical brigades, university-sponsored alternative spring break trips, and medical missions. People travel alone or with a group of classmates, families, parishes, hospitals, or medical specialists. In most cases the members of these groups are strangers seeking the same experience. They have two things in common—their Catholic faith and a belief that they can relieve suffering through a short-term engagement focused on providing medical services of the kind offered in the US.

The goal of this chapter is to examine how a Catholic, laity-led charitable entity from the US might choose to move beyond a colonial model of nonsurgical medical mission trips to a model of accompaniment; in other words, adopting a model that maximizes the value of such trips to participants and minimizes harm to the community they are intended to serve, all while maintaining their Catholicity. Such a change requires thoughtful self-examination, which should focus on three strategic questions:

- Is there a role for a Catholic, laity-led, faith-based entity to participate in meeting the health care needs of a local community?
- If there is a role for such an entity, how can it ensure that the missionary discipleship of the individuals who participate in its activities is centered on accompanying the community it serves?
- Should the focus of the mission shift toward health and prevention and away from a Western model of health care interventions?

This essay is organized into three sections. The first section focuses on the current model for short-term engagements in global health, reviewing relevant literature that outlines current thinking about such endeavors. It discusses the coalescence of views around the need for a new model of engagement and accompaniment. The second addresses the process of developing a better model. It examines the currently successful model of Partners in Health and is guided by the content of documents penned by Jorge Bergoglio/Pope Francis during his tenure as the archbishop of Buenos Aires and his papacy. These texts include the Aparecida Document, the apostolic exhortation *Evangelii Gaudium,* and the encyclical letter *Laudato Si'*. The final section discusses how an entity might take action to implement the new model for short-term engagements in global health and closes with a discussion of the challenges that might arise from such implementation.

I. Short-Term Engagements in Global Health

a. Socks and Beans

Several years ago, a medical mission team working in eastern Guatemala was seeing hundreds of patients every day. When they sat down to dinner, a group of resident physicians marveled at the number of patients they had seen that day. As the conversation drifted, the group recognized that neck pain was a common complaint among the women they treated. The group began to congratulate itself for the ingenious way they had treated the women for this complaint.

This treatment included stretching exercises and a two-week supply of the nonsteroidal anti-inflammatory drug (NSAID) ibuprofen. They dispensed modified tube socks that had been filled with beans earlier in the trip by a group of nonmedical volunteers. The patients were to place the sock as a heating pad on their neck as needed. The volunteer interpreters, some of whom were college students, would then dutifully translate instructions into Spanish and provide a written copy of the instructions. This interaction concluded with asking the patient if she had any questions. The answer invariably was "no, gracias." That night the Americans celebrated these outcomes. They were proud of their ability to relieve pain and to resolve what they perceived as simple medical problems for these patients.

A Spanish-speaking physician and leader of the group overheard the conversation and came to a different conclusion. Earlier in the clinic, one of the women who had received these instructions approached this physician with the bean-filled sock and asked her, "Why, when clothing and food are in short supply, would doctors suggest this?" The physician simply repeated the instructions and stated it would help to relieve her pain. The patient nodded her head in affirmation, and then requested a second bean bag. She received the second bean-filled sock and left the clinic happy about the outcome of the interaction—she now had a pair of socks for her son and beans for dinner the next day.

The physician turned away and engaged in another conversation without giving the woman's question much thought. The following morning when the group was driven out of the city in their air-conditioned motor coach, it happened to pass a group of women trudging up a dusty side road. The same physician saw these women carefully climbing the hill to their village all the while balancing large water jugs on their heads.

Like Saint Paul on the road to Damascus, the physician leader's belief in the value of the work the group had done had been struck down. It was only when the blindness resolved that the truth was revealed—the treatment for the neck pain was not medications, exercises, and improvised bean bags, but access to clean water.

I was that physician. Fifteen years later and after many more medical mission trips, I had become the leader of a Catholic NGO in Honduras, and I was called to act upon what I had learned that day in Guatemala.

b. Defining a Short-Term Engagement in Global Health

It is a challenge to give a name to, identify the participants in, and recognize the scope of a typical short-term medical mission trip. For the purposes of this essay, the term "short-term engagement in global health" (STEGH) will be used to describe short-term medical missions that are not surgical in nature. This designation has been promulgated by the collaborative Advocacy for Global Health Partnerships[1] and has been accepted by many entities involved in this work, including the Catholic Health Association of the United States (CHA).

Who participates and how? Just as the work of these excursions varies, so does the type of sponsor. A sponsor may be a charity, a faith-based foundation, a partnership, a nongovernmental organization (NGO), or a for-profit entity. Unfortunately, it is not unusual for these trips to be operated by global "voluntour" travel companies targeting college students, affluent families, and church groups. They tend to focus on the volunteer experience or an opportunity to bolster a college application or practice skills that they are not licensed to provide in the US. Preparation for the volunteers is often focused on immunizations and packing, not on cultural awareness, spiritual formation, or language skills. In this paper, all of these different kinds of sponsoring organizations will be referred to as "entities."

How much do these STEGHs cost? In a 2012 study, Maki et al. cited the work of Robert Wuthnow, who in 2008 used an internet search to identify 543 independent faith-based STEGHs. Wuthnow estimated that these trips generated $250 million in expenditures in one year.[2] Thirteen years later, the number of trips, participants, and destinations undertaken by Catholics or sponsored by Catholic entities remains unknown. However, it is possible to identify a small subset of STEGH experiences targeted at Catholic university students. These trips are organized by Global Brigades, Inc., a family-owned nonprofit that offers university students a chance to self-organize as medical brigades.[3] A review of its website in 2020 identified eighteen Catholic universities in which student-driven brigades facilitate participation in one- to two-week trips around the world. It is unclear if the universities are aware of, or sanction, this independent entity or others like it. This subset does not capture campus ministry–sponsored trips or those that are required for credit. This example is used to illustrate the participation of outside global entities in offering experiences to students in Catholic universities.

What is the scope of a typical STEGH? A typical nonsurgical STEGH usually consists of a one- or two-week experience in which volunteers, licensed health care professionals, those in training, and other individuals provide services in a low-income country.[4] They might work to screen

1. Advocacy for Global Health Partnerships, "About Us."
2. Maki et al., "Health Impact," 135.
3. Global Brigades, "Vision and Mission."
4. Martiniuk et al., "Brain Gains," 6.

adults and children, provide instruction on dental and personal hygiene, or perform clinical examinations. These encounters often end with dispensing a limited supply of medications brought from the US. These medications commonly include antiparasitic medications, vitamins, NSAIDs, and more recently, medications for treating hypertension or diabetes.

STEGHs are infrequently designed in consultation with the local community and they do not reliably connect patients to private or government health services. Groups often return to the same community each year and provide the same services. The cost for the trips tends to be the responsibility of volunteers, is often consumed by travel and lodging, and rarely trickles down to the community.

c. Criticism of the Model

In 2015, the Catholic Health Association of the United States (CHA) published *Guiding Principles for Conducting International Health Activities* in order to describe its international charitable mission in response to an increasing number of requests by employees to support medical mission efforts. The guide was based upon the results of a survey of Catholic hospitals and other entities involved in the provision of STEGHs.[5]

The findings of these surveys were in alignment with earlier research findings and further work done by Lasker.[6] STEGHs were designed based upon a colonial, paternalistic savior model, uninformed by actual community needs, dependent upon donations by individuals, disconnected from local health care systems, and lacking a means of measuring outcomes at the community level.

Criticism of these and other volunteer endeavors in Latin America is not new. In a famous 1968 address, "To Hell with Good Intentions" at the Conference on InterAmerican Student Projects, Ivan Illich delivered a stark message suggesting that North American volunteer armies should withdraw from Mexico. He closed with the statement, "Come to look, come to climb our mountains, to enjoy our flowers. Come to study. But do not come to help."[7] This message was in direct conflict with church-led efforts to recruit lay volunteers to work in Central America.

In 2007, Professor Laura Montgomery, an anthropologist and theologian working in Central America, spoke directly to the issue of short-term medical missions. Her opinion had not changed since 1993 when she

---

5. Compton et al., "Short-Term Medical Mission Trips," 77.
6. Lasker et al., "Guidelines," 8.
7. Illich, "To Hell with Good Intentions."

concluded that "short-term medical missions as currently constituted are neither the most appropriate nor the most effective means of providing health care or improving health status, regardless of the good intentions of those who plan, support, or participate in them."[8]

The voices suggesting revision of the model include theologians, medical leaders, and medical educators, and they have become stronger over time. A global consensus has emerged that the prevailing model of STEGH creates very few positive community outcomes and may cause harm. CHA has taken a leading role in promoting an alternative model through its active involvement in the Advocacy for Global Health Partnerships. CHA has embraced the principles outlined in the Brocher Declaration, which, among other things recommends that "global health engagements should be sustainable, asset based, bidirectional, adhere to appropriate legal standard and be adequately evaluated."[9]

This brief review of the shortcomings of the current model and of the voices of Catholic and other global commentators should cause entities to ask themselves the question of whether they should be in the STEGH business at all.

II. Developing a Better Model

The process of developing a better model for STEGHs requires two steps. It should begin with an examination of a proven model, followed by a separate, careful examination of its alignment with Catholic Social Teaching to ensure its adherence to its Catholicity and links to the local church. This second step is critical because without the influence and accompaniment of the local church, STEGHs will become what Pope Francis, in his first homily after election to pope, warned about: "Without faith in Christ's sacrifice on the cross, the church is nothing more than a 'pitiful NGO' focused on plans and projects."[10] The remainder of this chapter will attempt to answer a number of questions set forth in italics.

---

8. Montgomery, "Reinventing Short Term Medical Missions," 103.

9. Advocacy for Global Health Partnerships, Brocher Declaration. The AGHP website explains that "to build consensus amongst various stakeholders, AGHP arranged for a multi-party conference sponsored by Foundation Brocher to be held in Geneva, Switzerland in May 2020. This has been postponed due to the ongoing COVID19 pandemic. The 'Brocher Declaration' was to be launched at the conference. In lieu of a formal launch, AGHP held a series of priming conference calls and follow up conversations with stakeholders from around the world." The Declaration has been signed by numerous organizations active in the field.

10. Rocca, "Pope Francis," para. 1.

a. Reflection on a Proven Engagement Model

Is there a role for an entity led by the laity in addressing health care needs in the community? Any effort to reimagine its role and to predict the likelihood of success by a Catholic entity should begin with an examination of Partners in Health (PIH), the secular, international NGO founded by Dr. Paul Farmer and his colleagues in 1987. Although it is a secular entity, its mission was directly informed by Dr. Farmer's exposure to liberation theology and later by his personal friendship with Fr. Gustavo Gutiérrez. The mission of PIH is clearly informed by the tenets of Catholic social teaching, as illustrated by its embrace of the principles of accompaniment, solidarity, and subsidiarity. In a commencement address at Harvard University's Kennedy School of Government, Farmer elaborated on how PIH interprets the concept of accompaniment. "To accompany someone is to go somewhere with him or her, to break bread together, to be present on a journey with a beginning and an end. There's an element of mystery, of openness, of trust in accompaniment. The companion, the *accompagnateur* says: 'I'll go with you and support you on your journey wherever it leads. I'll share your fate for a while'—and by 'a while,' I don't mean a little while. Accompaniment is about sticking with a task until it's deemed completed—not by the *accompagnateur*, but by the person being accompanied."[11]

PIH explicitly states that its mission "is to provide a preferential option for the poor in health care." PIH accomplishes its work by establishing long-term relationships with local sister entities operating in settings of poverty and with national governments in order to bring the benefits of modern medical science to those most in need of them and to serve as an antidote to despair.[12] PIH is committed to equity. Its mission statement continues: "We draw on the resources of the world's leading medical and academic institutions and on the lived experience of the world's poorest and sickest communities. At its root, our mission is medical and moral. It is based on solidarity, rather than charity alone."[13]

It is unlikely that entities engaging in this self-examination will even contemplate replicating the PIH model as a whole. Yet this examination clearly points to the need for partnerships and sustainable goals. It is also informative to recognize what PIH does not do: provide services with untrained volunteers, distribute obsolete equipment, or provide drug samples that are nearing their expiration date.

---

11. Farmer, *To Repair the World*, 234.
12. Partners in Health, "Our Mission."
13. Partners in Health, "Our Mission."

There is a direct link between the mission of PIH and the principles set out in the Brocher Declaration. These principles state that STEGHs should embrace

- creating mutual partnerships with host communities with bidirectional input and learning;
- empowering host country–defined and community-defined needs and activities;
- focusing on constructing sustainable programs and capacity building;
- complying with applicable laws, ethical standards, and codes of conduct;
- fostering humility, cultural sensitivity, and respect for all involved; and
- accepting accountability for actions taken.[14]

b. Reflection on Catholic Social Teaching

Three documents penned by Pope Francis (Jorge Bergoglio), first in his role as archbishop of Buenos Aires and then after his election as pope, can provide guidance: the concluding document of the 2007 general conference of the Conference of Bishops of Latin America and the Caribbean (CELAM), commonly referred to as the Aparecida Document; the 2013 apostolic exhortation *Evangelii Gaudium*; and the 2015 papal encyclical, *Laudato Si'*. These documents were chosen for this exercise for three reasons: 1) they reflect the Latin American sensibility and experience that is a constant in the writings of Francis; 2) they refer to the same time period as the history of the involvement of STEGH entities in Central America; and 3) they are accessible to a lay reader. Each is directed at a different STEGH stakeholder: Aparecida at the leaders of the church and its people in Latin America; *Evangelii Gaudium* to the global church; and *Laudato Si'* "to every person living on the planet."[15]

1. *The Aparecida Document*

Pope Francis, then Cardinal Jorge Bergoglio, authored the Aparecida Document in his role as the president of the commission that drafted the final document. At its core, Aparecida reflects upon the call to missionary

---

14. Advocacy for Global Health Partnerships, Brocher Declaration.
15. Francis, *Laudato Si'*, 3.

discipleship. It is deeply informed by the journey of the Latin American church, stating in no uncertain terms that "the preferential option for the poor is one of the distinguishing features of our Latin American and Caribbean Church."[16] Aparecida's focus on missionary discipleship facilitates its use in reflecting on preparation of the laity, the responsibility of parishes, and a Catholic university's mission to teach and emulate missionary discipleship.

What is required for the formation of the laity? The Aparecida Document recognizes that "it is laymen and laywomen who carry out their evangelizing responsibility in forming Christian communities in building the Kingdom of God in the world."[17] This can be interpreted in the setting of global evangelization—lay Catholics should participate in efforts to build the bonds of community across the world. The document continues: "We emphasize that the formation of lay men and women must contribute primarily to an activity as missionary disciples in the world, from the standpoint of dialogue and transformation of society."[18] This is relevant for any entity considering the need for formation of those seeking to participate in a STEGH. It serves as a reminder that if participants are to have a significant impact, there is a need for unique formation for those in specialized fields like health care.

What should be the role of parishes in fostering a commitment to missionary discipleship? Entities providing mission experiences in the US often host parish-based groups. This provides them an opportunity to facilitate the call for parishes to become a community of communities: "The call for a renewal of parishes includes the need to foster participation in pastoral projects which go beyond an individual parish and alert to the world around them."[19] A specific call to "renewal of parishes at the outset of the third millennium requires reformulating its structures so that it may be a network of communities and groups, capable of being linked to one another, so that their members feel like they really are disciples and missionaries of Jesus Christ in communion."[20] This statement supports the conclusion that an entity engaged in Catholic mission must fulfill the need of parishes to form communities with parishes across international boundaries and to foster conversation and community among them.

---

16. CELAM, *Concluding Document*, 391.
17. CELAM, *Concluding Document*, 76.
18. CELAM, *Concluding Document*, 97.
19. CELAM, *Concluding Document*, 170.
20. CELAM, *Concluding Document*, 172.

Should Catholic universities be engaged in the provision of STEGHs? Youth seeking a missionary experience are often enrolled in Catholic colleges and universities. As the Aparecida Document recognizes, "The fundamental activities of a Catholic university must be linked and harmonized with the Church's evangelizing mission.... This entails a professional training that includes ethical values and the dimension of service to people and society [and] dialogue with the culture, which fosters better understanding and transmission of the faith."[21] It goes on to elaborate that "there must be a university ministry accompanying the life and journey of all members of the university community, promoting personal and committed encounter with Jesus Christ and multiple solidarity and missionary initiatives."[22] This is a call to entities providing STEGH to invite universities into partnerships that provide missionary opportunities for students and faculty to help fulfill the institution's Catholic mission.

2. *Evangelii Gaudium*

How does an organization ensure that the missionary discipleship of the individuals who participate in its activities is centered on accompanying the community it serves? Engagement with *Evangelii Gaudium* sheds light on how to strengthen and rebalance the relationship between participants in the STEGH and the local community. In this apostolic exhortation Francis speaks directly to the motivation of participants, the central tenet of serving the poor, and the need for long-term commitment.

What should be the motivation of the participants? What is the gift they receive? Is the act of going on a STEGH one of heroism or service? Francis reminds us: "Though it is true that this mission demands great generosity on our part, it would be wrong to see it as a heroic individual undertaking for it is first and foremost the Lord's work, surpassing anything which we can see and understand."[23] His perspective reminds an organization that its true calling is not to provide a *mission experience* for participants but a *mission engagement*.

What can serving the poor teach us? In *Evangelii Gaudium*, Francis explains the value of adopting a special option for the poor. "This is why I want a Church which is poor and for the poor. They have much to teach us. Not only do they share in the *sensus fidei* but in their difficulties they know

---

21. CELAM, *Concluding Document*, 341.
22. CELAM, *Concluding Document*, 343.
23. Francis, *Evangelii Gaudium*, 12.

the suffering Christ. We need to let ourselves be evangelized by them."[24] Participants often envision STEGHs as an opportunity to teach, to provide services, or to learn skills that will further their educational and professional endeavors. Francis reminds us that it is better to recognize that participants are acting as church, and that they must embrace their own poverty of knowledge and experience if they are to be rewarded.

How long is long enough? The scriptural passage, "Stay with us, for it is nearly evening, and the day is almost over" (Luke 24:29, NABR) is a call to accompany others, to promote openness to being evangelized by those we are serving, and to reconsider the length of service. Francis answers the question of how long is necessary: "An evangelizing community is also supportive, standing by people at every step of the way, no matter how difficult or lengthy this may prove to be."[25] This passage serves as an admonishment to any entity that supports visits to communities on a sporadic basis. True commitment includes developing and funding local staff or partnerships that are dedicated to long-term accompaniment.

There is always a risk that any Catholic organization involved in the provision of STEGHs will become a "pitiful NGO" focused on plans and projects. The only way to avoid this is through accompaniment with the local church community and dedication to keeping Christ's sacrifice on the cross at the heart of the mission. It is the suffering of the people who are served that will teach participants that they are not heroes, but humble servants.

In *Evangelii Gaudium,* Pope Francis calls organizations working on the peripheries to a commitment to provide participants with an encounter with the poor, an engagement in their lives, and a commitment to long-term accompaniment. This requires the encouragement of humility, fostering an openness to witnessing the suffering of the poor, and embracing a commitment to staying for more than a few weeks.

3. Laudato Si'

Should the focus of the mission shift toward health and prevention and away from the Western model of health care interventions? Laudato Si' speaks directly to the relationship between health and health care.

It is difficult to improve human health without addressing the factors that lead to poor health. But in practical terms, it is not clear whether a Catholic entity with finite resources should focus on health or health care. It

---

24. Francis, *Evangelii Gaudium,* 198.
25. Francis, "*Evangelii Gaudium,* 24."

is necessary to consider the impact of the environment on the community, the potential impact of traditional Western treatments on conditions suffered by the population, and the role of health care technology in addressing health care needs.

What is the likelihood of improving the health of individuals without addressing environmental issues? Is it enough to focus on teaching dental hygiene or dispensing medications in a country stripped of trees that were harvested for flooring in high-income countries or crisscrossed by rivers teeming with parasites and poisoned by heavy metals left from unregulated mines? Is it enough to teach diabetics about a healthy diet in a country blanketed in soil depleted from decades of churning out pineapples and bananas for foreign markets? Is it enough to screen children for malnutrition when their families live in visibly drought-ravaged places? The answer to these questions is clearly no.

Francis speaks of the need to embrace an ecology of daily life. "Authentic development includes efforts to bring about an integral improvement in the quality of human life, and this entails considering the setting in which people live their lives."[26] It is difficult to avoid concluding that any Catholic entity trying to develop a health care model in alignment with Catholic principles must do so in the context of local environments.

Is the provision of health care services enough? Francis reminds Catholic entities that "the fragmentation of knowledge proves helpful for concrete applications, and yet it often leads to a loss of appreciation for the whole, for the relationships between things, and for the broader horizon, which then becomes irrelevant. This very fact makes it hard to find adequate ways of solving the more complex problems of today's world, particularly those regarding the environment and the poor; these problems cannot be dealt with from a single perspective or from a single set of interests."[27] Health care professionals are important missionary disciples, yet intermittent visits and the exercise of specialized skills and knowledge are not enough to make a sustainable impact. It takes a diverse group of people that reflects the church to share in the work of missionary discipleship.

Is incorporating technical solutions enough? Technology can be used to improve pre-mission processes, the capture of data during an engagement, communications to address the need to work with the receiving community (via online video link), and post-trip surveys (using online survey tools). But is the embrace of technology enough to transform the model for STEGHs? Pope Francis warns that "merely technical solutions run the risk

---

26. Francis, *Laudato Si'*, 231.
27. Francis, *Laudato Si'*, 110.

of addressing symptoms and not the more serious underlying problems."[28] Dependence on technology increases the risk that a Catholic entity will adopt short-term solutions that may impact the process of care but will be unlikely to improve the health of the community or address environmental problems associated with poor health.

c. Summary

Examination of the PIH model and reflection on the chosen documents reveals that it is feasible to meet the needs of a Catholic entity hoping to convert from providing STEGHs based upon a colonial model to one that embraces a model of accompaniment. This process will facilitate the choice between suspending this work or transforming it in response to Francis's admonition that "it is useless to ask a seriously injured person if he has high cholesterol and about the level of his blood sugars! You have to heal the wounds. Then we can talk about everything else. Heal the wounds, heal the wounds. . . . And you have to start from the ground up."[29] The method recommended in this paper allows Catholic entities to begin from the ground-up and remain grounded in Catholic Social Teaching and in the community they serve.

III. Taking Action

In *Evangelii Gaudium*, Francis warns about committing the sin of *habri-aqueísmo*, which can be interpreted as focusing on what we have to do but omitting the work of making it a reality. "We waste time talking about 'what needs to be done'—like spiritual masters and pastoral experts who give instructions from on high."[30] Catholic entities that have the tools should undertake a self-examination and execute a plan to act upon this examination. There is no role in leadership for those who solely pronounce the words "make it so." An entity is called *to act*, either by suspending its work in this area or by working toward a conversion to the new model of engagement. *The exercise does not end with the decision.*

For some entities, the process will come to an end because the only feasible action is to suspend providing STEGHs that are unlikely to improve health and may harm individuals or their communities. Others will find

---

28. Francis, *Laudato Si'*, 98.
29. Spadaro, "Big Heart," para. 51.
30. Francis, *Evangelii Gaudium*, 96.

that they have the capability to embrace the new model. They will need a detailed plan of action prior to embarking on the journey. Although the development of a detailed plan of action is beyond the scope of this paper, it must be stated that the next step is to seek affirmation of this decision before proceeding. This should begin with thoughtful conversations with participants, donors, parishes, and staff, as well as the local receiving diocese. Successful transformation is a community effort not to be undertaken without the blessing of the participating entities in the US. At the same time, engagement with the receiving communities and local church officials is necessary to understand how they see what is needed, to gain their insight into best approaches, and to build consensus on the means of measuring outcomes.

Current Status

The Olancho Aid Foundation (OAF) is grounded in the soil of Latin America. It was founded over twenty-five years ago by a US diocesan priest working in rural Honduras. He emphasized the need for the organization to focus on educational initiatives and to be led by Hondurans who knew their own needs. Over time, US volunteers and funding organizations began to expand the mission based on their own ideas of what was needed in the community. It was this expansion that led to the adoption of the traditional medical mission model. Thus, it was necessary to find a balance between the desires of the North Americans seeking opportunities to participate in health care engagements and those of the community. This rebalancing was intentionally informed by texts written by those with Latin American blood in their veins and directly influenced by personal experiences in the region. A new approach to volunteer engagement beyond short-term medical missions was necessary.

Leadership embraced Henri J. M. Nouwen's feeling expressed in the foreword to the twentieth anniversary edition of Gustavo Gutiérrez's *We Drink from Our Own Wells*. Nouwen wrote, "I am increasingly struck by the thought that what is happening in the Christian communities of Latin America is part of God's way of calling us in the North to conversion." He continued, "I even feel that knowing God in North America can no longer be separated from the way God is making himself known in Latin America."[31]

After reflection, OAF made the difficult decision to suspend its medical mission program. Honduran leadership within the organization and members of the local community agreed. The board of directors also chose

---

31. Nouwen, "Foreword," xv.

to endorse the Brocher Declaration as a sign of their commitment to adopt its principles should they choose to reengage in STEGHs.

This discernment resulted in the revision of OAF's programs that provide opportunities for North Americans to encounter the people of Honduras. Volunteer engagement was reimagined within the context of a redefined mission. The focus shifted to accompanying the community through projects and encounters that help families to stay well, to stay together, and to have the option of staying at home in an economically sustainable community.

This refocused mission resulted in a shift from a program that once allowed volunteers to dispense a month's supply of medications for diabetes to one that has volunteers working at The Agape Farm, a site that grows lettuce in an effort to improve the community's diet. This farm and ongoing clean water projects will provide volunteers the opportunity to engage in vocational training for individuals with disabilities. In 2022, a program will be launched that provides students, teachers, and pastoral associates a chance to personally experience the effects of climate change on a vulnerable community. This program is being launched in the belief that once visitors see and feel the impact of global warming firsthand, they will be more prepared to engage in efforts to adopt the integral ecology outlined by Pope Francis in *Laudato Si'*.

The organization is full of hope and looking forward to welcoming North Americans back to Honduras to help carry out its commitment to improve the health of the community.

IV. Conclusion

In this essay I have illustrated how a US laity-led charitable Catholic entity might choose to move beyond a colonial model of medical mission trips to one of accompaniment. Such a model maximizes the value to participants and minimizes the harm to the community, while simultaneously maintaining its Catholicity. It moves, in other words, from a colonial or paternalistic model to one of accompaniment.

In the first section, I discussed how a Catholic entity involved in offering medical mission experiences for US groups and individuals must first see its model in the context of recommendations for change being promulgated by both Catholic and secular entities involved in STEGHs. The discussion in the second section illustrated how the successful entity Partners in Health has embraced accompaniment and how proceedings, papal exhortations, and encyclicals could be used to support the discernment process. The Aparecida Document was chosen to inform the involvement of laity-led Catholic entities in STEGHs in the Latin American context. *Evangelii Gaudium* provides guidance on ensuring that the missionary discipleship of participants is focused on accompanying the community they serve. *Laudato Si'* provides guidance on the need to answer the call to focus not just on the Western model of disease intervention, but to embrace the work of supporting the health of our common home.

The final section provided an example of how one Catholic entity chose to act when it recognized that it could not simply convert its traditional STEGH into an accompaniment model that embraced missionary discipleship and kept Christ at the center of its mission. The section concluded with an example of a new model for volunteer engagement that has been widely embraced.

I close on a hopeful note. OAF survived the early parts of the pandemic through the assistance of donors. These individuals, parishes, and foundations generously responded to a temporary broadening of its mission to include supplying food to employees, families, and the parishes it serves. In 2022, individuals and parish-led groups have committed to return to Honduras to participate in the revised volunteer engagement program.

Bibliography

Advocacy for Global Health Partnerships. "About Us." https://www.ghpartnerships.org.
———. Brocher Declaration. https://www.ghpartnerships.org/brocher.
Catholic Health Association of the United States of America. *Guiding Principles for Conducting International Health Activities*, 2022. https://www.chausa.org/internationaloutreach/guiding-principles.
Compton, Bruce, et al. "Short-Term Medical Mission Trips: Phase I Research Findings." *Health Progress* 96.6 (November–December 2014) 72–77.
Conference of Bishops of Latin America and the Caribbean (CELAM). *Concluding Document, Aparecida, May 13–31, 2007*, edited by Jorge Mario Bergoglio. Washington, DC: US Conference of Catholic Bishops, 2008. https://www.celam.org/aparecida/Ingles.pdf.
Farmer, Paul. *To Repair the World: Paul Farmer Speaks to the Next Generation*. Edited by Jonathan Weigel. Berkeley: University of California Press, 2013.
Francis, Pope. *Evangelii Gaudium: On the Joy of the Gospel*. Vatican City: Libreria Editrice Vaticana, November 24, 2013. http://www.vatican.va/holy_father/francesco/apost_exhortations/documents/papa-francesco_esortazione-ap_20131124_evangelii-gaudium_en.html.
———. *Laudato Si': On the Care of Our Common Home*. Vatican City: Libreria Editrice Vaticana, May 25, 2015. http://w2.vatican.va/content/francesco/en/encyclicals/documents/papa-francesco_20150524_enciclica-laudato-si.html.
Global Brigades. "Vision and Mission." https://www.globalbrigades.org/about-us/vision-mission/.

Illich, Ivan. "To Hell with Good Intentions." Conference on Interamerican Student Projects, Cuernavaca, Mexico, April 20, 1968. http://ciasp.ca/CIASPhistory/IllichCIASPspeech.htm.

Lasker, Judith, et al. "Guidelines for Responsible Short-Term Global Health Activities: Developing Common Principles." *Global Health* 14 (2018) 1–9.

Maki, Jesse, et al. "Health Impact Assessment and Short-Term Medical Missions: A Methods Study to Evaluate Quality of Care." BMC *Health Services Research* 8 (June 2008). https://doi:10.1186/1472-6963-8-121.

Martiniuk, Alexandra L. C., et al. "Brain Gains: A Literature Review of Medical Missions to Low and Middle-Income Countries." *BMC Health Services Research* 12.1 (2012) 1–8.

Montgomery, L. M. "Reinventing Short-Term Medical Missions in Latin America. *Journal of Latin American Theology* 2.2 (2007) 83–103.

Nouwen, Henri J. M. "Foreword." In *We Drink from Our Own Wells: The Spiritual Journey of a People*, by Gustavo Gutiérrez, vii–xv. Translated by Matthew J. O'Connell. Maryknoll, NY: Orbis, 2003.

Partners in Health. "Our Mission." https://www.pih.org/our-mission.

Rocca, Francis X. "Pope Francis: Without Faith in Christ, Church Is Just 'Pitiful NGO.'" Angelus, March 14, 2013. https://angelusnews.com/news/us-world/pope-francis-without-faith-in-christ-church-is-just-pitiful-ngo.

Spadaro, Antonio. "A Big Heart Open to God: An Interview with Pope Francis." *America Magazine*, September 30, 2013. https://www.americamagazine.org/faith/2013/09/30/big-heart-open-god-interview-pope-francis.

11

Fields, Forms of Capital, and Power in a Global North-South Health Partnership: Lessons from Ecuador

DAVID GAUS, MD, MPH/TM, DIEGO HERRERA, MD, AND FRANK HUTCHINS

Introduction

THE INTERFACE BETWEEN GOOD intentions and bad faith often involves a tempest of frustrations, accusations, and disappointments. This is certainly true for development projects, among which are global health initiatives scattered around the globe. The fuel for such flare-ups is often identified as corruption and dirty politics. David Clarke, writing about corruption as a "significant" problem in global health care, said it contributed to an estimated one hundred and forty thousand child deaths, global health financial losses estimated at 6.19 percent of total global health expenditures, and procurement losses for medicines and vaccines of 10–25 percent.[1] But certainly most of these situations are more complicated than a good guys/bad guys scenario. The following chapter uses a case study to explore how social relations, meanings, and power—particularly those pertaining to the hegemonic Western medical model—reflect a reality that exists between

1. Clarke, "Changing the Conversation."

good intentions and corruption. It emphasizes place dynamics, and analyzes these by applying Bourdieu's concepts of fields, capital, and habitus to develop a more nuanced sense of place. Special attention is given to a theological approach that emphasizes spiritual capital as a potentially important component in the local field. The case study reveals friction between a health NGO in Ecuador and the community where it built a small rural hospital and clinic, with the local church and priest—controlling significant spiritual capital—playing a pivotal role. The conclusion recognizes multifaceted interests and power relations that influence nearly every aspect of a health care project, and that have no doubt derailed more than one such initiative.

Although the project discussed here ultimately identified and successfully overcame power-related problems, there was a steep learning curve that involved a better understanding of social relations and meanings that emerge from distinct places. It also resulted in a deeper appreciation of how the hegemonic Western medical model exerts force on specific places. The authors use Bourdieu's concepts to discuss what they have learned about sociopolitical dynamics that impact health care in rural communities in a low-income country. The overarching argument is that place is not just constitutive of health conditions and outcomes, but of basic structural factors that impact both of these. Health care projects can face an especially perilous pathway to acceptance because place meanings and social relations are interwoven with politics, religion, economics, and cultural elements.

Fields, Forms of Capital, and Power

Bourdieu's ideas about the circulation of power and influence through particular social settings offer a pathway of analysis that is woven into the wide latitudes given to individual agency and into the boundedness of social structures. These social settings are, for Bourdieu, "fields" of action and interaction with dynamics with an internal logic familiar to those who are regular "players" in that social, political, and economic space.[2] The players are neither free to act as they please, nor are they programmed or disciplined to act in a totally predictable manner. Knowing the rules of the game (whether it be in politics, education, arts, religion, or business) means that they can accumulate valuable forms of capital and use them in their favor. Bourdieu refers to "overt struggles" over the form of capital at stake and the rules that govern exchanges.[3] While no field is ever entirely stable, as

2. Bourdieu, *Field of Cultural Production*.
3. Bourdieu, "Social Space."

political and economic events fire up and new and potentially powerful individuals enter the field, sufficient settling occurs to allow players to strategize, make moves, and respond to the moves of others. As John Levi Martin points out in his overview of field theory, "Every particular field has a coherence based on a working consensus as to the nature of the game, and people take predictable sides due to the more general structuring of social space."[4]

Every field has a competitive element, in which various forms of capital (whose nature and value differs with social, environmental, political, and historical contexts) are at stake. One's ability to act effectively within a particular field is determined in part by "habitus," which Wacquant defines as "the way society becomes deposited in persons in the form of lasting dispositions, or trained capacities and structured propensities to think, feel and act in determinant ways, which then guide them."[5] In the example discussed in this chapter, "players" are predominantly community members with some knowledge and experience that informs their sense of position within the fields that are of concern to them, and that guides their actions, strategies, and negotiations. For the most part, they know where they stand with regard to others active in the field, and they have a subjective sense of the forms of capital they possess. Outsiders are at a clear disadvantage, which can be exacerbated if they ally themselves with individuals or institutions whose habitus causes friction within certain fields—be they political, religious, economic, or social. This case study focuses on a relatively small community in which—as is commonly the case—there is a significant overlapping of these elements. More detailed discussion of religious and political actors follows a presentation of background on community dynamics, since both groups had interest in, and influence over, local health issues.

The Case Study in Rural Ecuador

In 1997, a small group of US and Ecuadorian health professionals partnered with a three-county rural Ecuadorian community with approximately fifty thousand inhabitants with high poverty levels (Table 1) and founded a nongovernmental organization. The vision was to provide an example of decentralized health care with a local community that the Ministry of Public Health (MOPH) of Ecuador had been promoting nationally. The decision to work in that particular community was, in part, influenced by the enthusiasm of the local Ecuadorian MOPH physician who shared the vision.

4. Martin, "What Is Field Theory?," 23.
5. Wacquant, "Habitus," 316.

Table 1. Focused demographics of a three-county community (Pichincha province: northwest region) in rural Ecuador

- Three counties cover 2,142 square kilometers at the base of the western slopes of the Andes mountains in a tropical, subtropical climate.
- Approximately 50,000 inhabitants in three predominantly rural counties, mostly of mestizo (mixed indigenous/Spanish heritage) culture with very few indigenous communities.
- 51 percent were below twenty years of age.
- 77 percent of the population lived in poverty, of which 12 percent was extreme poverty.
- Approximately 10 percent of the population was indigenous; the remainder mestizo.
- Illiteracy was 11 percent.
- 64 percent of the population had completed elementary education.
- 38 percent of housing in the capital of the canton under study had potable water.
- Agriculture and the informal work sector constituted the principal forms of employment.

Sources: (1) National Institute of Statistics and Census (INEC) 2001, and (2) Presidencia de la Republica del Ecuador, Mapa de Pobreza, 2008.

The NGO conducted a study to understand the health care needs of the community and to determine the feasibility of (1) creating a local health committee, (2) increasing the amount of health care infrastructure, and (3) attempting financial self-sustainability through partnerships with the public sector and through charging modest user fees (Table 2). The study revealed that the community believed that significant health care services, particularly hospital care, were lacking in the area. It also revealed that some members of the community had some disposable income to pay for health care services.

Table 2. Activities for initial community assessment and community oversight of NGO-initiated health care project

- Focus groups and key informant interviews with community members
- Community-wide meetings to learn of local health care needs
- Analysis of local epidemiology
- Interviews with local health care providers (private physicians, Ministry of Public Health physicians and nurses, and Ecuadorian Social Security Institute physicians and nurses)
- Interviews with national Ministry of Public Health officials, including the minister of public health
- Creation of a community health care committee with members chosen through local elections
- Subsequent creation of a three-county health council with participation of three mayors and the Ministries of Public Health, Education, and Agriculture

At that time, the MOPH of Ecuador was attempting to create a decentralized national health care system with wider community participation. This marked the beginning of a process of creating a postneoliberal framework, described by Sánchez and Polga-Hecimovich as a "transformation in the purposes, roles and capacities of political economic institutions."[6] A brief description of the national health care system is included (Table 3).

Hiring local Ecuadorians, the NGO opened a temporary outpatient clinic to confirm that certain members of the community would pay modest fees for medical services. The NGO and the newly created local health committee, chosen democratically by the community, attempted to partner with MOPH officials to convert the MOPH outpatient facility into a small hospital with supplemental funding from the NGO. Consistent with decentralization policy, the NGO and health committee would manage the facility in partnership with the MOPH. The MOPH initially agreed and signed a contract, but ultimately chose to rescind it.

---

6. Sánchez and Polga-Hecimovich, "Tools of Institutional Change," 383.

Table 3. Characteristics and brief history of the Ecuadorian National Health System

A mixed public/private delivery model:

- *Public sector* (85 percent of facilities): The Ministry of Public Health, which is the principal provider of services; the Ecuadorian Social Security Institute, which provides services to affiliates from the formal work sector; the armed forces and national police; municipalities; and an assortment of other smaller public institutions.
- *Private Sector* (15 percent of facilities): Private for-profit hospitals, clinics, and outpatient facilities, nonprofit nongovernmental organizations, and other social service organizations.
- The 1990s was a decade of attempted decentralization and wider participation in health services and policy, with little impact on inequalities, efficiency, and health care quality.
- In 2008, a new national constitution declared health an inalienable human right and the state as guarantor of free universal access.
- Public investment in the public health sector rose steadily from 2001 (USD 151 million) to 2014 (USD 2.5 billion).
- The Integral Public Health and Complementary networks, comprised of public sector and certain private sector providers, are fundamental components of universal access.
- Ecuador's National Health System in 2021 continues to be fragmented and the process of ensuring universal access has not been achieved.

Source: Chang Campos, "Evolución del sistema de salud de Ecuador"

Subsequently the NGO, in partnership with the local municipality, built and opened in 2001 a fifteen-bed hospital and clinic staffed with Ecuadorian health care personnel. The new hospital was the only one in the three-county area, but negotiations for a partnership with the local MOPH were unsuccessful. The local health committee approved a fee-for-service plan. Indigent patients were not charged. Various local financing mechanisms, such as microinsurance plans, were of limited utility. The NGO provided supplemental external funding to cover operating deficits.

The national Ecuadorian Social Security Institute (IESS) approached the NGO to provide care to its affiliates, which represented approximately 25 percent of the local population in the hospital's catchment area. Surpluses from that public-private partnership subsidized care for indigent patients.

The IESS contract, coupled with user fees for those able to pay, brought the hospital and clinic to self-sustainability after seven years of operations. In 2021, the community continues to use the hospital. A partnership was ultimately forged with the MOPH, and the NGO partnered with an Ecuadorian university to train over seventy Ecuadorian family physicians in a three-year residency program over a ten-year period. Many of these physicians came from the MOPH.

With community participation achieved through consensus-building activities and the creation of a democratically elected community health committee, the NGO and health committee believed that greater focus could be placed on clinical services to disrupt the cycle of poor health. With the preparatory community work completed, it was believed that they now only needed technical solutions: a small hospital, good physicians, access to medications, and diagnostic testing. However, that was not enough. The NGO understood community partnership and worked hard to maintain it, yet the NGO misunderstood power and the entanglement of various interests that characterized what Bourdieu identified as "fields."[7] In the most basic sense, fields contain actors, relationships, and various forms of capital that influence profits and power. They can be stable or become unstable as new actors with new objectives enter the field. Rules and forms of capital are often implicit and can be invisible to new actors. Health care institutions, characterized foremost by epistemic power rooted in scientific rationality, may be ill equipped to enter fields that evolve from vernacular forms of knowledge and power. The following examples illustrate the lack of understanding associated with this fact.

Ministry of Health

The early partnership with the MOPH to convert its facility into a small hospital was initially approved by the MOPH, which then reversed that decision weeks later. The NGO did not understand that the agreement proposed for a local, community-controlled health center would challenge the highly centralized national MOPH authority. The MOPH's reversal of its initial decision to partner with the NGO should have been a clear sign to the NGO that issues of power and authority were at stake. The NGO, not knowing who held the power in the MOPH, appealed to government officials at the national level, to no avail. Going to the wrong officials sealed the NGO's fate, as this violated the normative power relations in the field that included health care at the local and national levels.

7. Bourdieu, *Field of Cultural Production*; and Bourdieu, *Rules of Art*.

The NGO's relationship with local MOPH officials was further complicated by periodic new health initiatives coming from the central government, such as vertical disease programs having their own infrastructure, personnel, and budgets from international funding agencies. These disease-specific programs frequently distracted the rank and file of the MOPH from daily, unresolved challenges such as maternal morbidity/mortality, diabetes, and mental health. These programs, reflecting a field that had to be stretched to incorporate global actors and objectives, also prevented local MOPH officials from partnering with private NGOs.

Municipality

The municipality that is the focus of this article is led by an elected mayor and a council, with the council appointing a vice-mayor. The mayor chooses who will fill various administrative positions, and thus is in a key position within various overlapping fields. In addition to the various forms of capital that circulate through fields, there are social and cultural dynamics that constitute "the way things are done around here." Social actors, whose habitus can be thought of as the collective conditioning from lives lived in the overlapping fields of religion, economics, education, and politics, are agents whose ideas and behaviors are always subject to structural checks. Social and cultural capital is continuously expended, accrued, and diminished in exchanges between field actors. This circuitry can be quite complex at the municipal level. John Cameron, who has researched municipal politics in Ecuador, says that cleavages are based not only on rural/urban and mestizo/indigenous divisions, but also on "other important inequalities of power based on gender, generation, religion, migrancy and economic strata."[8] Cameron adds in a later article that municipal politics are worthy of attention for several reasons: this is where local elites establish and maintain economic and political privileges; municipal resource allocation has become increasingly important as the state continues to decentralize; and political activity at the municipal level is often key to understanding challenges and transformations at regional and national levels.[9] This all indicates that the structure and dynamics of fields of power operating at this level are hardly uncomplicated and that new actors attempting to enter these networks face a steep learning curve.

---

8. Cameron, "Municipal Democratisation," 371.
9. Cameron, "Hacía la Alcaldía."

Political Capital, Spiritual Capital, and Spheres of Exchange

In Ecuador—as in much of Latin America—the relative power of the Catholic Church and its relations with indigenous communities, have waxed and waned since colonial times. The church has in some periods and during certain administrations wielded significant political and economic power. It has also experienced land expropriations and governmental exclusion. As actors in various fields, the church as an institution, and individual religious and laypeople, continue to wield formidable power. During the colonial period and in the century after independence, the church was a significant force for assimilation, leading to the measurable erosion of indigenous cultures. With Vatican II and the emergence of liberation theology, some elements within the church took a dramatically different approach with regard to the poor in general, and indigenous groups in particular. Norget, documenting this process in Oaxaca, Mexico, refers to the evolution of a progressive church that became "an explicit alternative to the prevailing sociopolitical order," with some priests and nuns assuming roles as popular and indigenous activists.[10] In Ecuador, Leonidas Eduardo Proaño Villalba and others pushed for indigenous rights, bilingual education, and cultural protections that fundamentally reconfigured the social, political, and economic fields in some parts of the country.[11]

In this particular case study, social relations—often obscured to out-of-place actors—play a pivotal role. The NGO's initial Ecuadorian physician leader in the community was an adversary of the mayor and the local Spanish priest, who possessed significant political power in the community. The priest perceived the NGO's local physician as an enemy. Therefore, since the NGO failed to consult with the priest about the health project initially, the project also became his enemy. The relationship between the church and the mayor was described in an article in the national newspaper *La Hora* on May 18, 2000, which highlighted citizen discontent with the use of the church tower to exhibit political propaganda supporting the mayor's party. Witnessing strained dialogue between these various field actors in private and public settings, it became increasingly evident to the NGO that the awkward relationship between these three community leaders had a detrimental impact on the health project.

The influence of the local priest, which certainly extended into the power fields of politics and economics, should also be considered in relation to spiritual capital. Several theologians have used Bourdieu's concepts of

10. Norget, "Politics of Liberation," 97.
11. Martí i Puig, "Emergence of Indigenous Movements."

fields and capital in critical analyses of religion as praxis, or religion as one among several interacting fields of power-infused relations. Sanks argues that theology itself, and the conflicts and tensions within, could be analyzed through the fields/capital model. The history of liberation theology, for example, is filled with power plays and exchanges of various types of social and political capital. For the purposes of this chapter, his discussion of symbolic capital is useful insofar as it reveals how powerful religious symbols can mask systems of inequality or injustice.[12] For example, there are multiple contemporary examples of companies, governments, and religious institutions that are cloaked in righteous symbolism that is designed to obscure exploitative or oppressive behaviors. The more recent history of indigenous movements in Ecuador reveals that this symbolic power can also be wielded by the church to challenge extant structures and energize ethnic movements.

Spiritual capital, like other forms of capital, accounts for power and influence beyond money and property. Verter identifies it as a form of cultural capital that includes "spiritual knowledge, competencies, and preferences" that "may be understood as valuable assets in the economy of symbolic goods."[13] Priests and influential laypeople have a virtual monopoly on religious goods and services, often via symbolic capital that is the essence of rituals, behaviors, and certain material resources. In the case study under discussion, a relatively powerful (because it was foreign and offered its own form of salvation that is sometimes linked to the sacred and supernatural) health care institution could be seen as a threat to existing field relations and capital accounts. The monopoly on spiritual capital and the pseudomagical manipulation of the material world could be especially diminished by the arrival of doctors and administrators linked to powerful sources of knowledge and wealth. The symbolic power of the lab coat and stethoscope can be as compelling a force against maladies of the mind and body as the cassock and holy water are against maladies of the mind and soul.

The fields discussed in this study soon became destabilized and violent. The provincial vice-governor began looking into improprieties between the mayor's office and the church and was subsequently assassinated. The mayor was ultimately jailed, and the priest was ordered to return to his home country. The NGO worked with the municipality to get the derailed project on track again. It appeared that the municipal council members continued to be aligned with the mayor and with the NGO as an insurgent—albeit naïve—field actor.

12. Sanks, "Homo Theologicus."
13. Verter, "Spiritual Capital," 152.

Social Security (IESS)

Other networks of social relations were also fraught with complications. The partnership with the IESS, which drew a substantial number of patients into the NGO hospital, required the creation of a department within the hospital to audit medical records and process claims. The NGO created an electronic medical record, and the hospital went paperless in 2010. The hospital's financial well-being hinged on this critical public-private partnership, but there were consequences. At some point, it appeared the IESS was the hospital's client rather than the community, as the IESS's institutional financial power loomed large.

With time, the NGO began to see significant delays from the IESS in payments for services rendered to IESS patients. IESS gave budgetary shortfalls as an explanation, but the NGO began to appreciate a previously unnoticed sentiment in the IESS offices that were believed to be contributing to payment delays. Instead of growing their own infrastructure in the area, the IESS commissioned the NGO to care for IESS affiliates in the hospital's three-county area. The NGO became aware of discussions by angered employees within the IESS who believed that growing their own institution would be more strategic than outsourcing services. Why should an NGO be taking care of "their" patients? Within fields of social action, institutions can be understood as having their own habitus, much like entities in a "corporate culture." Symbolic capital may be particularly relevant at this level, with the behavior of an insurgent actor looked upon with suspicion or resentment. In contexts where global health actors are "foreign" by multiple definitions, field destabilization can be significant.

Nongovernmental Organization

That a US/Ecuadorian NGO could enter a community, set up a health project, and build a hospital, showed power that could be interpreted in a variety of ways by institutions in the community. The NGO certainly underestimated how that demonstration of power affected existing fields and altered the power dynamic in the community. The NGO's stated goal at the outset was to create a financially self-sustainable local model of high-quality health care for the community. The feasibility study suggested that the community generally would support that goal, which was pursued and achieved through a mix of user fees and the public-private partnership with the IESS.

However, with time, the NGO discovered that many in the community had an expectation that they would receive free health care. The

NGO-imposed, self-sustainable health care model represented a demonstration of its power. In spite of consensus building and significant, active community participation at the outset, some in the community perceived the NGO as setting the conditions of care in the community. The NGO acquired the legal status for the hospital and clinic by appealing to the president of Ecuador. While this tapped into a major power source within a state-level field to overcome the NGO's struggles at the local level, it may have also exacerbated suspicions toward an insurgent actor and violated norms of social relations.

An additional field of action in the community under study was managed by those who, while they may have been at the margins of formal power, were nevertheless integral to health care projects. Powerful informal leaders, through their opinions and ideas, can influence community thought. In this case study, the NGO did not recognize the power wielded by these informal leaders, nor did it understand how to build consensus in the community through them. These "influencers" are field actors not only in their local political roles, but also in the evolution of philosophies, ideas, and comportments that are the cultural substance of habitus and the generator of meanings.

An elderly gentleman who had lived for decades in the community commented, "Before the NGO came with the hospital, we were born here, we lived here, and then we died. It wasn't complicated. Since the NGO's arrival, we now have a lot of diseases, and everybody seems to be taking medications for something." With that, he succinctly summarized the sentiments of some within the community who pushed back on the power of the hegemonic biomedical model (described below). Could it be that certain members of the community with their own cosmovision were simply disinterested in the biomedical model? The NGO had to learn that from the community, but it took time. Training physicians to understand a patient's cosmovision was a long but necessary component of the family medicine residency.

Discussion

David Clarke's 2020 article on corruption in global health launched a discussion that spanned several issues of the *International Journal of Health Policy and Management*. After identifying the broad scope of the issue, he argued for a public health model that could address the multiple facets of corruption. This model, he said, "would include examining the influence of social, cultural, political, institutional and environmental factors that contribute to corruption in health systems."[14] In a May 2021 interview, the newly elected vice president of Ecuador, Alfredo Borrero, acknowledged that the health sector of his country is gripped by corruption, which the long-time family physician referred to as the "principal illness of the country."[15] While evidence, including various legal proceedings, points to corruption as a factor in the challenges discussed in this case study, it would be simplistic to leave it at that. Rather, lessons can be learned by a more deeply critical reflection on the complex nature of fields of action. This should include not just an accounting of local "obstacles" to health care projects, but also discussion of the hegemonic power of science-based medicine that dominates global health while obscuring other ways of knowing and acting.

This case study identifies health interventions as a potential source of place frictions. Power inequities, and competing meanings related to illness, wellness, and the body, energize these frictions. The dominance of the biomedical model (medical hegemony) often leads to the suppression of other medical alternatives. The biomedical model of health focuses exclusively on biological factors, excluding psychological, environmental, and social factors, and continues to be the prevailing paradigm in Western medicine. Engel characterized it as "embracing both reductionism, the philosophical view that complex phenomena are ultimately derived from a single primary principle, and mind-body dualism, the doctrine that separates the mental from the somatic. Hence the reductionist primary principle is physicalistic; that is, it assumes that the language of chemistry and physics will ultimately suffice to explain biological phenomena."[16]

Positivistic philosophy purports that true knowledge can only be derived from sensory, observational, and verifiable experience interpreted through reason, logic, and statistics. Therefore, society, like the physical world, operates through general laws. Positivism rejects intuitive knowledge, metaphysics, and theology because they cannot be verified by sense experience.[17] The challenge with positivism is that it looks to explain the clear world clearly, but it passes the unclear world over in silence.[18]

The biomedical model has accomplished much, particularly when infectious disease was at the forefront of global epidemiology. However, as noncommunicable diseases such as mental illness, cardiovascular disease, and diabetes, along with an aging population, become the major killers

14. Clarke, "Changing the Conversation," 258.
15. "Vicepresidente Borrero," para. 2.
16. Engel, "Need for a New Medical Model," 130.
17. Navarro Sada and Maldonado, "Research Methods in Education," 469–70.
18. Heisenberg, *Physics and Beyond*, 213.

globally, the biomedical model by itself falls short before these complex conditions involving interactions between the environment, sociocultural factors, the economy, and human psychology.

That the biomedical model is hegemonic can be understood through countless examples. The "medicalization" of disease prevention into risk factors and the subsequent lowering of thresholds for pre-disease have subtly blurred the boundaries between risk factor and disease, resulting in an explosion of pharmaceutical sales to treat risk factors such as dyslipidemia and prediabetes.[19] The pharmaceutical industry has also successfully moved from treating diseases to providing enhancements to what had previously been recognized as normal functioning, as in the case of erectile dysfunction. The *Diagnostic and Statistical Manual* creates new diagnoses for character traits not previously seen as illness, giving the biomedical model the power to determine conditions that are inherently normative.[20] This homogenization leaves little room for critical dimensions such as cultural diversity within communities, much less in the realm of global health. Shiffman suggests that the term "global health" itself confers a sense of universal legitimacy on the biomedical model, resulting in myriad problems with "input legitimacy." This creates imbalances in power and produces little epistemic and moral space for alternative ideas and practices.[21] The various forms of capital accumulated and expended in global health (cultural, social, financial, symbolic) are characterized by deep and extensive networks of power. These include health-related businesses, academia, and institutions of global health governance. The potential for incongruence with, and power over, local fields is substantial.

On the global health level, the hegemony of the biomedical model manifests through the great emphasis placed on specific disease management, such as vertical disease programs for malaria, tuberculosis, and HIV, and their medical therapies. Health systems in lower-income countries readily implement disease management and prevention policies used in high-income countries with little local contextualization, frequently creating discord between health sectors. The elderly gentleman's comment that "we all have diseases, and everybody is taking medications for something" illustrates the community's hesitation to accept with open arms the biomedical model because it had not been contextualized properly for them, thus creating friction as new ideas, expectations, and actors were being introduced into existing local fields of relation and meaning.

19. Starfield et al., "Concept of Prevention."
20. Lian, "Biomedical Hegemony."
21. Shiffman, "Global Health."

Power Dynamics in Literature

A deeper analysis of power in global health is necessary in order to appreciate its potential for affecting dynamics in local fields. This also helps make transparent any impacts on various forms of capital within a given field. Amidst the voluminous literature critical of the US health care system over the past fifty years, the ideas of three writers have stood the test of time. Their reflections have even greater relevance as the health care debate expands from national to global. They capture much of the health care dynamic the authors experienced in rural Ecuador. Paul Starr's timeless quotation, "The dream of reason did not take power into account," from *The Social Transformation of American Medicine* (1982) articulated the idea that "reason, in the form of arts and sciences, would liberate humanity from scarcity . . . , ignorance . . . , superstition . . . , and diseases of the body and the spirit. But reason is no abstract force pushing inexorably toward greater freedom at the end of history."[22] He argues that along with alleviating much burden in the world, reason, in the form of modern medicine, "cast up a new world of power."[23] He describes modern medicine as involving "extraordinary works of reason: an elaborate system of specialized knowledge, technical procedures, and rules of behavior," all revolving around the concept of power.[24]

Knowledge, coupled with a newly acquired professional competence (thanks to modern science), granted a dominating authority and professional sovereignty to physicians. Ultimately, "no one group has held so dominant a position in this new world of rationality and power."[25] But this scientifically driven authority has spilled "over its clinical boundaries into arenas of moral and political action for which medical judgment is only partially relevant and often incompletely equipped, . . . turning its authority into social privilege, economic power, and political influence."[26]

The power the medical community achieved through the biomedical model is not limited to the health sector, which suggests it can both influence and disrupt various of the fields as described by Bourdieu. The complexity of the health sector, including politics and economics, would suggest that those who maintain power over the health sector necessarily possess significant economic and political power. This has certainly been the case with physicians, although it could be argued that corporate America has

---

22. Starr, *Social Transformation*, 3.
23. Starr, *Social Transformation*, 3.
24. Starr, *Social Transformation*, 3.
25. Starr, *Social Transformation*, 4.
26. Starr, *Social Transformation*, 5.

usurped much of that physician-based power in recent decades. In low-income countries where physicians practice in small towns, it is not unusual to see them actively participate in local politics. But this more traditional field of power dynamics is rearranged, or even threatened, as more globally connected actors attempt to enter local fields.

While local and regional networks of power can complicate or even block projects—including health interventions—that ostensibly could improve living conditions, it is misguided to assert that these fields should cede a dominant role to "modern" global actors. As Shiffman argues, structural and productive power are elements of global health institutions that enhance the capacities of certain actors, while privileging ways of thinking rooted in Western and scientific epistemologies.[27]

In *Medical Nemesis: The Expropriation of Health* (1976), Illich illustrates through health care how modern responses to societal level challenges become counterproductive and even harmful.[28] "The threat which current medicine represents to the health of populations is analogous to the threat which the volume and intensity of traffic represent to mobility."[29] His main point is that health care can work against the healing process that patients seek—that health care can actually have a negative impact on health. "It is a social organization that set out to improve and equalize the opportunity for each man to cope in autonomy and ended by destroying it."[30]

Illich's argument centers around three types of iatrogenesis. Clinical iatrogenesis, known to all practitioners, is unintentional harm done to patients while attempting to restore health. Social iatrogenesis refers to the harm that "societal arrangements for health care (hospitals, physicians, pharmaceutical industry, insurers, government health agencies) can impose on patients, resulting in a 'standardization of health care' and the 'medicalization of life,' . . . when all suffering is 'hospitalized' and homes become inhospitable to birth, sickness, and death; when the language in which people could experience their bodies is turned into bureaucratic gobbledygook; or when suffering, mourning, and healing outside the patient role are labeled a form a deviance."[31] Illich's cultural iatrogenesis proceeds when societies succumb to "professionally organized medicine that has come to function as a domineering moral enterprise that advertises industrial expansion as a

---

27. Shiffman, "Global Health."
28. Illich, *Medical Nemesis*.
29. Illich, *Medical Nemesis*, 7.
30. Illich, *Medical Nemesis*, 275.
31. Illich, *Medical Nemesis*, 41.

war against all suffering."[32] When industrialized health care controls communities, those communities lose their authority and their will to manage their mounting suffering. This iatrogenesis appears when organized medicine replaces community responses to their health problems: "The siren of one ambulance can destroy Samaritan attitudes in a whole Chilean town."[33] Biomedicine, the far-reaching power it grants to the medical community, and a community's potential surrendering of their agency when it comes to their own health, introduces yet another element to the power dynamics of health care in any community, and certainly in the global South.

At the level of global health, Ferguson's *The Anti-Politics Machine* (1990) argues that the international aid industry depoliticizes social realities as a way of asserting control over them, effectively ignoring local social context.[34] Ferguson was influenced by Foucault's *The Birth of the Clinic* (1973), which argued that the medical encounter removes the human body from the social context and turns it into an object for technical investigation.[35] Ferguson describes the international aid community's ability to depoliticize and technicalize local social realities with generally accepted development strategies from the North. In doing so they remove local context and assert control over these communities. He suggests that this strategy of technical solutions without local context perpetuates structural inequalities.

These place-based contexts feature ways of doing and knowing that, we argue, can be understood via Bourdieu's concepts of fields and types of capital. They operate on sets of values, worldviews, and norms that may collectively represent a form of communication unintelligible to outsiders. Efforts to enter and influence these fields, and trade in these currencies, can confound nonlocal actors.

Conclusion: Lessons Learned and Lessons to Learn

The experiences of the Ecuadorian NGO discussed in this article suggest that power coming from various origins, circulating through actors and actions in multiple fields, contributes greatly to the health care dynamic in a community. Formal community leadership is not the only source of power in the community, as informal leadership and thought leaders can impact public opinion considerably. In the early years, the NGO remained unaware of the variety of thought leaders influential in different fields within the

32. Illich, *Medical Nemesis*, 127.
33. Illich, *Medical Nemesis*, 8.
34. Ferguson, *Anti-Politics Machine*.
35. Foucault, *Birth of the Clinic*.

community. Garnering their support might have brought the NGO's eventual success at an earlier moment. Rules and fluid dynamics in various local fields are also obscure and confusing for outsiders, at least initially. Sociological and theological perspectives can make transparent key players and rules of the game, which are influenced by economic, cultural, political, and religious factors.

The NGO also naively believed that institutions involved in health care delivery, such as the Ministry of Public Health, the social security system, municipal governments, and the private sector, would cooperate to achieve common health goals. Instead, each institution is embedded in particular field dynamics and acts to protect their bureaucracy and their assets, and therefore their power. IESS saw the NGO project as a threat to their power. The NGO attempted to access social and political capital to protect itself. The Ministry of Public Health has minimal collaboration with IESS, and it sometimes blocks municipalities interested in taking on a role in health care delivery. Attempts at decentralizing health care delivery to the local, community level are often met with great resistance, as extant power-based field relations are threatened.

Conversations with patients, physicians, nurses, and other health care professionals over the years reveal that most Ecuadorians feel powerless within their own public health care system. Part of the reason may be that people step into certain fields for relatively short-term events (a health crisis), or with a positionality largely formed in other field settings (medical education). The invisible walls and machinations of local fields can exasperate young, energetic physicians and nurses, as well as NGO personnel.

With time, the NGO and the community adapted to each other. The frequent emergencies that the hospital managed, and the biomedical model of the NGO, gained the respect of the community. The family medicine residency program brought sociologists, psychologists, and anthropologists whose influence resulted in the NGO's more sophisticated understanding of the complexities of the community and the local actors. The public-private partnership between the NGO and IESS grew stronger and broader as IESS decided against building additional health services infrastructure beyond their handful of small outpatient services in the area. The relationship with the local MOPH remained challenging at an administrative level. However, the high number of MOPH physicians who trained in family medicine at the NGO hospital and who continue to work in the region resulted in the creation of a de facto relationship.

Power should be part of any discussion of global health. The issue of power—who possesses it and who does not, where it hides, where it resides—is fundamental to a basic understanding of some of the complexities of health care systems and the cultures in which they operate, starting with one's own culture and health care system.

If true knowledge can only be derived from sensory, observational, and verifiable experience interpreted through reason, logic, and statistics, providing clarity to the clear world (positivism), what should students of global health do to approach an unclear world? Our current medical epistemology is out of synch with much of global health. We prefer to remain within the confines of clinical medicine with its skills and disease focus and a reductionist approach, rather than addressing complexities like as power relationships surrounding health in other cultures. Starr's description of ill-equipped medical authority extending to moral and political action still applies today. Illich's cultural and social iatrogenesis are more pervasive today than forty years ago. Ferguson's power dynamics of development and the resulting disengagement from local reality remain largely true.

Moving beyond positivism and the hegemony of biomedicine toward critical thinking and the social sciences may not provide answers to the complex challenges faced by students of global health, such as the medical residents mentioned above. However, a grounding in the social sciences will help students of global health begin to understand the uncertain world around them, much of which is driven by power. Contextualizing problems, and realizing that they have multiple points of origin, is a first important step in avoiding ill-fated solutions.

Understanding "the other," their culture, the systems in which they live and work, and how that "other" perceives your presence should be the initial goal for students and practitioners of global health. It is a disservice to global health students to tacitly imply that the other is strictly an object for intervention. Medical skills and disease-specific knowledge are useful only insofar as they are located within a cultural context and framework. Community power dynamics, envisioned here as fields of actors and actions, are a necessary component of that context.

Bibliography

Bourdieu, Pierre. *The Field of Cultural Production: Essays on Art and Literature*. Edited by Randal Johnson. New York: Columbia University Press, 1993.

———. *The Rules of Art: Genesis and Structure of the Literary Field*. Stanford, CA: Stanford University Press, 1996.

———. "The Social Space and the Genesis of Groups." *Theory and Society* 14.6 (November 1985) 723–44.

Cameron, John D. "Hacía la Alcaldía: The Municipalization of Peasant Politics in the Andes." *Latin American Perspectives* 36.4 (2009) 64–82.

———. "Municipal Democratisation in Rural Latin America: Methodological Insights from Ecuador." *Bulletin of Latin American Research* 24.3 (2005) 367–90.
Chang Campos, Caroline J. "Evolución del sistema de salud de Ecuador: Buenas prácticas y desafíos en su construcción en la última década 2005–2014." *Anales de la Facultad de Medicina* 78.4 (2017) 452–60. http://dx.doi.org/10.15381/anales.v78i4.14270.
Clarke, David. "Changing the Conversation, Why We Need to Reframe Corruption as a Public Health Issue: Comment on 'We Need to Talk About Corruption in Health Systems.'" *International Journal of Health Policy and Management* 9.6 (2020) 257–59.
Engel, George L. "The Need for a New Medical Model: A Challenge for Biomedicine." *Science* 196 (1977) 129–36.
Ferguson, James. *The Anti-Politics Machine: "Development," Depoliticization, and Bureaucratic Power in Lesotho*. Cambridge: Cambridge University Press, 1990.
Foucault, Michel. *The Birth of the Clinic: An Archeology of Medical Perception*. London: Tavistock, 1973.
Heisenberg, Werner. *Physics and Beyond: Encounters and Conversations*. New York: Harper and Row, 1972.
Illich, Ivan. *Medical Nemesis: The Expropriation of Health*. New York: Pantheon, 1976.
Lian, Olaug S. "Biomedical Hegemony: A Critical Perspective on the Cultural Imperialism of Modern Biomedical Perspectives on Human Life." Euro Academia, 6th Forum of Critical Studies Asking Big Questions Again, Lucca, Italy, November 23–25, 2017.
Martí i Puig, Salvador. "The Emergence of Indigenous Movements in Latin America and Their Impact on the Latin American Political Scene: Interpretive Tools at the Local and Global Levels." *Latin American Perspectives* 37.6 (November 2010) 74–92.
Martin, John Levi. "What Is Field Theory?" *American Journal of Sociology* 109.1 (July 2003) 1–49.
Navarro Sada, Alejandra, and Antonio Maldonado. "Research Methods in Education. Sixth Edition–by Louis Cohen, Lawrence Manion and Keith Morrison." *British Journal of Educational Studies* 55.4 (2007) 469–70.
Norget, Kristin. "The Politics of Liberation: The Popular Church, Indigenous Theology, and Grassroots Mobilization in Oaxaca, Mexico." *Latin American Perspectives* 24.5 (September 1997) 96–127.
Sánchez, Francisco, and John Polga-Hecimovich. "The Tools of Institutional Change under Post-Neoliberalism: Rafael Correa's Ecuador." *Journal of Latin American Studies* 51.2 (May 2019) 379–408.
Sanks, T. Howland, SJ. "Homo Theologicus: Toward a Reflexive Theology (With the Help of Pierre Bourdieu)." *Theological Studies* 68.3 (September 2007) 515–30.
Shiffman, Jeremy. "Global Health as a Field of Power Relations: A Response to Recent Commentaries." *International Journal of Health Policy and Management* 4.7 (2015) 497–99.
———. "Knowledge, Moral Claims, and the Exercise of Power in Global Health." *International Journal of Health Policy and Management* 3.6 (2014) 297–99.
Starfield, Barbara, et al. "The Concept of Prevention: A Good Idea Gone Astray?" *Journal of Epidemiology and Community Health* 62.7 (July 2008) 580–83.
Starr, Paul. *The Social Transformation of American Medicine*. New York: Basic Books, 1982.

Verter, Bradford. "Spiritual Capital: Theorizing Religion with Bourdieu against Bourdieu." *Sociological Theory* 21.2 (June 2003) 150–74.

"Vicepresidente Borrero asegura que la realidad de salud ecuatoriana es 'deplorable.'" *Expreso*, May 25, 2020. https://www.expreso.ec/actualidad/vicepresidente-borrero-asegura-realidad-salud-ecuatoriana-deplorable-105118.html.

Wacquant, L. "Habitus." In *International Encyclopedia of Economic Sociology*, edited by Jens Becket and Milan Zafirovski, 317–21. London: Routledge, 2005.

12

Solidarity with South Sudan: Paradigm of Promise in a Challenging Context

Joan Mumaw, IHM

Introduction

THE ORGANIZATION CALLED SOLIDARITY with South Sudan (SWSS) is a new model of ministry born of collaboration between the Union of Superiors General (USG, for men) and the International Union of Superiors General (UISG, for women).[1] It was formed in response to a request from the Catholic bishops of Sudan. The bishops' request, made in late 2004, was for Catholic religious men and women to come and see the situation in southern Sudan with a view toward encouraging religious congregations to send members to build the capacities of people in this war-torn country.

The bishops' request was made in connection with the International Congress on Consecrated Life held in Rome in 2004. The Congress had as its theme, "Passion for Christ, Passion for Humanity." The document that emanated from the Congress invited Catholic religious to "search for ... a new paradigm of mission ... born of compassion for the scarred and downtrodden of the earth—around new priorities, new models of organization and open and flexible collaboration between men and women of goodwill."[2]

---

1. USG and UISG are umbrella organizations of major superiors of congregations of Catholic priests, brothers, and sisters from around the world.

2. International Congress on Consecrated Life, *Passion for Christ*, 73.

During this journey to "come and see" in March 2006, the delegation became aware that "in the face of such enormous need, something new was needed . . . the 'new imagining' envisioned by the Congress on Consecrated Life."[3] A formal request was made to a meeting of the USG/UISG on May 15, 2006. Those who attended the meeting were asked "to consider whether international religious congregations could respond to the needs of southern Sudan in a way that would create a new paradigm, by responding collaboratively and by living and working together. This new initiative would not belong to any one congregation—it would belong to all of us, it would be shaped together."[4] This request was affirmed by those present at the meeting and initially thirty congregations responded with either personnel or funding.

A second assessment took place in March 2007, at which time it was decided, in consultation with the bishops, to focus on teacher training, training of health care professionals, and formation of diocesan pastoral teams. An agricultural project in Riimenze later received attention as a means to build the capacity of local farmers who had been displaced by conflict over many years and were without knowledge of appropriate and sustainable farming techniques.

The first team of religious went to southern Sudan in 2008. There have been, on average, twenty to thirty men and women religious, with a few laity coming from as many as nineteen congregations and twenty countries, working in South Sudan.[5] SWSS teams are presently working out of four sites to build the capacities of the people in this country, which has known only war since Sudan's independence from Britain and Egypt in 1956. The vision is to build the skills of the South Sudanese so that they will be able to assume responsibility for church institutions in the new country. More than sixty religious have been a part of this initiative over the past twelve years.[6]

My goal in this chapter is to explore a possible model for fruitful collaboration between church partners in the Global North and the Global South. In the first section, I lay out the historical context of South Sudan and the church there. In the second section, I describe what SWSS does and how it functions. I then discuss what we are learning from our work in the third section. In the fourth, I address some additional challenges and

3. *Origins and History,* 1–2.
4. *Origins and History,* 1–2.
5. As noted below, South Sudan became an independent nation in 2011.
6. See Stanislaus and Buhs, *Collaborative Mission in South Sudan,* for a history of Solidarity written in 2022 by participants in this initiative.

opportunities we are encountering in our work, and in the fifth and final section, I ask whether or not we are in fact forging a new paradigm for religious life.

I. The Context of South Sudan

a. History

The postcolonial period of Sudan (1956–2011) was dominated by the city of Khartoum in the north, an area which had been the focus of development under the colonial powers (Great Britain and Egypt). The north was predominantly Arab and Muslim and the south, African, Christian, and traditionalist. The north imposed Arabic and Sharia law on the south, while the south sought a measure of autonomy from the domination of the north. This period led to nearly continuous conflict and civil war (1955–72; 1983–2005) and exposed the serious lack of development in the south. Twice during this time expatriate missionaries were expelled from the country.

The signing of the Comprehensive Peace Agreement in 2005 allowed for self-determination for the people of the south. A referendum in early 2011 was nearly unanimous in the desire of the people for independence, which became a reality on July 9, 2011. The decision was backed by the United States of America, Britain, and Norway, "the Troika," that supported the newly independent nation. So much hope and so much promise! The decision clearly aligned the south with the rest of East Africa. Optimism was in the air! This nation, which is rich in oil, precious metals, and agricultural resources, would soon be self-supporting and less of a drain on the international community.

Opposition to the policies of the north and continuous conflict served to bond the ethnic groups in the South. However, historical animosities between major tribes in the south began to re-emerge in the post-independence period. A split along ethnic lines in the membership of the Sudan People's Liberation Movement (SPLM) in late 2013 immersed the new country in civil war. Attempts to build the skills of the South Sudanese in the fields of economics, politics, and social science were wiped out. Efforts to educate teachers and health care professionals were minimalized.

During the past eight years of conflict, two million people have been internally displaced and another two million have fled to neighboring countries, especially Uganda. Over half the country is food-insecure and, in many cases, bordering on famine. Schools, clinics, and hospitals in large areas of the country have been destroyed. Nongovernmental and humanitarian organizations have tried to respond but, when caught in the unrest, have often pulled their staff out of the country. SWSS staff have stayed through the thick and thin of these years, a fact not lost on the church and its people.

Several attempts to broker peace in this latest conflict have been made by the Troika (Britain, Norway, and the USA), the African Union, and the IGAD nations (the countries surrounding South Sudan). Most of these attempts have failed. In September 2018, a new peace deal was signed between the president, Salva Kiir (from the Dinka tribe) and the rebel leader and vice president, Riek Machar (from the Nuer tribe), who agreed to a power-sharing arrangement. After being postponed three times, a Revitalized Transitional Government of National Unity was sworn in on February 22, 2020. The cease-fire agreed upon is fragile and there have been outbreaks of violence in many parts of the country. The people have been traumatized by this conflict, which has been especially brutal, with looting and burning of houses; rape of women and children; murder; conscription of child soldiers, porters, and cooks; and the sexual exploitation of young girls. Unfortunately, the various "peace deals" have tended to focus on "power-sharing" rather than addressing the underlying causes of injustice and the best means of developing a prosperous, self-sufficient country.

b. Demographics

South Sudan is the third most fragile country in the world,[7] just ahead of Yemen and Somalia, and ranks 185th out of 189 countries with respect to human development.[8] This newly independent country lacks both physical and institutional infrastructure. During the colonial period, development was focused on the north, and little development occurred in the south. The latest civil war, beginning in December 2013, halted any efforts toward the development of a physical, economic, political, or social infrastructure. While statistics are poorly kept in South Sudan, we have, with the help of the United Nations and related agencies, some picture of the demographics of the country and the status of education and health care in the country.[9]

---

7. Fund for Peace, "Fragile States Index."
8. UNDP, "Economic Cluster."
9. Moran and Kahura, *Evolution of Solidarity*, 12.

Data: South Sudan[10]	
Independence	July 9, 2011
Population	12 million
Internally Displaced Persons (IDP)	1.9 million
Refugees outside the country since the beginning of conflict in 2013	2 million
Literacy rate	34.5 percent (female: 16 percent)
Maternal mortality rate	1,150 / 100,000 births (fifth highest in the world)
Human development index	185 of 189 countries
Livelihood	Agriculture and pastoralism (cows) Seven million in need of humanitarian assistance
GDP	2014: USD 1,111 2019: USD 2,003
Inflation	2020: 1 USD = 300 SSP 2019: 1 USD = 260 SSP (1400 percent over 2015 levels) 2015: 1 USD = 18.5 SSP (SSP = South Sudanese Pound)
Official Language	English since 2011 (before, Arabic)

c. Economy

The outlook for the economy at the time of independence was very promising. South Sudan is rich in oil, precious minerals, and agricultural products (horticulture and animal husbandry). Since 2013 and the current civil war, many items have been imported from Uganda and Kenya because the industrial base has not yet been developed. Food aid is imported into the most war-torn areas. Transportation has worsened due to insecurity and poor infrastructure. The only surfaced road leading into the country runs between Nimule, Uganda and Juba, and inside the country, between Juba, Wau, and Aweil towns. These roads have deteriorated significantly since the recent conflict began. The World Food Program operates the most important air transport system in the country, ferrying foodstuffs for humanitarian relief and taking those working for NGOs along for the ride. This service is very expensive, but it is considered safer than commercial air transport.

10. Moran and Kahura, *Evolution of Solidarity*, 12.

Since 2014, the South Sudanese economy has virtually collapsed. In 2013, the exchange rate of the SSP (South Sudanese Pound) to USD was approximately 13.5 SSP to $1 US. In 2017 it was 172 SSP to $1 US and in 2019, 260–320 SSP to $1 US, or twenty times the 2013 rate. For this reason, the costs of imported goods and locally grown foodstuffs have skyrocketed. Mobile phone networks have been closed down, as well as banks, in some areas of the country. Internet is expensive and often unreliable. Communication between SWSS projects and with offices in the US and Rome is difficult. Cash needs to be flown to Yambio and Riimenze in order for the projects to function. Construction materials are brought by road from Uganda via the Democratic Republic of the Congo to Yambio. The border with Sudan is, at times, open, allowing for goods from Khartoum to move to Wau and Malakal, but the projects managed by SWSS face difficult challenges and are expensive to maintain.

d. Education

According to UNICEF, the educational system has deteriorated further during the current civil war. The proportion of out-of-school children is the highest in the world at 72 percent;[11] in total, 2.2 million children are out of school,[12] and in rural areas, 76 percent of six-year-olds are not attending school, while in urban areas, that number is 64.5 percent.[13] For those who do attend school, the challenges are daunting: poor quality teaching, limited teaching materials and textbooks, absences due to displacement, a lack of food, the need to support families, early marriage, unsafe schools, long distances, and lack of transportation. The pandemic shut down existing schools for most of 2020 and from February through April of 2021. The capacity of the Ministry of Education to respond to the needs of children is limited.

Teacher qualifications are poor. It is estimated that there are nearly 52,000 teachers, 16 percent of whom are women.[14] Less than half have received a formal education. The ratio of qualified teachers to students is 1:1,171. Forty-four percent of teachers have some training, but many have as few as four years of primary school education. Thirty-five percent are government employees and the rest work for nongovernmental employers. Salaries are low—those employed by the government, when they are paid,

11. UNICEF, "Humanitarian Action for Children," 1.
12. UNESCO, *Global Initiative*, 11.
13. UNESCO, *Global Initiative*, 105.
14. South Sudan Education Cluster et al., "Education Cluster Assessment," 29.

earn the equivalent of $6–13 USD per month, paid in SSPs. Those working for diocesan schools may earn as much as $80 USD per month, paid in SSPs, and up to $120 USD working for NGOs, which often pay in foreign currency. The prolonged nonpayment and the insecurity in the country have led many teachers to abandon their posts for safer areas or other employment.[15]

There are eight teacher training colleges in the country, four of which were closed during the current civil war. The Solidarity Teacher Training College (STTC) has remained open, graduating teachers during this period, and in 2016 and 2017, it was the only college matriculating new teachers.

e. Health Care

Because of its experience of conflict over a nearly sixty-year period, the country has some of the worst health indicators in the world, with a child mortality rate of 63.7 per 1,000 live births, a maternal mortality rate of 1,150 per 100,000 live births,[16] and 75 percent of all child deaths being the result of preventable diseases. One in ten children dies before age five.[17] Two out of five children under five are malnourished and two out of five lactating or pregnant women are malnourished.[18] This is due to insecurity and conflict, as much of the country is very fertile and could sustain the food needs of the population. Half the population had insufficient access to health care services in 2019. In 2018, some five hundred attacks on health care facilities were documented. Of the nearly 1,900 health care facilities in the country, 22 percent are nonfunctional. Four out of five of these facilities are managed by faith-based organizations and NGOs,[19] but many of these are poorly resourced and often closed.

While the salaries of health care workers employed by the government are better than that of teachers, they are still extremely low, the equivalent of $12 USD per month paid in SSPs. Those working for NGOs make approximately $600 USD per month paid in foreign currency ($800 USD for a certified midwife). These pay rates are unsustainably low. Even so, most health care professionals are drawn to work for NGOs, thus depleting government and diocesan facilities of trained health care workers. The salary at the Daniel Comboni Hospital in Wau, the teaching hospital linked to the

15. Moran and Kahura, *Evolution of Solidarity,* 15.
16. Fund for Peace, "Fragile States Index."
17. See "Challenge" at https://www.unicef.org/southsudan/what-we-do/health, under "Health" on UNICEF South Sudan's website.
18. As quoted in Moran and Kahura, *Evolution of Solidarity,* 14.
19. As quoted in Moran and Kahura, *Evolution of Solidarity,* 14.

Catholic Health Training Institute (CHTI), is approximately $250 USD per month and for those working in diocesan facilities it is $100 USD (both paid in local currency). Retaining trained health care professionals in these health care facilities is challenging, to say the least.[20]

In 2009–10, there were eighty-three registered nurses, 1,110 certified nurses, and nineteen registered midwives in the country.[21] Most of these were poorly trained, with some having as little as nine months preparation. More recent figures for the country are not available, but CHTI alone has trained 170 registered nurses and 98 registered midwives since 2010. In 2019, CHTI trained 22 percent of all of the graduates in the country, all of whom passed the national exam with distinction or high credit. They are sought after by health care institutions throughout the country, not only for their outstanding academic results, but for the quality of the supervised, clinical practice training they have received. There is no legal framework for RNs and RMs working in the country, which means there is no national standard for health care personnel's qualifications. There are estimated to be eight health training institutions functioning in the country, the quality of which varies.[22] The CHTI enjoys the advantage of being a full-time residential program with excellent academic and hostel facilities developed by SWSS. Teaching practice in local hospitals is limited and there are few qualified senior trained professionals to supervise clinical practice.

f. The Roman Catholic Church

The Catholic Church is administered through seven dioceses, of which one bishopric is vacant and one bishop is due to retire. In 2019–20, four new bishops were appointed. The church has been severely impacted by the civil war and one diocese, Malakal, has had virtually all of its institutions destroyed and its clergy displaced. SWSS has worked to rebuild the pastoral presence in the country, working with diocesan pastoral teams and clergy. About 37 percent of the country is Catholic.[23] In the early history of colonial Sudan, specific areas of the country were designated for certain Christian denominations, including Catholic, Episcopalian, and Presbyterian. There is a strong ecumenical dimension to the Christian church in the country, and the South Sudan Council of Churches may be the most effective voice

---

20. Moran and Kahura, *Evolution of Solidarity*, 14.
21. Michael and Garnett, "Strengthening Nursing and Midwifery."
22. An accurate count of these facilities is impossible due to the conflict.
23. Sudan Relief Fund, "Pope Francis Set to Visit."

in the country, animating local churches and playing an important role in peacemaking and humanitarian relief.

The Religious Superiors Association of South Sudan (RSASS) estimates that there are forty-nine religious congregations in the country. Many are very small, indigenous congregations. One significant event in the life of RSASS was the building and opening of the Good Shepherd Peace Center in 2016, a much-needed venue for workshops and conferences. As of April 2020, the SWSS Pastoral Team of four religious had assumed responsibility for the management of the Good Shepherd Peace Center.

II. Solidarity with South Sudan: How We Operate and What We Do

a. North-South Partnership

The largest commitment to capacity-building in South Sudan has been made by the religious congregations and members of the USG and UISG located in Rome. The desperate state of education and health care in the country, the lack of resources in the church and in the society and the seeming promise of a new southern Sudan as per the Comprehensive Peace Agreement of 2005, coupled with the call of the Congress on Consecrated Life, impelled these congregations to take up the challenge of the invitation from the bishops of Sudan.

Many of the congregations were missionary or international in nature, with experienced and well trained members able to develop training institutions for education and health care. Lead congregations (the Comboni sisters in health care; the De La Salle brothers in education) were soon complemented by members of other religious congregations. Increasingly, lay associates and expatriate staff from Kenya and Uganda have taken up positions in the institutions.

The projects have been supported financially by religious congregations around the globe and Catholic agencies in Europe and the US. A legal structure is in place in Rome (ONLUS) and in the UK (UK Charity). In South Sudan, SWSS is registered as a faith-based organization, with the South Sudan Bishops Conference managing relationships (registrations, visas, etc.) with the government.[24]

Friends in Solidarity, the USA partner to SWSS and a legally separate, not-for-profit (501(c)3) organization, was established in late 2015 and has its office with the Leadership Conference of Women Religious (LCWR) in Silver

---

24. Solidarity with South Sudan, *Governance Manual*, 18:9.

Spring, Maryland. Friends in Solidarity is a new model of collaboration in the US. It was founded by the major superiors of various Catholic religious congregations, men and women. Its board of directors is made up of members of various congregations having an interest in SWSS. Friends in Solidarity supports the work of SWSS with funding that is sought and received from religious congregations, foundations, and generous individuals.[25]

The commitment from South Sudan is through a memorandum of understanding (MOU)[26] between SWSS and the Sudan Catholic Bishops Conference. This MOU makes clear that the institutions built and managed by SWSS are the property of the Sudan Catholic Bishops Conference. The costs of building and operating the institutions has been and continues to be borne by SWSS, which secures funding to meet these needs. The management and operation of these institutions (primarily the STTC and CHTI) will transfer to the Bishops Conference once sufficient South Sudanese capacity is in place and the bishops are ready to assume responsibility for the institutions. The original MOU called for a ten-year timeline (2008–18). This timeline was unrealistic given the civil war which has engulfed the country from 2013 to the present day, so the MOU has been extended from 2019 to 2026 with a review every three years. Most agree that it will need to be extended beyond 2026.

At the time of the signing of the MOU in 2008, the bishops were "on board" with the plans developed by SWSS. Diocesan land was provided in Yambio for the construction of the STTC and the bishops cleared the way with the government for the rehabilitation of the CHTI in Wau. Diocesan land was provided to SWSS for the Agricultural Training Project in Riimenze. In addition, the Daniel Comboni Hospital in Wau was reclaimed from the military and rehabilitated by the Comboni sisters as a teaching hospital for the training of those studying at the CHTI. Relationships have also been established between the Ministry of Health and the Wau Teaching Hospital, a poorly resourced government hospital, another site for clinical practice.

b. Financing

SWSS projects are sustained by religious congregations and Catholic funding agencies. The building of the STTCs in Yambio and Malakal and the rehabilitation of the CHTI in Wau was extremely expensive because a complete infrastructure for the institutes needed to be built from the ground up:

25. See the "All About Friends" page of the Friends in Solidarity website at https://www.solidarityfriends.org/about.
26. Solidarity with South Sudan, *Governance Manual*, 18:3.

buildings, provisions for water and electricity, security and furnishings, etc. It was originally envisioned that SWSS would be able to tap into existing water and electricity supplied by the municipalities. However, it was soon determined that municipal infrastructures were unreliable at best and most of the time nonexistent. Fuel for generators is exorbitantly expensive. Early on, solar systems were installed for the provision of electricity and the pumping of water, and planned upgrades to and the extension of these systems to meet the increasing number of buildings and students are in the offing.

Early construction needs were dependent upon expatriate engineers and contractors and the importation of construction materials either by road from Uganda (currently via the Democratic Republic of the Congo) or Khartoum or up the Nile to Malakal. Criminal activity on transportation routes has made it necessary to fly students, staff, and some imported goods to their destinations. The current conflict, corruption, and the collapse of the economy has only served to increase SWSS's costs and extend the timeline for the projects.

Donations from religious congregations funded the beginning of the work and European Catholic organizations have supported construction and operations since the early days. US donations have increased with the establishment of Friends in Solidarity in late 2015 and now contribute approximately 15–20 percent of SWSS's annual budget.

c. Accomplishments 2009–19+

1. Solidarity Teacher Training College (STTC)—Yambio

The initial vision was an STTC in every diocese (there are seven). The first college was built in Malakal and opened in 2013. This was taken over by the military at the end of 2013 and operations have been halted during the current conflict.

A second college was built and opened in 2013 in Yambio. This has become a national teacher training college accommodating students from all dioceses and states in the country. A two-year preservice program focuses on the training of primary school teachers. Beginning in 2021, an additional year will be offered, leading to a diploma in teaching.

The Ministry of Education requires in-service training leading to certification for existing teachers, many of whom have less than a primary school certificate. Nearly 550 primary teachers have been certified through the STTC to teach, either through the preservice (296) or in-service (248) programs conducted by STTC. There is a need for twenty-six thousand new teachers in the country.

The Ministry of Education has adopted a new curriculum for education, moving from a knowledge-based curriculum to an outcomes-based curriculum, stressing skills and behavior. (Good teachers have always taught this way.) This will necessitate additional, smaller classrooms for labs and in-service training for all the teachers in the system. STTC is already in the planning stages for this new development and is incorporating outcomes-based learning into their training of teachers. The ministry has yet to develop a new curriculum or to supply textbooks for the STTCs.

2. Solidarity Agricultural Training Project—Riimenze

The agricultural training project was not part of SWSS's original vision, but it has become an important part of the current work. An SWSS member, a sister from Vietnam with experience in sustainable methods of farming, initiated the project in 2010. Over seventy-five acres have been cleared by hand for planting and harvesting crops. More than eighty families directly benefit from the project as permanent employees and over five hundred farmers from the region have benefited from workshops held throughout the local area. Programs on the radio reach another group of listeners. Special workshops have introduced women to appropriate technology and sustainable methods. Animal husbandry, fish farming, and the drying and preservation of crops have also been introduced. Over forty tons of food are harvested annually. This work is generously supported by Caritas Austria, which has lent its expertise to the program.

Since 2017, SWSS has been assisting nearly eight thousand internally displaced people who have been encamped around the parish at Riimenze as a result of a conflict between the national army and rebels from the local tribe. Since there was little access to assistance from international humanitarian agencies in the area, SWSS reached out to assist the elderly and vulnerable people in the camp. Due to the cease-fire, many of these displaced persons have recently returned to their plots of land to rebuild their homes and livelihoods. SWSS has also renovated the parish primary school and hired qualified teachers, graduates of the nearby STTC in Yambio. One staff member has worked for several years developing a nursery school, which acts as a feeder to the primary school. This work is supported by religious congregations from the US and generous individuals supporting the humanitarian assistance to those in the camp.

3. Training of Diocesan Pastoral Teams—Juba

The people of South Sudan have been traumatized by war. The current conflict between ethnic groups in the country is perhaps the most destructive ever, with entire villages being destroyed, women raped, and men killed. Everyone in the country has been impacted by nearly sixty years of civil war: government leaders, bishops, priests, religious, and ordinary individuals. Children born today have known only war and its effects. SWSS has trained trainers for peace-building and trauma-healing workshops. They have worked to develop diocesan pastoral teams and trained catechists and initiated Christian base communities. So much more needs to be done to rebuild the church and provide resources to the catechists and laity who have sustained the church during these decades of war.

4. The Catholic Health Training Institute (CHTI)—Wau

The Catholic Health Training Institute is a two-story stone structure with staff bungalows built in late 1970s. It was virtually abandoned in 1983 when religious were driven out of the country and a skeleton staff left to guard the building. Following upon the signing of the Comprehensive Peace Agreement in 2005, refugees began to return to the area. Many took up residence, with their animals, in the institute. Since the resettlement of the refugees and very extensive renovation in 2010, new dormitories, a small chapel, and a security wall have been built; a small agricultural project has also been developed.

Initially the CHTI offered only a three-year registered nurse training program. The addition of a registered midwifery program in 2012 came at the request of the Ministry of Health and was originally funded by UNFPA.

Since the first graduation of registered nurses in 2013, 170 RNs and 98 RMs have graduated, most with distinction or high credit on state exams. Annually, graduates are sent for advanced degrees with the hope of their returning as tutors. Graduates from the CHTI can be found throughout the country, in the Nuba Mountains and Abyei and in disputed areas bordering Sudan. Over 85 percent are employed in the health care profession.

III. What We Are Learning

a. The Changing Scenario

When SWSS first sent staff to South Sudan there seemed to be great promise for the development of the country. The Comprehensive Peace Agreement signed in 2005 set the stage for independence in 2011. People began to return from exile and were positive about the future. Underlying ethnic tensions, however, were not addressed and soon resurfaced, resulting in the current civil war. During this period the economy has collapsed and corruption and misuse of funds are rampant. Travel by road is dangerous due to unmaintained roads and a lack of security on passable roads.

The government has also changed the rules and regulations applying to expatriate staff on several occasions. Regulations for visas and internal travel have become onerous. The ability of government institutions and ministries to develop adequate services is sorely lacking in both expertise and resources. Although it is recognized that the services of NGOs are urgently needed, the government has also imposed extra imposts on expatriates in an effort to generate revenue rather than facilitate the work of outside aid agencies.

The current civil war has further fragmented society, and civil society and government seem unable to foster reconciliation. The churches are best placed to take on this challenge because its parishes reach into all areas of the country. The South Sudan Council of Churches is the most effective organization of churches, seeking peace at all levels of society. Resources and a commitment to ecumenical activities and peace-making programs are needed.

SWSS has adapted its original vision and opted for national rather than diocesan institutions. This means that students from every ethnic group and from the border areas with Sudan are all studying together. They are learning to respect and appreciate people from cultures other than their own and developing friendships across ethnic boundaries. They are also witnessing SWSS staff members living and working together. This multinational, multicultural, and multicongregational witness of men and women religious working with the laity is not lost on the students who come from communities ripped apart by ethnic strife. It speaks powerfully to the major issue facing the country, ethnic strife. The leaders of the future of South Sudan are being formed in a values-centered culture through the ministry of SWSS staff.

b. Funding Challenges

The SWSS initiative is an expensive project to sustain over many years. A lack of local resources necessitates that students receive full support to attend SWSS institutions. There will be a need to support institutions once they are led by South Sudanese. Recognizing this from the beginning, SWSS has established an endowment for this support.

South Sudan has opted to become part of the East African Community. This has the potential for easing visa restrictions and facilitating trade across borders. The lack of reciprocity within the East African Community means that diplomas issued in South Sudan are not honored in Kenya and Uganda; this necessitates SWSS paying higher fees for those working on advanced degrees and students needing additional time to meet requirements, some of which they have already completed in South Sudan.

There are also different philanthropic patterns in Europe and the USA. European church collections and government grants flow to charitable organizations working in Africa and former colonies. SWSS has received significant support over many years from many Caritas-related organizations in Europe. In the US, there is a need to educate people about the needs of Africa and South Sudan. The traditional orientation of US funding seems to be its southern border, Central and South America, Haiti, and the Philippines. Funds in the US are held primarily by individuals and family foundations (over 90 percent); government funding is difficult to access for small groups and USAID assistance is often tied to US universities and US programs and businesses. Catholic Relief Services is the only Caritas-related organization in the country.

Friends in Solidarity, the US partner of SWSS, faces many challenges: communicating the vision and mission of SWSS for an area of the world engulfed in ongoing conflict; sharing the impact of the work in spite of the difficult situation; keeping the vision alive when there are frequent leadership changes in religious congregations; and developing a community of willing donors and volunteers.

Partnerships are being developed with congregations of women religious; currently these number forty-one and include Bon Secours Mercy Health System, parishes, schools, individuals, and foundations (e.g., the Hilton Fund for Sisters, the Loyola Foundation, etc.). Partnerships have been facilitated by the LCWR and IUSG-US Constellation. Partnerships with men's religious congregations and USG have been slower to develop.

A recent organizational evaluation of SWSS commissioned by a foundation that has supported SWSS from the beginning offers a sobering assessment of the long-term sustainability of its work. The commitment made by religious men and women to SWSS initiatives will need to be renewed and supported for the foreseeable future.

The context in South Sudan unfortunately does not support the establishment of sustainable programming. A fragile civil society, undependable state structures, high reliance on humanitarian aid and external funding, large numbers of displaced people struggling to survive, continually unsafe public spaces, and high living costs make it difficult for the Ministries of Education, Health, and Agriculture to support the programs. It is also challenging for many project participants to contribute financially because of their own tenuous livelihoods. The South Sudanese church has also suffered during the many years of war. Its structures and capacity to manage and to contribute to funding the existing Solidarity program appears to be limited and has to be further reviewed while developing a joint transition plan. The current uncertain political situation and the uncertain future scenario in South Sudan makes it doubly difficult to prepare the next steps towards sustainability, let alone plan for the long-term future.[27]

The extended length of SWSS's commitment to South Sudan is also challenging for congregations in the global North. There are fewer experienced religious to send to the global South. For US religious congregations, challenged by the situation at our southern border and recent climate-related catastrophes, funding is stretched thin, and personnel are nearly nonexistent. International congregations may be able to send members from their provinces in Asia and Africa, as is the case of the School Sisters of Notre Dame, longtime supporters of SWSS, who are in the process of establishing international communities in the country.

c. The Response of the Local South Sudan Church

Originally, it was the idea of the bishops of Sudan to attract religious congregations to South Sudan; they were not, however, sure that the model of collaboration among religious congregations, men and women, as proposed by SWSS would work. According to an original member of the board, at a meeting in 2009, the bishops felt that SWSS was moving too fast and had too little African experience. They reminded SWSS that the institutions belonged not to Solidarity but to the southern Sudan church. They asked if SWSS was empowering leaders to assume responsibility for the institutions.

Initially, SWSS was backed by several bishops, many of whom had been members of an international religious congregation. Later, issues of the control over external funding and diocesan control of land and institutions were raised by some bishops.

A question for SWSS and the bishops: Do the South Sudan bishops have the capacity to assume responsibility for the institutions created by SWSS? The answer has yet to be determined. There is a need for regular communication with the bishops regarding their needs for pastoral formation, the future of national institutions developed by SWSS in various dioceses, and the institutional needs of each diocese. The bishops provide one member to attend meetings of the SWSS board.

27. Moran and Kahura, *Evolution of Solidarity*, 65.

National church and diocesan coordinators for health and education have only recently been appointed. They are assisting SWSS institutions by vetting candidates to recommend to the STTC and CHTI. Research into the number and quality of parish schools and clinics operating in the various dioceses is only now being considered. How to sustainably support quality teaching and learning as well as quality health care is a question that urgently needs to be addressed. This also provides an opportunity to make policy recommendations to local, state, and national ministries with respect to support of qualified staff in schools and clinics.

IV. Additional Challenges and Opportunities

a. Role of Women in Society

SWSS has as one of its priorities fostering the education of young women. The STTC struggles to increase the enrollment of women interested in the teaching profession. In contrast to teaching, nursing and midwifery are professions that are in great demand. The CHTI has been successful in attracting women students, moving from 20 percent women in 2010 to nearly 50 percent in 2020. Keeping young women in school reduces the incidence of early marriage and childbearing and prevents human trafficking of young girls as child soldiers and sex slaves for armed men and the powerful.

b. Volunteers

Solidarity has been blessed with the presence of lay volunteers, whose time commitments have ranged from six months to several years. Because of the liability and cost, SWSS has refrained from seeking short-term volunteers. The real benefit of a short-term mission, unless volunteers come with specific expertise to share, is for the person who comes. For this reason, it is important to prepare persons who are coming and provide quality debriefing upon return. When done well, such experiences can be life-changing for those who come.[28] Short-term mission can also be a drain on local resources of time and energy. Hopefully, the local staff are not left with responsibilities they do not have the ability to handle.

---

28. The Catholic Health Association has excellent resources for the preparation and debriefing of short-term medical missions on their website, https://www.chausa.org/.

c. Ongoing Maintenance of Buildings

SWSS developed the STTCs from the ground up and renovated the CHTI, which had been used as informal housing (animals and all) by those returning to South Sudan after the signing of the 2005 Comprehensive Peace Agreement. This renovation included the introduction of solar energy and technology for the provision of water and electricity. Some of the early construction was substandard and needs upgrading or repair. The solar batteries are of varying quality and the lack of qualified local technicians has made repairs difficult and expensive. Training of on-site personnel responsible for maintaining such equipment is essential. It is also important to think long term: Will what we are building now be maintained when personnel from the global North are no longer on-site? Is this appropriate and sustainable technology for the long term?

d. Transportation and Security

Due to the ongoing conflict, SWSS has needed to increase its security arrangements. Walls have been built at great expense around the STTC and at the front of the CHTI to provide security for staff and students. There is little mobility outside the compounds, and a curfew is in place in the evening. Those who volunteer with SWSS need to be content with being campus-bound. Staff and students can be fearful and traumatized when they hear of localized fighting. Local primary schools close and teachers doing practice teaching move quickly back to the campus. In Wau, there is a plan for the evacuation of expatriate staff. UNICEF has a compound within walking distance of the CHTI, and they have agreed to ensure that expatriate staff needing to leave are taken to the airport. SWSS staff have chosen to remain with the South Sudanese staff.

Insecurity on the roads and their deplorable condition have affected transportation for students. Those who are not from the area need to be flown to Yambio and Wau at great cost to the colleges and to SWSS. The wear and tear on vehicles is immense.

e. Capacity-Building

SWSS contends that the greatest need in South Sudan is for education and capacity-building. In the face of the great need for humanitarian and development assistance, the temptation to do direct service is almost impossible to avoid. Many indigenous religious are able to do this better than SWSS staff;

many indigenous religious do not have the qualifications to do the training that is done by SWSS. Given this, when the need is on your doorstep, you must respond, as is the case in Riimenze with the internally displaced persons.

SWSS has also responded to humanitarian needs in Juba and Wau with the help of donors who respond generously to the need for food. The question is how to move away from this emergency response mode when there is nothing to replace these interventions. Such interventions need to be well thought out, with the long-term consequences of ending emergency help in mind. Direct service is a real need, but unless there is capacity-building, the people of South Sudan will never become self-sustaining and able to develop the resources that are present in the country. SWSS needs to continually focus on building capacity rather than "doing for."

V. A New Paradigm for Religious Life—or Not?

The model developed by SWSS draws its inspiration from the Congress on Consecrated Life (2004), which calls for greater collaboration between men and women in ministry among the poor. The intercongregational model is attractive to religious in the global North. Because of its collaborative model, it is sometimes seen as the future of religious life, especially in areas where religious are aging and fewer in numbers. The charism of religious life itself becomes the focus. From experience, the charism of a particular institute often becomes clearer in the midst of intercongregational community living. Interculturality, however, poses challenges as experienced in international congregations. The latter, a feature of SWSS, needs orientation and support and is characterized by an underdeveloped discourse.[29]

The question remains: Is this a new paradigm for religious life or an intensified collaboration for the purpose of building capacity among the poor, specifically among the people of South Sudan? An assessment that involves observation and experience indicates that the latter may be more accurate. It has become a challenge to find African indigenous religious congregations interested in having their members become part of SWSS. Members of African congregations are more comfortable living with their own members and establishing their own identity. SWSS is providing separate accommodations for members of two indigenous congregations interested in working alongside SWSS communities.

It should also be noted that few members of African congregations have the education and expertise to take on the administration of institutions.

---

29. This reflection comes from the author's own experience and the observations of Fr. Jim Greene, MAfr, the director of SWSS in Juba.

Their expertise is in direct service ministries. Few congregations have developed their own institutions and thus need their own educated personnel for internal and/or diocesan initiatives, and for this reason are not able to provide members to work with SWSS. SWSS sees mentoring and offering financial support to African religious in administration and management as an important aspect of building the capacity of the local church. It welcomes the capacity-building work being done by the African Sisters Education Collaborative (ASEC) and All Africa Conference Sister to Sister (AACSS).[30] And South Sudanese religious women are benefiting from these programs. One sister, supported by AACSS, will be working with SWSS beginning in 2021. Another is studying for a PhD in educational administration in Kenya, supported by Friends in Solidarity.

Given these personnel challenges, does SWSS offer something important for the rebuilding of society in South Sudan? A model that incorporates people from beyond Africa mirrors the universal church and witnesses to our oneness in Christ. International congregations with members in East Africa and beyond may be best suited to join SWSS as they witness to the possibility of living interculturally. Ethnic and religious differences are a source of conflict in South Sudan and many African countries. International congregations are committed to staying in the struggle in order to move beyond ethnic and cultural boundaries and conflicts in community. It is important for the future of their own congregations, and it models what we are called to by our faith. International congregations also have access to better training and resources, something desperately needed by African religious congregations and the people of South Sudan.

Keeping the vision of SWSS alive is also a challenge. Leadership changes in congregations often means that the commitment to SWSS is not sufficiently explained to incoming leadership. Screening of personnel is very important for SWSS. New members must be able to live in a multicultural community and be flexible in the use of their professional skills; at times this is overlooked in the face of the need for staff. There are fewer places in US for discernment for those considering mission in cross-cultural, conflict situations; still, it is important. Performance reviews and contact with the executive director regarding work and community are key to success of projects.

The model of SWSS has the potential to be beneficial for religious in both the global North and the global South. For those in the North, it is an opportunity to leave a legacy in the form of transferring skills from

---

30. ASEC is a collaborative ministry of US religious congregations of women and is funded by the Hilton Foundation. AACSS is an initiative of Sr. Margaret Farley, RSM, in response to the HIV/AIDS pandemic and works to build the capacities of religious congregations of women in Africa.

experienced religious in the North to religious in the South. A two- to three-year commitment by religious in the North brings new learning and skills to religious and laity in South Sudan, a country desperate for the infusion of such skills, and it reinvigorates a sense of mission for communities in the North. Religious from the North bring different models of leadership and administration, alternatives to African models, which are often patterned after that of tribal chiefs and authoritarian leaders. SWSS is a good venue for congregations wanting to begin a mission in the South Sudan but needing a good introduction to the country.

Conclusion

Pope Francis has described himself by saying, "I am flawed but chosen." Every person lives with inadequacies and human weakness, which are often more obvious to us than to others. But we need leadership . . . we need bishops . . . we need zealous Catholics . . . and some are chosen to lead. The biggest mistake in leadership is to try to pretend we are perfect. Rather, we need to see ourselves like Francis, as "chosen but flawed," needing support and encouragement from others and respecting others as equal human beings. As a new model of mission, SWSS is not perfect, but it is providing essential services for the severely disadvantaged people of South Sudan. Many of its members would not be in South Sudan were it not for this collaborative venture that provides an accountability structure and mutual support. SWSS has continued to provide services and development opportunities for the people of the country even when the violence of the conflict has been at its worst. SWSS members from diverse congregations and nationalities model unity among themselves and with the people of South Sudan. They rejoice in the strong faith of the people of South Sudan. They choose to accompany the South Sudanese people as sisters and brothers on their journey, not as global North and global South, but as one people seeking to move toward a sustainable future and a loving God.[31]

Bibliography

The Fund for Peace. "Fragile States Index 2020." https://fragilestatesindex.org/data.
International Congress on Consecrated Life. *Passion for Christ, Passion for Humanity.* Nairobi: Paulines Africa, 2005.

---

31. The author is indebted to Br. William Firman, FSC, a former director of SWSS, for his inspiration for this closing reflection.

Michael, Janet, and Gillian Garnett. "Strengthening Nursing and Midwifery in Southern Sudan: A Key Strategy for Improving Healthcare Beyond Independence." *Southern Sudan Medical Journal* 4.2 (May 2011). http://www.southsudanmedicaljournal.com/archive/may-2011/special-supplement-development-of-nursing-and-midwifery-services-in-south-sudan.html.

Moran, Nicole, and Nyokabi Kahura. *Evolution of Solidarity with South Sudan*. Rome, August 2019. Available upon request from info@solidaritysudan.org.

Origins and History of Solidarity with South Sudan: Extracts from Summary Report of the Delegation to Southern Sudan. Presented March 2006 to the International Unions of Superiors General (UISG/USG). Rome: UISG/USG Justice, Peace, and Integrity of Creation Commission, 2006. Available upon request from info@solidaritysudan.org.

Solidarity with South Sudan. *Governance Manual*. Rev. ed. Rome: SWSS, 2017. Available upon request from info@solidaritysudan.org.

South Sudan Education Cluster, Save the Children, and UNICEF. "Education Cluster Assessment South Sudan, October 2018." October 31, 2018. https://reliefweb.int/report/south-sudan/education-cluster-assessment-south-sudan-october-2018.

Stanislaus, Lazar T., and Carolyn Buhs, eds. *Collaborative Mission in South Sudan*. Sankt Ottilien, Germany: Sankt Ottilien, 2022.

Sudan Relief Fund. "Pope Francis Set to Visit South Sudan in July." March 25, 2022. https://sdnrlf.com/pope-francis-set-to-visit-south-sudan-in-july/.

United Nations Children's Development Fund (UNICEF). "Humanitarian Action for Children: South Sudan." Juba: UNICEF, December 2019. https://www.unicef.org/southsudan/reports/humanitarian-action-children-2020.

United Nations Development Program (UNDP). "Economic Cluster Urges Policies to Balance Development with Protecting South Sudan's Environment." December 16, 2020. https://www.undp.org/south-sudan/press-releases/economic-cluster-urges-policies-balance-development-protecting-south-sudans-environment.

United Nations Educational, Scientific, and Cultural Organization (UNESCO). *Global Initiative on Out-of-School Children: South Sudan Country Study*. New York: UNESCO, 2018. https://unesdoc.unesco.org/ark:/48223/pf0000265399.

United Nations Office for the Coordination of Humanitarian Affairs (UNOCHA). "South Sudan Situation Report." March 29, 2019. https://reliefweb.int/sites/reliefweb.int/files/resources/Situation%20Report%20-%20South%20Sudan%20-%2029%20Mar%202019.pdf.

PART FIVE

Healing Trauma and Invisible Wounds

13

Trauma Healing and Reconciliation in Post-Genocide Rwanda: A Complementary and Dialectical Approach

ELISEE RUTAGAMBWA, SJ

Introduction

FOLLOWING THE SHIFT FROM interstate to intrastate wars that has characterized the post–Cold War era, the world has been confronted with unprecedented complex situations while rebuilding societies after mass violence. Prominent among them is the controversy over the prioritization of either trauma healing or reconciliation in peace-building and national reconstruction. Focusing on the Rwandan post-genocide context, in this chapter, I first recall the egregious immediate post-genocide situation and its unprecedented challenges. Second, I highlight the disputes over the prioritization of either trauma healing or reconciliation in the process of reconstruction. Third, building on lessons learned from selected trauma healing and reconciliation initiatives—namely, the Healing Life Wounds (HLW) initiative conducted by Dr. Simon Gasibirege and his Life Wounds Healing Association (LIWOHA) and the Christian Gacaca (a Catholic Church reconciliation initiative)—I maintain that neither the exclusive prioritization of trauma healing nor that of reconciliation is a suitable course of action in addressing the post-genocide reconstruction challenges. Instead, I underscore a complementary and dialectical approach that simultaneously fosters trauma healing and reconciliation, and finally, I underline the contribution of theological ethics in sustaining both genuine and lasting trauma healing and reconciliation.

Post-Genocide Rwandan Context and Challenges

In 1994, Rwanda experienced one of the most atrocious genocides of the twentieth century. Following the Hutu extremist government refusal to implement the peace accords agreed upon with the Rwandan Patriotic Front, or RFP—a rebel group mainly composed by former Tutsi refugees who had been denied citizenship for thirty years—the government resorted to the "final solution of the Tutsi." It mobilized its resources and entire apparatus—namely its administration, security institutions ([military, police, and security services], its judiciary, its allied extremist political parties and their youth militia, the media, etc.)—and conducted the most horrendous extermination that the country had ever seen before. Using the entire arsenal within their reach, modern as well as traditional weaponry, and following pre-established lists of Tutsis, they moved from house to house and mercilessly hacked to death any Tutsi on their passage. These included unborn babies, children, men and women, youth, and elderly, etc. Women and girls were raped publicly and reduced to sexual slaves after the killing of their loved ones. As a result, many of them contracted HIV/AIDS, and others carried unwanted babies.[1]

Mass killings were mostly conducted in churches and Catholic school buildings, public halls and stadia, and other places that could gather as many people as possible. In most cases, victims were forced to march to their deaths, submitted to all kinds of humiliation, tortured physically and psychologically along the way, and eventually killed in the most abject ways. Those who managed to run away or hide were hunted down like savage animals until they were found. Eventually, they were butchered or left to die in the wilderness.[2] As Tutsis and Hutus lived together and were even mixed in families, the genocide against the Tutsi has been called the "intimate genocide." This explains how it took an extra mile in its inhumanity. It destroyed the most intimate relationships. Parents killed their children and vice versa, pastors their parishioners and vice versa, teachers their students and vice versa, medical doctors their patients, etc. Novice masters abandoned their novices, and religious superiors handed their inferiors to the killers. After

---

1. See des Forges, *Leave None*; and Dallaire and Beardsley, *Shake Hands*.
2. See Omaar, *Rwanda*; and Gourevitch, *We Wish*.

the killings, some victims were thrown into mass graves or pit latrines, and others were left to roast under the sun or served as animal fodder. Subsequently, all their properties were either stolen or destroyed. Their homes were either left in unrecognizable condition or totally erased. In only a hundred days, more than a million Tutsis—and Hutus who declined to partake in the killings or protected their Tutsi neighbors—were exterminated. According to the estimates, one-seventh of the Rwandan population perished, and ten thousand people were killed daily, thus making the genocide against the Tutsis one of the fastest genocides in history.

After the genocide was stopped, not only were a million people killed and their human remains still rotting under the sun or hidden, but two million others had also fled the country, thus prompting one of the most massive refugee crises in modern history. Hundreds of thousands of other people were internally displaced. The country counted hundreds of thousands of orphans and widows and uncountable war casualties, physical and mental patients, trauma victims, and disabled people. On the other hand, there were hundreds of thousands of genocide suspects awaiting trial in overcrowded jails while others remained unidentified among the rest of the population, including their victims. On the political front, none of the government institutions were functioning, as civil servants had either been killed or fled the country. Only members of the Rwandan Patriotic Front who had just stopped the genocide and the remnants of political opponents to the former regime were trying to cope with the untenable situation. On the economic front, all government coffers had been emptied by the fugitives of the former regime who later settled in neighboring Democratic Republic of Congo (DRC), then Zaire. From there, they were planning to return to Rwanda to finish off their genocidal agenda. It did not take long before they started infiltrating Rwanda, targeting genocide survivors, ambushing buses, and attacking boarding schools.

In the outside world, most of the nations who had stood by while the genocide was unfolding now considered the country as a failed state and were reluctant to mobilize funds to come to the rescue of the genocide survivors. Instead, they drew all their attention and humanitarian assistance to the refugee camps, disregarding the fact that they had been transformed into military camps by the genocide perpetrators.[3] It was under these circumstances that disputes over trauma healing and reconciliation prioritization emerged among many other dilemmas that the country was facing.

---

3. Martin, "Hard Choices after Genocide," 157–76.

Disputes over the Prioritization of Either Trauma Healing or Reconciliation

As Pearlman noted referring to the magnitude of the prevailing trauma in post-genocide Rwanda, "Nearly every citizen has been affected individually by violence, whether from direct involvement in perpetrating crimes, from personal injury, or from the injury or death of loved ones."[4] As a matter of fact, posttraumatic symptoms such as intrusive memories, flashbacks, nightmares, anxiety, suicide attempts, and hypervigilance were everywhere to be seen. Hence, although there were many priorities, trauma healing was one of them and certainly one of the most urgent.

Prominent among those who advocated for that priority were the different associations of genocide survivors. According to them, it was unthinkable to talk about reconciliation as a priority since they were still hurting from their unprecedented traumatic experience and being hunted down by unidentified perpetrators in their midst. Not only were the latter eager to finish up their genocidal agenda, but they were also trying to eliminate survivors to erase any possible testimony against them. Besides, given their anger, the survivors' outcry was much more in favor of seeing justice done rather than contemplating the idea of reconciliation.

Academically, some approaches to trauma healing justify the priority of individual trauma healing over concerns about restoration of social relationships such as those advocated for by community or national reconciliation. For example, as is argued in some approaches to psychotherapy, by its very nature, the process of healing from emotional trauma focuses primarily on individual healing. In this perspective, as David Brendel highlights,

> [t]he focus . . . is on what is best for the individual person, regardless of what might be best for other individuals in similar situations or what might be in the best interests of the patient's family or community. As such, the therapist avoids placing the patient on a procrustean bed of what would be helpful to victims of trauma as a general rule or to others in the social environment. In addition, when working with an individual patient, the therapist focuses on providing the patient with optimal care, even if that means excluding other equally deserving patients from his or her practice.[5]

For those who advocated for the prioritization of reconciliation (the new government and some church leaders), the major concerns were the

---

4. Clark, *Gacaca Courts*, 40.
5. Brendel, "Psychotherapy," 17.

survival of Rwanda as a nation and the future of its people. Indeed, the genocide had pushed ethnic division to its climax, and there were good reasons to believe that national unity was irreparable. On the one hand, most survivors were convinced that they would never live with their perpetrators again. On the other, while some bystanders were envisioning the partition of the country into Hutu and Tutsi lands,[6] some scholars justified it as the only lasting solution to end the conflict once and for all.[7] Others again simply deemed Rwanda a failed state. Therefore, reconciliation was the condition for survival, and it needed to be worked out before it was too late.

However, for realistic and optimistic leaders, things were not as clear-cut and absolutely desperate as they appeared. In fact, although the genocide had indeed escalated ethnic division to its climax and prompted trauma to the extreme, not all Hutu were anti-Tutsi and vice versa. During the genocide, there were signs of hope. Some Hutu heroically sacrificed their lives to save their Tutsi neighbors while others fought alongside the Rwandan Patriotic Front to stop the killings. Clearly, not everything was compromised. As these examples indicate, there were still chances to save the nation, and reconciliation was not only possible, but it was the only promising way forward.

Academically, the new developments in warfare and its destructive effects observed at the end of the twentieth century had led to revisions of the classical methods of conflict resolution and peacebuilding. With emerging hate crimes and their vicious circles, subsequent massive loss of life, psychological trauma, etc., the old ways of retaliation or retributive justice could no longer provide appropriate answers.[8] There were, therefore, sound arguments that fostered reconciliation as one of the most credible and pressing alternatives.

Although these two approaches present sound arguments, neither of them alone could have helped cope with the post-genocide situation. Initiatives taken both in trauma healing and reconciliation show that *each* of them was urgently needed. Therefore, they had to be pursued simultaneously. Let's now consider two of the initiatives—Healing Life Wounds and Christian Gacaca—that played a significant role in this process and show how they substantiate the point.

---

6. Already on April 18, 1994, in a manuscript note to President François Mitterrand, Hubert Védrine, then secretary to Mitterand, evoked Alain Juppé's project of the territorial partition of Rwanda along ethnic lines. See Védrine, "Lettre Manuscrite."

7. Byman, *Keeping the Peace*, 280.

8. Minow, *Between Vengeance and Forgiveness*, 2.

Selected Trauma Healing and Reconciliation Initiatives

To begin with, Healing Life Wounds (HLW) was initiated by Rwandan psychologist Dr. Simon Gasibirege in 1995 in the aftermath of the genocide against the Tutsi. In her article, Dr. Régine King, who closely worked with him, gives us a glimpse of the initiative. As she relates, the initial implementation of HLW was modeled on NGOs such as World Vision Rwanda. However, Gasibirege soon concluded that it was neither viable nor sustainable within such a framework and could hardly make the impact he intended. Probably due to the misunderstanding of the situation's complexities and the depth of hurt inflicted by genocide and other types of violence to the people, most Western NGOs envisioned the work of healing and reconciliation in terms of "business as usual." Underlying their methodologies was the rational technicality according to which healing and reconciliation were to be achieved following a managed process based on budgetary discipline and skilled mediators who had to help opposite parties identify issues of conflict and meet the pre-established goals in a timely manner. But as Schreiter rightly remarks, such a reconciliation is reduced to "a skill to be mastered" or "a tool to repair" a broken world. According to him, it should be instead more of an attitude than an acquired skill and more of a spirituality than a strategy.[9]

On the other hand, as King underscores, other types of interventions have been criticized for their narrow concept of suffering and their insensitivity to the complexities of local realities. Among other works, she cites Western trauma theory, which she accuses of "emphasizing individual mental health at the expense of the collective impact of violence on communities."[10] Therefore, in Gasibirege's view, envisioned as a Western process that was transient and bureaucratic in nature, healing and reconciliation in post-genocide Rwanda could never be accomplished. The process required more listening, repeating, going back and forth, as well as having the necessary patience to allow the concerned parties to articulate their burdens of pain or guilt. In addition, the people needed to engage the process according to their pace and in a manner that respected their cultural expression. This approach has been backed by medical anthropologists and cultural psychiatrists such as Paul Farmer and Laurence Kirmayer, who understand that mass violence does not only impact individual human lives but also destroys lifestyles and that it targets, as well as attempts to eliminate,

---

9. Schreiter, *Reconciliation*, 26.
10. King, "True Healing," 50.

"entire ethnic groups, eradicating cultures and social systems."[11] In the same vein, considering the divide between victims and perpetrators and the multilayered traumatic experiences resulting from the genocide, King deems it crucial to conjoin individual therapies and society-based interventions through which affected people can be supported to heal both their personal and collective wounds. That is why she joined her mentor, Gasibirege, in his decision to conceive their own model, taking the initiative to the grassroots and implementing it through the local organization he himself founded, namely Life Wounds Healing Association (LIWOHA). The intervention was conducted in two different sites: the Southern Province and the outskirts of the capital city Kigali in 2006 and 2009, respectively. What objectives did the initiative seek to achieve? How was it conducted? What was its outcome?

The Healing Life Wounds approach had two main objectives. The first was to facilitate the healing of individual wounds and rehabilitate communities affected by the genocide using the tools and language of their own context. The second was to address the subsequent impact of the post-genocide experiences of exile, repatriation, imprisonment, and family breakdown. As King explains, to achieve these objectives, the intervention adopted a threefold methodology. This methodology combines Western therapeutic procedures, the spiritual practice of confession and forgiveness, and Rwandan traditional reconciliatory practices. It proceeds by sharing experiences through storytelling, a guided series of exercises, and presentations of psycho-education.

While Western methodologies rely on universalistic and positivist perspectives, and spiritual practices were inspired by the Christian ritual of confession and forgiveness, Rwandan traditional reconciliatory practices are mostly community-oriented and exercised through critical ethnography. Since the two previous methods are quite familiar, let us focus on the last—Gacaca—and highlight its relevance to the context. In the traditional practice of Gacaca, which inspired the Rwandan reconciliatory practices after the genocide, elders bring together community members and attend to the following:

1. listening to the testimonies of parties who have outstanding grievances,
2. sharing painful experiences,
3. acknowledging wrongdoing,
4. exchanging apologies,
5. determining compensation,
6. and renewing the terms of peaceful coexistence.

---

11. Pedersen et al., "Sequelae of Political Violence," 214.

In King's intervention, HLW followed the same steps after people had initial preparatory sessions meant to create a safe environment for the exercise and to instruct them about social violence. At the end, the intervention had to evaluate the experience.

In addition to the assessment based on Western perspectives, King also introduced another appraisal mechanism that used critical ethnographic method. Unlike the previous approaches, which mostly relied on the objective assessment of intervenors' behavior throughout the intervention, the latter focused on historical and cultural tactics. Prominent among them was the narrative inquiry, which, according to King, "is a form of qualitative enquiry, interested in what human beings are doing or saying, and the meaning-making of the information in a given context as well as how the production of such information fits or does not fit in existing narratives."[12] As Vena Das and Arthur Kleinman fittingly point out, the strength of critical ethnography lies in its "careful attention to the details and the long-term engagement of the ethnographers with the places and people they describe; they demonstrate that there is no straightforward translation of social scripts into social action."[13]

In terms of its *modus operandi,* King points out, the HLW intervention used a bottom-up approach whereby workshops were organized at the grassroots and gathered people on a voluntary basis. Prior to the exchanges, the organizers created a safe space by establishing guiding principles for intervenors. These included, among others, the principles of confidentiality, autonomy, mutual respect, and support. During the workshop, small groups of Hutu and Tutsi, including victims and perpetrators or their respective relatives, were encouraged to share their personal stories. They were guided by a series of exercises aimed at helping overcome painful grievances.

In King's evaluation of the HLW intervention, which conjoined the findings of the original study and those of the subsequent follow-up, she noted remarkable progress made by participants over time. Not only did they become aware of their psychosocial wounds both personally and collectively, but they also recovered their voice and gained confidence in communicating their painful past experiences through shared stories. On the other hand, as they drew attention to others' experiences through storytelling and careful listening, they were able to recover a sense of mutuality and compassion. Another sign of progress that King highlights was the creative initiative participants came up with after the completion of HLW's initial intervention. As she points out, "With the support of other HLW

12. King, "True Healing," 52.
13. Kleinman, "Violences of Everyday," 1.

graduates, they decided to organize an annual community reconciliation event to inform their fellow community members about the importance of healing."[14] Furthermore, as a follow-up intervention later proved, there was an evolving and sustained personal and collective healing, which translated into participants' active engagement.

Christian Gacaca

For the church, the idea of Christian Gacaca emerged at a defining moment. The church had been blamed for her reluctance to speak out while innocent Tutsis were slaughtered in churches, and some clerics were involved in the killings. Moreover, another part of the church, including Hutu priests who associated with genocide perpetrators and some missionaries, had been denying or minimizing the genocide against the Tutsi.[15] As a result, the church's reputation was at its lowest, and her internal division was so deep that reconciliation was needed more than ever. In addition, like the rest of the society, the church was deeply hurting and needed healing. Not only had it lost many of its priests, religious, and faithful, but among its members were many Christians who still suffered from the horrendous violence and trauma inflicted during the genocide. Another factor that contributed to the emergence of Christian Gacaca was the 2000 Jubilee Year, a special year of forgiveness and reconciliation, which had been proclaimed by Pope John Paul II for the whole Catholic Church.[16] This coincided with the centennial of the arrival of the first missionaries in Rwanda. Rather than celebrating the successes, the church used the occasion for self-examination about its role during the genocide and its duty to reconcile a divided church. As Cardinal Antoine Kambanda later explains,

> However, under the circumstances of genocide, we could not celebrate the jubilee like others did. We had to find our way of living this important historical event of the universal church in general and of the Rwandan church in particular. It was a challenge for the pastors and theologians to find a way of doing pastoral work in a post-genocide society of Rwanda.[17]

That is how the church decided to organize a synod on ethnocentrism, which was identified as the major issue of concern for the church and

---

14. King, "True Healing," 54.
15. Denis, "Grief and Denial," 287–307.
16. See John Paul II, *Tertio Millenio Adveniente*.
17. Kambanda, "Role of the Church," 56–57.

society. However, as Philippe Denis remarks, due to the church's role during the genocide, it had a strained relationship with the new government and genocide survivors.[18] Therefore, the celebration of the Jubilee served as an opportunity for a public apology and the renewal of the church's relationship with the society. Now, what were the objectives of Christian Gacaca, and how did it help in social healing and reconciliation?

Unlike the official Gacaca, which mostly focused on popular justice, Christian Gacaca only concentrated on its reconciliatory mechanism. In the summary report of the preliminary research that he contributed to the commission on Gacaca cited by Philippe Denis, Catholic Bishop Smaragde Mbonyintege made it clear from the beginning that "[i]t was the task of the tribunals, and not of the *gacaca*, to judge the murders, rapes, and thefts committed during the genocide. Where *gacaca* could help was in establishing the truth and promoting the true values on which society could reconstruct itself."[19] The same position was echoed by Archbishop Thaddeus Ntihinyurwa in response to former cabinet minister Nayinzira Nepomuscene's concern that the church disregarded the punishment of perpetrators. The archbishop replied, "The church does not replace the instances responsible for punishment. It encourages people to confess and ask for forgiveness, so that love returns to the place from where it had disappeared. The church is careful not to hamper the work of justice."[20] In this view, its duty was not to judge wrongdoers but to facilitate Gacaca in healing and reconciling people whose relationships had been severely shattered because of the genocide. Hence, Christian Gacaca had two main objectives. The first one had to do with trauma healing, and it aimed at restoring a sense of humanity or, to use the literal Rwandan term, *Gusana Imitima*. The second concerned reconciliation, and it involved guiding people through the practice and rituals of forgiveness and reconciliation. How did the church proceed to achieve these objectives?

Placing Christian Gacaca in the context of the preparation of the synod on ethnocentrism, the Catholic Church first called a planning meeting which comprised four bishops and a hundred priests. This was held at Nyakibanda Major Seminary on July 4–7, 1998. It decided to focus on the topic of ethnocentrism and commended Gacaca as the methodology to follow. During the preparatory period, it was decided that each diocese would organize a synod in which the question of ethnic racism would be the focal point of analysis, and the Gacaca process would offer the space to different

---

18. Denis, "Christian *Gacaca*," 3.
19. Denis, "Christian *Gacaca*," 7.
20. Denis, "Christian *Gacaca*," 11.

Christian representatives to meet and tell the truth. On August 25, 1998, during the meeting of the national commission for the Jubilee, the Rwandan Bishops formally endorsed the recommendation of the Nyakibanda meeting and, three months later, they released a Jubilee preparatory letter that launched the synod.[21] Afterwards, they established structures from the diocese to the parish levels and synod facilitators, including priests and basic community leaders. The invited audience for Gacaca sessions included students, religious communities, prisoners, intellectuals, and families. On the opening day of the synod, there was a Mass, presided over by the bishop surrounded by all the priests of the diocese as a sign of their full support of the process. During Mass, the objectives and process of Gacaca were explained. The initial sessions consisted of creating a safe and trustful environment for participants to share their stories freely. They insisted on values of tolerance, confidentiality, truth telling, and mutual respect. In some instances, experts in history, psychotherapy, and sociopsychology—including founding members of the Life Wounds Healing Association—were invited to instruct participants. These provided them with relevant knowledge concerning the nature and dynamic of violent conflicts and illustrated their points using examples from other countries that have suffered mass violence.[22]

During the actual Christian Gacaca sessions, people were encouraged to tell the truth as they were sharing their painful experiences. Cardinal Kambanda notes that Christian Gacaca brought together both genocide perpetrators and survivors.[23] Workshops were organized that gathered small Christian communities and had them pray together. The people would all meditate on the word of God and later share, alternatively, their stories of suffering. While some were telling their stories, others listened quietly without judging them, even when the stories concerned gross human rights violations. Everyone was encouraged to ponder sympathetically the suffering endured by each without making comparisons. After sharing stories, people were invited to testify about their experiences as they listened and concluded by expressing whether they committed or not to ask or grant forgiveness. What was the concrete outcome of these sessions?

When the Christian Gacaca process came to its completion, people were able to shift their emotions and sympathize with the ordeal of their peers who belonged either to the perpetrators or the survivors' group. Some of those who perpetrated the genocide confessed their crimes and asked for forgiveness. In some cases, they were even ready to repair their wrongdoing

---

21. Denis, "Christian *Gacaca*," 11.
22. Denis, "Christian *Gacaca*," 11–12.
23. Rutagambwa et al., *Reinventing Theology*, 57.

or collaborate with civil justice. On the other hand, the genocide survivors were rehabilitated and regained their dignity. They even agreed to renew their interactions and forgive those who murdered their relatives. As these were genuine cases of confession and forgiveness, they favored mutual healing in church communities. The process gradually released the tension between opposite ethnic groups, and they started intermingling both in worship and pastoral activities. In some instances, they were even working together, former perpetrators offering supportive services and gifts to the survivors, or all of them engaging in common development enterprises or doing business together. This paved the way for the reconstruction of the Christian community and allowed significant normalization. Not everything was positive, however. There were also significant shortcomings, but overall, their efforts in leading the dual process of healing and reconciliation are appreciable. What lessons can be learned from their efforts to substantiate the relevance of their complementary and dialectical approaches in response to the post-genocide context?

For a Complementary and Dialectical Approach

Lessons from the Above Initiatives

After considering the two selected initiatives—Healing Life Wounds and Christian Gacaca—it is notable that both took seriously the complementary and dialectical approaches. First, in their objectives, they clearly stated that they aimed at both trauma healing and reconciliation. Even though the implementation proved harder than expected in some cases, the two initiatives linked trauma healing and reconciliation hand in hand and were able to produce tangible, positive results, which not only could help the country get back on track but also paved the way for continual efforts that have now revived the country irreversibly. It is also important to emphasize the mutual influence of both trauma healing and reconciliation operations. As has been witnessed, the more people were able to cope with their trauma, the better disposed they were to reengage in interactions with their foes and the more empowered they were to regain trust and reconcile with them. This explains why the two initiatives were among the most successful, although on an unequal basis and in need of continuous and creative improvement.

In regard to HLW, it is clear that it was more effective than and even instrumental to Christian Gacaca, probably due to its clearly determined targeted groups and the care put into preparing those groups. Not only did it lend a hand to it in helping train its facilitators, but it also shared its professional therapeutic skills. Certainly, it took longer as it required the patience to allow for voluntary participation, facilitate the conscientization of participants, and ensure prior training in relevant subjects to provide a broader understanding of the nature and dynamics of the violence the people went through. In addition, not only did HLW offer room for creativity as it allowed people to seek solutions from their cultural context, but it also conducted its evaluation within a sufficient length of time following participation in HLW to confirm the outcome. HLW even later extended its interventions to neighboring countries, thus leading the efforts of trauma healing and reconciliation beyond the Rwandan national borders.

As for Christian Gacaca, it also made a big difference, especially in terms of awakening the Christian community to the imperative of trauma healing and reconciliation. Further, it reenergized the Christian community, giving the church the impetus to reclaim its moral responsibility to reconcile society and partake in the efforts of reconstruction. Prior to this initiative, the church was paralyzed by internal divisions and burdened by the consequences of genocide. While some Christians were crushed by the pain and hopelessness that stemmed from the genocide, others were either ashamed of their unspeakable evildoing or self-defensive. Others were in denial of what had really happened. As Philippe Denis remarks, before Christian Gacaca, the church was enclosed within itself and could hardly play its social and spiritual role in society. The advent of Christian Gacaca helped the church seize the opportunity to play its dutiful spiritual role of caring and reconciling the faithful. In addition, the process contributed to interpersonal, communal, and social healing. In this respect, Christian Gacaca also helped the church to heal its relationship with both genocide survivors' associations and the new government, which contributed to renewed trust and interaction between the two institutions. Following this development, both the local and the universal church apologized for their role during the genocide and committed to supporting and promoting reconciliation efforts within the church, society at large, and even beyond. Certainly, though, not everything was perfect. Although Christian Gacaca made a significant contribution, it is nonetheless important to note that the outcome could have been far better if the church had deployed all of its potential resources. In this chapter's final point, we will see how such resources can enhance the complementary and dialectical approach for which I advocate.

It follows from the outcomes of these two interventions that the complementary and dialectical approach to trauma healing and reconciliation is a better response to post-genocide and other mass violent situations than an exclusive prioritization of either trauma healing or reconciliation. To substantiate the point, I will first elucidate the unusual and complex character of the post-genocide context that makes this dual approach compelling; then, I will highlight the insufficiency of the linear or circular progress approaches often used to back the prioritization of one over the other.

For a Complementary and Dialectical Approach

First, to appreciate the relevance of the complementary and dialectical approach, it is important to understand the situation following mass violence of genocide's magnitude and its unusual and complex character. Unlike any other situation, the post-genocide state is always replete with unprecedented challenges and complex dilemmas. Here, what is normal becomes abnormal, and what is abnormal becomes normal. That is why, as Priscilla Hayner rightly says, the killings are "unspeakable truths"—one hardly finds appropriate words to translate them.[24] On the one hand, given the massive destruction, when the effort of reconstruction starts, everything becomes a priority. For example, in a normal situation, it is obvious that trauma healing should precede reconciliation. But in the post-genocide context, given the massive numbers of people involved in the crime, those affected by it, and the imperative of relying on that same population to rebuild the country, neither trauma healing nor reconciliation is possible if they are not done simultaneously.

Second, given these unprecedented dilemmas, it is illusory to pretend to rely on classical ways of response. For example, in the ideal case, when a country is facing crimes against humanity, the proper way of dealing with it is recourse to the court of law. But in a post-genocide situation, not only is the judicial system destroyed, but the magnitude of the crime and the high number of culprits are also too much to cope with, even when operating within a well-functioning judiciary system. In the case of Rwanda in particular, it was not even possible to keep victims and perpetrators separate while figuring out what to do. They were all intermingled, and the potential for further harm needed only the slightest trigger. In addition, peace, security, and reconstruction were so imperative and compelling that they could not be disregarded in favor of caring for the victims, because they were precisely the preconditions for trauma healing and reconciliation everyone was longing for.

Finally, the approaches usually used to deal with minor trauma and reconciliation cases could not work. As mentioned above, the dynamics of trauma healing and the processes of reconciliation under post-genocide

24. Hayner, *Unspeakable Truths*.

conditions are so unprecedented that mechanisms typically used to address them either become useless or lead to additional catastrophes. One such approach is the linear progress approach that is often used by Western scholars and NGOs in post-violent societies. Guided by the principle of efficiency, the linear progress approach aims at achieving tangible measurable results in record time. Further, with a pre-established step-by-step plan and meticulously controlled budget calendar, it hardly conforms to the pace and process of genuine reconciliation and trauma healing. Another approach is the circular tactic often prevalent in indigenous communities. As John Paul Lederach explains, reconciliation and social healing are widely understood as processes involving some form of movement in a developmental progression. Hence, as a metaphor, movement has two perspectives. According to certain authors, Lederach points out,

> Reconciliation and healing encompass cyclical and circular movements. These are literally drawn out as images with circles, often in the form of a single iteration that seems to suggest the beginning of a spiral, the end point of the circle being somewhat higher than the beginning point. In addition, an emerging trend in recent years has documented the important contributions, perspectives, and practices of indigenous peoples that focus much more directly on the importance of *circle* per se, on native understandings of restoration and change, and on approaches based on ceremony and ritual.[25]

Most often, those who envision reconciliation and healing as cyclical in nature also indicate that the processes follow a linear progression. In other words, they identify discernible stages. Here, the analytical assumption is to identify patterns that emerge when one considers several cases to understand the functioning of reconciliation and healing. Although most authors admit an inherent tension between the circular and linear movements, some deny the linearity of circular movements while suggesting the stages they follow. As Lederach further observes, seeking to create scientific and pragmatic concepts, the academic literature has often overlooked the tension. Thus, while reconciliation and healing have gained prominence even as political categories referring to deeply complex social realities, Lederach notes that a paradigm undergirded by "a metaphor structure of linearity, with its sequential notion of social change and progression in time, has become increasingly prevalent."[26] In this view, he remarks, the underlying assumption of the linear structure is that "reason, maturity, and

25. Lederach and Lederach, *When Blood and Bones Cry*, 5.
26. Lederach and Lederach, *When Blood and Bones Cry*, 5.

individual and social health develop towards the latter stages of the sequential progression, whereas unhealthy patterns of reactivity, denial, being stuck, repetitiousness, and irrationality are prevalent in the earlier stages."[27] Consequently, the literature on social healing and reconciliation disregard other metaphors or deem them irrelevant while privileging linear structure as the necessary matrix to understand or deal with them. Despite the inadequacy of linear metaphors, Lederach does not dismiss them altogether. Instead, he emphasizes the fact that they fail to account for more hidden aspects of healing and reconciliation that are prevalent specifically in contexts of protracted, mass violence and deep-rooted conflicts. Further, he insists that linearity is inadequate on its own to penetrate the nature of social healing. Hence, gaining insights from the tactics of communities emerging from horrendous violent conflicts in different parts of the world, he proposes a metaphor shift from linearity to the sound metaphor. Unlike linearity, "[s]ound rises and falls in joy and in sorrow, in loss and in triumph, in fear and in courage."[28] In other words, such a dialectical approach illustrated by the sound metaphor better captures the complex and unpredictable reality of the post-violence condition while providing insights and helping understand the multifaceted nature of reconciliation and social healing.

It is in this same vein, looking at the problem within the context of the South African Truth and Reconciliation Commission (TRC) and from the perspective of psychotherapy, that Brendel affirms that individual and community-wide healing from emotional trauma are not mutually exclusive processes. Although he concurs that one or the other may be prioritized in specific cases, he nonetheless recommends that mental health clinicians must seriously consider both individual and collective factors when determining the appropriate way to help traumatized people and communities to heal and reconcile. It is crucial, Brendel insists, that the clinician take into consideration, in an individual's therapy, the role played by other people in that patient's life and the implications of the therapy for those other people. Conversely, in reconciliation processes such as the TRC that follow a long, drawn-out violent history, clinicians should not overlook the individual experiences and needs of specific traumatized people participating in national reconciliation processes. For Brendel, it is therefore crucial to have recourse to a dialectical approach. As he argues, "A dialectical approach to healing emotional trauma—in which individual and collective factors deeply shape

---

27. Lederach and Lederach, *When Blood and Bones Cry*, 6.
28. Atkinson, "Foreword," xi.

and influence one another—can help mental health clinicians to balance all of these disparate concerns."[29]

The advantage of such an approach lies in its integration of individual and collective concerns. Not only does it protect individuals, but it also promotes the sociopolitical process of national reconciliation. As he puts it, "The individual/community dialectic applies as much to psychotherapy of patients with trauma histories as it does to devastated societies trying to heal themselves through processes such as the TRC."[30] In other words, the psychotherapist's work consists of dialectically empathizing with the patient's reported experience as it also considers other people's perspectives and the overall sociocultural context where both trauma and the subsequent therapeutic interaction occurs. Envisioned in these dialectic terms, trauma healing and reconciliation processes pay equal attention to trauma victims, perpetrators, and the complex communities in which they share their lives.

Certainly, these approaches offer relevant insights and necessary practical guidance. However, like any human enterprise, they also bear the marks of human finitude and limitations. Viewed from the perspective of faith, independently of these approaches' potential effectiveness, they cannot satisfy or fulfill the kind of healing and reconciliation that human beings deeply long for, especially when confronted with existential questions such as those raised by the troubling crime of genocide and its consequences. That is why, to enhance this dialectical method, it is important to rise to a spiritual approach and consider what theological ethics has to offer in this respect.

Role of Theological Ethics in Enhancing the Complementary and Dialectical Approach

The critical problem at the heart of trauma healing and reconciliation and which the complementary and dialectical approach wrestles to address is what Geiko Müller-Fahrenholz calls the "bondage" that keeps the perpetrator and the victim locked together—and the need for them to set each other free. As he puts it, "Every act of transgression constitutes a bondage that keeps the perpetrator and the victim locked together. The more violent the transgression, the deeper the bondage."[31] Transgression is inherent to human activity, and there is no way we can act without getting in someone's way. Therefore, we need to assume it and constantly find reasonable ways to

29. Brendel, "Psychotherapy," 22.
30. Brendel, "Psychotherapy," 24.
31. Müller-Fahrenholz, *Art of Forgiveness*, 24.

deal with it. But as Müller-Fahrenholz states, the major problem is that "the heavier the guilt and the more painful the hurt, the more difficult this mutual unburdening becomes."[32] Whether we attempt to silence our conscience or have recourse to the psychologist's "power of numbing," extended forms of repression and denial do no more than generate either character distortions or various illnesses that worsen the situation. How, then, do trauma healing and reconciliation—envisioned from the theological, ethical perspective— add value to the complementary and dialectical approach? How do they help unlock the painful bondage that tie together perpetrators and victims, thus leading to their mutual liberation? To respond to these questions, I suggest three important ways. First, the theological, ethical perspective presents genuine trauma healing and reconciliation not simply as a human tactic but as God's gifts. Second, grounding them in the christological event shows how authentic healing and reconciliation are fundamentally achieved through Christ's incarnation and the redemptive action of his Passion and Resurrection. Third, this perspective elucidates the relevance of scriptural and sacramental resources available to the church and their instrumental ethical role in the praxis of trauma healing and reconciliation.

Healing and Reconciliation as God's Gifts

Although unlocking the bondage between perpetrator and victim constitutes an arduous task that is often doomed to failure, it is nevertheless not an impossible one. As Müller-Fahrenholz explains, it is achieved at the price of experiencing a cathartic moment which imposes upon the two parties a process of kenosis. To articulate the process, he uses an old German term referring to "repentance"—*Entblössung*—which literally means "denuding oneself." This is a process by which perpetrators return to the point where they committed the original evil act. To revisit this moment implies not only admitting the shameful implications of the act, but also being compelled to go through the more painful exercise of confessing the very act in the face of the victims. This involves self-humiliation that threatens the perpetrator's pride and self-esteem. That is why people don't like to appear in their nakedness before others, especially their victims, but rather prefer to run to the extremes of denial or rationalization. It is a crucial moment, however, that allows the perpetrators to liberate themselves.

On the side of the victims, a similar process takes them back to the original place of their hurt and compels them to reexperience the humiliation, the anger, the hatred, and the dehumanization they suffered. To

---

32. Müller-Fahrenholz, *Art of Forgiveness*, 24.

appreciate the level of such nakedness, Müller-Fahrenholz explains: "Hurt is an impairment of the core of our personhood and leads to an almost cosmic sense of insecurity. Consequently, there are many good reasons why victims want to avoid returning to the depth of their traumatic hurt."[33] Similar to the perpetrators, they also prefer to hide behind barricades of repression, anger, and self-righteousness. The realization of such a painful and yet liberating moment is what opens a mutual understanding of each one's pain and the struggle with the bondage in which they are locked. In other words, the overwhelming liberation takes place when one enters the pain of the other and breaks into tears. This is the cathartic moment that corrects the evil between the perpetrator and the victim and restores their human dignity.

Referring to Martin Buber's renowned book, *I and Thou*, Müller-Fahrenholz recalls the author's assertion that "[w]herever there is a genuine encounter between persons something new emerges, an energy which neither possesses within himself or herself or in isolation from the other, but which originates in their coming together. Whenever two human beings reveal themselves to each other, an 'energy-field' is established between them which transcends their individual strengths."[34] Although in secular discourse this may be given a different name, in the religious lexicon, this is recognized as God's Spirit, a power that enables people to discuss things that they would otherwise deem impossible. Since it is not *sui generis* but comes from outside, that power is an indication that God is at work in a mysterious way. Hence, the capacity to unlock the bondage between the perpetrator and the victim is fundamentally God's gift. This is what Esau and Jacob experienced when they met after twenty years of enmity and broke into a tearful embrace (Gen 33:4). It is also the experience of Joseph when reunited with his brothers (Gen 50:17) and that of Peter after realizing his betrayal of Jesus and weeping bitterly (Matt 26:75). As Müller-Fahrenholz underscores, "From the tears emerge the power that transcends the accustomed patterns of hatred, distrust, and prejudice, a power that overcomes deep-seated barriers and lays the ground for new trust."[35] This explains why reconciliation is first and foremost the work of God and cannot be a mere human labor. Certainly, God's Spirit also works and speaks through culture. That is why there is a need for a cultural hermeneutical critique that restores people's dignity as it revisits their cultural values. In this regard, it is crucial to rediscover the Rwandan concept of Ubuntu—"to be is to be together" (*Kubaho n'ukubana*)—as a resource for rethinking genuine Rwandan healing and

---

33. Müller-Fahrenholz, *Art of Forgiveness*, 26.
34. Müller-Fahrenholz, *Art of Forgiveness*, 33.
35. Müller-Fahrenholz, *Art of Forgiveness*, 28.

reconciliation. Now, how does such God's work translate into the christological event?

The Roots of Healing and Reconciliation in the Christological Event

The God who sparks his Spirit among former conflicting parties and prompts their mutual liberation is the very God who was incarnated in Jesus and humbled himself by becoming human. He is also the one who reconciled us with himself in the fundamental act of reconciliation through the Passion of his Son. As St. Paul makes clear, it is God who takes the initiative, and this is precisely what he asserts in his letters to the Philippians and Corinthians. In his letter to the Philippians, Paul describes Jesus's kenotic moment and enjoins Christians to emulate him in their relationships: "In your relationships with one another, have the same mindset as Christ Jesus who, being in very nature God, did not consider equality with God something to be used to his own advantage; rather, he made himself nothing, by taking the very nature of a servant, being made in human likeness. And being found in appearance as a man, he humbled himself by becoming obedient to death, even the death on a cross" (Phil 2:5–8 NIV). As we sing in the Easter Exsultet, this is the moment "when things of heaven are wed to those of earth, and divine to the human."[36] It is the moment Jesus empties himself to espouse the human condition in its brokenness and heals it by introducing humans into the divine life.

In Paul's second letter to the Corinthians, emphasizing God's initiative and referring to Christ's redemptive act, he states: "All this is from God, who reconciled us to himself through Christ, and has given us the ministry of reconciliation; that is, in Christ God was reconciling the world to himself, not counting their trespasses against them, and entrusting the message of reconciliation" (2 Cor 5:18–19 NIV). As we can see, reconciliation is not simply a planned process or a set of skills to achieve. It is instead, first and foremost, an invitation to experience the new world that God makes possible. As Paul further reveals, rather than returning to the original position, the telos of healing and reconciliation is rooted in God's new creation. In other words, genuine healing and reconciliation consist of partaking in God's life, which implies a conversion to a new way of seeing and being in the world. This is precisely what Paul says: "From now on, we regard no one according to the flesh. Although we once regarded Christ in this way, we do so no longer. Therefore, if anyone is in Christ, he is a new creation. The old has passed away. Behold, the new has come" (2 Cor 2:16–17 NIV). That is

---

36. "The Exsultet."

why, as stated in the 2009 African synod, "[r]econciliation involves a way of life (spirituality) and a mission."[37] More than the mere fruit of negotiations and diplomatic agreements, Paul Béré emphasizes, "It is the peace of a humanity reconciled with itself in God, a peace of which the church is the sacrament."[38] This peace is a moment of grace that enables both parties to reconnect face to face and have their dignified and equal humanity restored. Now, how should theological ethics help translate this vision of healing and reconciliation into practical actions?

The Relevance of Scriptural and Sacramental Resources and Their Instrumental Ethical Role in the Praxis of Trauma Healing and Reconciliation

First, to translate the above vision of healing and reconciliation into practice, theological ethics should not content itself with providing normative directives or abstract reconciliatory discourses. It should engage hearts and minds and, as Pope Francis would suggest, lead a work of mercy. Keeping in mind the traumatic burden that still weighs on people's hearts, mere discourse can indeed hardly heal their profound wounds or dispel the fears, shame, guilt, and resentment which stand in the way of reconciliation. It is crucial to engage with people's emotions and attend to their concerns with a caring dedication. As Johann Baptist Metz would say, it is vital to have recourse to the "mysticism of open eyes"[39] to be able to understand their cry and hear their lament. One of the ways of achieving that goal—and this is the second task of theological ethics—is to help them rediscover the relevance of the scriptural and sacramental resources and their ethical impact.

For too long, the church has privileged proclamation and pastoral letters as ways of conveying its message to the faithful. Whenever there was a particular concern, pastoral letters were issued, and dioceses were invited to read them to the faithful during Sunday Masses. Although this method proved somewhat viable, it has had its own shortcomings. Once the message was released and delivered to the public, it was assumed that the mission was over and people understood. In most cases, the church did not elaborate any means of breaking the message down to make it accessible to the grassroots or translating it into concrete policies that could be implemented in church institutions and structures.

37. Synod of Bishops, Second Special Assembly for Africa, "Elenchus Finalis," Propositio 9.
38. Benedict XVI, *Africae Munus,* 50, as cited in Béré, "Word of God," 48.
39. Metz, *Passion for God,* 163.

Given the complexity of the problem at stake and the increasing sophistication of societies, it is crucial to develop new ways of communicating and creatively convey the message. It is also necessary to use all appropriate media to reach as many people as possible and speak to the depth of their concerns. Of course, this does not mean rewriting the Scriptures, reforming the sacraments, or casting them aside as outdated. Instead, it is crucial to use technical skills where necessary but, more importantly, to revitalize the Scriptures and sacraments by articulating the depth of their content and adapting them to people's context. For example, regarding healing and reconciliation, the Scriptures contain eloquent narratives, metaphors, and symbols that speak to the heart of people's concerns. It is, therefore, essential to elaborate educational and pastoral programs, prayerful recollections, and liturgical and sacramental practices that make use of those tools to bring together people in need of mutual healing and reconciliation. For instance, just to give one example, the symbols of death, the cross, and blood which mediate the Passion of Jesus as a means of reconciliation provide profound insights. As Robert Schreiter highlights, "They show us, first of all, that the efforts needed to bring about reconciliation take us to the limits of human existence. They bring us to death, to violent death, to the relinquishing of the very source of life. Only an enmity that brings us to the utter limits of possibility could dare elicit such a strong means of reconciliation."[40]

Schreiter shows how the cross, generally seen as a sign of death, is transformed into a sign of life for believers who trust in Christ's passage from death to resurrection. Thus, it helps people who have undergone the ordeal of genocide to contemplate the possibility of a new life in Christ. Schreiter quotes Paul's first letter to the Corinthians, which exposes the irony of the cross: "For the message about the cross is foolishness to those who are perishing, but to us who are being saved it is the power of God" (1 Cor 1:18). Such a paradox of symbols help makes sense of dire realities that otherwise leave people numbed and incapable of recovering from their unspeakable wounds. Using these symbols in the liturgy and sacramental practices plays an instrumental ethical role in regenerating courage and hope, without which it is almost impossible to recover from the horrendous experience of genocide and its perpetration.

Conclusion

It follows from the above initiatives and subsequent reflections inspired by theological ethics that the response to the complexity of post-genocide—or

40. Schreiter, *Reconciliation*, 47.

any other situation of mass violence—requires us to conduct trauma healing at the same time as reconciliation. Nonetheless, it is important to remember that each case has a distinctive context and presents its own particularities. Therefore, it is not wise to assume that there is a universal recipe valid everywhere and at any given time, however sound and reasonable a course of action it is. While I highly recommend a complementary and dialectical approach and appreciate its holistic character so important for societies under similar circumstances as Rwanda, it is crucial to pay attention to each case in its distinctiveness and always keep a window open for flexibility and creativity. More importantly, it is vital to be open to the theological ethical approach, which offers not only a wider and deeper vista for thinking about trauma healing and reconciliation beyond human immediate concerns and possibilities but also provides significant resources—including symbolic and metaphoric tools—that help articulate the problems and discover God's transformative power at work even in the worst of situations.

Bibliography

Atkinson, Judy. "Foreword." In *When Blood and Bones Cry Out: Journeys Through the Soundscape of Healing and Reconciliation,* by John Paul Lederach and Angela Jill Lederach, ix–xiv. New York: Oxford University Press, 2010.

Benedict XVI, Pope. *Africae Munus: On the Church in Africa in Service to Reconciliation, Justice, and Peace.* Vatican City: Libreria Editrice Vaticana, 2011. https://www.vatican.va/content/benedict-xvi/en/apost_exhortations/documents/hf_ben-xvi_exh_20111119_africae-munus.html.

Béré, Paul. "The Word of God as Transformative Power in Reconciling African Christians." In *Reconciliation, Justice, and Peace: The Second African Synod,* edited by Agbonkhianmeghe Orobator, 48–58. Maryknoll, NY: Orbis, 2011.

Brendel, David H. "Psychotherapy and the Truth and Reconciliation Commission: The Dialectic of Individual and Collective Healing." In *Trauma, Truth, and Reconciliation: Healing Damaged Relationships,* edited by Nancy Nyquist Potter, 15–27. New York: Oxford University Press, 2006.

Byman, Daniel L. *Keeping the Peace: Lasting Solutions to Ethnic Conflicts.* Baltimore: The Johns Hopkins University Press, 2002.

Clark, Phil. *The Gacaca Courts, Post-Genocide Justice, and Reconciliation in Rwanda: Justice Without Lawyers.* Cambridge: Cambridge University Press, 2010.

Conference Episcopale du Rwanda. "Message from the Catholic Bishops of Rwanda to the Faithful at the Closure of the Special Year of Reconciliation: Be Reconciled with God (2 Cor 5:20)." November 17, 2018. https://eglisecatholiquerwanda.org/IMG/pdf/message_from_the_catholic_bishops_of_rwanda_to_the_faithful_at_the_closure_of_the_special_year_of_reconciliation.pdf.

Dallaire, Roméo, and Brent Beardsley. *Shake Hands with the Devil: The Failure of Humanity in Rwanda.* New York: Carroll and Graf, 2005.

Denis, Philippe. "Christian *Gacaca* and Official *Gacaca* in Post-Genocide Rwanda." *Journal for the Study of Religion* 32.1 (2019) 1–27. https://www.jstor.org/stable/26900032.

———. "Grief and Denial among Rwandan Catholics in the Aftermath of the Genocide Against the Tutsi." *Archives de Sciences Sociales des Religions* 183 (2018) 287–307.

des Forges, Alison. *Leave None to Tell the Story: Genocide in Rwanda*. New York: Human Rights Watch, 1999.

"The Exsultet: The Proclamation of Easter." US Conference of Catholic Bishops, n.d. https://www.usccb.org/prayer-and-worship/liturgical-year-and-calendar/easter/easter-proclamation-exsultet.

Gourevitch, Philip. *We Wish to Inform You that Tomorrow We Will Be Killed with Our Families*. New York: Picador, 1999.

Hayner, B. Priscilla. *Unspeakable Truths: Facing the Challenge of Truth Commissions*. New York: Routledge, 2002.

John Paul II, Pope. *Tertio Millenio Adveniente: On Preparation for the Jubilee Year 2000*. Vatican City: Libreria Editrice Vaticana, 1994. https://www.vatican.va/content/john-paul-ii/en/apost_letters/1994/documents/hf_jp-ii_apl_19941110_tertio-millennio-adveniente.html.

Kambanda, Cardinal Antoine. "The Role of the Church in the Process of Reconciliation in Rwanda." In *Reinventing Theology in Post-Genocide Rwanda: Challenges and Hopes*, edited by Elisée Rutagambwa et al., 55–62. Washington, DC: Georgetown University Press, 2023.

King, Régine U. "The True Healing Is Healing Together: Healing and Rebuilding Social Relations in Postgenocide Rwanda." *Peace and Conflict: Journal of Peace Psychology* 25.1 (2019) 49–60.

Kleinman, Arthur. "The Violences of Everyday Life: The Multiple Forms and Dynamics of Social Suffering." In *Violence and Subjectivity*, edited by Veena Das et al., 226–41. Berkeley: University of California Press, 2000.

Lederach, John Paul, and Angela Jill Lederach. *When Blood and Bones Cry Out: Journeys Through the Soundscape of Healing and Reconciliation*. New York: Oxford University Press, 2010.

Martin, Ian. "Hard Choices after Genocide: Human Rights and Political Failures in Rwanda." In *Hard Choices: Moral Dilemmas in Humanitarian Intervention*, edited by Jonathan Moore, 157–76. Lanham, MD: Rowman and Littlefield, 1998.

Metz, Johann Baptist. *A Passion for God: The Mystical-Political Dimension of Christianity*. New York: Paulist, 1998.

Minow, Martha. *Between Vengeance and Forgiveness: Facing History after Genocide and Mass Violence*. Boston: Beacon, 1999.

Müller-Fahrenholz, Geiko. *The Art of Forgiveness: Theological Reflection on Healing and Reconciliation*. Geneva: WCC, 1997.

Omaar, Rakiya. *Rwanda: Death, Despair, and Defiance*. London: African Rights, 1995.

Pearlman, L. A. "Psychological Trauma." Lecture given for the John Templeton Foundation's "Healing, Forgiveness, and Reconciliation" Project. West Conshohocken, Pennsylvania, March 13, 2000.

Pedersen, Duncan, et al. "The Sequelae of Political Violence: Assessing Trauma, Suffering, and Dislocation in the Peruvian Highlands." *Social Science and Medicine* 67.2 (2008) 205–17. https://www.sciencedirect.com/science/article/pii/S0277953608001834?via%3Dihub.

Rutagambwa, Elisée, et al. *Reinventing Theology in Post-Genocide Rwanda: Challenges and Hopes.* Washington, DC: Georgetown University Press, 2023.

Schreiter, Robert. *Reconciliation: Mission and Ministry in a Changing Social Order.* Maryknoll, NY: Orbis, 1999.

Synod of Bishops, Second Special Assembly for Africa. "Elenchus Finalis Propositionum" [Final List of Propositions]. Vatican City, October 23, 2009. https://www.vatican.va/roman_curia/synod/documents/rc_synod_doc_20091023_elenco-prop-finali_en.html.

Védrine, Hubert. "Lettre Manuscrite au Président de la République [April 18, 1994]." France Génocide Tutsi. https://francegenocidetutsi.org/Vedrine18avril1994.pdf.

14

"It Is Like That": The Moral Imagination of Maggy Barankitse

DAVID TOOLE

As death began to lose its sanctity, so too did life. The primary reason the dead have an afterlife in so many cultures is because it falls to them to come to the rescue and provide counsel when the debilitating darkness falls. Where the dead are simply dead, the living are in some sense already dead as well. Conversely, where the afterlife of the dead receives new life, the earth as a whole receives a new blessing.
—ROBERT POGUE HARRISON

The living are at the service of the dead, and the dead deserve not only cemeteries but moral institutions.
—MICHAEL BARNETT

ON OCTOBER 25, 1993, Maggy Barankitse buried seventy-two bodies in a mass grave. She knows the number because, she says, "I counted." The site was a simple cemetery near the compound of the Catholic bishop in Ruyigi, Burundi. A day earlier, Maggy—stripped naked, beaten, and tied to a chair—had watched as the people she was now burying were murdered in a fit of ethnic violence. For the burial, Maggy had the help of a few men from the local prison and Chloé, her oldest daughter. They moved the bodies from the bishop's compound to the gravesite in a wheelbarrow and worked in a hurry, fearful that the perpetrators would return. Among the dead was Maggy's friend Juliette. Just before she died, Juliette had asked Maggy to care for her one- and three-year-old daughters, Lydia and Lysette. Then Maggy watched as a man swung a machete and severed Juliette's head from her body. Hours later, after the killers had departed and Maggy was free from the ropes that bound her to the chair, she gathered up Lydia and Lysette, thirty other surviving children, and Juliette's head, and found shelter in the house of a German aid worker. "It was hard to go with Juliette's head, but I couldn't leave her for the dogs." When Maggy returned to the scene of the massacre the next morning, she went into the bishop's chapel to retrieve the cloth from the altar and used it to rejoin Juliette's head with her body before she buried her in the mass grave.[1]

---

1. This essay is excerpted from "The Morgue in the Garden of Eden, or Hope in the Dark," a much longer account I have written of Maggy Barankitse as part of a manuscript with the working title *Outposts of Hope: Theological Dispatches from the Frontlines of Poverty and War*. My primary sources are formal interviews that I or others conducted between 2009 and 2022, as well as notes from many informal conversations I have had with Maggy. I have also relied on three published accounts that tell parts of Maggy's story: Katongole, "Gathering the Fragments of a New Future: Maggy Barankitse and Maison Shalom," in *Sacrifice of Africa*, 166–97; Katongole, "Maggy Barankitse and the Politics of Forgiveness in Burundi," in *Born from Lament*, 225–42; and Martin, *Haine n'aura pas le derniere mot*. I owe special thanks to Emmanuel Katongole, who has written insightfully about Maggy, and through whom I first met her in Burundi in 2009. Emmanuel also helped me think methodologically by alerting me to Lawrence-Lightfoot and Davis, *Art and Science of Portraiture*. On that score, a few words:

My account of Maggy is what Lawrence-Lightfoot and Davis in *Art and Science of Portraiture* would call a *portrait*, that is, "from an outsider's purview, an insider's understanding of the scene" (25). Portraits, they suggest, require "a difficult vigilance to empirical description and aesthetic expression. . . . Portraits are constructed, shaped, and drawn through the development of relationships. It is in the building of relationships that the portraitist experiences most pointedly the complex fusion of conceptual, methodological, emotional, and ethical challenges" (12, 135). What I have written has emerged from a relationship I developed with Maggy over more than a decade. In keeping with a practice of portraiture, I have departed from using only verbatim quotations from the many transcripts that served as my main source. I sometimes reorder Maggy's words and finish her thoughts, never by making things up, but by combining words from different interviews or from my notes of our informal conversations. Maggy speaks in French-constructed English, in a staccato way that sometimes leads her to stop speaking in the middle of a thought, and with frequent flights into French that do not always get transcribed. When I was confident that I could draw on the full scope of resources at my disposal to finish those thoughts or reorder her words in a way that captures her life, I did so. Generally, when I am quoting someone other than Maggy, I am reciting that person's words as Maggy recited them. When that is not the case, I have

I first heard the outlines of that story on January 17, 2009, when a group of colleagues and I went with Maggy to the site of the mass grave. We arrived at the small, unkempt cemetery on the outskirts or Ruyigi at about 2:15 in the afternoon. The gray of the morning had given way to a blue sky, half full of shape-shifting clouds. The cemetery glowed green in sunlight, with knee-high grass and weeds entangling weathered wooden crosses. Much later, I would learn that those crosses marked the graves of mothers and infants Maggy had buried after they had died of AIDS while in her care. The focus of the moment, however, was the mass grave, which was capped in a large concrete slab decorated with white tiles. We followed Maggy as she picked her way across the cross-cluttered space to a drab stucco memorial at the far end of the grave. We stopped there, and Maggy stepped up onto the concrete overlay and began to tell us what had happened in the compound of the Catholic bishop on October 24, 1993.

According to the date stamps on my photographs, it took Maggy seven minutes to tell the story of the events that led to the mass grave around which we were gathered. When she got to the part about Juliette, she held up pictures of Lydia and Lysette as young children and as grown women, letting us know, without quite saying it, that she had fulfilled her promise to her friend. She did not tell us on that occasion about taking Juliette's head with her as she led the children to safety, or about hiding it from Lysette that night, or about taking the cloth from the altar in the chapel the next day to use as a burial shroud, or about what she said to God in that moment, or about having to identify Juliette's body and that of her husband by their hands and the rings on their fingers, which she removed and gave to Lydia and Lysette when they were older. These intimate details came later, during the many conversations I would have with Maggy in the years to come, as her story became something of an obsession of mine—not because of what she said while standing on the mass grave but because of something she had said a few hours earlier.

Before Maggy took us to the gravesite, she gave us a tour of the things she had built in Ruyigi in the years following the events of 1993—things that were the physical embodiment of Maison Shalom, the House of Peace, an organization she had founded to care for Burundi's orphans.[2] The tour included a visit to Rema Hospital, which had opened just a year earlier. On the way there, Maggy stopped the cars in our procession and had us get out so that she could show us the hospital from a distance. The high ground in

---

included the source in a note.

2. For background on the events of 1993, see United States Institute of Peace, "International Commission."

front of us, she said, was Nyamutobo Hill. We could see the hospital sprawled across the flat hilltop—a collection of single-story buildings connected by covered walkways, courtyards, and verandas in typical African fashion. Just to the left of the hospital, Maggy pointed out, was the maternity center she had constructed first, near the end of the long civil war unleashed by the events of October 1993. She explained that the whole hill had been the site of her family's village; it was destroyed two days before the massacre she had survived in the compound of the Catholic bishop. We had stopped in the middle of the road so that Maggy could give us perspective. She wanted us to know that, during the war, the site of the maternity center had been the preferred location of the government's artillery, and that the hospital now sat on the ruins of her ancestral village.

Maggy often says things that are hard to process in the moment, when her words first hit your ears, and I remember distinctly that, as we walked from the cars to the entrance of the hospital, one of my colleagues asked if we had heard correctly. Had she really built the hospital on the ruins of the village where all but one member of her extended family had died in October 1993? "Yes," she said, "I will show you where my mother's house used to be." As we toured the hospital—a state-of-the-art facility that surpassed anything my medical colleagues had seen in rural Africa—Maggy said another remarkable thing. She pointed to one of the buildings with great pride, a prominent presence behind the wards, and told us it was the morgue. Then she showed us how this building was positioned in relationship to the others, suggesting, it seemed, that the whole hospital complex had been designed around the morgue. She added that she had spent more money on the morgue than on the pediatric ward, which included a neonatal intensive care unit with four incubators. In the months following my first encounter with Maggy Barankitse lots of things stuck with me, but it was the morgue of Rema Hospital that caused me to spend years chasing down the details of Maggy's story.

That story, where I pick it up, begins on Friday, October 22, 1993, the day after a faction in the Tutsi-led military assassinated Hutu President Melchior Ndadaye, the first democratically elected president of the country.[3] That morning, Maggy woke up in her village on Nyamutobo Hill and walked a little over a mile with her seven adopted children into Ruyigi. Chloé, twenty-six years old and attending university, was home on holiday.

---

3. For a good account of events in 1993 and into the mid-1990s, see Krueger and Krueger, *From Bloodshed to Hope in Burundi*. Bob Krueger was the US ambassador to Burundi from June 1994 to September 1995 and served heroically in that capacity by traveling the country documenting genocide, until he was called back by Washington following a failed assassination attempt.

The other children were on their way to school, and Maggy was on her way to work at the bishop's office. When they arrived in town, Maggy found that school had been canceled, and then she heard news of the president's assassination. With no school and with warnings from people in Ruyigi that vengeful Hutus were wreaking havoc on Tutsi villages in other parts of the country, Maggy went to the bishop's house to retrieve valuable documents related to her adopted children. She then headed to her village, telling Chloé to gather food and take the children back to the bishop's house.

When Maggy got to the ravine that marks the low point before the gentle rise of Nyamutobo Hill—near where she had stopped to show us the maternity center and the hospital—she could see that her house and many others in the village were in flames. She met members of her family fleeing. She wanted to continue to the village, convinced that she could stop the violence, but fleeing family members told her not to go. About this time, Chloé arrived with her six siblings. Too much time had passed for her to wait at the bishop's house, so she had come searching for Maggy. With increasing chaos and her village in flames, Maggy was now convinced she too needed to flee, so she asked family members if she could join them. They were unwilling to take Maggy with them unless she left behind her four Hutu children. After all, Hutus were, at that moment, destroying their village. Maggy rejected this idea and moved on. She encountered some Hutus who were fleeing as well, headed for the nearby Tanzanian border. She asked if she could join them. "Only if you leave your three Tutsi children here." Maggy's village was on fire. Ruyigi itself was chaos. And no one wanted anything to do with Maggy and her Hutu and Tutsi children. "Suddenly, we were alone."

Maggy decided to return to the Catholic bishop's compound, thinking it would be safe there. Along the way, she met her friend Juliette Bigirimana, a Tutsi married to a Hutu. Juliette was a nurse and her husband, Cyprian Ndimurwanko, was a physician. They had two young children. "Come with me to the bishop's compound," Maggy told Juliette. "I am a Tutsi with both Tutsi and Hutu children. You are a Tutsi married to a Hutu. We must be prophets. Now is the time for us to show people that Tutsis and Hutu don't need to kill each other." By evening Maggy, Juliette, Cyprian, and all the children were in the bishop's compound, along with a growing number of others, mostly Hutus.

By Sunday, October 24, well over a hundred people, a mix of Hutus and Tutsis, had gathered in the bishop's compound for safety. The bishop was out of town, but the vicar general—the primary leader of a Catholic diocese in the absence of its bishop—was there. About 9 AM, Maggy and others were preparing breakfast and planning for Mass. Amid continued chaos and confusion in Ruyigi, they had decided to celebrate Mass in the garden outside the bishop's residence instead of risking the quarter-mile walk to the cathedral. Looking out a window from the building that contained the bishop's great hall, Maggy was the first to see what appeared to be a mob of Tutsis entering the bishop's compound. She told everyone to run or to hide, suspecting that it was more than a mob. The Burundian military had long been led by Tutsis, and the day before, Maggy had watched a military plane land in Ruyigi. "Normally the military protects all the people, but the arrival of the military in Ruyigi meant that revenge was going to be very hard."

The implication, Maggy explains, was that the military would organize killing squads with specific instructions to target Hutus, with a special focus on Hutu intellectuals, an aim that harkened back to the genocide of 1972. "That's why I told the father of Lydia and Lysette to go hide in the ceiling." The vicar general, a Tutsi like Maggy, was hiding under a bed. Maggy tried to hide, too, in a way that later became laughable: she and eight other women tried to fit under a single bed. But then Maggy heard familiar voices. Looking out the window, she saw her cousin's husband and students she knew from a nearby college. Grabbing Juliette, she stepped outside, thinking, as she had two days earlier, that she could intervene to stop the impending violence. She was wrong.

Maggy had locked the door to the great hall. When she refused to open it, one of the men slapped her face while others forced the door open. Maggy tried to negotiate, but they were undeterred. "You and your ideas. We'll burn everything; we'll show you." They proceeded to splash gasoline throughout the great hall and then set the building on fire. Maggy continued to plead and protest, but to these Tutsi men, some of whom were her relatives, the fact that she was seeking to protect Hutus made her a traitor. They yelled at her; she screamed back. They beat her; she hit back. And so, they stripped her and tied her to a chair. By this time, the building was on fire, and there was only one exit. As people fled into the open to escape the flames and smoke, the killers separated Hutus from Tutsis. The latter ran away. "They abandoned me," Maggy says. Some of the Hutus were also able to escape unnoticed. "It was chaos. The building was burning. Some people came out on fire, but not everyone was there to kill. Some were just robbers. Some were also the survivors of the machete of Hutu from two days before. They had spent two days without eating and were looking for food, and for alcohol, because they were in despair."

Amid this chaos, Maggy watched helplessly as those who had come to kill got on with their business. Some of them had guns, but mostly they had clubs, stones, bamboo spears, and machetes. Because Juliette was a Tutsi, the killers were going to spare her life, but not her husband's. Juliette responded, "I married not a Hutu but the man I love. If you are going to kill my husband, you should kill me too." Then she told the killers to untie Maggy, so that Maggy could take her children. As one of the men loosened the ropes, Juliette said to Maggy, "I want to die with my husband. Please raise Lydia and Lysette like your own children, love them, give them kindness." Then to the killers, "Kill me." Now untied, Maggy tried to shield the eyes of Lydia and Lysette as one of the men swung his machete.

What transpired next was continued chaos. No longer tied, Maggy began to fight to save Lydia and Lysette and other children. Men with weapons of one kind or another had already killed some children, and it was clear to Maggy that they were about to kill more. "Don't kill, don't. I'll give you money." As secretary to the bishop, Maggy had access to the church's cash. "I'll take you to the coffer where the bishop keeps the money." The offer was attractive. Some of the men followed Maggy to the office, where she gave them the money in the safe in exchange for the lives of Lydia, Lysette, and some of the other children scattered throughout the compound. But that wasn't the end of it. "I began also to fight in order to take this child or that child away from a killer, saying 'Take this' and giving wine or whiskey, or the key to the storeroom, or some little bit of money, and then, in the chaos, I hid the children."

Maggy says that she was tied to the chair for about an hour, until 10 AM, and that her fight to save children lasted until about 1 or maybe 2 PM. At times, while fighting to save children, she entered the burning building "until I could no longer stand the heat." The fire became her reference for time. "I can remember, because the fire stopped about 3 PM." She also remembers that, after helping children hide, she turned her attention to helping a priest who was trying to save documents from the fire. "I tried to help take all those documents and then to one old priest, also a Tutsi, I said, 'You go and then hide.'"

Sometime between 1 and 3 PM, the killing stopped, the killers departed, and Maggy began looking for the children she had sent into hiding, as well as for her own children, whom she had not seen since she left the building to confront the mob hours earlier, when Chloé was still in her pajamas preparing breakfast. When Maggy couldn't find Chloé or any of her own children among all the bodies strewn around the garden, she panicked. Distraught, she went into the nearby chapel and unloaded her emotions on God: "My mother lied to me. She told me you were love, but where is love in what I have just witnessed? Where is love in being spared death, in being the one who had to watch everyone else being killed? Where is love in the loss of my own children?" As she was railing against God in this way, she heard a voice from the sacristy. It was Chloé. "Mama, we are here. We're alive."

"When I found my children, immediately I understood how sublime my vocation was. I will never have the same strength as I had in that moment." Maggy was thirty-seven years old and the survivor of an ethnically charged massacre of Hutu at the hands of Tutsi, which was itself revenge for a massacre of Tutsi at the hands of Hutu. And God had spared not only Maggy but her seven Hutu and Tutsi children. "Oh, God, how strange that I discovered my vocation among atrocities." Up to this moment, everything had been loud and chaotic and confused for hours. Now chaos gave way to calm as Maggy, on her knees in front of the tabernacle that holds the Eucharist, apologized to God for misunderstanding his love. Were this a movie, the camera would linger on the scene, a subtle foreshadowing of a life to come. "The Eucharist," Maggy says, "is the source of my true courage."

The moment of calm was brief. More confusion and fear followed. "We cried together, and then we went out of the little chapel. I showed them the bodies and said, 'Where we can go?' Fabrice, who was five, said, 'But we can go to the German.'" Fabrice was a Rwandan whom Maggy had adopted after he had been abandoned as a baby. "He was very clever," Maggy says. "You know, Fabrice, if we go from here to there, they will kill us." But then Fabrice helped Maggy hatch a plan. She would write a note to Martin Novak, a German aid worker who had a house not far away, and Fabrice would go alone with the note. Meanwhile, Maggy—still mostly naked and surrounded by thirty-one children—was worried the killers would come back. "If they find us here, they will kill us." Lysette, three-and-a-half years old, suggested they move to the cemetery. "Hutu and Tutsi are together there."

The cemetery wasn't far, but getting there took time. They travelled with caution, avoiding streets as much as possible, moving through the bush, and taking advantage of the coming dusk of evening. Martin found them there at half past six in the evening. Then he and Maggy returned to the bishop's compound and did their best to cover up the bodies—to hide them, fearing that the perpetrators would come back and make the bodies disappear. It's unclear whether Maggy recovered Juliette's head at this point, or if she had taken it with her to the cemetery. When, in my disbelief, I asked Maggy why she took it with her, she said, "Because I could not bear to leave my friend behind." She also told me that she hid the head from view for the night when three-year-old Lysette kept trying to touch it, saying, "I see that you have the head of my mom." The next morning, Maggy took Chloé and returned to the bishop's compound to bury the dead.

A few days later, Martin's organization pulled him out of Burundi, but Maggy continued to live in his house and collect orphans. By May 1994, she was caring for hundreds of children, and the numbers were escalating quickly because of the genocide that had started next door in Rwanda in

April. With the help of the bishop, Maggy secured an old school building in Ruyigi, and what had begun as an impromptu relief effort for Burundi's growing population of orphans became Maison Shalom. Of the early days, Maggy says, "I was the only adult with the children. Life was hard. I had no money. Sometimes I had to lie and steal to secure food for all the children." Exact numbers are uncertain. In this case, Maggy was not counting, but the numbers would eventually rise into the tens of thousands.

When Maggy tells her story, she doesn't sort out dates; it's as if everything is happening at once. Her story resists precise chronology. Some dates, however, are secure—among them, May 28, 1996. On that day, Hutu rebels attacked a camp of internally displaced Tutsis in Butezi, killing forty-nine people.[4] Butezi is only ten miles from Ruyigi and was home to one of Maggy's three orphan centers. When she heard of the massacre, Maggy made the short trip to Butezi to see what had happened. The dead were mostly women and children. "I went to see them. All those bodies. Again, they killed so many people. So many mothers. I found their bodies. Again, I buried them in the same grave. I took many children, mutilated children without moms." Caught up in a scene all too familiar, Maggy was overwhelmed. When she returned to Ruyigi a few days later, something was wrong. She had trouble breathing. She lost her voice. She couldn't speak. She went to a doctor, thinking she was having an asthma attack and that she needed an inhaler. He said, "It's not asthma. You have another problem. Something an inhaler won't fix."

Unable to function, Maggy sought refuge in a Carmelite monastery in Musongati, twenty miles to the southwest of Ruyigi. Since 1993, she had not prayed nor cried, not really; she had been too busy. Now she did both. "I stopped. I was alone. The nuns brought me food. I mourned. I began to cry and cry. I went to chapel and mourned for my family. I read my Bible. I reconciled with myself and my story. I prayed." Maggy prayed at first for understanding, to make sense of the human capacity for cruelty, and then, when that remained a mystery, simply for the ability to go on. She remained silent for a month. Her time in the monastery was a time of conversion. "I was a new person. I began to dream good things for my children. I wanted Burundi to become a paradise. I discovered that, if I accepted in my heart that God is God, that God is powerful, that God is love and tenderness, that God forgives even all this, then I could go on." She means that last bit quite literally. "On many occasions, if it weren't for my faith, I would have killed myself." Instead, she says, "I decided to turn the page, to write new

---

4. Reports of the number of dead vary. Maggy herself uses a much larger number. I am using the number as reported in Human Rights Watch, "Human Rights Watch World Report."

pages with children. The children taught me so many things; for example, it's children who showed me how I must love them."

Maggy is fond of saying that love made her an inventor. "Every morning," she says, "we invent how to live with dignity." During the war in Burundi, her inventions were many, but chief among them was the City of Angels. Inaugurated in April 2003, it marked the culmination of Maggy's post-conversion imaginative response to a world in which the violence of war and terror had become the norm. Anchoring the small campus was *Le Cinéma des Anges*—the only movie theater in a country of six million people, other than one in the capital city. Attending the inauguration were the ambassador of Belgium, emissaries from the French embassy, UNICEF's country director, Ruyigi's provincial governor, various other local dignitaries, and as many people from the community as could fit alongside hundreds of Maggy's children inside the compound of the small campus. The ceremony opened with a ribbon-cutting, then came the speeches, followed by music and dancing and tours.

The welcoming speech fell to one of the children Maggy had taken in during those first few months when she was living in Martin Novak's house and collecting orphans. Justine was only nine years old in October 1993 when a neighbor set the family's house on fire, killed her parents and her sister, and left her wounded with machete blows to the head. That's how she ended up with Maggy. She was now a young woman of eighteen and living back in her village in the house of her birth, next door to the man who had killed her parents and sister, with whom she had reconciled. Indeed, he had helped her rebuild the home he had destroyed, and sometime later she cared for him as he was dying. To those who knew her story, Justine's welcoming speech would not have been a surprise: "Dear parents, brothers, and sisters, welcome to our home. The Cinema of Angels will be a challenge to war and a challenge to AIDS, a return to hope, and a place of reunion and conviviality between two ethnic groups in conflict."[5]

Moving Justine from an orphan center to her home village was an early experiment in what would become another of Maggy's inventions, one she was scaling up during the same years she was creating the City of Angels: *Fratrie*. The key to this invention was that children would live in houses, not in orphan centers, and that, where possible, the houses would be in the children's home villages and constructed with the help of the community. The impetus for this change was something that happened one day when a woman stopped Maggy at Mass: "I want you to hear what my son just said to me." Then to her son, "Go ahead. Tell Maggy what you said." The boy spoke,

---

5. Speaking in Nutchey and Bitamba, *Cinéma des anges*. My translation.

"I asked mama when she would die so I could go live with you." Maggy was horrified. Amid war and poverty, the children in Maison Shalom's orphan centers were better off than children in the villages.

Maggy saw immediately that her model of caring for orphans was flawed. "Children belong to the community, to the village, not to my centers." Maison Shalom had always conducted searches for the village of a child's origin—a kind of proactive lost and found. But enlisting members of a village to build houses for children and turning these houses into homes occupied by both biological and "adopted" siblings—*Fratrie*—was an invention, one Justine had influenced. When Maggy proposed to Justine that Maison Shalom return her to the village and rebuild the house of her parents, Justine objected. "No, I think we will call the man who killed my parents and show him the burned house." Maggy replied, in disbelief, "We call this killer?" Justine insisted, "Yes, of course, because I want to rebuild first the heart not the house. I will tell him what he must do for us to make reconciliation. If I hate him, I can't live."

Maggy often tells the story of Justine by summarizing what she learned from the children of Maison Shalom. "Forgiveness is the key to life. Hatred in your heart will kill you. Without forgiveness, there is no future. This is what the children taught me. They taught me how to forgive. Forgiveness is a process; it was not easy for me." Maggy admits that, prior to her breakdown and the month she spent in the monastery, she had been consumed by anger. When a soldier called her children snakes, she threatened him aggressively. When at Mass one day she saw a man walking up for communion wearing the clothes of Cyprian, Juliette's husband, she lost it. The priest had to intervene. "Maggy, now you come to church to beat people?" She replied, "Yes, even you I will beat." Reflecting on this time, Maggy says, "It was like that. I was horrible. Even with God, I was violent. I was so angry with God that sometimes in front of the tabernacle I would tell God that if I could beat him I would." Maggy clarifies, "I didn't strike anyone. I killed them in my heart."

Forgiveness was not easy for Maggy or her children. She says that what would have been easy is for Maison Shalom to have become a house of rebels, of children waiting to grow old enough to kill the killers of their parents. In an earlier speech at a ceremony dedicating eighty-five *Fratrie* that Maison Shalom had built in Ruyigi, Justine underscored the point: "If I hadn't met Maggy, I myself would have become a killer."[6] Children like Justine taught Maggy that, to love them, "I must change their life and make them like candles among the darkness."

---

6. Quoted in Martin, *Haine n'aura pas le derniere mot*, 155. My translation.

A few steps away from the *Le Cinéma des Anges*, Maggy built a swimming pool—again, the only one in the country outside the capital city. At the inauguration of the City of Angels in April 2003, the main attraction was the theater. The swimming pool wasn't finished; it was a deep, rectangular hole in Ruyigi's red clay that a small army of workers were digging by hand. By the end of the year, however, the pool was an aqua-colored wonder surrounded by a skirt of red tile with a shining chrome ladder at each end. "For those people who suffered so much in war, I built a swimming pool. We were not just there to give out food and clothes but to distribute dignity and hope. All the time, my children were afraid. They had no place to play. They had become victims. I wanted to give them dignity. Children need a future. And not just orphans. When I looked around, I saw that there was no dialogue between the military and the rebels, between Tutsi and Hutu. I wanted to act, to show them that they can come and swim together. I even invited the rebels. I told them, 'You have a right to play. You must not always be thinking about killing your enemies.'"

Maggy also invited both government soldiers and rebels to the theater, where fixed to the door was a red circle and slash painted on top of a black silhouette of an AK47. "I saw that Hutus and Tutsis couldn't talk to each other. I said, 'Tomorrow another war will begin because people are not together. How can I give them the opportunity to dream?' In town I saw fear. They were all so anxious. They had no idea what was happening outside Burundi. I built a cinema so they could talk together, watch a movie together, heal each other, leave the trauma behind." The goal of showing films to children was the same. "To offer children an image that is not of war, that is not of AIDS, of death, but an image of hope. There have to be people who believe in reconciliation."

To complete the City of Angels, Maggy added other things, among them a library and vocational training for tailors. Next door, in 2005, she started *Le Garage des Anges*, where child soldiers who were being decommissioned as a step toward peace could become car mechanics. Maggy rattles off the sequence of causes and effects that created the City of Angels and the other inventions of Maison Shalom:

> People came in the evenings to watch films. I saw that they began to stop killing, so I said, "Oh, I can also put in a library." Then they came to read, and I said, "I see that they need internet" so I built a cybercafé to give them a window on the world, because they were thinking only about war. Then I put in a reception hall for weddings, and they had their pictures taken near the pool. Then I saw that women needed nice clothes and also their hair done—so I opened a tailor shop and a beauty salon. Then I paid

the rebels to give me child soldiers, but I needed something for them to do, so nearby I built a mechanics' garage to fix cars. Still, there was so much unemployment, so I said, "Oh, I can make a little restaurant." I created a restaurant, and a bakery, for all the young people to come to after swimming. And I talked with them, "What can you do?" Some said, "I can learn to sew." Others, "I can learn to cook." So, I started vocational training. Then I also built a guest house where visitors could stay. It was like that.

It was like that is one of Maggy's favorite phrases. She uses it often at the end of such summaries of her life and work, a kind of punctuated pause that allows her to catch her breath and gather her thoughts. It's a verbal ellipsis standing in for all the things she could go on to say were she not out of breath. When she catches her breath, Maggy has a lot more to say, much of which focuses on mothers and infants.

One day in 2001, Maison Shalom received sixteen newborns because sixteen mothers had died. At the time, Maison Shalom was already caring for more than 250 infants. In 1995, Maggy had opened a center in Gisuru, near the Tanzanian border. Chloé, then on her way to becoming a physician, remembers the impetus for opening the center. "Fleeing people were trying to reach refugee camps just across the border. Women were dying while fleeing or trying to return to Burundi. Newborn babies were abandoned on the roads or left to their fathers who were unable to feed them."[7] Maggy opened a center to try to save infants like these, but that was 1995. It was now 2001, and the influx of so many newborns on a single day caused Maggy to wonder why sixteen mothers had died. She decided to find out.

This was now eight years into a protracted civil war. "It was dangerous. I went to see the villages. I slept in the villages. I talked to mothers." A description of what things were like in Ruyigi about this time offers helpful context for Maggy's travels. "Ruyigi was still a small village with an archaic economy in a war zone, with a sanitary infrastructure lower than the vital minimum, with little food provisions, with an overfilled prison, and with hills devastated by fire. This region is the one most harmed by the civil war. The positions of Burundian rebels in Tanzania obliged them to pass systematically through the area around Ruyigi where the chaos was intense: raped women, hundreds of dead bodies, destroyed schools, a ravaged health center, and devastated villages."[8] Maggy has her own description. She saw women with no food, with no shelter, and no clothes. She saw babies with

---

7. Chloé Ndayikunda, speaking in Nutchey and Bitamba, *L'Armée des anges*. My translation.

8. Martin, *Haine n'aura pas le derniere mot*, 166. My translation.

no milk. She saw men who were drunk. "Hardcore." When Maggy returned from her trip to the villages, she asked herself, "What can I do?"

Her answer was to build a maternity center and a hospital. Construction of the maternity center started in January 2007 and ended in April. As she had showed us during our tour in 2009, the building site was the leading edge of Nyamutobo Hill where, only a few years before, government troops had launched mortars and shells from its artillery batteries. Maggy had also convinced the Burundian military to build the center themselves. "And then in this place where they used to kill people, they themselves built the maternity center." When the center opened a short time later, it brought into full view what Maggy had encountered in the villages. "So many women came. Very ill. They came, many returning from refugee camps in Tanzania. And then I saw that I must build a hospital. Because I saw the miserable situation of these women."

Rema Hospital opened in January 2008, just a few hundred feet away from the maternity center, on the ruins of Maggy's ancestral village. The hospital came to be because, "It is like that," as Maggy is wont to say. One thing led to another. Orphan centers and houses, a swimming pool and movie theater, a mechanics' garage, a library, a vocational training school, a restaurant, a bakery, a guest house, a maternity center . . . and then a hospital. First a maternity ward and a lab. Then a surgery. Then pediatrics, followed by neonatology, and soon, "The hospital was the center of everything. For me, these buildings, this hospital, the plans were in my heart. When the architects came, I said, 'I don't want to build near the street. When people come to the hospital, I want them to feel like we sing in the psalm, 'We're going up to Jerusalem.' I told the architects, 'I want a chapel here because the morgue is there, and people will pass this way, because we are not a hospital only. Maison Shalom is a message: we believe in life. It's life that has the last word."

Rema Hospital came to be exactly as Maggy envisioned it. The entrance sits a football field away from the street. The natural progression from entrance to exit passes around the wards to the morgue, which sits just at the point where the road takes a sharp turn back toward the exit and the chapel, the last stop before arriving at the street. Noting the location of the chapel, Maggy says: "From the morgue, the family and community can bring their loved one here to say farewell and give the gift of life back to God." For Maggy, a morgue without a chapel nearby would be unthinkable, but it's the morgue, the building that sits at the greatest distance from the street, that tethers Rema Hospital to Nyamutobo Hill.

"Because you have witnessed so much dying, is that why you built such a prominent morgue?"

Yes, because I have seen my brothers and sisters trivialize life. I have seen people taking machetes and—foompf—like that. . . . In 1993, I saw dogs with the hands of my friends in their mouths. And I said, "I am Christian, I know that human life is sacred. You can't vandalize it. How can I show my brothers, my Burundian brothers and sisters, that life is sacred, that bodies are sacred?" And that is why the morgue is important for the hospital, for me. That is why, in the hospital, the morgue is more expensive than pediatrics. All the people told me I was crazy, but for me, it is not a hospital. It is a sacred place. We heal people. Our human vocation is to heal our brothers and sisters. It is a unique vocation. It is not to build stupid things. God gave us Eden. And now we can rebuild, even in our hearts, the garden. You see, everybody comes to the hospital.

When we visited Ruyigi in 2009, Rema Hospital was clearly the crowning achievement of Maison Shalom and of everything Maggy had created. Even if it took me time to figure out the details, it was clear that this achievement, although embodied in a set of buildings that was recognizable in every respect as a hospital, was more than a hospital—or, rather, it was a hospital of an entirely different sort, one constructed around a morgue, in contrast to hospitals in the United States, where the morgue is generally in the basement near the laundry and the garbage so that all three can share a loading dock as a requirement of industrial efficiency. The hospital Maggy built was not the product of industrial efficiency but of a moral imagination that displayed deep truths about what it means to be human. "In my hospital," Maggy says, "it's not just that you go to see the doctor and then get medicine and leave. When you enter, there are social workers and psychologists. Beyond that, there are baths. And it is beautiful, with flowers. Then when you continue, there is a place for massage. Because of the war, the trauma, people are afraid to touch each other. We say, 'We can give you a little massage. Take a break. Sit.' Then we bring oil, and we sing. We put on music for the baby who is there. We heal all trauma. . . ." Her words trail off into another "And it is like that."

Only after many conversations with Maggy did I come to understand the mechanics of her imagination. One of the keys was the swimming pool, the slightly tardy companion to the theater as anchor of the City of Angels, which Maggy built on a large lot across from Ruyigi's soccer stadium in one direction and its open-air market in the other. The lot had been the site of a small hotel. "During the war, the proprietor lost money, and then the bank took this place. It was a waste, a ruin—empty and broken and a dumping ground." This abandoned lot was also right next to an army camp. When

Maggy tried to buy the land, the minister of defense said he would not allow it, so she went to court to secure it. She had a reason for choosing this lot over others and fighting for its purchase. She knew that government soldiers were using the site for the secret disposal of the bodies of rebel fighters, and she remembered how beautiful that part of Ruyigi had been when she was a child. Now it was a wasteland on its way to becoming a mass grave, and she wanted to intervene. From the start, the City of Angels was just what Justine would later say of it. It was a challenge to war.

Maggy figured that, if she bought the land and built something on it, she would at least disrupt the operations of the army. "I was thinking about how I could break the cycle. Maybe I could stop the military from killing people because they would not have another place to put the bodies. As a Christian, I was also thinking about how I could clean up the mass grave. I didn't want all of Ruyigi to become a cemetery. It was such a wonderful place when I was a child." That's how the swimming pool came to be. Maggy disinterred the bodies of the rebels stashed away in shallow graves on the overgrown lot and then buried them in the city cemetery. "I wanted to clean the town, to purify Ruyigi, every citizen." Maggy created the pool not only as a place for the children and others to play, but as a mechanism for overcoming violence and despair and death with love and hope and life. "A swimming pool," Maggy says, "is symbolic of baptism."

It took time and a careful search through my own photographs, like a detective analyzing pictures of a crime scene, for me to see that, at every turn, the tour Maggy gave us of Maison Shalom in 2009 moved from one gravesite or site of violence and death to the next. When we arrived in Ruyigi at noon, after a three-hour drive across the country from Bujumbura, our first stop was the mass-grave-become-swimming-pool; our second stop was the razed-village-become-hospital; our third stop was the mass grave and memorial in the small cemetery: "Here rest the 72 victims of 24 October 1993. Dear parents, dear friends, rest in peace." Our final stop was a morgue, not Maggy's morgue but the one at the government hospital.

In a strategic move that mimicked what she had done with the swimming pool, the maternity center, and the hospital, Maggy had built her house on the lot next door to the government hospital, which had been a dumping ground for medical waste. Just a few feet from the ramshackle shack that served as the government morgue, Maggy had constructed a chapel. We were in this chapel in 2009 when Maggy summarized for us what she had learned since 1993. In English accented and constructed like French, she said almost the same words as those in the epigraph of this essay: "As death began to lose its sanctity, so too did life. Where the dead are simply dead, the living are in some sense already dead as well."[9] That's why Maggy built a chapel right next to the government morgue. "They call us when a person or a baby dies. And we go, and we bring the body here, and we pray, and we prepare it for burial." In Burundi, she explained, bodies had become nothing than more corpses to discard or to step over in the street. What she had learned was that, to teach people to care for the living, she had first to teach them to care for the dead.

The lesson was lost on me, in part because, by that point in our whirlwind tour of Maison Shalom, I was overwhelmed. But the lesson was also lost on me because I was not conceptually equipped to make sense of what Maggy was saying. I got help a few years later from Robert Pogue Harrison's *The Dominion of the Dead*. "Let me put forward a premise," Harrison says, "to the effect that humanity is not a species; it is a way of being mortal and relating to the dead. As human beings, we are born of the dead, of the regional ground they occupy, of the languages they inhabited, of the worlds they brought into being. To be human means above all to bury."[10] Harrison's premise has a metaphorical component, but he also means for us to take it literally: the practice of burying our dead marks us as distinct among the life forms that have evolved on this planet.

The city of Çatalhöyük—first inhabited nine thousand years ago in the region that is now southwestern Turkey—is instructive. Beneath the floor of house after house, archaeologists have found the skeletal remains of the dead. Similar burial practices characterized other Neolithic cities, where archaeologists have found skeletal remains under floors, in walls, next to walls, in or near ovens and hearths, and under thresholds. With altars and hearths in their homes dedicated to ancestors, the ancient Greeks and Romans continued this practice, at least in spirit, and Christians in Europe, for the better part of a thousand years, modified the practice by burying the dead beneath the floors of their churches and by venerating the relics of saints.[11] Harrison again: "It is as if we the living can stand only because the dead underlie the ground on which we build our homes, worlds, commonwealths."[12] Maggy's

---

9. Harrison, *Dominion of the Dead*, 122–23.

10. Harrison, *Dominion of the Dead*, xi.

11. For an account of Çatalhöyük, see Jarus, "No Family Plots"; and Newitz, *Four Lost Cities*, 19–75. For Neolithic burial practice, see Goce Naumov, "Housing the Dead," in Barrowclough and Malone, *Cult in Context*, 255–56. For a broad overview of the role the dead have played and continue to play in the formation of culture, especially in the Christian West, see Laqueur, *Work of the Dead*. On the relics of saints, see Brown, *Cult of the Saints*. For an interesting account of altars and hearths in ancient Rome that makes their connections to ancestors more complicated than has often been assumed in the past, see Flower, *Dancing Lares*.

12. Harrison, *Dominion of the Dead*, 22.

riff on the reality that these ancient practices capture is the morgue at Rema Hospital, which itself is a scale model of Maggy's theological worldview.

I think Maggy would say of her hospital what Pope Francis said when asked, "What kind of church do you dream of?" Francis replied, "I see clearly that the thing the church needs most today is the ability to heal wounds and to warm the hearts of the faithful; it needs nearness, proximity. I see the church as a field hospital after battle. It is useless to ask a seriously injured person if he has high cholesterol and about the level of his blood sugars! You have to heal his wounds. Then we can talk about everything else. Heal the wounds, heal the wounds. . . . And you have to start from the ground up."[13] When it opened in 2008, Rema Hospital was Maggy's crowning achievement; but all along, from the first orphan centers to the theater and swimming pool to the maternity center, Maggy had been building a field hospital from the ground of a mass grave, keenly aware that the dead deserved not only a cemetery but a moral institution.

Coda

After our visit in 2009, we learned that Maggy always took visitors to the site of the mass grave and that she had never stopped visiting it herself. "Not to relive the trauma, but so that I may see the future more clearly." That future took a shocking turn on May 14, 2015, when the president of Burundi, a former rebel commander, sent men to kill Maggy. He had survived an unsuccessful coup attempt the day before, and Maggy had become such a vocal critic of his government that he aligned her, falsely, with the generals who attempted the coup. Maggy escaped the assassination attempt and fled to Rwanda, where she remains a refugee living in exile. After she left Burundi, Maison Shalom continued its work for another six months, until November 2015, when the government seized its assets and suspended its activities, effectively declaring it an enemy of the state. Many of its 270 employees fled and joined Maggy in Rwanda, where Maison Shalom International became a Rwandan NGO dedicated to Burundian refugees.

When I first met Maggy after she had become a refugee, I asked, "How do you think about what you left behind? For more than twenty years Maison Shalom was building, building, building. You probably didn't imagine it would end in this way. Was that a surprise?" Maggy laughed. "No. Because for me, the buildings were not important. I was not working to build buildings. I was distributing love and happiness. Who can stop me? Nobody can stop love. I have never put importance in things that are brick. I've never

---

13. Spadaro, "Big Heart."

cried over the buildings, just the babies who were in the hospital. I've lost nothing. I have fled with my treasure, my faith that our home is in heaven, and I laugh, because they tried to bury us, but they forgot that we are seeds."

Bibliography

Barrowclough, David, and Caroline Malone, eds. *Cult in Context: Reconsidering Ritual in Archaeology*. Oxford: Oxbow, 2007.

Brown, Peter. *The Cult of the Saints: The Rise and Function in Latin Christianity*. Chicago: University of Chicago Press, 1981.

Flower, Harriet I. *The Dancing Lares and the Serpent in the Garden: Religion at the Roman Street Corner*. Princeton: Princeton University Press, 2017.

Harrison, Robert Pogue. *Dominion of the Dead*. Chicago. University of Chicago Press, 2003.

Human Rights Watch. "Human Rights Watch World Report." Human Rights Watch, 1997. https://www.hrw.org/reports/1997/WR97/AFRICA-02.htm#P126_61234.

Jarus, Owen. "No Family Plots, Just Communal Burials in Ancient Settlement." *Live Science*, June 29, 2011. https://www.livescience.com/14824-communal-human-burials-ancient-settlement.html.

Katongole, Emmanuel. *Born from Lament: The Theology and Politics of Hope in Africa*. Grand Rapids: William B. Eerdmans, 2017.

———. *The Sacrifice of Africa: A Political Theology for Africa*. Grand Rapids: William B. Eerdmans, 2011.

Krueger, Robert, and Kathleen Krueger. *From Bloodshed to Hope in Burundi: Our Embassy Years during Genocide*. Austin: University of Texas Press, 2007.

Laqueur, Thomas W. *The Work of the Dead: A Cultural History of Mortal Remains*. Princeton: Princeton University Press, 2015.

Lawrence-Lightfoot, Sara, and Jessica Hoffman Davis. *The Art and Science of Portraiture*. San Francisco: Jossey-Bass, 1997.

Martin, Christel. *La haine n'aura pas le derniere mot: Maggy la femme aux 10000 enfants*. Paris: Albin Michel, 2005.

Newitz, Annalee. *Four Lost Cities: A Secret History of the Urban Age*. New York: W. W. Norton, 2021.

Nutchey, Thierry. *Le cinéma des anges, un cinéma humanitaire*. Ivry-sur-Seine, France: El alors Production, 2000. https://vimeo.com/356710016.

Nutchey, Thierry, and Joseph Bitamba. *L'Armée des anges*. Dijon, France: Production Lorelei, 2000.

Spadaro, Antonio. "A Big Heart Open to God: An Interview with Pope Francis." *America*, September 30, 2013. https://www.americamagazine.org/faith/2013/09/30/big-heart-open-god-interview-pope-francis.

United States Institute of Peace. "International Commission of Inquiry for Burundi: Final Report." Washington, DC: United States Institute of Peace, 2002. https://www.usip.org/sites/default/files/file/resources/collections/commissions/Burundi-Report.pdf.

15

Gendered Wounds That Clamor for Healing

Kochurani Abraham

It is significant that the "Rise Up and Walk" conference participants, in discussions about the conference's subtitle, "Catholicism and Health Care across the Globe," raised issues related to gender and sexual violence. This is particularly noteworthy, as these discussions call the official church to address these issues in all sincerity and in a prophetic manner so that ecclesiastical health and integrity can be restored.

Participants in the roundtable "Healing Trauma and Invisible Wounds" examined why some wounds remain invisible. Wounds gain visibility depending on where they are inflicted, who or what is responsible for causing them, and the sociocultural setting of the afflicted person. While wounds caused by domestic violence may be physically visible, women tend to mask the reasons behind their injuries. Thus, it is not surprising that many wounds resulting from sexual violence remain mostly invisible.

Trauma that is consequent to gender violence goes beyond the question of visibility. Women who are trapped in the gendered molds cast by patriarchy find themselves totally confused and powerless when they find themselves in situations of intimate partner violence or incest. An anecdote from my experience of working with women in India illustrates this. Some years ago, when I was working with the organization Streevani, which means "Voice of Women," in Pune, central India, a woman was brought to our center from the nearby locality. She was bleeding profusely from a deep and fresh cut on her forehead. After giving her first aid and while I was accompanying her to the hospital, I told her that after getting her wound dressed, we could go to the police station and lodge a complaint against the perpetrator, who was none other than her husband. She held my hand tightly and pleaded with me in loud sighs not to do this. I wanted to file a case because he was an alcoholic and a regular abuser, and I feared that his frequent bouts of rage put her life in danger. But her reasoning was different. For her, it was important that she safeguard the honor of the family, particularly of her children, even if it meant risking her own life.

Because gender is the sociocultural characterization of how human beings ought to behave as men and women in a given society, it is loaded with meanings having diverse implications for their lives. The intersectionality of gender with markers of identity such as class, caste, religion, ethnicity, and other factors serve as the foundation for either enhancing people's opportunities or denying their prospects for growth. The impact of gender definitions is most acutely experienced by women and those belonging to LGBTQI+ groups, a fact that becomes intensely manifest in their experiences of violence.

This paper offers a critical assessment of women's experience of gendered violence by discussing a particular instance of sexual violence within the ecclesiastical framework as a case analysis. It unveils the intricacies of sexual violence and the layers of woundedness experienced by women, particularly when gender intersects with religion. In exploring possible ways of facilitating healing, it calls into question the gendered framework of the ecclesiastical reality and suggests a serious rethinking of the church's theology and praxis.

The Traumatic Underbelly of Invisible Wounding

Given that women—particularly in countries like India—do not disclose their experiences of sexual violence easily, the inside story of their trauma is little known to the outside world. While the #MeToo movement has helped crack the hardened shell of silence to some extent, women still recoil from divulging their anguish, particularly if it has an incestuous character and can shatter the grounds on which their lives and those of their loved ones are built. This silence induced by fear becomes more intense and complex when there are systemic concerns with religious overtones. I will refer to the experiences of a survivor from the Indian setting whom I have been accompanying closely over the last three years in order to identify some aspects of the invisible trauma endured by women who are victims of sexual violence within the church.

I refer here to a concrete case of sexual violence involving a bishop in India, a case that attracted widespread media coverage across the globe. Toward the end of June 2018, a nun belonging to a diocesan congregation in India filed a case against her bishop, accusing him of abusing her sexually over a period of two years between 2014 and 2016. It took the nun almost a year to disclose her ordeal to anyone and the first person to whom she confided was her spiritual director, a nun of another indigenous congregation. This person advised her to speak to the priests with whom she made confession, hoping that someone within the ecclesiastical framework would advise her about dealing with the issue in an appropriate manner. In her distress, the survivor confessed to six different priests in the course of one year, but none helped her to find a way forward. To her shock, some of these priests scolded her and made her feel guilty for what had happened to her. Some said that she was at fault for giving the bishop a chance to use her, whereas others spiritualized it by saying that if a priest or bishop has this weakness, God intends that nuns pray for them that they may overcome it. Utterly confused and numb with a sense of shame mixed with fear, guilt, anger, and sadness, she could do nothing but indulge in self-pity. She was petrified of the consequences if this was brought to light, the offender being none other than the bishop of her diocese and the patron of her congregation, which followed the diocesan rite.

When the inner turmoil of remaining helpless before the abuse became intense, the nun went on retreat and there a priest to whom she confessed finally gave her the courage to call a spade a spade. He told her that even under threat of being killed or getting her congregation suppressed, she had a moral responsibility to report the bishop's crime to the relevant authorities. This became the turning point in her life and upon her return, she summoned the courage to resist his advances and report the abuse to her congregational leadership and church authorities.

While the trauma of concealing her suffering was unbearable for this nun, revealing it meant tasting the bitter cup of hostility, primarily from her own sisters, whose growth she had accompanied as a mother, since she was their former superior general. Except for five younger nuns who decided to stand by her come what may, the rest of the congregation turned hostile because she had dared point a finger at the bishop who was their patron. The first move by her congregational leadership was to incapacitate her and her companions by taking away from them their mission of managing a senior citizens home and a working women's hostel. Her role as the superior of the local community was terminated, and a group of three sisters was appointed to take over the administration of the local community and its apostolate. It became a rare case of a religious community of nuns having two warring groups under the same roof and sharing the same table, with one group explicitly on the side of the perpetrator and the other explicitly on the side of the victim.

The next move of her congregational leaders was to attempt to transfer the small group of her sympathetic companions so that she would be totally isolated while fighting the case. This plan did not, however, succeed because some of these sisters were witnesses in the case and could not be transferred without the permission of the court. Despite being under an obligation to provide food, shelter, and medicines to the survivor and her companions (who were under police protection in their own convent), the congregation deleted their names from the congregation's directory. The trauma that arose from this harassment continues up until the present, with the congregational leaders under the hegemonic control of the perpetrator bishop.

Adding to the agony of this survivor nun was the experience of estrangement she encountered in the church, the space that should have been her home. She took the radical step of approaching the civil courts after having knocked on many ecclesiastical doors in search for justice—first her parish priest, who directed her to the local ordinary of the diocese where she was based, who in turn directed her to speak to the head of the local church (which is one of the three Catholic rites in India). This prelate washed his hands of the problem, finding that the accused bishop belongs to another rite and is not under his jurisdiction. He suggested that she contact the police; however, blindly believing that approaching higher authorities in the church would make a difference, she then wrote to the nuncio. When this letter was met by silence, she approached the Holy See, sending letters to the prefect of the Congregation for the Doctrine of Faith, the prefect of the Congregation for Bishops, and to Pope Francis himself. Even though she tracked the letters and confirmed they were delivered to the Vatican, she was again met with silence. Finally, she mustered the courage to file a FIR against the bishop when he began threatening her family members by filing false claims against them.

The trauma experienced by the nun was intensified when new stories were invented and circulated by those with vested interests and whose motive was to punish her for daring to speak out. In an attempt to divert attention from the offender, some tried to corner the survivor nun, claiming that she entertained a relationship with the bishop for money and that she began to assert charges against him when he stopped paying her. Others asserted that she was taking revenge on him after he turned his attentions to someone else. Many of the loyal faithful of the church insisted that her silence in the face of abuse for two years clearly signaled her consent. While the blame game continued, she continued to suffer with silent tears, shattered by the duplicity of a system that defended the offender while defaming the victim. Only the few who reached out to her with genuine care could see the truth of what had happened and take a stand in solidarity with her.

The suffering ensuing from invisible wounding, as in cases of sexual violence, could be very intense for any woman, and her lived experience is very different from how it is perceived by others. Perceptions are colored by the lenses worn by those who observe situations from the outside. In a country like India, which is deeply wired by patriarchal gender norms, sexual assault is a crime for which the victim is blamed. Often, questions like what she was wearing, why she was out at that time, why she invited trouble by meeting the offender alone at the wrong time, etc., are shot like arrows at the victim without any hesitations. Consequently, when women are afflicted by sexual violence, they undergo unspeakable difficulty in voicing their experience as their trauma is deeply tangled up with a sense of shame, guilt, denial, and anger. It becomes evident that physical rape is but one aspect of the total experience of rape, with the psychological, emotional, and spiritual implications of the ordeal also weighing heavily on them.[1] Many women succumb to silence because "the penalties for complaining are high."[2] This silencing, whether self-imposed or the result of external threats, serves to further fuel the invisibility of the torment, which in turn makes the victims vulnerable to further abuse.

The Persistent Woundedness of the Church

Invisible wounding resulting from experiences of sexual violence becomes an affliction not just for the survivors but for their families and the communities to which they belong. Within the ecclesiastical framework, the trauma experienced by many Catholics who are concerned about the integrity and credibility of the church points to this. This trauma is the outcome of a systemic problem, an invisible wound on the ecclesiastical body that is not diagnosed and healed because it continues to be masked. The many instances of clergy sexual abuse and the inappropriate ways of handling the crisis by church authorities have been very traumatic for many of the Christian faithful across the globe.

One basic problem behind the ecclesiastical wounding is the double standard exercised by the official church, which generally protects abusers while keeping the victims alienated. This causes the sore spot that becomes a festering wound on the ecclesiastical body. To use another metaphor, clergy

---

1. Logue, "Treatment of Rape," 59.
2. McColgan, *Case for Taking*, 21.

sexual abuse has become like a virus eating into the entrails of the church. The inability of the all-male church leadership to deal with this problem in a healthy manner has deeply affected those who love the church and care about its integrity and mission in the world. The suffering continues because of the disconnect between those who are authorized to function as the heads of the church and those voicing the groans emanating from the many layers of the traumatic and unhealed wounds of clergy sexual abuse. The apparent numbness or lack of sensation of the head to the wounds that are still sore in the body is symptomatic of a sickness that can have fatal effects as it becomes a malignancy in the body of the church. The deep-rooted gender bias that can be seen in the case of the nun abused by a bishop raises the question: Would a daughter of the ecclesiastical family cease to be one if she dares expose the incestuous experience of sexual violation by one of the sons of the same mother church?

Woundedness of the ecclesiastical body becomes very grave because of its religious, spiritual, and theological implications. A study investigating the experiences of people who were sexually abused by Roman Catholic priests indicated that the majority of the respondents considered "God" to have been integral to the abuse, manipulated by design or default by the clerical or religious perpetrator. This creates significant anxiety and distress, leading to a crisis of faith.[3] Sexual abuse by clergy is considered especially traumatic because of the devastating effect it has on the victim's spirituality and religiosity.[4] This is because the vast majority of victims are (or were) devoted members of their churches, having an exceptional degree of trust in their clergy and in the religious system. Many times, the priest is viewed by the victims not only as a representative of God, but *as* God. This belief is not based on free-floating Catholic mythology but is solidly grounded in church teaching, with priests themselves believing they are ontologically different from the rest of the Christian faithful because of their ordination.[5]

In order to comprehend why priests hold so much power over the Christian faithful, we need to look into its theological underpinnings. The theology of ministerial priesthood is founded on the basic principle that the priest functions *in persona Christi*/in the person of Christ. This theology is based on an understanding of the church as the body of which Christ is the head and the ordained priests act in his person.[6] While this theology of the priest becoming "another Christ" holds the possibility of affirming the

---

3. Farrell, "Sexual Abuse," 39.
4. McLaughlin, "Devastated Spirituality."
5. Doyle, "Spiritual Trauma," 248.
6. Paul VI, *Presbyterorum Ordinis*, 2.

sacredness of the priestly vocation, it is potentially dangerous because of the possible abuse of the "sacred power" they are vested with. Even if the priests do not abuse this power, the exaltation of the priest as *alter Christus*/another Christ[7] can be spiritually intimidating to the Christian faithful. For those who are religiously socialized to see the priest as another Christ, this conception is imprinted on their minds to the extent that they attribute a divine status to him and consequently desire to please him without counting the cost. In such situations, the priest could very well abuse the *potestas Sacra*—sacred power—that becomes his privilege through the rite of ordination.[8] The power a priest has over his victims as well as erroneous beliefs about the nature of the priesthood contribute to create a toxic bond between victim and perpetrator, commonly known as a "trauma bond," which is especially strong when fortified by religiously based beliefs and fears.[9]

Catholic historians like Massimo Faggioli identify the crisis ensuing from clergy sexual abuse as a "theological crisis" that has long-term consequences on the theological standing and balance of the Catholic Church throughout the world. In his opinion, a theological rethinking in light of the abuse crisis is necessary—not only from the lens of those who have suffered, but also from the lens of the changes caused by this global crisis for the whole Catholic community.[10]

The symptoms of this crisis/sickness afflicting the church have been felt for four to five decades or more. It is ironic that the church engages actively in a healing ministry through its numerous health care institutions, outreach programs, and individual initiatives, yet is negligent of the grave infirmity that is sucking out the vital energies from its body.

What is lacking in the church is not an awareness of the crisis but the will to act on it. The 1983 Code of Canon Law contains legislation that deals directly with sexual abuse and lays down procedures for dealing with such situations. Canon lawyers are of the opinion that the issue is not the absence of legal structures to meet this vexing problem but the failure of church leadership to follow its own rules.[11] Canon 1389 acknowledges that clerical sexual violence is an abuse of authority as a minister and officeholder in the institutional church, and Canon 1395 establishes that sexual contact with a minor qualifies as one of four classifications of sexual offenses for which a man may be permanently removed from the clerical state. Further, the Code

7. Pius XI, *Ad Catholici Sacerdotti*, 12.
8. Abraham, "Unmasking Integrity," 401.
9. Julich, "Stockholm Syndrome."
10. Faggioli, "Catholic Sexual Abuse Crisis."
11. Coughlin, "Clergy Sexual Abuse Crisis."

of Canon Law outlines a specific procedure for investigating allegations of clergy sexual abuse, which entrusts the bishop to deal with them after sufficient investigation as provided for in Canon 1341 of the 1983 code. In spite of having all these legal provisions in place, it is an undeniable fact that the crime of clergy sexual abuse has continued unchecked over the last five decades.

According to some scholars, the governmental structure of the Catholic Church is primarily responsible for this phenomenon. These scholars argue that understanding the church's hierarchical system of governance is essential to understanding the practical role of the canon law in the day-to-day life of the church.[12] All too often, persons abused by clergy report that their complaints to bishops and other diocesan officials have been met with varying degrees of denial, arrogance, and/or incompetence. Such attitudes only serve to intensify the psychological damage caused by the abuse.[13] In light of everything we have said above, it is clear that clergy sexual abuse in the Catholic Church is a multidimensional crisis that is deeply problematic for the personal and systemic issues that are at stake. This crisis has led to a situation that calls for an ecclesiastical emergency that must be addressed using a multipronged approach.

Tracing the Pathways to Healing

Healing from the trauma caused by any form of sexual violence involves a slow and difficult process that calls for a critical diagnosis of the problem in all of its complexity. In situations of clergy sexual abuse, as was described above in the case of the nun who was violated by the bishop, the process of healing is especially complex because it involves not only healing the victim but also dealing with the system that perpetrates the sickness. Within official church circles, clergy sexual abuse is not seen as an ailment that needs healing. If the issue has caught media attention and turned scandalous, the tendency is to mask it in piety by increasing the dose of prayers for clergy that they are strengthened and safeguarded from temptation. It is treated as a sin that can be erased with absolution. For those who see it as a symptom of a major sickness affecting the system, healing is not possible without taking decisive steps that involve identifying the causative elements, calling them by their true names, and addressing them squarely without spiritualizing the matter.

---

12. Doyle and Rubino, "Catholic Clergy Sexual Abuse," 558.
13. Coughlin, "Clergy Sexual Abuse Crisis," 979.

Sexual abuse in any form is traumatic and often confusing for the victims because it is the most intimate and arguably the most profound of all violations that a human being could experience, as was observed in the Texas Association Against Sexual Assault (TAASA) in its *Guidebook for Clergy on Healing Victims of Sexual Abuse*. It is noted in this guidebook that sexual assault victims are left with various types of wounds from which they must recover. Some victims may be left with physical injuries and scars. All victims of sexual trauma will be left with some form of emotional or psychological wounding. Perhaps most troubling of all, however, is the spiritual injury that results from this most intimate form of violation and betrayal. A sexual violation might be understood as a wounding of the soul—it does violence to one's very spirit. Because these injuries are so personal and so profound, they often result in painful existential searching and questioning. However, because religious communities have often avoided these issues, the sense of isolation and betrayal can be even more profound for sexual assault victims seeking spiritual support and guidance.[14]

Healing for any trauma is directly correlated to diagnosing correctly its causative factors. In the case of those traumatized by sexual violence, the emotional and mental conditioning of the victim directly influences their ability to recover. Survivors observe that recovery is often experienced as a slow process, and some people will never fully recover from such a profound abuse of power and trust, especially when the abuser is a priest. Ongoing support, friendship, and a willingness to listen time and again to the anger and fragility that remains will require considerable patience. For some people, healing is a very distant hope.[15]

When accompanying survivors through the healing process, it is important to take note of the basic stages of a crisis. Therapists identify the first stage as the "impact" stage. This occurs in the immediate aftermath of the traumatic event or when victims initially confront what has happened to them. At this stage, some victims experience denial, which ranges from a total inability to recall what has happened to simply viewing the situation as not as bad as it is in reality. Therapists believe that this is nature's way of protecting those affected from the full impact of a traumatic event until they are more able to cope with the situation. Victims have been known to repress memories of sexual trauma for days, months, and even years. The goals of crisis intervention in the impact stage include addressing the immediate needs of the victim, such as the needs for physical safety, emotional support, and information. Helpers must suspend judgment, listen with

14. Thueson, *Guidebook for Clergy*, 1.
15. Collins and Hollins, "Healing a Wound."

empathy, normalize the victim's reaction, and predict and prepare the victim for future reactions. Further, it is important to begin to return a sense of control to the victim as soon as possible.[16]

Following the impact stage comes the "recoil" stage. This is characterized by a flood, a great upheaval, of emotions. This is seen as a natural reaction to being suddenly struck, that is pulling away from or recoiling from the trauma. Victims often reel from overwhelming and chaotic emotions. They may feel anger and rage and then sorrow and depression. Victims may feel relief that they are alive or that the abuse is over and then be struck with fear and feelings of panic. This emotional roller coaster is exhausting; many victims describe feeling that they are "going crazy." Victims often experience a kind of existential crisis during this period. Questions about who they are, what they believe in, and the purpose of things often arise. Some question the very foundation of their beliefs as they struggle to make sense of what has happened to them. Issues of grief, trust, and faith are often prevalent. The goals of crisis intervention during this stage include validation of the victim's reactions to the trauma, support, empathic listening, and normalizing and predicting their reactions to traumatic stress. Helpers must be patient in the face of the wide range of the victim's often-changing emotions and thoughts. Thoughts and feelings may seem chaotic during this stage, but this is simply the victim's attempt to grasp the situation and attribute meaning to a new and horrible experience. Remember to suspend judgment and offer unconditional love and positive words to those you are assisting.

The final stage in the therapeutic process is identified as "reorganization." During this phase, victims must reconstruct their beliefs and sense of equilibrium. The reorganization stage is where victims begin to regain a sense of equilibrium in their lives. This involves coming to terms with the losses they have experienced, regaining a sense of control and personal empowerment, reestablishing trust, redefining the future, finding meaning again, rediscovering the self, and often redefining their values and beliefs. These are the goals of crisis intervention during this stage. This is the stage in which victims hope to achieve real spiritual healing and find peace and direction once again. Crisis intervention at this stage may involve helping victims identify strategies that will help them feel safe and secure. It is important that the therapist reassures victims that they are safe when they are with them; for this reason, it is imperative to be sensitive to their insecurities and fears. If some victims do not feel safe behind closed doors, or in being alone with a man, it is important that meetings take place in an open space with others nearby or within view. Victims need the assurance

---

16. Thueson, *Guidebook for Clergy*, 9–10.

that conversations are confidential, and it is essential to always keep their confidences (with the exception that information needs to be shared with those who can offer professional intervention; this needs to be done with the knowledge of the victim). It is important to identify support systems because people in crisis need a great deal of emotional support, which might include support from family members, old friends with whom they have lost touch, coworkers, or members of their congregation. Survivors can be helped to identify their support systems.[17]

Therapists encourage survivors to pay special attention to taking care of themselves as they work on healing. Places and activities that make them feel safe and secure, warm, and loved and nurtured need to be identified, and survivors need to be encouraged to engage in these activities often. They should focus on getting a good night's sleep, exercise, and eating healthy and regular meals. Spending time outside in the sunlight and appreciating the beauty of God's creations can be quite healing. Some victims find writing poetry or keeping a journal to be therapeutic and healing. Prayer and meditation are also soothing and can help victims find a sense of calm and peace. At every stage of the healing process, empathic listening is imperative—as victims discuss their thoughts and feelings, it is important to suspend all judgment. Nonjudgmentally listening with genuine compassion and empathy will help the victim feel safe and begin to trust again. Providing a safe place that is free of judgment allows victims to explore their true thoughts, feelings, and fears. This is the beginning of regaining some sense of control and reestablishing meaning in their lives.[18]

Healing the Ecclesiastical Body

The healing of individual survivors cannot be separated from the healing of the church as an institution, since the ecclesiastical body that we understand theologically as the body of Christ is an organic whole. The woundedness of one part would certainly affect the health of the whole body and this is true also of the healing process. Unfortunately, when survivors dare to disclose their experience of clergy sexual abuse, they are often blamed for being instrumental in tarnishing the image of the ecclesiastical institution. And this trying to save the institution from scandal has caused the greatest of all scandals and has perpetuated the harm of the abuse, destroying the faith of many victims.[19] Because clergy sexual abuse has caused lifelong

17. Thueson, *Guidebook for Clergy*, 9–10.
18. Thueson, *Guidebook for Clergy*, 11–13.
19. Collins and Hollins, "Healing a Wound," 28.

trauma to survivors and their families and communities, many Christian faithful have lost trust in the church as a community founded on integrity. When the credibility of an institution like the church, which is expected to provide a moral grounding to the faithful, becomes eroded, it precipitates not just an ecclesiological crisis but also a theological crisis and an urgency to address concerns openly to bring about healing.

Healing processes are effective only when there is a proper diagnosis of the causative factors underlying any sickness. Many scholars who have examined the pathology of clergy sexual abuse identify clericalism as a major issue behind the inability of the church to address it. Although these clergy constitute a minuscule fraction (approximately 0.0004 percent) of the world's Catholic population, they wield all of the power in the church. This is because the institutional church has constructed a theology of sacred orders (deacons, priests, and bishops) that supported the separation of clerics into a special caste, leading to the theology that bishops are the direct descendants of the apostles.[20] Or, to put it differently, clericalism is the culture that created the climate in which Catholic men and women of conscience have routinely not been heard or understood, and in which the self-preserving power of the clerics was given sanction.[21] Because of the presence of these dynamics in the phenomenon of clergy sexual abuse, initiating a healing process implies tackling the iniquity of clericalism. Pope Francis has consistently spoken against clericalism, seeing it as "a perversion" that is "the root of many evils in the Church," for which "we must humbly ask forgiveness . . . and above all create the conditions so that it is not repeated."[22]

It can be observed that the toxic and un-Christian culture of ministerial superiority that is consequent to clericalism allows clerics to avoid being held accountable. This leads to a lack of transparency and the misuse of power and raises issues that cannot easily be addressed.[23] The noted moral theologian James Keenan identifies *hierarchicalism* as the culture emerging at the center of the sexual abuse scandal and argues that the hierarchical culture has exercised its power and networking capabilities in order to cover up their own actions. In his opinion, hierarchicalism and its attendant lack of accountability and ability to act with impunity will be harder to dismantle than clericalism and in fact will guarantee the survival of clericalism, for it is the father and promoter of clericalism.[24]

20. Doyle, "Clericalism," 149–50.
21. Keenan, "Vulnerability and Hierarchicalism," 132.
22. Francis, "Address at the Opening."
23. Boorstein, "What Caused the Clergy Sex Abuse Crisis?"
24. Keenan, "Vulnerability and Hierarchicalism," 134–35.

In light of this state of religious politics in the church, there is a real question about the possibility of bringing healing to the ecclesiastical system. Because ecclesiastical leadership is structured as a hierarchy, it will not be easy to address hierarchicalism, even though it is imperative to do so, in order to facilitate dialogue on the present crisis in the church between different groups making up the people of God. In this situation, it is necessary to advance conversations about sexual abuse beyond the well-worn path of discussing issues of accountability and develop an ecclesiology based on the risk-taking vulnerability of God.[25] As an alternative to the culture of hierarchicalism and clericalism that dominate not only the ecclesiastical leadership itself but also the life of the church generally, Keenan proposes another culture—a "culture of vulnerability." He sees this as a path that will facilitate "servant priesthood" and a "servant episcopacy" and argues that it is precisely vulnerability that our clerics and hierarchs ignored during the course of this scandal.[26] Formation of clergy in this "culture of vulnerability" would certainly herald a path for the emergence of a new way of being church, freed of imperialistic pretensions and a patriarchal worldview.

In the aftermath of clergy sexual abuse, the Evangelical Lutheran Church in America (ELCA) recommends that the pastoral leadership work toward reestablishing trust in a spirit of honesty and respect so that church becomes a safe space for all. As a therapeutic measure, the ELCA has suggested gospel resources that promise and promote healing, which implies openness to listening attentively and making available real opportunities for communication in all frankness. In this process, it is important to avoid identification with factions and cliques and to prevent triangulation. Healthy interaction needs to be promoted at congregational meetings. Healing can occur whenever members are gathered at council meetings, Bible study, committee meetings, and educational or social events, always beginning with prayer for God's Spirit to guide and enlighten the conversation.[27]

While the "culture of vulnerability" proposed by Keenan as an alternative to the self-imposing power structures of the church is certainly appealing as a healing mechanism, feminist theologians in India have consistently argued for making a distinction between sin and crime in dealing with clergy sexual abuse. For many holding ecclesiastical authority, the issue is not so much about the abuse. They see abuses of this nature as sin, as a moral deviation that can be absolved at the confessional if the abuser expresses repentance, or as the result of a personality disorder that needs to be treated.

---

25. Roberts, "Vulnerability as Strength."
26. Keenan, "Vulnerability and Hierarchicalism," 135.
27. Erickson-Pearson, *Healing in Congregations*, 85–86.

From the perspective of the survivors, it is not a sin that can be absolved but a crime that needs to be addressed in all its gravity. In ecclesiastical crimes of this nature, it is not just the abuse of religious power but also of economic and political power, as the perpetrators of the crime generally have access to enormous resources.

Bringing the offenders to trial in the state's legal systems is crucial for restoring justice and for facilitating the healing process of the affected persons in the ecclesiastical community. As noted by a survivor:

> The beginning of recovery for me was the day in court when my abuser took responsibility for his actions and admitted his guilt. This admission had a profound effect on me. It led in time to my being able to forgive what he had done and no longer feel him as a presence in my life. I attended therapy for nearly two years and through this came to understand how this abuser had twisted my view of myself. This had come at a crucial time in my development. My feelings of guilt and a very poor self-image led me to turn away from those nearest to me and isolate myself. My deep-seated anxiety led to depression. Gaining insight into all these areas helped me to believe things could change. I could be in control of my life rather than have my past control me. I was able to leave the wasted years behind. I have not been hospitalized with any mental health issue since that time.[28]

As far as survivors are concerned, being believed is in itself healing, especially if it is associated with an admission of guilt or responsibility, and even more so if there is an attempt at reparation. This demands putting in place structures like an Internal Complaints Committee (ICC) that play a vigilant role against abuse and provide other measures that facilitate redress. Since recovery from an experience of abuse is a slow process for the victim and for the community, ongoing support and friendship is necessary. This entails a willingness to listen time and again to the anger and fragility that remains, which requires considerable patience because for some people healing seems very far away.[29]

Conclusion

Handling sexual conflicts within the church implies going beyond the avoidance syndrome and seeing it as a crisis calling for renewal and an authentic humanization of the church as an institution. This is a crisis that offers the

---

28. Collins and Hollins, "Healing a Wound," 28.
29. Collins and Hollins, "Healing a Wound," 27.

church a tremendous opportunity for growth because the healing process—if assumed in truthfulness—entails deep purification and liberation from its patriarchal and imperialistic fetters. Tackling this situation of ecclesiastical emergency calls for bridging the clergy-laity divide and necessitates the restoration of women and other excluded persons to their rightful places of decision-making and leadership in the church. All this becomes possible only through a return to the gospel vision of being church as a Christian community founded on the ever-renewing ways of the Spirit, which implies a radical turning back to the founding charism of the church according to the mind of Christ. If this were to happen, the church would rediscover its rightful vocation and mission as a wounded healer in the world.

Bibliography

Abraham, Kochurani. "Unmasking Integrity: The Challenge Before Clergy Sexual Abuse." *Asian Horizons* 14 (2020) 393–406.

Boorstein, Michelle. "What Caused the Clergy Sex Abuse Crisis? Catholic Universities Are Pushing for Debate on the Answer." *Washington Post*, March 27, 2019. https://www.washingtonpost.com/religion/2019/03/27/what-caused-clergy-sex-abuse-crisis-catholic-universities-are-pushing-debate-answer/.

Collins, Marie, and Sheila Hollins. "Healing a Wound at the Heart of the Church and Society." In *Toward Healing and Renewal: The 2012 Symposium on the Sexual Abuse of Minors Held at the Pontifical Gregorian University*, edited by Charles J. Scicluna et al., 15–28. New York: Paulist, 2012.

Coughlin, John J. "The Clergy Sexual Abuse Crisis and the Spirit of Canon Law." *Boston College Law Review* 44 (2002–2003) 977–97. https://scholarship.law.nd.edu/law_faculty_scholarship/45/.

Doyle, Thomas. "Clericalism and Catholic Clergy Sexual Abuse." In *Predatory Priests, Silenced Victims: The Sexual Abuse Crisis and the Catholic Church*, edited by Mary Gail Frawley-O'Dea and Virginia Goldner, 147–62. Mahwah, NJ: Analytic, 2007.

———. "The Spiritual Trauma Experienced by Victims of Sexual Abuse by Catholic Clergy." *Pastoral Psychology* 58.3 (2009) 239–60.

Doyle, Thomas, and Stephen C. Rubino. "Catholic Clergy Sexual Abuse Meets the Civil Law." *Fordham Urban Law Journal* 31.2 (2004) 549–616. https://ir.lawnet.fordham.edu/ulj/vol31/iss2/6.

Erickson-Pearson, Jan. *Healing in Congregations after Clergy Sexual Abuse: A Resource to Assist Synodical Leaders and Local Congregations of the Evangelical Lutheran Church in America*. Chicago: ELCA Division for Ministry, 2007. http://download.elca.org/ELCA%20Resource%20Repository/Healing_In_Congregations_After_Clergy_Sexual_Abuse.pdf.

Faggioli, Massimo. "The Catholic Sexual Abuse Crisis as a Theological Crisis: Emerging Issues." *Theological Studies* 80.3 (2019) 572–89.

Farrell, Derek P. "Sexual Abuse Perpetrated by Roman Catholic Priests and Religious." *Mental Health, Religion, and Culture* 12.1 (2009) 39–53.

Francis, Pope. "Address at the Opening of the Synod of Bishops on Young People, the Faith and Vocational Discernment." Speech given in Synod Hall, Rome, October 3, 2018. http://w2.vatican.va/content/francesco/en/speeches/2018/october/documents/papa-francesco_20181003_apertura-sinodo.html.

Julich, Shirley. "Stockholm Syndrome and Child Sexual Abuse." *Journal of Child Sexual Abuse* 14.3 (2005) 107–29.

Keenan, James F. "Vulnerability and Hierarchicalism." *Melita Theologica* 68.2 (2018) 129–42.

Logue, Pauline. "The Treatment of Rape in Theology." *ITB Journal* 1.2 (2000) 59–64.

McColgan, Aileen. *The Case for Taking the Date Out of Rape*. London: Pandora, 1996.

McLaughlin, Barbara. "Devastated Spirituality: The Impact of Clergy Sexual Abuse on the Survivor's Relationship with God and the Church." *Sexual Addiction and Compulsivity* 1.2 (1994) 145–58.

Paul VI, Pope. *Presbyterorum Ordinis: Decree on the Ministry and Life of Priests*. December 7, 1965. https://www.vatican.va/archive/hist_councils/ii_vatican_council/documents/vat-ii_decree_19651207_presbyterorum-ordinis_en.html.

Pius XI, Pope. *Ad Catholici Sacerdotii: On the Catholic Priesthood*. December 20, 1935. https://www.vatican.va/content/pius-xi/en/encyclicals/documents/hf_p-xi_enc_19351220_ad-catholici-sacerdotii.html.

Roberts, Tom. "Vulnerability as Strength: Keenan's Key to Dismantling Clericalism." *National Catholic Reporter*, December 31, 2019. https://www.ncronline.org/news/ncr-connections/vulnerability-strength-keenans-key-dismantling-clericalism.

Thueson, Helen. *A Guidebook for Clergy on Sexual Assault, Trauma, and Spiritual Healing*. Austin: Texas Association Against Sexual Assault. https://www.cbshouston.edu/assets/files/sexual-assault-trauma-spiritual-healing-clergy-guidebook.pdf.

16

The Pandemic in the Context of Necropolitics and Liberation Spiritualities

Claudio de Oliveira Ribeiro

Introduction

The pandemic caused by the coronavirus has had different consequences for the world in different dynamics of life. These consequences generated crises, not only in the scope of public health and in the economic sphere, but also in the most diverse subjective, interpersonal, and social aspects. The physical and emotional fragility of human beings has never been so explicit and exposed—at least, not in recent times. Traumas and invisible wounds abound in our reality. At the same time, however, different forms of human solidarity and creativity also emerged from this picture.

The concerns and fears surrounding the pandemic have sparked reactions of varying degrees around the world. Among them, I highlight here the reinforcement of different forms of spirituality—religious or otherwise—to help face issues related to death, physical and emotional fragility, and social isolation. Likewise, especially due to the confinement and economic implications of the pandemic, different aspects of human coexistence impacted social, collective, and interpersonal relationships with the most diverse results, underscoring and accentuating the difficulties in human relationships and social insensitivity, now favoring acts of solidarity and fostering reflections on new possibilities for understanding and organizing life.

All of these aspects, both complex and challenging, highlight significant paths for life in general and in particular, for spiritual experience. The diversity of religious responses to the pandemic situation was not—and has not been—small. They have encompassed everything from the presence of negationist and ideological religious forms to others that are characterized by dialogue with science, human sensitivity to suffering, and maturity in the search for attitudes that emphasize social responsibility in the face of the harmful effects of this situation.[1]

The Pandemic in the Context of Necropolitics

It is necessary to look at the pandemic that has plagued the world in the context of necropolitics. Among the various negative aspects of the difficult and dramatic situation generated by the pandemic, there are some aspects that reveal possibilities for a reorganization of society, both in terms of personal experiences in daily life, as well as in our social structures. Portuguese sociologist Boaventura de Souza Santos called these possibilities "a cruel pedagogy of the virus," the title of one of his recent books.[2]

The pandemic revealed that the economic system that structures society, even with variations between countries and continents, does not meet the demands of human dignity or basic human rights.[3] The situation in Brazil, but also in several other parts of the globe, has shown that the risks and major problems are concentrated in the poorest sectors of society, and the realities of prison populations, slum areas, and homeless people have become even more dramatic. The peripheries, with their precarious housing, overcrowding, and lack of sanitation are the communities that suffer the most from the pandemic's outbreak. A virus, bacteria, or any other microorganism responsible for an outbreak like this does not choose people. Everyone is subject to contagion. However, it can be more serious for those who are already vulnerable or have chronic diseases.[4] Brazilian society, for example, which is racialized and marked by inequality, illustrated how racial division, forms of machismo, and economic disparities were exacerbated by the pandemic's devastating impact, amplifying and intensifying the genocide of black and indigenous Brazilians.[5]

---

1. For an overview of this theme, see Usarski and Py, "Religion and the Pandemic"; Renders and Wolff, "Fé e o Sagrado"; and Barsalini et al., "Quem e o Que Se Perde."
2. Santos, *Cruel Pedagogia do Vírus*.
3. Cf. Dowbor, "Além da Pandemia," 25–47.
4. Cunha, "Esperança em Tempo de Pandemia," 484.
5. For a specific analysis of the vulnerability of indigenous peoples aggravated by

Luis Augusto de Paula Souza draws attention to the fact that

> [f]orms of life under the current capitalist system are based on consumerism and consumption for consumption as an absolute value; in biopower, Michel Foucault's concept, we see the extensive and intensive control of life—including biological life—by incorporating the logic of capital: bodies phagocytized by capitalism, "naked life" in the expression of Giorgio Agamben; and in necropower, Achille Mbembe's concept, we see the rule of government, by which the greatest expression of sovereignty is granted by the ability to decide who should live and who should die. To give just one example from the pandemic: in Brazil, is there any doubt about which social segments will be protected and which ones will be on their own?[6]

Necropolitics, with its ideological background and colonial origin, permeates social life. The organization of urban space, for example, generates "non-places," where the law has no validity. Death is trivialized, and there is no justice or accountability for murders and deaths. The pandemic has made this reality even more evident. In large urban centers, the levels of contamination and mortality as well as the amount of people who cannot adopt social distancing (especially due to working and transportation conditions) reflect this division of space. "In the virus, necropolitics finds an alibi to kill even more intensely. Hands are not dirty. Death is outsourced to an invisible 'being' that is everywhere. As a result, responsibility is also outsourced. It's the virus. It is a biological fact."[7] It is an "ancient colonialist necrophilia . . . with the objective of expressing the undisguised sympathy for the death of black and indigenous people, as well as the poor and the elderly in the Brazilian context, in the face of the pandemic [through] strategic and arbitrary actions promoted in the current conjuncture of a policy deliberated by death."[8]

The concept of necropolitics can be related to the sacrificial logic that emerges in the context of the pandemic, mainly due to some of its structuring elements such as the fictional creation of an enemy (China's communism, for example), the strengthening of ties of enmity, and the notion of the state of exception. This is the religious dimension of necropolitics. The

---

COVID-19, see Xavier and Delfino, "Pensar, Sentir e Agir," 177–92; and Barreto Jr., "COVID-19 Pandemic," 417–39.

6. Souza, "Cura ou Qual Mundo," 178; translation mine. Throughout the rest of this chapter, all of the English translations from Portuguese sources are my own.

7. Gabatz and Angelin, "Ponderações Críticas," 470.

8. Gabatz and Angelin, "Ponderações Críticas," 470.

pandemic has revealed this racist and antidemocratic face, allowing us to perceive, in the expiatory sacrifice, a face of the necroreligion.[9]

The causes of the pandemic have been analyzed by numerous people from different sectors of knowledge. Such analyses are not within the scope of this text, but they are important. Along these same lines, there are the scientific reflections synthesized by Leonardo Boff in various works. Boff states that "the coronavirus pandemic reveals to us that the way we inhabit our common home is harmful to its nature. The lesson it transmits to us echoes in our lives: it is imperative to rethink the way we live together, as a living planet."[10] He stresses that the land "is warning us that we cannot continue to live the way we have been. Otherwise, the Earth itself will get rid of us, beings that are excessively aggressive and harmful to the life-system."[11]

Many of the reflections have highlighted the consequences of the pandemic, although it is recognized that an in-depth view of its causes is imperative for raising awareness about other forms of political-social, cultural, and spiritual views. These could reinforce the sustainability of life and of the world, as well as indicate the necessary criticism of the current economic system and the exclusive way in which society is organized. It is not insignificant that there were signs of decreased pollution in large cities during the initial period of social isolation (from March to July 2020) and a reduction in unrestrained consumption. The expression used by the Brazilian theologian Leonardo Boff in the title of one of his articles is an example of this reality: To return to "normalcy" is to condemn yourself to yourself.[12]

This reality applies mainly to women. The situation of social isolation transferred professional activities to the home environment, creating problematic situations for many women (and children), being forced to live with abusive men. The restriction of travel made it impossible for women to visit or seek refuge in their closest networks—whether family or friends—and they were exposed to the most diverse forms of violence. "Violence, which is already a historical, chronic, structural, and pandemic problem, according to the UN, is intensifying in the context of the pandemic."[13] Therefore, this pandemic is one of serious global and planetary impact, crossing several dimensions of daily life.

---

9. Pieper et al., "Necropolítica," 533.
10. Boff, "Terra Se Defende," para. 2.
11. Boff, "Terra Se Defende," para. 2.
12. Boff, "Voltar à 'Normalidade.'"
13. Ulrich et al., "Mulheres em Tempos de Pandemia," 561.

In this perspective, the expression "crisis" has become central to the most consistent reflections on the pandemic and its consequences. It reveals the dialectical opposition of the aforementioned "cruel pedagogy of the virus."

João Décio Passos calls attention to the fact that every crisis creates an urgent question for the future. The pandemic has dominated the public world scene with an abrupt end to life as we knew it. This planetary crisis has revealed the limits of life, economies, and governments, in their ability to offer immediate solutions. For Passos, the functioning of society had been devised for decades within the logic of a supposedly given economic regime and, in recent times, by an epidemic crisis of powers that has tested authoritarian regimes around the world. And still, it was nothing like this pandemic. The planet stopped and put itself in a posture of urgent review of its economic, political, and cultural practices.[14]

Passos also points out that

> the pandemic woke the planet up from some of its illusions. At least immediately, some truths proved, in fact, to be illusions: the illusion of progress and limitless consumption; the illusion of universal well-being and a regime ready to dispense it by all means; the illusion of a world capital that saves the world; the illusion of a dominant science always available to intervene in any health crisis; the illusion of an omnipotent God of religion that intervenes when the natural order plays against prosperity.[15]

In this same direction, Boaventura de Souza Santos proposes a new political-social articulation that must have as its primary assumption an epistemological, cultural, and ideological shift. It would require forging political, economic, and social solutions that would guarantee maintaining dignified human life for all people on the planet. Such a change would have multiple implications. One of them—of an urgent and planetary character—would be the creation of a new common and critical awareness that, especially in the last decades, there has been a political and cultural "quarantine," with a strong ideological accent, forged by the capitalist economic system in its exclusionary and discriminatory structures with respect to the racist and sexist contexts in which it exists. "The quarantine caused by the pandemic is, after all, a quarantine within another quarantine. We will overcome the quarantine of capitalism when we are able to imagine the planet

---

14. Passos, *Pandemia do Coronavírus*, 232.
15. Passos, *Pandemia do Coronavírus*, 233.

as our common home and Nature as our original mother to whom we owe love and respect."[16]

Regarding interpersonal relationships and issues related to family contexts and aspects of daily life, the pandemic does have one positive aspect. At the level of human solidarity, our common pain seems—at least in part—to awaken our sensitivities and a spirit of solidarity. Despite a greater indifference in some groups (some people are more protected than others), the current situation reveals everyone's vulnerability. The crisis, therefore, seems to be an aid in awakening our solidarity with our elderly neighbors, with the most vulnerable people in society, and with patients who are in hospitals.

During the COVID-19 pandemic, we have experienced for the first time (at least in our lifetime) social isolation on a global level. The attitude of staying away leads, paradoxically, to self-protection as a social group. Being apart became an act of care and affection. COVID-19 has also created a large amount of fear. Confronting the idea of death causes us to deal with what the existential interpretation of the human condition calls anguish. And such a condition, "by extension, brings up this inevitable understanding that we have to survive. . . . It is this challenging time that produces certain skills, whether you like it or not, and forces you to develop a great mental discipline, giving rise to new social skills."[17]

In Brazil, the streets and squares of the city of São Paulo know the protests of Father Julio Lancelotti and his team in working with people living on the streets. In their work, health is understood in a holistic, integral way, ranging from addressing the hunger and illness of the homeless to defending their basic human rights. In the pandemic crisis, all of these efforts needed to be multiplied; they are a concrete example of inviting people to "rise up and walk."

When defined as a global crisis, the pandemic of the new coronavirus—more than in other dramatic social situations—reveals the crisis of the economic system that creates grave health risks and shows more clearly the signs of necropolitics established in various parts of the world. Such a framework requires new sensitivities, a different global policy, and the confrontation of local and national administrations, all based on the supreme value of life.

16. Santos, *Cruel Pedagogia do Vírus*, 32.
17. Gabatz and Angelin, "Ponderações Críticas," 479.

The Pandemic and Religious Experiences

Let us look more closely at the relationship between the pandemic and religious experiences. In the social and cultural context of the pandemic, many religious themes and arguments have stood out in conversations and debates, whether due to the atmosphere of negating the virus that some groups have sparked, or due to the search for broader and well-founded understandings of the phenomenon that are also social in nature. A question that several groups have asked is, "How can we better understand this situation?" And different sectors have dedicated themselves to reflecting on it.

Both the most spontaneous forms of spirituality and the most traditional or institutionalized religious expressions are present in the debate about the pandemic and social isolation. Both have marked the lives of many people and groups, and have been present, in different ways, in each situation they face. The forms and characteristics of these spiritualities and religious experiences are very different. Some of them, with many variations and nuances, are articulated by ideological elements. They are also traversed by economic readings, almost always as a "fundamental solution key and, often, as the main criterion for deciding on contagion containment strategies. And there was no shortage of people who stated, explicitly or otherwise, that saving the economy was more important than preserving lives."[18]

This first set of religious views has at least four vigorous expressions, most of them with strong popular attachment, and they are present in the Latin American Catholic context. One of its expressions is characterized, following emerging views in society's political arena, by the denial of the pandemic's drama.[19] In this perspective, the relationship with the relativism of the truth present in political discourses about the pandemic becomes clear and, even more, it illustrates the challenges for understanding the Christian life, in coherence with the evangelical truth. At the same time, "a negationist reading of the COVID-19 pandemic, present in government discourse [in Brazil], contributes to a process of reinforcing the dimension of death, with an emphasis on its trivialization and the silencing of grief in society."[20]

18. Passos, *Pandemia do Coronavírus*, 18.

19. In Brazil, such a religious vision is closely linked to several statements by the president of the republic, Jair Bolsonaro, and members of his political party that denied or mitigated the dramatic effects of the pandemic, accompanied by absence or timidity in formulating and implementing consistent public policies to combat the pandemic. For that, see Bandeira and Carranza, "Reactions to the Pandemic," 170–93; Kibuuka, "Complicity and Synergy," 288–317; and Lellis and Dutra, "Programmatic Crisis and Moralization," 335–59.

20. Paula and Souza, "Tabu da Morte," 165.

Another religious expression attributes the spread of the disease to God's wrath and punishment for human sins, especially those associated with sexual freedom and the use of blasphemous humor or the relativization of traditional religious values. In this view, the pandemic and its respective health and economic impacts signify an action by God to punish humanity which has lost its moral course. Several Catholic priests and evangelical pastors, especially those who have a certain presence in the media, publicized this view.

Another belief, also related to ideologies of denial, attributes the pandemic to supposed communist interests to defy the Christian faith: "COVID-19 has given rise to false prophets in order to contaminate the intricacies of political action, causing reverie and discomfort in confirming one of our greatest paradoxes: the painful social inequality."[21] In this sense, it is necessary to analyze the constant need to point out enemies, either real or imagined, who threaten the faith, something that is always present in religious interpretations of a more fundamentalist character. Constantly identifying enemies is necessary to sustain and maintain violent speeches, feelings of rivalry, and even exclusivity of faith and reason. During the COVID-19 pandemic, one of the primary enemies that religious groups chose are the protagonists of agendas identified as belonging to the political left.[22]

Another expression of this set of religious views highlights the religious element as opposed to the scientific one in the context of the pandemic. Generally speaking, such religious readings persist parallel to the sciences, and sometimes they take their place. Those who hold this viewpoint "put God or the devil as the cause of the virus and, therefore, offer solution rituals: worship services, anointing with oil, novenas, prayer chains, crucifixes on the door, holy water sprinkled on the street, procession with the Blessed Sacrament."[23]

There is a second set of spiritual approaches of a more intimist character that focuses on devotional life, prayers, and meditation as a way to achieve inner balance, considering that the current era is one of uncertainty and insecurity. Intensely disseminated by secular media, these intimist spiritualities are not necessarily anti-scientific, but they do not have the critical scope that the time and circumstances of the pandemic require. Marked by

---

21. Gabatz and Angelin, "Ponderações Críticas," 466.

22. See generally Stern, *Interpretações Religiosas*, for a detailed description of the reasons presented by different religious groups for the "divine punishment" that the pandemic represents. They include such things as the film *The First Temptation of Christ*, by the well-known Brazilian comedy troupe Porta dos Fundos, as well as society's acceptance and affirmation of the LGBTQ community.

23. Passos, *Pandemia do Coronavírus*, 18.

the search for overcoming (or, in some cases, escaping) their own limits and anxieties, they do not always highlight the most critical religious tenets for coping with crisis situations. In this sense, it is necessary to be aware of the limits of strongly intimist spiritualities.

There is a third set of spiritual expressions whose interpretations of faith are more consistent and are also present in different Christian groups as well as in different religions. Connected with the sociopolitical aspects evidenced in the social crisis that the pandemic revealed, these spiritualities are anchored in the principles of responsibility, solidarity, and communion with the destinies of human life and the world. This view has a broad theological foundation. João Décio Passos, for example, draws attention to the fact that "the question and the religious response [to the pandemic] will have to be coherent and ethical, consistent with the principles of reality offered by science and ethics for placing life as a value prior to any other. Anything that escapes this parameter will contribute to the reinforcement of naivete and fanaticism."[24] In a similar way, the Brazilian theologian Maria Clara Bingemer stresses that talking about God in the context of the pandemic requires—in a more intense and responsible way—a dialogue with science, recognizing its full autonomy in its own area of competence. "This requires not mixing epistemologies or treating what concerns the biological field with falsely spiritual instruments, which kill rather than cure and feed genocidal policies capable of pushing people to contagion and, probably, to death."[25]

Magali Cunha, a Brazilian journalist and an outstanding leader within the ecumenical movement, refutes supernaturalistic religious interpretations when analyzing the causes of the pandemic and highlights the importance of a faith articulated with social and human conscience. She criticizes the market society, based on the capitalist need for endless profit growth, emphasizing that this needs to be, instead, a time of opportunity, redemption, and hope, to "think about an ecological and fair world organized around care, not centered on humans, but that seeks the harmony of all beings that inhabit the same Earth, our common home."[26]

Ascribing to this view makes several social service and health care initiatives possible. Among Catholic groups, for example, is the very beautiful work and witness of the Franciscan team led by Fr. Diego Atalino de Melo. In both Rio de Janeiro and São Paulo, they attend to the health care needs of people living on the streets. Their Franciscan vision understands that health includes housing, food, work, and other basic necessities of life,

---

24. Passos, *Pandemia do Coronavírus*, 18.
25. Bingemer, "Deus em Meio a Pandemia," 205.
26. Cunha, "Nem 'Obra de Satanás,'" para. 5.

for which the homeless struggle but are denied. There is a wide range of such groups across the country, including Catholics and Protestants and secular groups, many of them led by women; they concretely represent the expression, "Rise up and walk."

Spirituality, the Pandemic, and Otherness

When reflecting theologically on the effects of the pandemic, Fernando Altemeyer Junior underscores another aspect when affirming the urgency of a provisional spirituality: "It is in the ephemeral love of ephemeral things and in the love for people marked by time that we find the portal to eternal life in God. The only hope of integrating us into the finite, while attaching ourselves to the eternal, is to love the passing things around us."[27] Junior recalls the biblical reference, "Look at life, and live it like the lilies of the field. The true return to God resides in patience in uncertain times. In earthly love, in fleeting times. Living with God, without imprisoning or manipulating God. Using things without being their owner or lord. Believing in the love of a creator knowing that He became a crucified God, as Jürgen Moltmann says in his exemplary work."[28]

These reflections emphasize a vision of spirituality that is essential for the future of humanity: a spirituality that values life and is sensitive to caring for nature and the poor, concerned for the whole, open to the mysteries of the universe, and attentive to the main social and political challenges that present themselves to the world today. Care is a collective and historical construction that belongs to all people, groups, and institutions. A new ethics of care is needed to transform both human being and doing. Care needs to be taught and learned in different life cycles. "This ethical principle, which has to do with human and planetary existence, needs to be reinvented in our pandemic daily life and even be considered in our economic models. Life is more than the market, based only on capital. It is necessary to break with the circle of capitalist, hierarchical, misogynistic, racist, militarized, and femicidal patriarchy."[29]

What has been illustrated so far reveals an openness to a sensitivity to others, as well as cooperation and respect for human life and nature. Thus, it is possible to perceive the natural, material, and human world as living sources of energy and move toward the call for communion between them. The contribution of different faiths to eco-spirituality is fundamental to the

27. Altemeyer Junior, "Silêncio de Deus," 226.
28. Altemeyer Junior, "Silêncio de Deus," 226.
29. Ulrich et al., "Mulheres em Tempos de Pandemia," 565.

dimensions of personal, community, and ecological integration, as well as vital for the survival of the biosphere.[30]

An authentic and profound spirituality cannot be dissociated from the other. This is the human possibility of relating to realities, groups, and people that are different from ourselves, and this is a fundamental element of the Christian faith. Though rooted in the Bible, the formal concept of "other" comes from the fields of anthropology and philosophy. *Alter*, a word of Greek origin, refers to that which is different. Therefore, the capacity for otherness is to recognize an "other" that is beyond the subjectivity of each person, group, or institution. It is a posture, method, or system of scientific tools that allows us to resize, in perspective, reality. Thus, the plausibility of a given system (religious or cultural) would be evident in the coexistence with the "other" and not in an apologetic confrontation, trying to disqualify it. This allows for a creative possibility of approximation and living together, from which will arise a better understanding of the "other," which will no longer be seen as exotic, inferior, or as an enemy or any other form of disqualification. In order to reflect on otherness as a fundamental opening to the other, we must effectively consider the power differentials that mark social and political relations.[31]

Otherness lives in strong harmony with anthropological studies including the challenges of the practice of communion, the concrete consequences of divine love for human life and history and the destinies of nature and of all creation. The notion of otherness is fundamental to spirituality. The communal and relational experience of different religious traditions, once perceived and assumed as a value, enables egalitarian relationships between different human groups, creating a favorable environment (although not free from tensions) for ecumenical dialogue in all its dimensions.

Such perspectives are directly linked to deep existential questions. Ivone Gebara emphasized that thinking about religion in times of COVID-19

> is to feel and know that the same virus inhabits us in many ways, the same mortality lurks in us, the same hunger and the same thirst inhabit our bodies, the same shortness of breath plagues us, and we need to open our hands so that our hearts may also open and let COVID disappear. Perhaps this is how COVID fulfilled its mission, the mission of reminding us of what we had forgotten, that of "being siblings" in the same life and death. This condition cannot be avoided; this is the secret hidden in us, engraved in all the cells of our being, a perennial and at the

---

30. Cf. Pui-Lan, *Globalização, Gênero e Construção da Paz*.
31. Cf. Ribeiro, "Alteridade, Espiritualidade e Pandemia," 231–48.

same time temporary tattoo. It is this condition that identifies us, that makes us who we really are—a fragile little reed that today breathes and moves, but that tomorrow will be manure in the renewal of the earth/life. That is why the ancients liked to meditate on death, both their own and that of others, to indicate the need to remember that the world does not belong to me and that this life, no matter how brief or long, will eventually take its last breath, returning to the Earth so that life may be renewed and move forward.[32]

In addition to the real data and threat of death, social isolation during the pandemic also kept a large number of people in their homes. This situation in and of itself has had several consequences. For families with small homes, living together became tense, with a greater rate of domestic violence and conflicts. The large number of people working remotely from home reinforced the precariousness of working relationships, increased the volume of work-related tasks, and subverted the notion of home as a space of comfort and rest.[33]

As already mentioned, the pandemic showed the inhuman side of social inequalities, mainly due to unfavorable conditions for women; it has increased the burden of care on their shoulders. "Measures to contain the disease through physical isolation, suspension of classes, and mandatory stay-at-home orders weighed heavily on women. . . . In addition, violence against women also grew during the pandemic."[34] This analysis clearly emphasizes that "men need to take care of themselves and others, overcoming inequalities in gender, race, and social class. It is necessary to fight for public policies that also care for women with children, the elderly, people with disabilities, health, education, security, and promote a new way of relating to nature. Caring, therefore, is not necessarily a natural task for women."[35]

---

32. Gebara, "Religião e a Pandemia COVID-19," para. 25.

33. Cf. Pochmann, "Trabalho," 49–61.

34. Ulrich et al.,"Mulheres em Tempos de Pandemia," 556. And the authors add: "Women, even when working outside the home, do much of the housework. The work of caring for children, elderly family members, and the disabled still largely remains the responsibility of women. Many of them have to do their professional work at home (home office) and have little help from their husbands, partners, and other family members. Not all women can stay at home. In many professional categories, it is the women who are on the front lines. There are, for example, teachers, social workers, cleaning women, day laborers. In the health system, at the forefront of care provided to people infected by the virus are women, such as nurses or nursing technicians and social workers" (556).

35. Ulrich et al., "Mulheres em Tempos de Pandemia," 565.

On the other hand, there has simultaneously also been a very significant social movement with initiatives and campaigns of solidarity involving broad social sectors, health professionals, and groups that defend human rights and citizenship. Among the various examples are community campaigns that provide poor families with necessary social assistance along with the firm defense of rights and citizenship. Due to social isolation, many people felt more acutely aware of the value of human relationships, friendship, a more humanizing vision of life, and the need to pay more attention to their children.[36]

When reflecting on otherness, the encounter between human beings, nature, and history has an important role. This encounter makes it possible to question forms of individualism, contempt for cosmology and holistic views, refusal to confront issues about the meaning of life, and utilitarian forms of technical and scientific knowledge. In contrast to these reductionisms, there is an eco-spirituality that fosters relationships of interdependence and vital cooperation, as well as respect for human integrity, personal formation, and the totality of life-generating processes, and the valorization of the body as a source of pleasure.

The spirituality that arises from and is committed to the creation and recreation of life reaches beyond the personal dimension to a cosmic perspective. This spirituality is also committed to history. It does not become a form of escapism or individualism but instead, relates to life in all its human, community, and social scopes. It marks a broad vision of salvation, which helps us keep in mind the Judeo-Christian biblical tradition of the beautiful figure of the shepherd who, in the dangers of life, saves the injured sheep. Talking about salvation mobilizes all human beings, regardless of creeds, cultures, political, or philosophical beliefs. It is something decisive, fundamental in human existence, that brings questions and expectations to all people.[37] Such perspectives have gained great prominence in the context of a pandemic that has plagued the world.

Final Words

In conclusion, I would like to emphasize once again how much the coronavirus pandemic has evidenced the crisis and the injustices of the economic

---

36. There are several theological and pastoral reflections on these aspects. For example, see Teixeira, "Dimensão Espiritual" for an analysis of the pandemic's global impacts, highlighting the crisis as an opportunity to face human precariousness and fragility.

37. Cf. Ribeiro, "Alteridade, Espiritualidade e Pandemia," 231–48.

system in which society is structured, as well as the erosion of life-generating processes and nature caused by destructive human actions based on profit. As I have shown here, the main victims of this health crisis are the poor who are living in vulnerable conditions. The dramatic situation they faced, resulting from the established necropolitics in line with the economic system, should serve as a guide to navigate the challenges of building a civilization based on rights and justice.

It is also important to highlight the otherness that is necessary for forms of spirituality that intend to develop in an authentic and profound way, and that both establish and reinforce dialogical and plural paradigms. The pandemic revealed that human beings are in a state of rupture, which threatens the integrity of our communion with society, with bodies, with nature, and with all that is sacred. In this sense, spirituality marked by otherness shows itself as a channel and expression of human life in the search for overcoming limits while experiencing joy, well-being, and happiness.

Otherness presents itself as a path to a just relationship not only between people, but also between different realities and groups, religious or not, as well as the corporeal, historical, and cosmic dimensions that permeate humanity. The relationship between spirituality and otherness is evident as a contribution, albeit a modest one, to attempts to respond to the current world crisis. It is also evident in the post-pandemic world's reconstruction of society, which definitely must seek new ways of valuing human life and its dignity.

In this context, religious experiences—including those of Catholic groups—underscore the simultaneous presence of obscurantist and denialist forms, on the one hand, and others that, in contrast, are characterized by dialogue with the sciences, a mature social responsibility, and human sensitivity. Growing out of this last set of religious experiences is a social movement of groups (organizations?) who are attuned to expressions of human fragility and open to the tasks of confronting them. Such experiences have been marked by spontaneous, creative, and plural expressions of spirituality that, in their own way, favor perspectives of hope. There are many voices saying, "Rise up and walk."

Bibliography

Altemeyer Junior, Fernando. "O Silêncio de Deus No Grito das Vítimas." In *A Pandemia do Coronavírus: Onde Estivemos? Para Onde Vamos?*, edited by João Décio Passos, 213–29. São Paulo: Paulinas, 2020.
Bandeira, Olívia, and Brenda Carranza. "Reactions to the Pandemic in Latin America and Brazil: Are Religions Essential Services?" *International Journal of Latin*

American Religions 4 (2020) 170–93. https://link.springer.com/article/10.1007/s41603-020-00116-0.

Barreto, Raimundo Cesar, Jr. "The COVID-19 Pandemic and the Ongoing Genocide of Black and Indigenous Peoples in Brazil." *International Journal of Latin American Religions* 4 (2020) 417–39. https://link.springer.com/article/10.1007/s41603-020-00126-y.

Barsalini, Glauco, et al., eds. "Quem e o Que Se Perde No Contexto da Pandemia da COVID-19." *Estudos Teológicos* 60.2 (2020) 363–69. http://www.periodicos.est.edu.br/index.php/estudos_teologicos/issue/view/330.

Bingemer, Maria Clara Lucchetti. "Deus em Meio a Pandemia." In *A Pandemia do Coronavírus: Onde Estivemos? Para Onde Vamos?*, edited by João Décio Passos, 197–221. São Paulo: Paulinas, 2020.

Boff, Leonardo. "A Terra Se Defende." *Instituto Humanitas Unisinos*, March 25, 2020. http://www.ihu.unisinos.br/78-aoticias/597421-a-terra-se-defende-artigo-de-leonardo-boff.

———. "Voltar à 'Normalidade' é Auto-Condenar-Se." *Brasil de Fato*, May 4, 2020. https://www.brasildefatorj.com.br/2020/05/04/artigo-voltar-a-normalidade-e-auto-condenar-se-por-leonardo-boff.

Cunha, Carlos Alberto Motta. "Esperança em Tempo de Pandemia: Apontamentos da Escatologia Contemporânea No Contexto da COVID-19." *Estudos Teológicos* 60.2 (2020) 483–98. https://revistas.est.edu.br/periodicos_novo/index.php/ET/article/view/52/42.

Cunha, Magali do Nascimento. "Nem 'Obra de Satanás' nem 'Castigo de Deus': A Pandemia é Oportunidade." *CartaCapital*, March 18, 2020. https://www.cartacapital.com.br/blogs/nem-obra-de-satanas-nem-castigo-de-deus-a-pandemia-e-oportunidade.

Dowbor, Ladislau. "Além da Pandemia: Uma Convergência de Crises." In *A Pandemia do Coronavírus: Onde Estivemos? Para Onde Vamos?*, edited by João Décio Passos, 25–47. São Paulo: Paulinas, 2020.

Gabatz, Celso, and Rosângela Angelin. "Ponderações Críticas acerca da COVID-19: Contribuições para Ampliar o Entendimento No Contexto Brasileiro." *Estudos Teológicos* 60.2 (2020) 466–82. https://revistas.est.edu.br/periodicos_novo/index.php/ET/article/view/51/41.

Gebara, Ivone. "Religião e a Pandemia COVID-19." *Instituto Humanitas Unisinos*, June 23, 2020. http://www.ihu.unisinos.br/78-noticias/600224-religiao-e-a-pandemia-COVID-19-artigo-de-ivone-gebara.

Kibuuka, Brian Gordon Lutalo. "Complicity and Synergy Between Bolsonaro and Brazilian Evangelicals in COVID-19 Times: Adherence to Scientific Negationism for Political-Religious Reasons." *International Journal of Latin American Religions* 4 (2020) 170–93. https://link.springer.com/article/10.1007/s41603-020-00124-0.

Lellis, Nelson, and Roberto Dutra. "Programmatic Crisis and Moralization of the Politics: A Proposal to Define the Bolsonarism from the Experience with the COVID-19 Pandemic." *International Journal of Latin American Religions* 4 (2020) 335–59. https://link.springer.com/article/10.1007/s41603-020-00113-3.

Passos, João Décio, ed. *A Pandemia do Coronavírus: Onde Estivemos? Para Onde Vamos?* São Paulo: Paulinas, 2020.

Paula, Blanches de, and Lindolfo Alexandre de Souza. "O Tabu da Morte na Modernidade: A COVID-19 Como um Reforço ao Interdito." *Caminhos de Diálogo* 8.13 (2020) 466–82. http://dx.doi.org/10.7213/cd.a8n13p165-176.

Pieper, Frederico, et al. "Necropolítica e sua Lógica Sacrificial em Tempos de Pandemia." *Estudos Teológicos* 60.2 (2020) 531–53. http://revistas.est.edu.br/index.php/ET/article/view/55.

Pochmann, Marcio. "O Trabalho Sob o Impacto da COVID-19." In *A Pandemia do Coronavírus: Onde Estivemos? Para Onde Vamos?*, edited by João Décio Passos, 49–61. São Paulo: Paulinas, 2020.

Pui-Lan, Kwok. *Globalização, Gênero e Construção da Paz: O Futuro do Diálogo Interfé.* São Paulo: Paulinas, 2015.

Renders, Helmut, and Elias Wolff. "A Fé e o Sagrado no Contexto de Pandemia da COVID-19." *Caminhos de Diálogo* 8.13 (2020). https://periodicos.pucpr.br/index.php/caminhosdedialogo/issue/view/2040.

Ribeiro, Claudio de Oliveira. "Alteridade, Espiritualidade e Pandemia." *Caminhos de Diálogo* 8.13 (2020) 231–48. https://periodicos.pucpr.br/index.php/caminhosdedialogo/article/view/27475.

Santos, Boaventura de Souza. *A Cruel Pedagogia do Vírus.* São Paulo: Boitempo, 2020.

Souza, Luis Augusto de Paula. "Cura ou Qual Mundo Queremos (Re)construir." In *A Pandemia do Coronavírus: Onde Estivemos? Para Onde Vamos?*, edited by João Décio Passos, 171–83. São Paulo: Paulinas, 2020.

Stern, Fábio L. "As Interpretações Religiosas para o Novo Vírus." In *A Pandemia do Coronavírus: Onde Estivemos? Para Onde Vamos?*, edited by João Décio Passos, 151–67. São Paulo: Paulinas, 2020.

Teixeira, Faustino. "A Dimensão Espiritual da Crise do Coronavírus." *Instituto Humanitas Unisinos*, March 20, 2020. http://www.ihu.unisinos.br/78-noticias/597292-a-dimensao-espiritual-da-crise-do-coronavirus.

Ulrich, Claudete Beise, et al. "Mulheres em Tempos de Pandemia: A Cotidianidade, a Economia do Cuidado e o Grito Uterino!" *Estudos Teológicos* 60.2 (2020) 554–72. http://periodicos.est.edu.br/index.php/estudos_teologicos/article/view/4101.

Usarski, Franklin, and Fábio Py, eds. "Religion and the Pandemic—Latin American Responses." *International Journal of Latin-American Religions* 4.2 (2020) 165–69. https://link.springer.com/article/10.1007/s41603-020-00127-x.

Xavier, Donizete José, and Claudio Antonio Delfino. "Pensar, Sentir e Agir: Interpelações e Perplexidades no Contexto da Pandemia do Novo Coronavírus." *Caminhos de Diálogo* 8.13 (2020) 177–92. http://dx.doi.org/10.7213/cd.a8n13p177-192.

Index

Abraham, Kochurani, 8
absinthe, 153
abundant life, 45, 144
abuse, 8, 296–308, 314
    sexual, 299–303, 305–7 (*see also* violence, sexual)
academia, 92, 118, 151, 195, 219, 234, 254–55, 265
    literature, 190, 220, 265–66
accompaniment, 6, 8, 36–37, 41, 45, 146, 189–90, 194–95, 199, 201, 203–4
    accompagnateur, 195
accountability, 51, 172, 196, 247, 306–7, 313
affordability, 21, 44–45, 63, 82, 159, 169–70, 173–74
Africa
    administration models, 247
    African Christian Health Associations Platform (ACHAP), 76
    African Initiated Churches, 138
    Africanization, 61
    architecture, 279
    Catholic Church, 74–75, 77, 85, 139, 242, 245–46
        African synod (2009), 271
        women religious, 55, 57–58, 61, 246, 246n30
            African Sisters Education Collaborative (ASEC), 246, 246n2
            All Africa Conference Sister to Sister (AACSS), 246, 246n30

cities, 42
continent, 2n3, 41, 67–69, 70, 72–76, 82, 85, 128, 241, 246
countries, 5, 70–71, 75, 77–83, 246
    North African, 70
cultures, 4, 57
East, 79–80, 229, 246
    East African Community, 240–41
foreign missionaries, 55, 57
gender issues, 36
health care, 5, 57–58, 67–68, 70, 72–74, 77, 129–31, 130n5
    biomedical knowledge, 135
illness, 42, 44, 69, 128, 133
MDGs, 71
oppression, 139
people, 129–30, 139, 144, 229
prosperity gospel, 144
proverb, 30
rural, 132, 279
southern, 141
sub-Saharan (SSA), 3–4, 50, 55, 57–58, 61, 68, 70, 72, 74–75, 78
traditional medicine, 61, 129, 135, 136, 139–40, 145–46
    faith healers, 140
traditional religion, 141
Union, 230
villages, 42
West, 79, 96
Africa Christian Health Associations Platform (ACHAP), 76
Agamben, Giorgio, 313
Agape Farm, 203

agency, 22–24, 26, 40, 43–44, 57, 121, 131, 139, 179, 213, 222
  Christian, 145
  individual, 30, 207
alcohol, 281–82, 296
Alexian Brothers, 50
Algeria, 70
Alma Ata Declaration, 42
American Maryknoll Sisters, 57, 62, 93
Americas, 72, 148–49
  Central, 6, 154, 193, 196, 241
  Latin, 2n3, 5, 11n1, 42, 110, 193, 196–97, 202, 204, 214, 317 (see also CELAM)
    Latino, 12, 17
      Hispanics, 51
  native peoples of, 149–50
  New World, 148
    Columbus, Christopher, 148
  North, 2n3, 68, 193, 202–3
  South, 241
ancestors, 121, 136, 138, 279, 289, 292, 292n11
animals, 36, 148, 153, 238–39, 244, 252
  cows, 231
  dogs, 277, 290
  husbandry, 82, 231, 238, 253
  sheep, 18, 89, 323
anointing, 17, 19–20, 25, 31, 318
anthropology, 102, 121, 193, 223, 256, 321
Apollonius of Tyana, 172
Arabic (language), 229, 231
Arabs, 165, 229, 231, 255, 297
architecture, 157, 289
Arendt, Hannah, 43
ARHAP, 78
Ascension Health, 13
ashram, 176n35
Asia, 2n3, 74, 103, 171, 242
assassination, 215, 279–80, 279n3, 293
Australia, 2n3, 119
  New South Wales, 119
  Oosterhuis, Paul, 119
Austria, 55, 238
  Vienna, 109
authoritarianism, 247, 315
autonomy, 44, 149, 221, 229, 258, 319

axioms, 120, 123

babies, 57–58, 135, 154, 278, 283, 288, 290, 292
Bacon, Francis, 110
Badiano, Juan, 153
baptism, 19, 57–58, 291
beauty, 24, 157, 287, 290–91, 305, 319, 323
Belgium, 285
Benedict XVI, 104
benediction, 112
Benin, 96
Béré, Paul, 271
Bernardin, Joseph Cardinal, 97n18
Bible, 2, 4, 9, 29, 41, 68, 284, 307, 320–21, 323
  Beatitudes, 14, 18
  Capernaum, 17, 34
  centurion's servant, 34
  Esau and Jacob, 269
  foundations, 12–13, 16
  Galilee, 17–18, 31
  Good Shepherd, 14, 89, 323
    ministry of Jesus to the vulnerable, 4, 11–26
  historical Jesus, 13–14, 24, 32
  Israel, ancient, 32, 89
  Jairus, 29, 34–35, 37–40
    daughter of, 29, 34, 37, 39–40
  Jerusalem, 31, 35, 289
    Beautiful Gate, 32–33
  Jordan River, 19
  Joseph (Genesis), 269
  Joseph, Saint, 17
  Judea, 31
  Last Supper, 39
  Lazarus, 13
  lilies of the field, 320
  Messiah, 19, 31
  Moses, 72, 76
  narratives of healing, 17, 26, 29–46
    Jairus's daughter, 29, 34–35, 37–38, 40
    paralyzed man, 29, 31–34, 37–38, 40, 173
    woman with the flow of blood, 29, 33–34, 37–38, 40, 173

INDEX   329

Nazareth, 17–18, 26, 33
New Testament, 17, 20, 31, 116,
    173–74
  Acts, 32, 68
  1 Corinthians, 270, 272
  2 Corinthians, 270
  Gospels, 2–3, 13, 15, 17–20,
      24, 29, 35, 89–90, 103–4,
      172–73, 309
    John, 32, 39, 68, 173
    liberation, 20
    Luke, 4, 14, 17–20, 17n15,
        18n16, 20, 31–33, 35, 173
    Luke-Acts, 29–30
    Mark, 18, 40, 68, 173
    Matthew, 18, 32, 34, 68, 173
    resources, 307
    "Rise up and walk," 8, 28–29,
        33, 41, 68, 295, 316, 320,
        324
    synoptic, 18, 173
    witnessing, 45
  Philippians, 270
Nicodemus, 15
Old Testament, 2
  Isaiah (prophet), 17–19, 18n16,
      26
  Leviticus, 40
parables, 13, 29, 90
Passion of Jesus, 18–19, 268, 270, 272
Paul, Saint (apostle), 40, 191, 270, 272
  Damascus, road to, 191
Peter, Saint (apostle), 32–33, 173, 269
  mother-in-law, 173
Pharisee, 31, 38
Resurrection of Jesus, 35, 39, 268, 272
sabbath, 17
Samaritan, 14–15, 56, 222
  good, 13, 29, 90
scholars, 18n16
Scribe, 38
Scriptures (*see* scripture, Christian)
Septuagint, 18
study, 13, 41, 307
synagogues, 17–19, 26, 31, 37–38,
    40, 89
theology, 28
year of the Lord, 16–20, 25

bilingualism, 156, 214
Bingemer, Maria Clara, 319
bioethics, 12, 40, 101–2, 156
biology, 121n35, 136, 140–42, 144, 218,
    286, 313, 319
biomedcine, 100–102, 128–30, 130n5,
    133–35, 137–40, 143–45, 158–
    59, 222–24
  data science, 118
  establishment, 5
  ethics, 45, 100
  knowledge, 56, 135
  model, 5–7, 32, 36, 128–30, 130n5,
      133, 140, 151, 217–20, 223
  religion and, 50
biotechnology, 101
blame, 36, 131, 136, 142–43, 145, 259,
    298–99, 305
  culpability, 142
  culprits, 142, 264
  guilt, 136, 142–43, 145, 256, 268,
      271, 297, 299, 308
  shame, 148, 263, 268, 271, 297, 299
Boff, Leonardo, 24, 314
bone marrow, 94, 101
botany, 148, 153, 153n25, 155, 166
Boyle, Robert, 120
Brazil, 4, 8, 23, 42, 312–14, 316–19,
    317n19
  Bolsonaro, Jair, 317n19
  First Temptation of Christ, The, 318n22
  machismo, 312
  Porta dos Fundos, 318n22
  Rio de Janeiro, 319
  São Paulo, 316, 319
    Lancelotti, Julio, 316
bread, 22, 195
Brendel, David, 254, 266–67
Britain. *See* Great Britain
Brocher Declaration, 194, 194n9, 196,
    203
  Foundation Brocher, 194n9
Buber, Martin, 269
budgets, 72, 104, 213, 216, 237, 256,
    265
Buenos Aires, 190, 196
bureaucracy, 111, 156, 221, 223, 256
Burkina Faso, 96

Burns, James MacGregor, 44
Burundi, 7, 276, 277n1, 278, 279n3, 281, 283–85, 287–90, 292–93
  Barankitse, Maggy, 7–8, 276–94, 277n1, 284n4
    Chloé (daughter), 277, 279–80, 282–83, 288
    Fabrice (son), 283
    Ndimurwanko, Cyprian (husband), 280–82, 286
  Bigirimana, Juliette, 280–82
  Bujumbura, 291
  Butezi, 284
  Catholic bishop, 277–80, 282–83
  Catholic cathedral, 281–83
  Catholic vicar general, 280–81
  City of Angels, 285, 287, 290–91
    Fratrie, 285–86
    Le Cinéma des Anges, 285, 287
    Le Garage des Anges, 287
  civil war, 279, 285–88, 290–91
  Gisuru, 288
  government, 279, 285, 287, 289, 291–92
    military, 281, 287, 289–91
    president, 279, 293
  Hutu, 279–84, 287
  Juliette, 277–78, 283
    Lydia and Lysette (daughters), 277–78, 281–83
  Justine, 285–86, 291
  Krueger, Bob, 279n3
  Maison Shalom, 7, 278, 284, 286–93
    Maison Shalom International, 293
  Musongati, 284
    Carmelite monastery, 284
  Ndadaye, Melchior (president), 279–80
  Novak, Martin, 283, 285
  Nyamutobo Hill, 279–80, 289
  Rema Hospital, 7–8, 278–80, 289–91, 293–94
    maternity center, 279–80, 288–89, 291, 293
    incubators, 279
    morgue, 7, 279, 289–93
    swimming pool, 287, 289–91, 293
  Ruyigi, 276, 278–81, 284–88, 290–91
  Tutsi, 279–84, 287

Câmara, Dom Hélder, 23
Cambodia, 103
  Cambodian Mobile Clinic Project, 103
Cameron, John, 213
Cameroon, 81
  Federation of Protestant Churches and Missions in Cameroon (CEPCA), 81
  Foundation ad Lucem (FALC), 81
  Organisation Catholique pour la Sante au Cameroun (OCASC), 81
Canada, 112, 118, 120, 124, 149
  Canadian Broadcasting Corporation, 118
    Cross-Country Checkup, 118
  Manitoba, 118
    Kettner, Joel, 118
  Ontario, 119–20
    College of Physicians and Surgeons, 119
    Ford, Doug (premier), 120
    Ontario Civil Liberties Association, 120
    Toronto, 110
  Quebec, 125
    Montreal, 125
      Herron Nursing Home, 125
  Trudeau, Justin, 124
Canadian Broadcasting Corporation, 118
capital, 206–8, 212–13, 215, 219–20, 222, 313, 320
  cultural, 213, 215, 219
  financial, 219
  political, 214–15, 223
  social, 219, 223
  spiritual, 207, 214–15
  symbolic, 215–16, 219
capital city, 91, 176, 209, 257, 285, 287, 315
capitalism, 313, 315, 319–20
Caribbean, 14, 109, 149, 196–97

INDEX   331

bishops (*see* CELAM)
Church, 197
Caritas, 175, 238, 241
   Austria, 238
   Catholic Relief Services, 241
   Europe, 241
   India, 175
   United States, 241
Cayley, David, 5
CELAM (Episcopal Conference of Latin American and Caribbean Bishops), 14, 16, 196–98
   Aparecida Document, 16, 24, 190, 196–98, 203–4
century, 2, 74, 214
   early, 73
   eighth, 165
   sixteenth, 6, 64
   seventeenth, 50, 120
   eighteenth, 151, 164
   nineteenth, 3, 50, 73, 166
   twentieth, 51, 53–55, 114, 252, 255
   twenty-first, 153
CHA. *See* United States, Catholic Health Association
Chad, 81, 96
Chang Campos, Caroline J., 211
chapels, 7, 239, 277–78, 282–84, 289, 291–92
charism, 128, 245, 309
charity
   acts of, 16, 22, 43, 56, 63, 94, 102, 189, 195
   Christian, 73, 102
   international, 193
   organizations, 84, 91–92, 192, 203, 241
chemistry, 132
Cheong, Nicholas Cardinal, 100
Chile, 222
China, 165, 313
Christian Medical Commission, 61
Christology, 11n1, 16–18, 17n15, 20–21, 23, 25, 31, 268, 270–71
Christus Health, 13
Church of Science, 121n35
citizens, 50, 119, 130n4, 149, 169, 214, 252, 254, 291, 323

senior, 297
Clarke, David, 206, 217
class (social), 23, 52, 165, 296, 322
   caste, 175, 296, 306
clericalism, 8, 300–301, 306–7
   See also hierarchicalism
Coburn, Carol, 52
Colombia, 103
colonies, 2n3, 58–59, 73, 93, 150, 229, 234
colonization, 3, 55–56
   era, 58, 110, 130, 150, 152, 163–65, 167, 169, 214, 229–30
   mentality, 3, 4, 22, 57, 139, 189, 201, 203, 313
   neocolonial, 110
   paternalism, 3, 6, 23, 203
   postcolonial, 139, 150, 163, 167–70, 229
   precolonial, 163–65
commerce, 35, 43, 45, 95–96, 148, 159, 231
   businesses, 51, 63, 120, 144, 152, 194, 207, 219, 241, 262
   corporations, 1, 103, 166
   enterprises, 92, 262
commodities, 3, 5, 97, 100, 122
common good, 3–4, 4n4, 14n8, 16–17, 20–22, 24–26, 104, 117
communion, 8, 15, 20, 39, 197, 286, 319–21, 324
communism, 8, 23, 313, 318
community health, 86, 156, 170, 174, 177–78, 210, 212
Conference on InterAmerican Student Projects, 193
congregations, religious, 55–57, 60, 62, 175, 178, 297–98, 305–7
   Comboni sisters, 235–36
   Congregation of Servants of Mary, 175
   Congregation of the Holy Spirit, 91
   Holy Rosary Sisters, 60
      Agbasiere, Joseph Theresa, 60
   IHM (Sisters, Servants of the Immaculate Heart of Mary), 7
   Medical Missionaries of Mary, 59, 61
      Dean, Pauline, 59
      Nolan, Margaret Mary, 61

congregations, religious (continued)
  Nazareth nuns, 176
  Society of Catholic Medical
    Missionaries (Medical Mission
    Sisters), 55, 57, 61–62, 175, 177
    Dengel, Anna, 55–57, 62
      Mission for Samaritans, 56
    Kerschbaumer, Rose, 61
  South Sudan and, 227–28, 227n1,
    235–38, 240–42, 245–47, 246n30
consumption (of resources), 92n11,
  313–15
continents, 74, 312
corpses, 41, 253, 288, 292
corruption, 155, 206–7, 217–18, 237, 240
cosmos, 164, 177, 269, 323–24
  cosmology, 323
  cosmovision, 217
Côte d'Ivoire, 96
counseling, 94–95, 119, 176, 276
courage, 30, 40, 43, 55, 142, 266, 272,
  283, 297–98
COVID-19
  coronavirus, 117, 119–20, 124, 311–
    12, 314–19, 322n34, 323
    pedagogy of, 312, 315
  disinformation, 119
  Great Barrington Declaration, 119,
    119n30
    Bhattacharya Jayanta, 119,
      119n30
    Gupta, Sunetra, 119, 119n30
    Kulldorff, Martin, 119, 119n30
  lockdowns, 117–20
  masking, 119–20
  misinformation, 8, 118–19, 118n28,
    158
  mortality, 111, 119–20, 321
  pandemic, 8, 12, 83, 116, 120, 156–59,
    313, 316–17
  religion and, 317–20, 318n22
  responses to, 8, 118, 121–22, 124–25,
    246, 312, 319
  quarantine, 117–18, 315
  social distancing, 118–20, 313
  vaccination, 119, 129
creativity, 23, 98–99, 101, 258, 262–63,
  272–73, 311, 321, 324

crime, 113, 139, 237, 261, 264, 299
  clerical, 297, 302, 307–8
  genocide and, 254, 261, 267, 291
  hate, 255
crisis, 97n18, 113, 124, 129, 176, 223,
  253, 311, 315–17, 319, 323–24
  abuse, 8, 299, 301–2, 306–8
  economic, 150
  faith, 300
  HIV/AIDS, 132
  intervention, 303–5
  marriage, 135
Croatia, 109
  Adriatic Coast, 109
  Split, 109
crucifixion, 24, 318, 320
  cross, 90, 144, 145, 194, 199, 270,
    272, 278
Cruz, Martín de la, 153
culture of life, 101–3
culture of vulnerability, 307
Cunha, Magali, 319
current health expenditure (CHE), 70–71
customs, 149, 151–52, 170

Daniels, Norman, 12n3
Das, Vena, 258
De La Salle brothers, 235
Dean, Pauline, 59–60
decision-making, 21, 24, 41n11, 78,
  171–72, 309
dehumanization, 103, 139n13, 159, 268
democracy, 51, 121, 210, 212, 279, 314
Democratic Republic of the Congo
  (DRC), 232, 237, 253
  Zaire, 253
demography, 42, 68–69, 209, 230
demons, 6, 73, 90, 104, 138–42, 155, 173
Denis, Philippe, 260, 263
DePaul University, 8
  Center for World Catholicism and
    Intercultural Theology, 8
Depression, Great, 54
determinants of health, 21–22, 30–33,
  35, 42–43, 45, 62, 69, 78, 117
determinism, 23

diagnosis (medicine), 53, 96, 111–13,
       154, 166, 170, 177, 180, 219,
       299, 306
   Diagnostic and Statistical Manual, 219
   equipment, 166
   testing, 212
   undiagnosed, 120
   wrong, 111, 132
dialectic, 315
   See also Rwanda, complementary and
       dialectical approach
dialogue, 2, 21, 21n18, 25, 31, 172,
       197–98, 214, 287, 307, 324
   ecumenical, 321
   with science, 312, 319, 324
diet, 138, 162, 165, 176, 200, 203
dignity, 12, 14, 22, 33–34, 36, 95, 103,
       149, 158–59, 269, 287
   genocide and, 262
   human, 14, 25, 30, 39, 95, 99–100,
       103, 182, 269, 312, 324
dioceses, 29, 202, 234, 237, 242–43,
       260–61, 271, 280, 297–98
   See also specific diocese names
disciples, 14–15, 17, 20, 24, 32, 35, 90,
       190, 197–98, 200, 204
discrimination, 93, 150, 158, 315
disembodiment, 115, 123
displaced persons, 58, 229, 231–32,
       234, 238, 241, 245, 253, 284
Djibouti, 70
doctrine, 3, 62, 218
donations, 53, 70–72, 77, 82, 101, 193,
       202, 204, 237, 241, 245
dreams, 138, 152, 220, 284, 287, 293
dualism, 39, 144–45, 218, 262, 264
Dugan, John, 43–44

earth, 18, 20, 24, 39, 77, 116, 152, 164,
       227, 320, 322
   earthquakes, 175
   mission of Jesus to, 31, 35, 270
   planet, 148, 314, 319, 322
Easter, 270
   Exsultet, 270
ecclesiology, 8, 20, 306–7
eco-spirituality, 320, 323
ecology, 116, 177, 200, 203, 319, 321

ecosystems, 101, 115
Ecuador, 7, 103, 206–18, 220, 222–23
   decentralization, 7, 208, 210–11, 213,
       223
   Ecuadorian Social Security Institute
       (IESS), 210–12, 216, 223
   Integral Public Health and
       Complementary networks, 211
   La Hora (newspaper), 214
   Ministry of Agriculture, 210
   Ministry of Education, 210
   Ministry of Public Health (MOPH),
       208, 210–13, 223
   National Health (Care) System,
       210–11
   National Institute of Statistics and
       Census (INEC), 209
   Pichincha province, 209
   president, 209, 217
       Mapa de Pobreza, 209
   vice president, 218
       Borrero, Alfredo, 218
       Villalba, Leonidas Eduardo Proaño,
           214
ecumenism, 58, 60, 234, 240, 319, 321
efficacy, 44, 152n23, 158, 162–63,
       181–82
Egypt, 70, 228–29
electricity, 150, 237, 244
emotion, 132, 176, 179, 261, 271,
       277n1, 282, 299, 304
   care of, 95, 173, 176–77, 179–81,
       303–5
   fragility, 311
   trauma, 254, 266, 303
empathy, 45, 96, 135, 181, 183, 267,
       304–5
empowerment, 20, 23, 35, 40–41, 97,
       158, 181, 183, 242, 262, 304
   communities, of, 35, 42–43, 104, 196
   women, of, 101
end-of-life issues, 39, 41
enemies, 15, 60, 76, 214, 287, 293, 313,
       318, 321
Engel, George L., 218
English (language), 2n3, 231, 277n1, 291
entrepreneurs, 50, 53, 113

334 INDEX

environment (nature), 36–37, 92,
    92n11, 100, 159, 177, 181,
    200–201, 208, 217–19
epidemics, 5, 119, 167–68, 315
    See also medical specialties,
        epidemiology; COVID-19
episcopacy, 307
Episcopal Conference of Latin
    American and Caribbean
    Bishops. See CELAM
equilibrium, 19, 164, 179, 304
equity, 42, 118, 159, 195
    inequity, 41–43, 70, 150, 171, 218
    See also inequality
establishment (control)
    hospital, 50, 53
    medical, 5, 111, 115, 129
    political, 5
    religious, 115
eternal life, 3, 143–45, 320
ethnic, 103, 154, 156, 215, 229, 239–40,
    255n6, 257, 262, 296
    division, 7, 240, 246, 255, 260, 277,
        283, 285
ethnography, 257–58
    critical, 257–58
    ethnomedicine (see Mexico, ethno-
        medicine)
    ethnobotany, 153
    ethnocentrism, 259–60
    ethnoveterinary techniques, 170
Euclid, 120
Europe, 2–3, 50–51, 56–57, 68, 74, 117,
    165–66, 235, 237, 241, 292
    Western, 2n3, 3
euthanasia, 77, 100–101
    right-to-die movements, 39
evangelization, 18n16, 67, 95, 103,
    197–99, 317
evil, 22, 31, 35, 85, 90, 263, 268–69, 306
    eye, 155
    spirits, 58
        devil, 148, 173, 318
            Satanism, 130, 140
        exorcism, 36, 140, 173
exegesis, 17, 31
exercise (physical), 171, 176, 190–91, 305

existential, 24, 132, 145, 267, 303–4,
    316, 321
exploitation, 15, 40, 43, 56, 215, 230
expropriation, 110, 214, 221

Faggioli, Massimo, 301
failed states, 3, 253, 255
Farley, Margaret, 246n2
Farmer, Paul, 6, 23, 195, 256
farming, 59–60, 82, 153n25, 203, 209–10,
    228–29, 231, 236, 238–39, 241
    See also animals, husbandry
feasibility, 201, 209, 216
Felkin, R. W., 79
feminist, 307
Ferguson, James, 222, 224
    The Anti-Politics Machine, 222
fever, 132, 153
field, 2, 269, 289
    hospital, 38, 52, 293
    of knowledge, 52, 57, 98, 104, 118,
        182, 194n9, 197, 229, 319, 321
    power, of, 206–8, 212–24
        action, of, 218
        Bourdieu, Pierre, 7, 207, 212,
            214, 220, 222
        habitus, 207–8, 213, 216–17
        local, 219
        Martin, John Levi, 208
        power, of, 7, 213, 215
financing, 7, 69–72, 82, 86, 211, 236–37
Firman, William, 247n31
Fleck, Ludwik, 121
    *Genesis and Development of a
        Scientific Fact*, 121
floods, 175
Florence (Italy), 109, 152, 152n23
flourishing, 14, 16, 22, 101
food
    access, 150
    cost, 232, 284
    hunger, 14–15, 22, 91, 125, 316, 321
        famine, 50, 53, 60, 229
        malnourishment, 233
    lack, 59, 191, 229, 232, 281, 288
    necessity, 4, 159, 165, 170, 233, 245,
        298
    preparation, 134

provision, 51, 133, 204, 238, 280, 284, 287, 298
war and, 58, 60, 231
foreign, 3, 55, 91, 155, 200, 215–16, 233
Foucault, Michel, 43, 222, 313
The Birth of the Clinic, 222
France, 50, 91, 285
Juppé, Alain, 255n6
Mitterand, François, 255n6
Védrine, Hubert, 255n6
Francis, Pope, 1, 6, 16, 182, 194, 196, 247, 271, 293, 298, 306
Bergoglio, Jorge, 190, 196
archbishop of Buenos Aires, 190, 196
church as field hospital, 38, 293
Evangelii Gaudium and, 11n1, 16, 64, 190, 196, 198–99, 201, 204
Laudato Si' and, 11n1, 190, 196, 199–201, 203–4
Franciscans, 319
Melo, Diego Atalino de, 319
Freire, Paulo, 23
Pedagogy of the Oppressed, 23
French (language), 277n1, 291
fruit, 8, 21n18, 23, 35, 153, 228, 271
funding, 5, 69–71, 71n12, 82–85, 199, 202, 210–11, 213, 228, 236, 240–42
under-, 128
funerals, 122n40, 125, 145
burial, 276–78, 283–84, 291–92, 292n11

Gadenz, Pablo, 35
Gaus, David, 7
Gebara, Ivone, 321
gender, 8, 36, 56, 175, 213, 295–96, 299–300, 322
generations, 42, 154–55, 166, 213
Geneva Convention, 100
genocide, 279n3, 281, 312, 319
See also Rwanda, genocide
Gentiles, 172
geography, 42, 149
climate, 123, 209, 242
change, 42, 203
subtropical, 209
tropical, 209
deserts, 153
forests, 153, 155
mountains, 138, 140, 193, 209, 239
Andes, 209
Nuba, 239
oceans, 140, 153
Pacific, 154–55
Germany, 113, 277, 283
Bremen, 122n40
language, 268
Ghana, 62, 79
CHAG (Christian Health Association of Ghana), 79
global
health, 11–12, 16, 22, 24, 162, 190–92, 194, 196, 206, 216–17, 219–24
North, 2–3, 2n3, 6, 187, 206, 228, 242, 244–47
South, 2, 67–68, 70, 76, 84, 85, 187, 222, 228, 242, 246–47
Catholicism in, 3, 6, 76, 85
definition, 2n3, 68, 76
Global Brigades, Inc., 192
good manufacturing product (GMP), 100
good news (Christianity), 14, 17, 19–20, 25, 31, 89
grassroots, 6, 44, 174, 257–58, 271
graves, 253, 276–78, 284, 291, 293
mass, 253, 276–78, 291, 293
Great Britain, 55, 57–59, 79, 114, 117, 121, 165–67, 178, 228–30
London, 119, 121, 124
Imperial College, 124
Queen Mary University, 119
Oxford, John, 119
Oxford University, 119
Oxford Centre for Evidence-Based Practice, 182
UK Charity, 235
Greece
ancient, 292
language, 28, 35, 321
Greenleaf, Robert, 44–45
gross domestic product (GDP), 70, 231
Guatemala, 190–91

336 INDEX

Gutiérrez, Gustavo, 23, 195, 202
  We Drink from Our Own Wells, 202

Haiti, 241
handicaps, 93
Harper's Magazine, 111
Harrison, Robert Pogue, 292
  The Dominion of the Dead, 292
Harvard University, 119, 195
  Kennedy School of Government, 195
Hayner, Priscilla, 264
healing ministry, 28, 140, 142, 144
  Catholic, 5, 21, 85, 129, 135, 139–40,
    143, 145–46, 301
  Jesus, of, 4, 13, 16–21, 30–32, 68, 76,
    173
  Zambia, 128, 133, 139
hearth, 292, 292n11
hegemony, 114, 298
  medical, 206–7, 217–19, 224
herbal medicine, 61, 138, 152–53, 162,
    164, 170, 176
  Sahagún, Fray Bernardino de, 152
hermeneutics, 17, 269
Hernández, Francisco, 153
heroism, 131–32, 198–99, 255, 279n3
Herrera, Diego, 7
hierarchicalism, 306–7
  See also clericalism
hierarchy, 171, 302, 306–7, 320
Hilton Foundation, 246n2
  Hilton Fund for Sisters, 241
Hobbes, Thomas, 120
holistic, 4, 37, 177, 273, 323
  care, 83, 95, 98–99, 101
  healing, 35, 174, 178, 182–83
    Jesus and, 6, 30–31, 33, 172–73,
      183
  health, 32, 36, 175, 183, 316
  health care, 5–6, 36, 83, 90, 153, 165,
    173, 177, 181
  See also India, Pune, Holistic Health
    Centre
Honduras, 6, 191, 202–4
Horton, Robin, 141
hospice, 92, 94–96, 101
hospitality, 2, 73
  inhospitable, 111, 221

hospitals
  Catholic, 1n1, 5, 41, 49–55, 62–63,
    81, 128, 133, 193
    Catholic Hospital Association
      Convention, 54
  hostels, 234, 297
  human resources for health, 69–70, 72,
    77, 103, 169
  humanitarianism, 16, 43, 58, 60, 159,
    229–31, 235, 238, 241, 244–45,
    253
  Hutchins, Frank, 7
  hygiene, 36, 92, 128, 193
    dental, 193, 200

Ibo (Igbo), 58
identity, 31, 34, 55–56, 95–99, 97n13,
    102, 131, 134–35, 146, 245, 296
ideology, 5, 59, 116, 123, 312–13, 315,
    317–18
Illich, Ivan, 5, 7, 109–17, 114n15, 121–
    25, 193, 221–22, 224
  Age of Systems, 115, 122
  Becker, Hellmut, 122
  Deschooling Society, 110
  disestablishment, 111
  funeral, 122n40
    Duden, Barbara, 122n40
    Nagel, Muska, 122n40
  iatrogenesis, 7, 111–12, 114, 116,
    125, 221–22, 224
    clinical, 111, 221
    cultural, 111–12, 125, 221
    social, 111, 221, 224
  *Medical Nemesis: The Expropriation
    of Health*, 5, 110–16, 114n15,
    122–23, 125, 221–22
    Limits to Medicine, 110
  rain dance, 124
  Sachs, Wolfgang, 123
  "To Hell with Good Intentions," 193
  Tools for Conviviality, 121
illnesses and conditions, specific
  acute, 57, 129, 159, 167, 179, 183
  anemia, 137, 175
  arthritis, 158, 178, 180
  asthma, 170, 180, 181, 284
  back pain, 136, 178, 180

INDEX

blindness, 13–14, 17, 19, 25, 31–32, 90, 114, 191
bone fractures, 62, 166, 170
cancer, 2, 158, 175, 177, 181
cardiovascular, 150, 218
cholera, 167
cholesterol, high, 201, 293
chronic, 13, 38, 103, 136, 150, 159, 175–76, 178, 180–81, 183, 312
communicable and noncommunicable, 37, 41–42, 69, 162, 167, 174, 218
dermatologic, 13, 178, 180–81
diabetes, 150, 193, 200–201, 203, 213, 218–19, 293
    prediabetes, 219
disability, 19, 111, 113–14, 116, 128, 174, 180, 203, 253, 322, 322n34
dyslipidemia, 219
gastrointestinal, 94, 170, 180
    diarrhea, 131, 169–70
    irritable bowel syndrome (IBS), 179–80
Hansen's disease (*see* leprosy)
hypertension, 193
kidney, 94, 178
leprosy, 1n1, 15, 73, 76, 90n4, 93–94, 94n12, 104, 145, 167, 173
liver, 94, 178, 180
measles, 169
mental, 37, 62, 93, 95, 136, 157, 213, 218, 253, 256, 307–8
    anxiety, 50, 95, 120, 154, 179–80, 254, 287, 300, 308, 319
    clinicians, 266–67
    depression, 179, 304, 308
    despair, 30, 130, 179, 195, 281, 291
    spirituality and, 138–39, 171, 177, 181
musculoskeletal, 180
neck, 190–91
plague, 167
pneumoconiosis, 92
polycystic ovarian disorder (PCOD), 179–80
psychosomatic, 139, 175, 181
smallpox, 124, 167
thyroid, 178
tropical, 166
tuberculosis (TB), 71, 81, 131–32, 154, 156–58, 230, 232, 238, 268, 289, 312
typhoid, 169
illusion, 315
Ilo, Stan Chu, 4
immunity
    circumstances, of, 22, 113–14, 125
    disease, from, 42, 93, 156, 192
    immunization, 156, 192
imperialism, 3, 57, 307, 309
Incarnation (of Jesus), 116, 268, 270
inclusion, 25, 37, 67, 159
income, 82, 91, 209
    high-, 200, 219
    low-, 68 70, 189, 192, 207, 221
    lower-, 219
    lower-middle, 70
independence, 22–23, 25, 59, 102n30, 140, 192, 267
    national, 55
        Biafra, 59
        Latin America, 214
        Nigeria, 59
        South Sudan, 228–31, 228n5, 240
        Sudan, 228
India, 6, 8, 148, 162–81, 183, 295–99, 307
    Bangalore, 174, 176n35
        Bengaluru, 176n35
            Vidyanan Ashram, 176n35
        St. John's Medical College, 174
    Bihar, 176
        Mokoma, 176
        Patna, 176
    British rule, 165–67
        British East India Company, 165
    Capuchin friars, 176
    Caritas India, 175
    Carmelites of Mary Immaculate, 176–77
        Vadakethala, Francis Vineeth, 176, 176n35
    Catholic Church, 173–75, 178, 182–83
        Catholic Bishops' Conference of India (CBCI), 174
            CBCI Health Commission, 174–75

338 INDEX

India (continued)
   Catholic Health Association of India
      (CHAI), 6, 174–75, 177–78
      core values, 174
      Health Action, 178
   Catholic Medical Mission Board
      (CMMB), 175
   Catholic Relief Services (CRS), 175,
      241
   Central Council of Research, 181–82
   central India, 295
   constitution, 169
   Gandhi, Mahatma, 167
   government
      national, 168–69, 171, 181
         Bhore Committee, 168
         Central Council of Research,
            181
         Chopra, R. N., 168
         health care policy, 168
         National AIDS Control
            Programme (NACO),
            175
         National Rural Health
            Mission (NRHM), 171
         Revised National
            Tuberculosis Control
            Programme (RNTCP),
            175
      provincial, 167
   Hinduism, 164, 167
   Indus Valley Civilization, 165
   International Hospice and Palliative
      Care Workforce Training, 95–96
   Karnataka, 176
      Deralakatta, 176
   Kerala, 170, 175, 177
      Kottayam, 175
      Thrissur, 177
         Amala Ayurvedic Hospital,
            177
         Amala Institute of Medical
            Sciences, 177
   medical systems, 164–67, 169–71,
      175, 180–81
      allopathy, 172, 180–81
      alternative medicine, 171–72,
         175, 178, 181, 183
      Ayurveda, 164–68, 170–71,
         176–77, 180
         Atharva Veda, 164
         *Journal of Ayurveda or
            the Hindu System of
            Medicine, The*, 167
         universe elements, 164
      AYUSH, 171–72, 175
         Ayushya Centre for Healing
            and Integration, 175
         complementary and
            alternative medicine
            (CAM), 175
      chloroform, 166
      district- and *taluka*-level
         hospitals, 172, 172n23
      flower remedies, 6, 164, 178–80
         Bach, Edward, 178
         Bach flower remedies
            (BFRs), 178
         impatiens, 179–80
      homoeopathy, 164, 171, 176–77
         Father Muller Homeopathic
            Medical College
            Hospital, 176
      humors, 166
      literature, 164
      naturopathy, 164, 171, 176,
         176n33
         Sangamam, 176, 176n33
      non-Western and Western, 6,
         162–63, 165–72, 175, 177–
         78, 180–83
         Eastern, 163, 171, 178
      reflexology, 178
      rural, 6, 162–63, 166, 169–75,
         178, 183
      Siddha, 164–65, 170–71, 175
         alchemy, 165
         Taoism, 165
            patrology, 165
      traditional, 165–72, 175, 178,
         180–83
      Unani, 164–66, 168, 171
         health factors, 165
      yoga, 164, 171, 176, 176n35, 178
         hatha, 171
         Indian Christian yoga, 176

Nama Japa, 180, 180n45
north India, 170
Pune, 177, 295
    Holistic Health Centre (HHC), 177
    Streevani, 295
    Revised National Tuberculosis Control Programme (RNTCP), 175
    Sister Doctors Forum of India (SDFI), 6, 174–75
        Cancer Prevention in Women through Screening and Awareness Creation program, 175
        continuing medical education (CME), 175
        Save the Girl Child campaign, 175
south India, 178
Tamil Nādu (state), 170, 175–76, 178
    Kaveri River, 176
    Perugamani, 176
    Perumalmalai, 176
    Tiruchirappalli, 176
Tamils, 165
    Siddhars, 165
Vedic culture, 164
vipassana meditations, Indian Christian, 176
Zen, 176, 178
    Bodhi Zendo, 176
    Indian Chrstian meditation, 176
individualism, 15, 39, 323
industry, 92, 92n11, 97, 100, 122, 129, 155, 221–22, 231, 290
    pharmaceutical, 219, 221 (*see also* pharmaceuticals)
    pollution, 35
inequality, 12, 103, 122, 159, 213, 215, 222, 262, 312, 322
    health, 14–15, 21–22, 24, 211
    social, 103, 318, 322
    See also equity, inequity
infantilization, 22
infection, 36, 42, 120, 129, 166, 218, 322n34

infrastructure, 73–74, 76, 169, 209, 213, 216, 223, 230–31, 236–37, 288
injustice, 8, 12, 14–15, 20, 22, 24–25, 215, 230, 323
innovation, 53
    health, 45, 92, 94, 99, 123
inpatients, 92, 156
insects, 62, 153
insurance, health, 21, 63, 94, 102, 211, 221
    microinsurance, 211
integral, 17, 200, 217, 300, 316
    development, 17, 19–20, 24, 26
    ecology, 203
    healing ministry of Jesus, 17–21
integrity, 103, 115, 295, 299–300, 306, 323–24
interculturality, 6, 8, 109, 155–57, 245–46
International Congress on Consecrated Life, 227–28, 235, 245
International Journal of Health Policy and Management, 217
intimist spiritualities, 318–19
Ireland, 50, 53, 56, 58–61
Iron Age, 164
isolation, 8, 40, 42, 90, 94, 120, 138, 144n21, 269, 298, 303
    areas, 151, 156
    physical, 322
    self-, 158, 308
    social, 4, 311, 314, 316–17, 322–23

Jesuits, 7, 176
    Cyril, Mathew, 176
    Samy, Ama, 176
Jews, 2, 19, 109, 172–73
    Sabbatical Year, 19
John Paul II, 11n1, 14, 14n8, 89, 259, 265
Josephus, 173
Journal of Patient Safety, 111n5
journalism, 116–19, 122, 214, 252, 297, 302, 318–19
Judeo-Christian biblical tradition, 323
Junior, Fernando Altemeyer, 320

Katongole, Emmanuel, 277n1

INDEX

Keenan, James, 306–7
Kenya, 83, 103, 231, 235, 241, 246
   Kenya Conference of Catholic Bishops (KCCB), 83
   Mission for Essential Drugs and Supplies (MEDS), 83
   Protestant Christian Health Association (CHAK), 83
Kim, Pyeong Man, 5
Kim, Soojung, 5
Kim, Souhwan Stephen, Cardinal, 95, 97
kingdom of God, 14–15, 31, 73, 89, 90n4, 144, 197
Kirmayer, Laurence, 256
Kleinman, Arthur, 258
Korea. *See* South Korea
Kroesbergen, Hermen, 141
Kuhn, Thomas, 121
   The Structure of Scientific Revolutions, 121

laboratories, 93, 131, 154, 156, 238, 289
Lancelotti, Father Julio, 316
Lancet, The, 12n2
Lasker, Judith, et al., 193
Latour, Bruno, 121
law, 42, 55, 102, 113–14, 116, 150, 158, 196, 218, 264, 313
   biology, of, 141
   courts, 136, 264, 291, 298, 308
      trials, 253, 308
   informal, 217
   judiciary, 114, 136, 252, 260, 264
   labor, 151
   legality, 59–60, 85, 151, 194, 217–18, 234–35, 301–2, 308
   religious, 31
      Canon, 301–2
      Sharia, 229
   servant, 4, 43–45
lay (laity), 1, 6, 63–64, 173–74, 195–97, 214–15, 228, 239–40, 247, 309
   associates, 235
   -led, 189–90, 203–4
   volunteers, 193, 243
Leadership Conference of Women Religious (LCWR), 235, 241
leadership, servant, 4, 43–45

Lederach, John Paul, 265–66
left (politics), 318
   progressive, 176, 214
Lesotho, 78
LGBTQ, LGBTQI+, 296, 318n22
liberal (politics), 114, 125
   neoliberalism, 21–22, 97, 155, 210
liberation, 4, 8, 13, 16–21, 18n16, 21n18, 23–26, 89–90, 220, 309, 311
   mutual, 268–70
   theology, 2, 195, 214–15
libertarian, 39
liberty, 17, 19, 25, 31, 90
Libya, 70
lifestyle, 149, 162, 165, 175, 177–78, 256
literacy, 150, 209, 231
liturgy, 34, 95, 139, 272
loneliness, 130–31, 179
Louise de Marillac, Saint, 50
   Daughters of Charity, 50
Love, Stuart, 32–33
Loyola Foundation, 241

magic, 130–31, 152n23
   pseudomagic, 215
Maki, Jesse, et al., 192
malaria, 42, 44, 71, 129–32, 167, 219
Mali, 73, 131
margins (social), 122, 217
   marginalization, 5–6, 12–15, 33, 90, 92, 96, 102, 119, 149, 154, 177
      cultural, 68
      historical, 21–22
market, 24, 97, 200, 290, 319–20
   health, 4, 15, 21–22, 25, 51–52, 84, 97
marriage, 135–36, 144, 232, 243, 280–81
   adultery, 134–35
   spouses, 132, 134
      husbands, 36, 40, 134–36, 140, 179, 278, 280–82, 286, 296, 322n34
      wives, 56–58, 61, 134–37
   weddings, 287
Martins, Alexandre, 4
Mary, Blessed Virgin, 51
Maryknoll of America, 93
   Sweeny, Joseph A., 93

Mass (Catholic), 34, 95, 261, 271, 280, 285–86
Mbembe, Achille, 313
McCauley, Bernadette, 52
McGuinness, Margaret, 52
medical education, 41, 56, 93, 166–68, 174–75, 194, 223
   medical schools, 5, 56, 91, 118, 159, 167, 174, 176–77, 279
   medical students, 93, 151, 168
   nursing schools, 5, 91, 128, 167, 174
   nursing students, 54, 93, 95
medical missions, 73, 89–91, 98–99, 103–4, 175, 243
   model, 6, 189–91, 193–94, 202–3
      Short-Term Engagement in Global Health (STEGH), 189–94, 196–204
         Advocacy for Global Health Partnerships (AGHP), 192, 194, 194n9
         Global Brigades, Inc., 192
         sponsors, 192, 194
   women religious and, 55–59, 61–62, 175, 177
medical specialties, 94, 151, 156–58, 174–75, 177, 189
   anesthesiology, 119, 145
   blood tests, 130, 130n4, 156, 201, 293
   cardiology, 175
   chemotherapy, 93
   dentistry, 174
   dermatology, 94n12, 157, 178, 180
   epidemiology, 41, 42n12, 71, 118–19, 158, 210, 218
   family medicine, 157, 175, 217, 223
   general medicine, 175
   genetic engineering, 100
   immunology, 93
   midwifery, 56, 59, 61, 170, 174, 233, 239, 243
   obstetrics and gynecology, 56–57, 101, 157, 166, 175, 178
   pathology, 168, 175, 183, 306
   pediatrics, 94, 175, 279, 289–90
   radiology, 54, 156–58, 175, 178
   rehabilitation, 93
   rheumatology, 157
   surgery, 54, 56–57, 74, 93–94, 111, 119, 156, 165–66, 174–75, 178, 289
      American College of Surgeons, 54
   urology, 157
   virology, 119
medicalization, 219, 221
medicine
   complementary, 6, 20, 162–63, 175, 178, 180–182
   Eastern, 163, 171
   non-Western, 2, 5, 107, 151, 159, 162–63, 169–71, 177, 180–82
   India, in, 166–71, 177, 181–83
   Northern, 2n3
meditation, 8, 171, 176, 178, 180, 180n45, 261, 305, 318, 322
mercy, 18–19, 34, 252, 271
mestizo, 150, 209, 213
metaphor, 35, 38, 265–66, 272–73, 292, 299
Metz, Johann Baptist, 271
Mexico, 6, 109, 148–54, 156, 158–59, 193, 214
   Aztecs, 153
   Na'huatl, 160
   Nahua, 152n23, 153, 156
   Chiapas (state), 6, 154–56, 158
      Altamirano, 155–56
         Hospital San Carlos, 6, 155–59
            Castañeda-Chávez, Abraham, 6, 155–56
            Daughters of Charity, 155–56
            directly observed therapy (DOT) program, 155
            Martínez Haro, Carolina, 6, 156
            posada, 158
            services, 156, 158
            St. Vincent Social Work Foundation, 155
            translators, 157–58
      OMIECH (Organization of Indigenous Doctors of the State of Chiapas), 156

Mexico, Chiapas (continued)
   peoples (Ch'oles, Kakchikeles, Lacandón-Caribes, Mámes, Mochos, Tojolabales, Tzeltales, Tzotziles, Zoques), 154–56
   San Cristobal de las Casas, 156
   Zapatista Army of National Liberation (EZLN), 149
Cuernavaca, 109
   Center for Intercultural Documentation (CIDOC), 109–10
Constitution, 151
ethnomedicine, 148, 151–54, 164
   iloles, 153, 155
   ointments and poultices, 152
   self-Attention, 154
   treatments, 154
Mayans, 155
   Tzeltal, 159
      language, 157, 160
   Tzotzil, 153, 155
   Yucatec, 153
National Autonomous University of Mexico (UNAM), 153
National Institute of Statistics and Geography (INEGI), 149–50
Oaxaca, 214
Pacific coast, 154–55
Texcoco, 153
      Universidad Autónoma Chapingo (UACH), 153
         Departmento de Fitnotecnia, 153n25
         horticultural sciences, 153n25
Middle East, 70
   migration,109, 213
   emigration, 50
   immigration, 50–51, 53, 171
military, 52, 59–60, 113, 236–37, 252–53, 279, 281, 287, 289, 291, 320
   army, 52–53, 149, 173, 238, 291
   militia, 242
   paramilitary, 149
   soldiers, 53, 59, 166, 230, 243, 286–88, 291
   troops, 165, 289

miracles, 4, 29–35, 29n2, 37–40, 58, 137, 172–73
misogyny, 320
missionaries, 2, 34, 55–59, 61, 90–91, 103–4, 110, 156, 229, 235, 259
   discipleship, 190, 196–98, 200, 204
Moltmann, Jürgen, 320
Mongolia, 95, 103
monopolies, 110, 123, 129, 215
Montgomery, Laura, 193–94
morbidity, 213
morgues, 7, 41, 279, 289–93
Morocco, 70
Morrow, Diane Batts, 52
mortality, 96, 150, 167, 213, 231, 233, 313, 321
   See also COVID-19
mourning, 37, 110, 112, 221, 284
Müller-Fahrenholz, Geiko, 267–69
   Entblössung, 268
multicausality, 144
multiculture, 240, 246
Mumaw, Joan, 7
municipalities, 41, 156, 158, 211, 213, 215, 223, 237
   mayors, 210, 213–15
murder, 148–49, 230, 260, 262, 276, 313
Muslims, 58–59, 81, 229
   See also law, religious, Sharia
mysticism, 133, 138–39, 271
myth, 38, 120, 300

Nader, Ralph, 111, 111n5
narratives, 1, 9, 14, 17–18, 26, 29–30, 61, 129, 173, 258, 272
   See also Bible, narratives of healing
nativism, 50
natural resources, 155
   minerals, 231
   mining, 200
      heavy metals, 200
      precious metals, 229
   oil and natural gas, 155, 229, 231
      gasoline, 281
   uranium, 155
   water, 36, 123, 135, 164, 191, 215, 237, 244

clean, 44, 52, 123, 155, 177, 191, 203, 209
  holy, 215, 318
necrophilia, 313
necropolitics, 311–16, 324
necropower, 313
necroreligion, 314
Nedza, Susan, 6
negation, 312, 317
Nelson, Sioban, 52
Nepal, 103
Nigeria, 4, 41, 56, 58–61
  Achi Joint Hospital, 41
  Biafra, 58–60
  Civil War, 58–61
  Federal Military Government, 59
  Urua Akpan, 59
    St. Mary's Hospital, 59
Nightingale, Florence, 52
nightmares, 124, 254
Nile River, 237
nongovernmental, 229
  organization (NGO), 7, 84, 191–92, 194–195, 207–17, 222–23, 231–33, 240, 256, 265, 293
    pitiful, 194, 199
  provider, 1, 76
Norway, 229–30
Nouwen, Henri J. M., 202
nutrition, 156, 170, 175–76
  malnutrition, 59, 150, 157, 200

Obama, Barack, 63
Oceania, 74
Okure, Teresa, 29n2
Olancho Aid Foundation (OAF), 6, 202–4
ontology, 115, 300
oppression, 11, 14, 16–26, 63, 93, 139, 159, 215
Orach, Sam Orochi, 4–5
Organization of American States (OAS), 149
otherness, 320–21, 323–24
out-of-pocket expenditures (OOPs), 70–72, 82, 169
outpatients, 59, 79–81, 92–93, 156, 210–11, 223

paganism, 8, 148, 155
palliative care, 20, 95–96, 174–75
paradox, 96, 119, 125, 272, 316, 318
parasites, 153, 193, 200
  antiparasitic medications, 153, 193
  necropolitics and, 312–16
  worms, 131, 154
Paris Foreign Missions Society, 91
  Maistre, Father, 91
parishes, 78, 128–29, 136, 139, 189, 197, 202, 204, 238, 240–41, 261
  communities, 183, 197
  parishioners, 252
  priest, 109, 298
  schools, 238, 241, 243
Partners in Health (PIH), 6, 190, 195–96, 201, 203–4
passivity, 22–23, 132
Passos, João Décio, 315, 319
paternalism, 3, 6, 23, 193, 203
pathogens, 37, 115, 125
  bacteria, 37, 312
    antibiotics, 53, 132
  microorganisms, 312
  viruses, 3, 37, 74, 77, 117, 181, 300, 312–13, 321 (*see also* COVID-19)
    antiretroviral therapy (ART), 3, 74, 81
    Ebola, 36–37, 42
    HIV/AIDS, 3, 36–37, 49, 77, 82, 84, 177, 252, 278, 285, 287
      antiretroviral drugs, 3, 74, 81
      condom use, 3
      crisis, 132
      HIV, 130–31, 158, 219
      National AIDS Control Programme (NACO), India, 175
      pandemic, 246n30
      tuberculosis and malaria, and, 71
      U.S. President's Emergency Plan for AIDS Relief (PEPFAR), 84
    Zika, 42
patriarchy, 8, 295, 299–300, 307, 309, 320

344 INDEX

Paul VI, 17, 109
Pearce, Craig, 43
Pearlman, L. A., 254
Pennsylvania State University, 114n15
pericope, 17–20
peripheries, 173, 175, 199, 312
Persians, 165
personnel, 102, 159, 211, 213, 223, 228, 234, 242, 244, 246
Peru, 1
phagocytosis, 313
pharmaceuticals, 1, 69, 91, 128, 132, 156, 174, 219, 221
   drugs, 3, 61, 83, 93, 111, 129–30, 154, 158, 170, 190, 195
      trafficking, 149
      wonder, 53
   pharmacies, 1, 69, 91, 128, 132, 156, 174, 219, 221
      apothecaries, 152
      drugstores, 132
philanthropy, 4, 22, 103, 241
Philippines, 103, 241
philosophy, 97–98, 101, 109, 120–21, 141, 164–65, 170, 172, 217–18, 321, 323
   epistemology, 212, 219, 221, 224, 315, 319
   metaphysics, 218
   Scholasticism, 140
   Thomism, 141
physics, 218
Pilch, John, 173
placebo effect, 139, 179
   /nocebo, 139
players, 84, 207–8, 223
Polanyi, Karl, 117
Polga-Hecimovich, John, 210
police, 102, 211, 252, 296, 298
pollution, 35, 314
pope, 50, 56, 194, 196, 203
Portugal, 312
positivism, 218, 224, 257
postmodern, 139–40
power dynamics, 7, 216, 220–22, 224
praxis, 19–20, 21n18, 25, 215, 268, 271, 296

prayer, 51–52, 135–36, 138–39, 144–46, 152–55, 261, 284, 292, 297, 302, 307
   chains, 318
   meditation and, 305, 318
   recollection, 272
   vocabulary for, 141
preferential option for the poor, 3–4, 11–13, 11n1, 15–16, 19, 21, 23–25, 45, 195, 197–98
prejudice, 94, 269
preternatural, 139–42
prison, 52, 117, 215, 253, 257, 261, 277, 288, 312
private sector, 150, 169, 211, 223
privileged, 58, 213, 220, 271, 301
   health care, 21–22, 44, 82, 97, 102–3, 122, 132
   recipients of the Gospel, 14, 17, 19–20
   under-, 5, 102–3
professors, 96–97, 118–19, 193
profit, 21, 41, 63, 192, 211–12, 319, 324
   for-profit, 192, 211
   nonprofit, 80, 84, 102n30, 192, 211, 235
   not-for-profit, 63, 80, 84, 235
progress, 61, 71, 83, 158, 168, 179, 182, 214, 258, 264–65, 315
   progression, 265–66, 289
prophets, 16–19, 25–26, 38, 45, 110, 139, 280, 295, 318
proselytization, 85
prosperity gospel, 2, 144–45
Protestantism, 50–51, 53–55, 59, 81, 83, 139, 320
   Adventists, 81
   African Initiated Churches, 138
   Anglicans, 73, 75
   born-again Christians, 75
   charismatic, 36, 138
   Episcopalians, 234
   Evangelicals, 75, 318
   Jehovah's Witnesses, 81
   Lutheran church, 116
      Evangelical Lutheran Church in America (ELCA), 307
   Pentecostals, 36, 75, 129, 134, 138

"languages of health," 134
Presbyterians, 234
Zion, 129, 138
psychiatry, 62, 175, 256
psychology, 174–75, 219
   psycho-education, 257
   psychological, 30, 95, 103, 139, 179, 218, 252
      difficulties, 179, 255, 299, 302–3
      well-being, 164, 176
   psychologist, 223, 256, 268, 290
   psychosocial, 258
      biopsychosocial, 130n5, 139, 152
      sociopsychology, 261
   psychosomatic, 139, 175, 181
   psychospiritual, 176
   psychotherapy, 176, 254, 261, 266, 267
public health, 57–58, 93, 117–19, 163, 175, 208, 211, 311
   care, 169, 223
   global and, 12–13, 21, 25, 45
   leadership, 41, 45
   policy, 117–18, 123, 159, 210, 217
   professionals, 44–45, 62, 117–18, 119n30, 223
   response, 36
   system, 78, 169, 171–72, 223
public sector, 209, 211
public-private partnership, 211, 216, 223
pumpkins, 59, 154
punishment, 30, 32, 260, 298, 318, 318n22

race, 56, 61, 135, 150, 312, 322
   blacks, 312–13
   racism, 158, 260, 314–15, 320
   whites, 56, 61
radicalism, 110
reagents, 91, 93
   lepromin, 93
reciprocity, 44, 166, 241
reconciliation, 7, 15, 144, 168, 240, 284–87
   See also Rwanda, reconciliation
reconstruction, 251, 260, 262–64, 304, 324

redemption, 2, 14, 30, 39–40, 268, 270, 319
refugees, 59, 231, 239, 252–53, 284, 288–89, 293
rehabilitation (non-medical), 93, 236, 257, 262
Replenish+, 83
reproduction, 42, 101
   Natural Procreative Technology (NaPro) method, 101
      Creighton Model Fertility Care System, 101n27
      Hilgers, Thomas, 101n27
   pregnancy, 63, 101, 131, 134, 154, 179–80, 233
      abortion, 77, 85, 100, 134
         pro-life, 63
      birth, 42, 110–11, 134–35, 155, 221, 231, 233, 285
         breech, 135–36, 154
         cephalic, 154
         cesarean, 79, 135
         newborns, 288
      conception (of children), 39, 179–80
      contraception, 77, 85
      fertility, 68, 101, 179–80, 233
      maternity center, 279–80, 289, 291, 293
      menstruation, 101, 134, 173
      miscarriage, 134
      unborn child, 134–35, 252
research, 6, 49, 92–95, 97–102, 166–68, 172, 177, 181–82, 193, 243, 260
   AAHRPP (Association for the Accreditation of Human Research Protection Programs), 102, 102n30
   Pew Research Center, 75
   political, 213
   stem cells, 93–94, 100–101, 101n26
      embryonic stem cell research, 100–101, 101n26
   trials, 181–82
      N-of-1 (single-subject), 181–82
      randomized control trial (RCT), 182

346   INDEX

research, trials (continued)
    single-case experimental designs (SCEDs), 182
    workers, 61, 92, 167, 181–82
resuscitation, 38, 170, 173
revolution, 58–59, 110, 110n1, 120–21, 166–67
    innovation as, 166–67
    institutional, 110, 110n1
    insurgency, 215–17
    political, 110
    rebels, 60, 230, 238, 252, 284, 286–88, 291, 293
    scientific, 120–21
    See also war
Ribeiro, Claudio de Oliveira, 8
right (politics), 110
rights, 4n4, 15, 149, 287, 324
    constitutional, 112
    human, 42, 93, 139, 144, 149, 159, 211, 323
        basic, 55, 151, 312, 316
        violation, 93, 149, 261
    indigenous, 214
    to die, 39
    to health care, 1, 3, 22, 40, 43, 45, 55, 151, 159, 178, 211
    to self-care, 111
    worker's, 151
risk (management), 71, 92n11, 115–16, 122–25, 199–201, 219, 312, 316
Robin, Arul J., 172–73
Rockefeller University, 118
Rome
    ancient, 2, 2n3, 144, 173, 202, 292, 292n11
        Byzantine, Eastern, 2n3
        goddess, 144n21
            Salus, 144n21
        Latin (language), 144n21, 153
        Western, 2n3
    modern, 109–10, 227, 232, 235
    ONLUS, 235
rural, 6, 84, 155
    areas and regions, 96, 129, 131, 159, 232
        Africa, 132, 279
        Ecuador, 207–9, 213, 220

        Honduras, 202
        India, 6, 162–63, 166, 169–75, 178, 183
        Zambia, 5
    communities, 151, 154–55, 207, 209
Rutagambwa, Elisee, 7
Rwanda, 7, 81, 251–57, 259–61, 263–64, 269–70, 273, 283, 293
    bishops, 260–61
    Gacaca, 257, 260–61
        Christian, 7, 251, 254–55, 257, 259–63
    circular and linear movements, 264–66
    complementary and dialectical approach, 7, 252, 262–64, 267–68, 273
        complementary approach, 7
        dialectical approach, 266
    genocide, 7, 251–57, 259–65, 267, 272–73, 283
        post-genocide, 7, 251–52, 254–57, 259, 262–64, 272
    Gusana Imitima, 260
    Healing Life Wounds (HLW), 7, 251, 255–59, 262–63
    Hutu, 7, 252–53, 255, 258–59
    Kambanda, Antoine, Cardinal, 259, 261
    Kigali, 257
    Life Wounds Healing Association (LIWOHA), 251, 257, 261
        Gasibirege, Simon, 251, 256–57
        King, Régine, 256–59
    Mbonyintege, Smaragde, Bishop, 260
    Nepomuscene, Nayinzira, 260
    Ntihinyurwa, Thaddeus, Archbishop, 260
    Nyakibanda Major Seminary, 260–61
    perpetrators, 253–55, 257–62, 264, 267–69, 272
    reconciliation, 251–73
    refugees, 252–53
    Rwandan Patriotic Front (RFP), 252–53, 255
    small Christian communities, 261
    Southern Province, 257
    torture, 252

INDEX   347

trauma, 253–57, 259, 262, 264, 266–67, 269, 271
   healing, 7, 251–56, 260, 262–65, 267–68, 271, 273
   Tutsi, 7, 252–53, 255–56, 258–59
   Ubuntu, 269
   victims, 252–54, 257–58, 264, 267–69
   World Vision Rwanda, 256

sacrament, 7, 95, 145, 268, 271–72, 318
sacred, 64, 113, 164, 215, 290, 301, 306, 324
sacrifice, 125, 145, 194, 199, 255, 313–14
saints, 22–23, 51, 191, 292, 292n11
salvation, 2, 28, 31, 35, 89–90, 144, 144n21, 172–73, 215, 272, 323
   ersatz, 111
   eschatological, 14
   historical, 14
Sánchez, Francisco, 210
sanitation, 36, 44, 123, 128, 174, 288, 312
Sanks, T. Howland, 215
Santos, Boaventura de Souza, 312, 315
scandal, 101n26, 114, 302, 305–7
scapegoat, 8
Schmitt, Carl, 113–14
   Political Theology, 113
scholarship, 1, 12–13, 45, 52, 110, 255, 265, 302, 306
   biblical, 18n16
Schreiter, Robert, 272
scripture
   Christian, 2, 20, 34, 67, 72, 199, 268, 271–72
   Hindu, 164
secular, 25, 51–52, 55–56, 64, 103, 195, 203, 269, 318, 320
Seon Woo, Gyeong-sik, 99
   Joseph House, 99
servants, 34, 165, 199, 253, 270, 307
   See also leadership, servant
Sessé, Martín de, and Mociño, José Mariano, 153
Seton, Elizabeth, Saint, 51–52
Shapin, Steven, and Schaffer, Simon, 120–21

Leviathan and the Air-Pump: Hobbes, Boyle, and the Experimental Life, 120–21
Sheldrake, Rupert, 121n35
Shiffman, Jeremy, 219, 221
sin, 15, 18n16, 30–32, 38, 90, 113, 148, 201, 302, 307–8, 318
Sister doctors, 6, 56, 58–59, 61, 174–75
Sister nurses (nuns), 49–53, 57, 60–62, 178
Sisters of Charity, 51–52
   Clark, Mother Xavier, 52
Sisters of St. Joseph, 53
   Keating, Mother de Chantal, 53
slavery, 15, 148–49, 173, 243
   sexual, 252
Smith, Martha, 52
snakes, 62, 170, 286
social justice, 16, 25, 35, 43, 62
social media, 119
social service, 72, 78, 151, 174, 211, 319
social teaching, Catholic, 4, 11–12, 11n1, 19, 24, 194–201
social workers, 155, 158, 290, 322n34
sociology, 7, 25, 110, 123, 223, 312
   sociocultural, 219, 267, 295–96
   sociodemography, 68
   socioeconomic, 12, 22–25, 42, 77, 111
   sociopolitical, 207, 214, 267, 319
   sociopsychology, 261
solar energy, 237, 244
solidarity, 8, 30, 37, 189, 195, 198, 299, 311, 316, 319, 323
   biblical, 14, 33
   transnational, 6
   virtue as, 14, 14n8
   See also South Sudan, SWSS
Somalia, 70, 230
sophistication, 1, 22, 223, 272
soul, 2, 57–58, 122, 141, 153, 155, 215, 303
   body and, 2–4, 32, 52, 95, 134–35, 138, 145
South Africa, 73, 85, 266
   Somerset Hospital, 73
   Truth and Reconciliation Commission (TRC), 266–67

348   INDEX

South Korea (Korea), 5, 89, 91–94, 96, 101–3
   Catholic University of Korea, 95–96, 101
      Catholic Institute of Bioethics, 101
      College of Medicine, 92
         Catholic Industrial Medical Center (CIMC), 92, 92n11
      College of Nursing
         International Hospice and Palliative Care Workforce Training, 95–96
         Research Institute for Hospice and Palliative Care, 95–96
         Yong, Jinsun (Julianna), 96
         WHO Collaborating Center for Training in Hospice and Palliative Care, 95
      Nicholas Cardinal Cheong Graduate School for Life, 101
   Gyeonggi-do, 93
   Han River, 93
   Korea Occupational Safety and Health Agency—KOSHA, 92
   Korea-France Treaty, 91
   Korean Catholic Church, 93, 103
      Catholic Leprosy Service, 93
      Korean Catholic diocese, 91
         Catholic Diocesan Youth Union, 91
   Ministry of Health and Welfare, 93
      Center for Disease Control, 93
      national health insurance system, 102
   Seoul, 2n3, 100
      Archdiocese of, 100
         Catholic Institute of Cell Therapy, 100, 101n26
         Hwang, Woo Suk, 101n26
      Committee for Life, 100
   St. Mary's Hospital, 5, 91–95, 102–3
      Catholic Medical Center (CMC), as, 5, 91–92, 94–103
      AAHRPP certification, 102 (see also research, AAHRPP)
      Catholic Clinical Medical Ethics Guidebook, 102
      core values, 5, 95, 97–99
      educational modules, 97–99
      family nursing team, 102–3
      Medical Ethics Committee, 102
      Task Force Team (TFT), 97–99
      Window of Communication, 97–99
   Hansen's Disease Research Center, 93, 94n12
      Department of Medical Treatment, 93
      medical research, 94
      pastoral care and hospice, 94–95
      social concern and charity, 94
      St. Najaro village, 93
South Sudan, 7, 227–36, 228n5, 239–42, 244–47
   Abyei, 239
   agriculture, 238
      Ministry of Agriculture, 241
   Aweil, 231
   Council of Churches, 234–35, 240
   Dinka tribe, 230
   education, 232–33, 235–38, 241, 243–44
      Ministry of Education, 232, 237–38, 241
      Solidarity Teacher Training College (STTC), 233, 236–38, 243–44
      teachers, 232–33
   fishing, 238
   IGAD nations, 230
   independence, 228–31, 228n5, 240
   Juba, 231, 239, 245
   Kiir, Salva, (president), 230
   Machar, Riek, (vice president), 230
   Malakal, 232, 234, 236–37
   military, 237–38
   Ministry of Health, 236, 239, 241
   Nimule, 231

Nuba Mountains, 239
Nuer tribe, 230
Religious Superiors Association of (RSASS), 235
    Good Shepherd Peace Center, 235
Revitalized Transitional Government of National Unity, 230
Riimenze, 228, 232, 236, 238, 245
South Sudan Bishops Conference, 235, 242
South Sudan Council of Churches, 234, 240
SSP (South Sudanese Pound), 231–33
SWSS (Solidarity with South Sudan), 7, 227–28, 228n6, 230, 232, 234–47, 245n29, 247n31
    agricultural training project, 238
    Bon Secours Mercy Health System, 241
    Friends in Solidarity, 235–37, 236n25, 241, 246
    Greene, Jim, 245n29
    Hilton Fund for Sisters, 241
    Loyola Foundation, 241
    memorandum of understanding (MOU), 236
    role of women, 243
    School Sisters of Notre Dame, 242
    services, 244
    volunteers, 243
Troika (Britain, Norway, USA), 229–30
war, 227–34, 236, 239–40, 242, 251
Wau, 231–33, 236, 239, 244–45
    Catholic Health Training Institute (CHTI), 234, 236, 239, 243–44
    Daniel Comboni Hospital, 233, 236
    Wau Teaching Hospital, 236
Yambio, 232, 236–38, 244
Souza, Luis Augusto de Paula, 313
sovereignty, 59, 114, 220, 313
Spain, 6, 148 153, 155, 209, 214
    Carlos the Fifth, King, 148
    New Spain, 152–53

Spanish (language) 152n22, 155n30, 191
spirit world, 3, 5, 21n18, 78, 155
spirits, 6, 58, 73, 139–41
spiritual healing, 78, 103, 128, 133, 135, 152, 176, 304
spirituality, 6, 8, 98, 157, 256, 271, 300, 311, 317, 320–21, 323–24
Stanford School of Medicine, 118–19
    Ioannidis, John, 118
Starr, Paul, 220, 224
The Social Transformation of American Medicine, 220
statistics, 73, 112, 115, 123–24, 140, 149, 182, 209, 218–19, 224, 230
    probability, 112
stereotyping, 36, 93, 112
steroids, 180, 190
    NSAIDs, 190, 193
Stewart, Angus, 43
stigmatization, 36, 93
subsidiarity, 92, 195
Sudan, 227
    Catholic Bishops Conference, 227–28, 235–36, 242
    memorandum of understanding (MOU), 236
    civil war, 229–30, 233
    Comprehensive Peace Agreement, 229, 235, 239–40, 244
    Khartoum, 229, 232, 237
    north, 229–30
    People's Liberation Movement (SPLM), 229
    southern, 227–30, 232, 234–35, 239–40, 242
suicide, 100–101, 130n4, 254
superiors general, religious, 227–28, 227n1, 235–36, 241
    International Union of Superiors General (UISG, for women), 227–28, 227n1, 235, 241
    IUSG-US, 241
    Religious Superiors Association of South Sudan (RSASS), 235
    Union of Superiors General (USG, for men), 227–28, 227n1, 235, 241

350   INDEX

supernatural, 53, 139–42, 152n23, 215, 319
  ghosts, 136
superstition, 5, 134, 220
surveillance, 71
  biosecurity, 123
  biosurveillance, 122, 125
sustainability, 7, 68, 84–85, 194–96, 200, 203, 228, 238, 241–44, 247, 314
  management, 99
  self-, 209, 212, 216–17
  unsustainability, 233, 256
  See also United Nations, Sustainable Development Goals
Swaziland, 73
  Bremersdorp (Manzini) Hospital, 73
Sweden, 117, 124
  Giesecke, Johan, 124
Switzerland, 194n9
  Geneva, 100, 194n9
symbols, 113–14, 135–36, 215–16, 219, 272–73, 291
symptoms, 124, 132, 134, 178–80, 183, 201, 254, 300–302
synods, 259–61, 271

taboos, 131, 134, 142
Tanzania, 57, 62, 81, 280, 288–89
tattoos, 137, 322
TB. *See* illnesses and conditions, tuberculosis
teams, 97–99, 102, 112, 124, 158, 190, 228, 234–35, 239, 316, 319
  leadership, 43, 319
  pastoral, 228, 234–35, 239
  Task Force Team (*see* South Korea, St. Mary's Hospital, Catholic Medical Center, Task Force Team)
  teamwork, 97–98
technocracy, 122
theory, 11n1, 45, 53, 102, 130, 133–35, 140, 165–66, 208, 256
Third World, 2n3
thirst, 125, 321
tobacco, 35
Togo, 96

Lomé, 96
Toole, David, 7
total government expenditure (TGE), 71, 72
trafficking, 149, 243
transgression, 152, 267
trauma, 7, 230, 239, 244, 249, 290, 293, 295–304, 306, 311
  healing of, 4, 7, 239, 287, 290, 295, 302–3
  See also Rwanda, trauma
tribes, 170, 175, 229–30, 238, 247
Trinity, 20
tsunamis, 175
Tunisia, 70
Turkey, 292
  Çatalhöyük, 292, 292n11
Two-Thirds World, 2, 4
Tylor, Edward, 141

Udelhoven, Bernhard, 5–6
Uganda, 67, 70–73, 75–81, 82–83, 85, 131, 229, 231–32, 235, 237, 241
  Catholic health services, 67, 82
  Christian health associations (medical bureaus), 78
  Church of Uganda (Anglicans), 75
  human resources for health (HRH), 69, 70, 72
  Joint Medical Store (JMS), 83
  Kahura (Western Uganda), 79
  Kampala, 80
    Lubaga Hospital, 73, 80
    Mengo Hospital, 73, 80
  Ministry of Health, 78
  "nodding disease," 83
    seleno-excel (selenium), 83
  private not-for-profits (PNFPs), 80–81, 84
  Protestant Medical Bureau (UPMB), 83
  savings and internal lending communities (SILCs), 77
  Uganda Catholic Medical Bureau (UCMB), 5, 78, 80–84
unclean, 40, 73, 173
United Kingdom. *See* Great Britain

INDEX 351

United Nations, 67, 77, 104, 149, 230, 314
  General Assembly, 149
  International Indigenous Peoples Day, 149
  Millennium Development Goals (MDGs), 71, 71n11
  Sustainable Development Goals (SDGs), 67, 71n11, 77, 104
  UNICEF, 232, 244, 285
  World Food Program, 231
  World Health Organization (WHO), 12n2, 42, 61, 68–70, 72, 162–63, 173, 183
    African Region, 72
    African Religious Health Assets Program, 74
    Commission on Social Determinants of Health, 42
    definition of health, 183
    health system "building blocks," 68–69
    Member States, 92n11
    Region of the Americas, 72
    Regional Office for Africa, 70
    WHO Collaborating Center (WHO-CC), 92, 95–96
      WHO-Collaborating Center in Occupational Health, 92n11
    WHO-WPRO [Western Pacific Region Office], 92n11
United States
  9/11, 117
  African Americans, 12
  American Hospital Association, 55
  Americans, 114, 191
  Army, 52–53
  Boston, 51
  Catholic Health Association of the (CHA), 13, 63, 63n57, 192–94, 243n28
    as Catholic Hospital Association of the, 54–55
    Schwitalla, Alphonse, 55
    Guiding Principles for Conducting International Health Activities, 193
  Keehan, Carol, 63
  Chicago, 8, 51, 116
    Archdiocese of, 97n18
  Civil War, 52–53
  continental, 51
  corporate, 220–21
  currency, 70, 232
  Hospital Survey and Construction Act (Hill-Burton Act), 55
  Maryland, 51–52, 236
    Baltimore Infirmary, 51
    Emmitsburg, 51–52
    Silver Spring, 235–36
  Medicare and Medicaid, 62
  Midwest, 51
  Navy, 52
  New York City, 2n3, 51, 109, 118
    Manhattan, 109
    Rockefeller University, 118
      Wittkowski, Kurt, 118, 118n28
  Patient Protection and Affordable Care Act, 63
  Philadelphia, 51
  President's Emergency Plan for AIDS Relief (PEPFAR), 84
  Protestant Hospital Association, 55
  Puerto Rico, 109
    Ponce, 109
      Catholic University, 109
  St. Louis, 51
  St. Paul, 51
  Texas, 51
  Union government, 53
  USAID, 74, 241
  USCCB (United States Conference of Catholic Bishops), 28, 39
  Utah, 51
  War Department, 53
  Washington, DC, 53, 111, 279
  West Virginia, 53
    Wheeling, 53
  White House, 63, 113
universal health coverage, 41, 45, 67–68, 150, 159, 211
universe, 164, 320
University of California, Los Angeles (UCLA), 157

352 INDEX

urban, 154, 163, 169, 213, 232, 313
user fees, 82, 209–10, 212, 216

vaccination, 166, 206
   See also COVID-19
Vasantha, Maria, 6
Vatican, 1, 74, 84, 298
   Congregation for the Doctrine of
      Faith, 298
      Holy Office, 110
   Congregation for Bishops, 298
   documents
      apostolic exhortations
         Evangelii Gaudium (Francis),
            11n1, 16, 64, 190, 196,
            198–99, 201, 204
      Catechism of the Catholic Church,
         4, 143
      encyclical letters
         Sollicitudo Rei Socialis (John
            Paul II), 11n1
      encyclicals
         Laudato Si' (Francis), 11n1,
            190, 196, 199–201, 203–4
         Redemptoris Missio (John
            Paul II), 89
   Jubilee Year, 16, 19, 259–61
   nuncio, 298
   Pontifical Council for Pastoral
      Assistance to Health Care
      Workers, 1n1
   Second Vatican Council, 4, 62, 214
   World Day of the Sick, 104, 182
Verter, Bradford, 215
vertical programs, 71, 71n12, 82, 85,
   213, 219
Vietnam, 94n12, 95, 238
   National Dermatology Hospital, 94n12
   Huyen, My Le, 94n12
Vincent DePaul, Saint, 50
violence, 7, 57, 130, 139n13, 215, 230,
   247, 261, 266–67, 272, 318
   cycles of, 25
   domestic, 295, 322
   ethnic, 254, 277–78, 280–81, 285–86,
      291
   gender, 8, 295–96, 314, 322
   genocide and, 259, 263

   healing, 36–37
   intimate-partner, 295
      spousal, 295–96
   mass, 251, 256, 261, 263–64, 266, 273
   post-, 265–66
   sexual, 295–97, 299, 301–9
      clerical, 296–309
         Internal Complaints
            Committee (ICC), 308
      healing, 302–9
      incest, 295–96, 300
      invisible wounds, 249, 295–96,
         299
      #MeToo movement, 296
      rape, 230, 239, 252, 260, 288, 299
      Texas Association Against Sexual
         Assault (TAASA), 303
         *Guidebook for Clergy on
           Healing Victims of Sexual
           Abuse*, 303
   social, 258
   structural, 3, 12, 22, 24
vitamins, 193
vocation, 28, 30, 34, 136, 143, 145, 203,
   283, 287–90, 301, 309
volunteers, 93, 95, 156–57, 174, 191–
   93, 195, 202–4, 241, 243–44

Wacquant, Loïc, 208
Wall, Barbra Mann, 4
war, 2, 117, 149
   American Civil, 52–53
   Burundi, 279, 285–88, 290–91
   Cold, 251
   First World War, 117
   Nigerian Civil, 58–61
   Rwanda, 253
   Second World War, 53, 55, 109
   South Sudan, 227–34, 236, 239–40,
      242, 251
Washington Post, 111n5
Wassenaar, Christina, 43
wealth, 2–3, 12, 18n16, 23, 42, 109, 130,
   215, 229, 231, 292
Western (the "West"), 2, 2n3, 59, 117,
   121, 139, 256, 258, 265, 292n11
   Christian, 292n11
   culture, 151

INDEX   353

science, 141
WHO. *See* United Nations, World Health Organization
witchcraft, 36, 131, 133, 136–43, 139n13
  curandero, 157
  shaman, 155, 157
  sorcerers, 155
  spells, 136
  witch hunt, 142–43
Wittgenstein, Ludwig, 140–41
workshops, 98, 175, 235, 238–39, 258, 261
World Bank, 12n2, 69–70, 74
  Wolfensohn, James, 74

World Christian Database, 75
worship, 180n45, 262, 318
Wuthnow, Robert, 192

Yemen, 230

Zambia, 5, 78, 128–44, 130n4, 131
  Chifunda, 129
  Luangwa Valley, 129, 136
  Ministry of Health, 129–30
  musutula, 135–36
  rainy season, 132
  Zewe, 137
    Chipyera, Doctor, 137

www.ingramcontent.com/pod-product-compliance
Lightning Source LLC
Chambersburg PA
CBHW032012300426
44117CB00008B/1004